Women's Fiction and the Great War

Women's Fiction and the Great War

EDITED BY
SUZANNE RAITT
AND
TRUDI TATE

CLARENDON PRESS · OXFORD

OXFORD
UNIVERSITY PRESS
Great Clarendon Street, Oxford OX2 6DP

Oxford University Press is a department of the University of Oxford
It furthers the University's objective of excellence in research, scholarship,
and education by publishing worldwide in

Oxford New York
Athens Auckland Bangkok Bogotá Buenos Aires Calcutta
Cape Town Chennai Dar es Salaam Delhi Florence Hong Kong Istanbul
Karachi Kuala Lumpur Madrid Melbourne Mexico City Mumbai
Nairobi Paris São Paulo Singapore Taipei Tokyo Toronto Warsaw
and associated companies in Berlin Ibadan

Oxford is a registered trade mark of Oxford University Press
in the UK and in certain other countries

Published in the United States
by Oxford University Press Inc., New York

Reprinted 1999

ISBN 0-19-818283-X
ISBN 0-19-818278-3 Pbk

Printed in Great Britain
on acid-free paper by
Bookcraft (Bath) Short Run Books
Midsomer Norton

Contents

Introduction

TRUDI TATE AND SUZANNE RAITT

Why Women?

In a curious poem published in 1917, Violet Hunt describes a kind of darkness which has descended during the Great War:

It is all shiny and black, like bombazine or taffeta,
Or the satin of my grandmother's gown, that stood alone
It was so thick;
A screen between us and knowledge,
That sometimes, when we are very good, gets on to the placards.[1]

Something stands between civilians and knowledge; a screen which Hunt likens to the surfaces of femininity: shiny cloth; a Victorian gown. The gown conceals forbidden knowledge from the viewer; and knowledge itself is figured as a female body, hidden and impenetrable. Yet the metaphor is even more complex, for the gown is remembered as empty, standing alone, supported by the weight of its fabric. Knowledge is figured as an absent female body; an empty space inside a woman's gown. 'Woman' simultaneously represents an invisible body of knowledge, and the subject (the speaker of Hunt's poem) prevented from knowing.

No one knew what was going on throughout the Great War.[2] Censorship, propaganda, and the sheer scale and complexity of the event made it impossible to grasp what was happening at any particular moment. Even combatants were often unsure whether they were winning or losing a particular engagement, and had no knowledge of the progress of the war overall, apart from what they read in the papers. Lack of knowledge was not gender-specific, nor even specific to civilians. But ignorance was often figured as feminine: a woman indifferently beautifying herself while soldiers die 'To save her light blue eyes from dreadful scenes', as May O'Rourke puts it.[3] As Nosheen Khan points out, many of the most famous war writers blamed women for unthinkingly supporting the war.[4]

This is a new collection of essays on women writers and the Great War. It is no longer true to claim that women's responses to the war have been ignored. Several important and broad-ranging studies have appeared in recent years, most notably Nosheen Khan's *Women's Poetry of the First World War* (1988), Claire Tylee's *The Great War and Women's Consciousness* (1990), *Women and World War I*, edited by Dorothy Goldman (1993), and Sharon Ouditt's *Fighting Forces, Writing Women* (1994).[5] However, some feminists are becoming slightly uneasy about writing separately about women as if women were a unified group, requiring special pleading; or as if 'woman' were an unproblematic category for organizing knowledge. For, as Diane Elam argues, 'what it means to be a "woman" is hardly self-evident'; this is particularly true of the period surrounding the Great War. And, as Denise Riley points out, 'being a woman' is a contested and various position even in societies which are not facing the trauma of war.[6] Rather than trying to present a 'woman's view' of the war, we have compiled this volume on the assumption that there is no such thing; that women, like men, occupy a range of political, philosophical, and aesthetic positions. The historian Gail Braybon sets out the problem in a recent essay:

> 'Women in the First World War' are often referred to as though they are a clearly defined, coherent group. It cannot be reiterated too often that the experiences of women differed dramatically between geographical areas, trades, age groups and classes. The 15-year-old Belfast flax worker who went to work at Woolwich Arsenal, the middle-aged Scottish crofter with no family at the Front, the domestic servant who took up road sweeping, the laundry worker who went into munitions—all these are 'typical' women workers of one kind or another, yet all of them had very different war experiences.[7]

Similarly, middle-class women writers such as Edith Wharton, Virginia Woolf, Mrs Humphry Ward, and HD all had remarkably different experiences of the Great War, and produced very different kinds of writing about it. None the less, Braybon concludes, we *can* talk about women as a group 'by virtue of their gender', on the one hand, and because of 'society's expectations of them', on the other.[8] Here the argument becomes somewhat circular: we can group women together because of their gender, that is, because they are women. But what does this mean? Braybon suggests that what women had in common during the Great War were social expectations: what we might call discourses of femininity. Yet, as Braybon's examples indicate, social expectations differed according to class, region, age, and so forth. In other words, the discourses which constructed 'woman' and 'femininity' were not coherent or consistent; we will argue this point in more detail in the next section.

This volume is particularly interested, then, in the *differences* among women; it also attempts to rethink what it means to look at a collection of 'women's writings'. Much feminist work of the past two decades has suggested that writing by women is concerned mainly or even exclusively with questions of gender. We have tried to challenge this orthodoxy, for it fails to address the wide range of issues which concerned women, then as now, and tends to imply that gender is something unique to women, and that only women write about gender—assumptions feminist criticism surely aims to challenge. Other scholars have shown that women were interpellated in specific (though also contradictory) ways during the Great War; that the war produces particular—and conflicting—discourses of femininity. Important work remains to be done if we are to understand how gender is constructed, especially in relation to significant historical events, such as war.[9] And perhaps we need to start asking why gender has become a critical orthodoxy; why critics rarely feel the need to justify an analysis of gender, especially in writing by women, to the exclusion of many other issues. For to focus exclusively on gender can produce a curiously depoliticized reading of our culture, its history, and its writing.

Much recent work on gender and the writing of the Great War is responding, in one way or another, to an essay by Sandra Gilbert, first published in 1983 and reprinted several times since. Gilbert reads the Great War as a form of sex warfare; a 'climactic episode in a battle of sexes'; a 'war between the front and the home front'.[10] It is easy to apply metaphors of crisis and warfare to every aspect of the Great War, including gender, but an approach which is sensitive only to drama and to violence actually misses much of what the war and its writings were about. Rather, we need to ask how the war located women and men as citizens; in Britain, for example, the war brought new levels of policing, internal surveillance, and coercion, including conscription in 1916. At the same time, it can be argued that the war provided new work opportunities, especially for women, and eventually led to the extension of the franchise.[11] The gap between rich and poor was reduced after the war and the standard of living for working-class and poor people was substantially improved.[12] Whether these social changes occurred because of the war or in spite of it remains a matter of debate among historians.[13] Nor is there agreement on such issues among the writers discussed here. As Gertrude Stein comments, 'war makes things go backward as well as forward';[14] it produces contradictions which are almost impossible to reconcile. An extended franchise, better housing, safer pregnancies, and improved dentistry are accompanied by the invention of the tank and the first use of poison gas.[15] Technology brings relief as well as suffering on a scale much greater than in previous wars, and writers struggle to understand how to place themselves, and their culture, in this new phase of industrialization.

Technological and imaginative boundaries were shifting, for better and for worse; so were political borders. The peace settlements transformed the shape of Europe, as the defunct Ottoman, Russian, and Austro-Hungarian empires were replaced with new independent nations such as Yugoslavia, Czechoslovakia, Hungary, Poland, Austria, Lithuania, Latvia, and Estonia.[16] Attempts were made to establish 'ethnic-linguistic nation-states'; as Eric Hobsbawm argues, small nationalistic states were encouraged as a bolster against Bolshevik Russia.[17] The consequences of the peace settlements after the Great War can still be felt today in the former Yugoslavia as well as in Armenia, the Baltic states, and elsewhere in central and eastern Europe. The new discourses of nationalism filtered strangely into Britain and the United States during this period, and we find writers meditating on notions of nation, citizenship, and service as Europe embarked on what historians are beginning to describe as the second Thirty Years War, 1914–45.[18] Many writers were also concerned with the ways in which subjectivity is constructed (and damaged) by the trauma of war. All these issues were addressed by women as well as by men; in other words, women were not concerned exclusively with questions of gender, as the chapters which follow attempt to demonstrate.

War, Perversity, Femininity

The chapters in this book expose the sheer unmanageability both of women's writing as a category and of 'woman' as a cultural condition. We are used to thinking of Vera Brittain, Virginia Woolf, Katherine Mansfield, perhaps, as typical of women's literary expression of the war. Yet these are reconstructions defined as much by the pressure of our interpretations and mythologies of the First World War as by our understanding of the historical development of women's experience and women's writing. What has Vernon Lee's *Satan the Waster* to do with Woolf's Lily Briscoe or HD's Julia? As Tracy Hargreaves points out, war, like woman, is difficult to locate. What might constitute authentic reportage, authentic war experience? And similarly, how might we recognize authentic femininity, the real thing? Woolf was to pose this question to herself with some anguish throughout her life, writing in 1925 of Vita Sackville-West 'being in short (what I have never been) a real woman'.[19]

The chapters that follow demonstrate the extent to which war only intensified the pressure on women to inhabit a cultural, social, and sexual paradox. In *Fighting Forces, Writing Women*, Sharon Ouditt argues that the VADs of the Great War 'found themselves [. . .] at an ideological junction between a traditional, idealised value system and a radical new order of experience: a complex and ambiguous subject position that was frequently the source of breakdown'.[20] 'Woman' as a category became ever more contested as government propaganda struggled both to mobilize and to renegotiate femininity to serve its purposes, and to cling on to a fundamental continuity with peacetime versions of Edwardian womanhood. Without this continuity the ideological imperatives behind Britain's involvement in the conflict, controversial at the best of times, would have seemed flimsy indeed. As the editors of *Arms and the Woman* point out, war cultures must invest in an image of a peace worth fighting for, a peace which is imagined through images of an idealized and nostalgic pre-war Golden Age.[21] Jane Potter's chapter (4) shows that popular forms such as the romance and the memoir were especially well placed to respond to these cultural demands, but we see femininity reinvested and reconstituted in a variety of the texts discussed here: in the propaganda and fiction of Mrs Humphry Ward, in the variety of images of feminine creativity and labour in *To the Lighthouse*, and in the extraordinary invocation of fabrics and textures in Mary Butts's 'Speed the Plough'. The problematic continuity with, and anticipation of, a culture at peace becomes emblematic of a society's relation to historical process. Wars are fought in the name of their consequences, their end-results; military and other strategies plan for and anticipate them. War then calls into question a nation and a culture's relation to its own past and its own future, as we have seen so clearly in the recent conflicts in Bosnia. Femininity is variously invoked as an index of war's traumatic commitment to change and to consolidation. 'Woman' becomes a fundamentally perverse identity, constituted both for and against itself. More than this: the aims of the Great War were never clear to any of the combatant nations; millions of people suffered and died—for what purpose? For an old bitch gone in the teeth, in Pound's characterization of Britain, the British empire, European civilization? The war itself was a highly perverse entity, an astonishing feat of organization as well as of bungling, producing remarkable acts of courage and sacrifice as well as cruelty and barbarism in what came to seem a self-sustaining system of 'total war'.

The perversity of warfare and the perverse category 'woman' intersect in the writing of May Sinclair, one of the war's most greedy and excited supporters. In an article for *Woman at Home* in February 1915 she writes: 'the British woman at her best is very like the British soldier'.[22] Woman's relation to military action is problematized along with her gender:

> For sacrifices are of two kinds, voluntary and involuntary, and they cover the whole ground. I do not mean to say much about women's involuntary sacrifices, about the great and terrible and tragic part they have played in this war, and have still to play, about the mothers and wives and sweethearts of soldiers and of sailors; nor about the women whom the war has thrown out of work; nor yet about the multitude of refugee women who are crowding into England for shelter and protection. You may say that these have not made any sacrifice. They *are* the sacrifice.[23]

The war, fought to protect women and the domestic ideal, also delivered them up as damaged objects in which they became not inspiration but reproach, destroyed in order to secure their own safety. Sinclair goes on to explain the thinking behind her title (assigned to her, not invented by her): 'I do not think that this is what the author of my title meant by women's sacrifices. He really means women's work, what women have done and are ready to do for the war and because of the war.'[24] Women's work, so heavily emphasized in stereotypical images of women in the First World War—as VADs, munitions workers, land-girls, and so on—becomes the only available image for their decisive participation in the war as autonomous subjects. But even here, of course, as Sharon Ouditt has shown, the cultural connotations of what they did were recuperated for an ideal of woman as subordinate and self-sacrificing. As the editor of the memoirs of the 'Heroines of Pervyse', the Baroness de T'Serclaes and Mairi Chisholm, comments: 'both young themselves, one very young, they yet have mothered Belgian soldiers through their trials'.[25] Women become soldiers, soldiers become mothers, and mothers become children.

The anxiety and possible exhilaration of this kind of fluidity is emphasized by writers other than those discussed in the chapters in this volume. In the memoirs of de T'Serclaes and Chisholm, for example, the symbolic cutting of long hair is also absorbed into a discourse about mothering. Chisholm and de T'Serclaes, impatient with their lack of autonomy working for Hector Munro in the ambulance corps with which May Sinclair was also travelling, resolved to set up their own emergency dressing station just behind the front line and ritually cut off their long hair, wove it together into one thick plait, and sent it floating off down the canal. With the loss of their hair, they say, they 'became soldiers'.[26] And yet this ritual too is a sacrifice. The Baroness de T'Serclaes was both hurt and glad when troops marched straight past her and Chisholm without acknowledging them as women.[27] Deprived of their identity as spectacle for a moment the women become curiously invisible, moving back into focus only as nurses and mothers.

A similar preoccupation appears in Helen Zenna Smith's extraordinary *Not So Quiet* (1930). The ambiguously sexed Tosh cuts off her own hair to the horror of her co-workers in the French ambulance unit:

> I watch her now running a comb through her hair, softly damning and blasting the knots. Generous hair, Tosh's, as generous as the rest of her, thick, long, red as a sunset in Devon when not grime- and grease-blackened. As I stare she parts the strands over her right ear,

peers anxiously into the square of looking-glass, and emits a string of swear-words before turning to the Bug.

'Lend me your scissors, Bug.'[28]

Here the erotic gaze between women, phobically repudiated throughout much of the book, is animated by a vision of the pastoral England which the war and twentieth-century urbanization are simultaneously destroying (grime and grease) and securing. As Claire Buck shows in relation to Radclyffe Hall's work, the rhetorical discourses of war (service, the Devon sunsets that soldiers are supposedly fighting to protect) can offer narrative and ideological points of identification for same-sex erotic identities. But the narrator's love for Tosh is expressed in the language of military comradeship, something like the homoeroticism of many soldiers' writings of the same period. The characters' only moment of physical contact is a version of the Pietà which was used on the Red Cross poster 'The Greatest Mother in the World': 'Tosh lies in my arms dead, soaking my overcoat with blood. [. . .] Tosh the brave, the splendid, the great-hearted. Tosh is dead' (160). The symbolic castration of the haircut is graphically realized here as blood seeps from Tosh's head wound, 'big brave Tosh with her head hanging childishly on one side' (159). The association with castration is only strengthened by the narrator's assumption and hope that the wounded woman is not Tosh but the hated Commandant, 'Mrs Bitch', the quintessential phallic mother: 'They say she is a married woman with daughters of her own . . . I cannot believe it. No woman who has suffered the pangs of childbirth could have so little understanding of pain in other women's daughters' (49). Where the Commandant's motherhood is vitiated by her ruthlessness and megalomania ('why is it that women in authority almost invariably fall victims to megalomania?'), Tosh's symbolic self-castration is recuperated by the maternal beauty of her breasts: '"You'll look awfully unsexed, Tosh," warns the B.F. "Unsexed? Me? With the breasts of a nursing mother?" Tosh winks behind the B.F.'s back' (17). Tosh's breasts, like her hair, become the site of a paradoxical femininity, at once signifying the women's home (Devon sunsets), their potential or anticipated motherhood, and the possibility of a subversive and eroticized 'stare' which displaces lesbian desire on to the repulsive Skinny and Frost and finds its justification in an image of sacrificial and soldierly maternity as Tosh dies.

Not So Quiet reads this paradoxical femininity through the lens of class as well as sexuality: Tosh is aristocratic, the cook a 'fat, common, lazy, impertinent slut' (51). Although it reads very unsympathetically, the discourse of class is one of the few ways in which the novel manages to invest women with authority and agency. In a classic move, *Not So Quiet* buys into one image of feminine power at the expense of another, just as Virginia Woolf does in *To the Lighthouse*, with the beautiful Mrs Ramsay and the creaking, witless Mrs McNab.

The inflexion of femininity with class, always crucially determining of the material conditions of women's lives as well as of their experience and sense of themselves, was of great significance to women who made their money by writing. Writing could, if you were lucky, insert you into the labour market, and the demand for fiction increased during the war. Almost all of the war fiction and the memoirs which have come down to us were written by middle-class women for whom a sense of their own class was intimately bound up with their identity as publishing writers, as professionals. Mrs Humphry Ward, as Helen Small tells us in Chapter 1, used her writing experience to serve the British government during the war, thereby endowing herself with the status of authorized observer, as well as of professional writer. But this authority was elusive for many of the women discussed here: May Sinclair, too old to become a VAD, never invited to become an official propagandist, was quickly sent home by her Commandant like a disgraced child. Although she intended to finance her ambulance corps by writing journalism, very little was ever produced, and certainly not while she was actually in Belgium. The problem for these women was to find a way of authorizing themselves as artists as well as women. Edith Wharton and Gertrude Stein side-stepped the issue of the relevance of art to war by undertaking their own projects of relief and assistance; Radclyffe Hall used her writing skills to produce recruitment leaflets; Vernon Lee implicitly suggested the priority of art over war in the curious satire *Satan the Waster*, as Gillian Beer tells us in Chapter 5. Many of the images we find of feminine power and vulnerability in novels and other texts by women during and after the war hinge on an almost shamanic power to rescue and to heal. The relation between the quotidian and the magical, or the intoxicating, in war is confused and problematic, as Con Coroneos shows (Chapter 9). But women had available to them certain iconic identities (the wife, the mother, the nurse) which could draw together the mundane and the inspirational. Even a text like *Not So Quiet,* with its violence, aggression, and disgust, invests the figure of Tosh with a subversive and healing energy which, until Tosh's death, seems to sustain the narrator. As Nathalie Blondel shows in Chapter 7, the traumatic losses and griefs of war are interpreted in Frances Bellerby's fiction as part of a cosmic ebbing in which memory and fantasy take on a ghostly and magical aspect.

One consequence of this sense of healing power, of living close to the experience of death, was a feeling of predestination for many of the women who did come into close contact with the front lines. The Baroness de T'Serclaes echoed the emotions of many, among them May Sinclair, when she wrote: 'ten years of my life had slipped away in groping, and now I felt that I had, literally, a date with destiny'.[29] Olive Schreiner was to reiterate this sense of women's vocation, their privileged knowledge, in an article extracted from *Woman and Labour* (1911) and included in *Woman at Home*: 'on this one point, and on this point almost alone, the knowledge of woman, simply as woman, is superior to that of man. She knows the history of human flesh; she knows its cost; he does not.'[30] Schreiner's argument is that women, because they give birth, are instinctively conservative of human life, but also the repository of an arcane knowledge of it. Once again motherhood is invoked as part of what is threatened by war, which goes against the biological and moral instincts of the women on whose behalf it is fought. Indeed war can remake the world in terms of maternity—a figure also found in men's writing: the image of soldiers mothering one another appears in a surprising number of soldiers' novels of the Great War.[31] In writing by both women and men, maternity is oddly displaced from gender and re-emerges as a fantasy of tenderness and power. The Baroness de T'Serclaes writes of the way in which her effectiveness and her fame during the war compensated for a neglected and deprived childhood with foster-parents: 'I felt that I was in the way, that I had no right to be in the world.'[32] She longed for a mother who could love and console her; she found herself 'mothering' Belgian soldiers with a preternatural ability to bring them back from death: 'The stress of the life we were living had begun to reveal something in me which I had never suspected and which could not, surely, have been the product of the few absurd years on earth of which I was aware. I possessed a kind of power which seemed to be able to drag men back literally from the jaws of death.'[33] The Baroness loved to be wanted, loved to preside over the leaving and giving of life in a strange modulation of her own experience of loss and desertion.

By far the best-known war novel to explore women's healing power is Rebecca West's *The Return of the Soldier* (1918). In this novel, Chris Baldry returns from the war with shell-shock, having forgotten the years between 1901 and 1916. He returns to his first love, a working-class woman called Margaret Allington, and a strangely redemptive narrative is played out under the distorting pressures of class and gender. Margaret is regarded with horror by the narrator and Chris's forgotten wife, Kitty: 'For a long time we watched her as she went along the drive, her yellowish raincoat looking sick and bright in the sharp sunshine, her black plumes nodding like the pines above, her cheap boots making her walk on her heels; a spreading stain on the fabric of our lives.'[34] Yet Margaret has the telepathic healing powers of a mother and a lover, and the story seems to replay many of the assumptions about the regenerative powers of working-class women's labour that Tracy Hargreaves has identified in *To the Lighthouse.* But here it is the labour of love which is needed: 'the woman has gathered the soul of the man into her soul and is keeping it warm in love and peace so that his body can rest quiet for a little time' (144). As in a number of the narratives discussed here, women's love involves their martyrdom: Margaret agrees to use her spiritual knowledge of Chris to cure his amnesia, and to lose his love. As he renounces his love, he regains his masculinity, absorbed until then into a childlike dependency on his childhood sweetheart. Women and their magic are both central to, and cast aside by, the novel's movement, as, in a more general sense, their creativity and love were drawn on and hurt by all the war's violence and grief.

This volume begins with writers we might characterize as Edwardian, and continues with modernists and anti-modernists of the 1920s and 1930s. In Chapter 1 Helen Small considers Mrs Humphry Ward's thematics of censorship and speech, both in her propaganda writing and in her fiction. Mary Condé continues (in Chapter 2) the theme of payment and Franco-

American relations in a reading of Edith Wharton's *A Son at the Front*, arguing that the novel explores questions of representation and the role of the non-combatant. Suzanne Raitt (Chapter 3) examines the war journals of May Sinclair, who spent a few weeks with the Munro Corps in Belgium in 1915. Sinclair's writing demonstrates the perversity of some women's sexual investment in the war, a theme continued in Jane Potter's account, in Chapter 4, of the conservative gender politics of romance writers Ruby M. Ayres and Berta Ruck, and memoirists Kate Finzi and Olive Dent. Gillian Beer (Chapter 5) examines how knowledge is figured in the remarkable writing of Vernon Lee, an intellectual who placed herself very firmly within a tradition of European thinking. Tracy Hargreaves (Chapter 6) looks at the politics and aesthetics of Woolf's account of post-war regeneration in *To the Lighthouse*, arguing that while Woolf's account of Mrs McNab and Mrs Bast is inflected by her own social distaste for them, they none the less raise issues that lie at the heart of Woolf's artistic project. Nathalie Blondel (Chapter 7) introduces the little-known writer Frances Bellerby, and explores Bellerby's aesthetics of grief, loss, and remembrance in the context of her comment that the war simply 'goes on happening'. Claire Buck (Chapter 8) analyses the way in which the invocation of an ethic of service allowed Radclyffe Hall to imagine the war as a peculiarly liberating event for patrician lesbians such as Stephen Gordon in *The Well of Loneliness* (1928) and Miss Ogilvy in 'Miss Ogilvy Finds Herself' (1934). In Chapter 9 Con Coroneos reads the only two of Katherine Mansfield's stories to deal explicitly with the war, 'An Indiscreet Journey' and 'The Fly', as forms of inoculation against suffering which make her writing possible. Mary Hamer (Chapter 10) gives readings of three texts by Mary Butts, arguing that Butts exposes the extent to which war makes evident a cruelty already structured into the social arrangements between women and men. Finally, Trudi Tate (Chapter 11) looks at the relationship between witnessing and war neuroses in HD's fiction, and Elizabeth Gregory (Chapter 12) explores the encounter between Gertrude Stein's utopian project of tenderness and a world at war in which tenderness and the rights of individuals seem to have small importance.

This book is both a supplement and a complement to existing studies of women and the First World War. The chapters look closely at specific writers, analysing their work in considerable detail, and addressing some of the conceptual and historical questions which arise from their writing. The collection is necessarily selective and does not try to provide an overview of women's writing about the war.[35] Rather, the chapters trace the different ways in which women writers engaged with the problems of knowing and not-knowing as they faced the contradictions and trauma of the Great War. Like men, women took up a very wide range of positions. Some supported the war enthusiastically; others were deeply opposed. Some were ambivalent, or changed their views in the course of the war. We have tried to represent this range of response, from pacifists such as Vernon Lee and Virginia Woolf to active supporters of the war such as Radclyffe Hall and May Sinclair.

The collection has several aims. It rereads pieces by well-known modernists such as Woolf, Stein, Mansfield, Wharton, and HD, arguing that we need to pay more attention to their work as 'war writing'.[36] It reintroduces writers such as Mary Butts and Frances Bellerby whose responses to the war have largely been forgotten. And it looks closely at other kinds of war writings produced by women—works which were influential at the time, but which have received very little attention since: the propaganda of Mrs Humphry Ward, the popular fiction of Ruby M. Ayres and Berta Ruck, and the pacifist work of Vernon Lee. What interests us is how women positioned themselves, and their writing, in relation to the troubled status of knowledge in the Great War. And the writing itself raises further questions about knowledge. What constitutes a *response* to the war, asks Con Coroneos; how should we read what is not said? How is the writing driven by its knowledge, and lack of knowledge, of the disaster of the war? These are also important questions for reading Mrs Humphry Ward, a propagandist who is, perhaps unexpectedly, deeply concerned about the effects of censorship during the Great War. Ward's war fiction sets up a counter-discourse to the certainties of her own propaganda, as Helen Small demonstrates. Ward is a particularly interesting figure: an anti-suffrage campaigner whose propaganda work gave her privileged access to precisely the kinds of power and knowledge which she felt ought to be the preserve of men. Her complex responses to this paradox can be usefully read alongside the pro-war romances and memoirs of Ruck, Ayres, Finzi, and Dent, discussed by Jane Potter. These works, too, prove to be more complex than we might anticipate, as they intersect in striking ways with other discourses of the period, notably the eugenic anxieties of the decade immediately prior to the war.

The Great War produced terrible and often purposeless suffering, both for women and for men: around 9 million killed and millions more injured, bereaved, or rendered war neurotic. War neurosis was a serious problem for the medical authorities during the Great War, as large numbers of soldiers were incapacitated by hysterical paralysis, deafness, blindness, insomnia, terrifying nightmares, hallucinations. This has been well documented in recent studies of the war. What is overlooked, however, is the fact that civilians, too, were susceptible to war neuroses, as Trudi Tate points out. This complicates the differences between combatants and civilians, and raises difficult questions about who suffers and who bears witness to suffering during the Great War. And who pays the price?, as Mary Condé asks of Edith Wharton's war writing. In *A Son at the Front* (1923), Wharton explores the ways in which civilians invest fantasmatically in the war, and at what cost. Wharton worked tirelessly for civilian refugees during the war through charities such as the American Hostels for Refugees and the Children of Flanders Rescue Committee.[37] She visited the front lines on several occasions; her letters about Verdun to her old friend Henry James in 1915 were a source of deep fascination for James. To James, Wharton occupied a position closer to combatant than civilian; she had access to a kind of knowledge which James, an elderly civilian, found intensely exciting—as did Wharton herself.[38]

Some of the fantasies which surface in women's war writings are quite perverse, as we see in the work of May Sinclair, discussed by Suzanne Raitt. But to claim that women simply gloated over men's suffering, as Sandra Gilbert suggests, seems an inadequate account of the strange ambivalences in writing such as Sinclair's. Rather, Sinclair, like many other writers of this period, explores *how femininity is constituted* in relation to the war. And this in turn is modified by other structures of difference; Raitt shows that age, for example, is a highly significant factor in the experience and writing of the Great War. Furthermore, the differences between civilians and combatants, or between pacifists and jingoists, often outweigh, or at the very least reconfigure, the differences between women and men. In other words, gender is not always the fundamental organizing category of either experience or subjectivity, and this emerges, in different ways, in war writing by women. Femininity, like masculinity, is a contested site of meaning during and after the Great War. But the war is not 'about' gender; nor is it a metaphorical battle of the sexes. To transform the actual violence of the Great War into a trope of sex warfare is to deny the specificity of its trauma, both for women and for men.

NOTES

1. Violet Hunt, 'What the Civilian Saw', *Poetry*, 9/6 (Mar. 1917), 295.
2. The First World War (Great War) of 1914–18 mobilized 70 million combatants, of whom approximately 9 million died. The allied side and its associates included Britain and its empire, France, Russia, Serbia, Montenegro, Italy, Greece, Romania, Portugal, Japan, China, Brazil, and the United States. The central powers included Germany, Austria-Hungary, Bulgaria, and the Ottoman empire. The land war was fought in France, Belgium, Prussia, the Balkans, Italy, Turkey, and Africa. See J. M. Winter, *The Experience of World War I* (Oxford, 1988); Martin Gilbert, *The Routledge Atlas of the First World War* (1970; 2nd edn. London, 1994).
3. May O'Rourke, 'The Minority: 1917', repr. in Catherine Reilly (ed.), *Scars upon my Heart: Women's Poetry and Verse of the First World War* (London, 1981), 86. The woman is addressed as 'Fool!' and accused of forgetting the men who are suffering for her.
4. Nosheen Khan, *Women's Poetry of the First World War* (London, 1988), 2, 190 n. Khan cites works by Siegfried Sassoon, Wilfred Owen, and Richard Aldington.
5. Full details are provided in the bibliography. Other works that include important essays on women and the Great War are M. R. Higonnet, Jane Jenson, Sonya Michel, and Margaret C. Weitz (eds.), *Behind the Lines: Gender and the Two World Wars* (New Haven, 1987), Helen M. Cooper, Adrienne Auslander Munich, and Susan Merrill Squier (eds.), *Arms and the Woman: War, Gender and Literary Representation* (Chapel Hill, NC, 1989), and Lynne Hanley, *Writing War* (Amherst, Mass., 1991).
6. Diane Elam, *Feminism and Deconstruction* (London, 1994), 22; Denise Riley, *Am I that Name? Feminism and the Category of 'Women' in History* (London, 1988), 96–7.
7. Gail Braybon, 'Women and the War', in Stephen Constantine, Maurice Kirby, and Mary Rose (eds.), *The First World War in British History* (London, 1995), 145.
8. Ibid.
9. See Joan Scott, 'Rewriting History', in Higonnet *et al.* (eds.), *Behind the Lines.*
10. Sandra Gilbert, 'Soldier's Heart: Literary Men, Literary Women, and the Great War', *Signs*, 8/3 (1983), 422–50; repr. in Sandra Gilbert and Susan Gubar, *No Man's Land: The Place of the Woman Writer in the Twentieth Century*, ii: *Sexchanges* (New Haven, 1989), 260, 302. Claire Tylee offers a powerful

critique of this essay in '"Maleness Run Riot": The Great War and Women's Resistance to Militarism', *Women's Studies International Forum*, 11 (1988), 199–210. See also Jane Marcus, 'The Asylums of Antaeus: Women, War and Madness—Is there a Feminist Fetishism?' in H. Aram Veeser (ed.), *The New Historicism* (London, 1990).

11. Arthur Marwick argues that the establishment of a Ministry of Munitions in 1915 and the introduction of conscription in 1916 'transformed the [work] opportunities open to women' in Britain (*Women at War 1914–1918* (London, 1977), 51). Gail Braybon takes a more cautious view. She points out that many historians have found that 'women were still paid less than men, that their working conditions were often appalling, and that there remained many areas of work from which they were excluded completely, and that it proved impossible for women to hold on to their wartime jobs when peace returned' ('Women and the War', 143). Deborah Thom has argued that the war actually harmed women's economic and social position ('The Bundle of Sticks', in Angela John (ed.), *Unequal Opportunities* (Oxford, 1986)). Claire Tylee notes that working-class women suffered from greater *unemployment* at the beginning of the war, as middle-class people economized; this changed with conscription in 1916. Overall, approximately 1.5 million extra women entered the work-force (Tylee, *The Great War and Women's Consciousness*, 11). See also Gail Braybon, *Women Workers in the First World War* (London, 1989); Gail Braybon and Penny Summerfield, *Out of the Cage: Women's Experiences in Two World Wars* (London, 1987).
12. J. M. Winter argues that in Britain the war 'was the occasion of a completely unanticipated improvement in the life expectancy of the civilian population'; this was due mainly to better public health services and improved nutrition for working-class people (*The Great War and the British People* (Basingstoke, 1986), 2, 4).
13. For an outline of the historians' debate, see Braybon, 'Women and the War', 142–4; see also the intro. to Constantine *et al.* (eds.), *The First World War in British History*, 1–3.
14. Gertrude Stein, *Wars I Have Seen* (1945; London, 1984), 5.
15. For improvements in civilian health during the war, see Winter, *The Great War and the British People*, ch. 4.
16. Eric Hobsbawm, *Age of Extremes: The Short Twentieth Century, 1914–1991* (London, 1994), 33; Gilbert, *The Routledge Atlas of the First World War*, 152, 155.
17. Hobsbawm argues that the attempts to create 'neat nation-states' were a disaster; the terrible conflicts in central Europe in the 1990s are 'the old chickens of Versailles coming home to roost' (*Age of Extremes*, 31).
18. Ibid. 22; Winter, *The Great War and the British People*, 5. The writing of American expatriates such as Stein and Wharton in France and HD in England is particularly interesting in this context. See also Samuel Hynes, *A War Imagined* (London, 1990).
19. *The Diary of Virginia Woolf*, iii: *1925–1930*, ed. Anne Olivier Bell and Andrew McNeillie (New York, 1980), 52; 21 Dec. 1925.
20. Ouditt, *Fighting Forces, Writing Women*, 7.
21. Cooper *et al.* (eds.), *Arms and the Woman*, 16.
22. May Sinclair, 'Women's Sacrifices for the War', *Woman at Home*, 67 (Feb. 1915), 7.

23. Ibid.
24. Ibid.
25. *The Cellar-House of Pervyse: A Tale of Uncommon Things from the Journals and Letters of the Baroness de T'Serclaes and Mairi Chisholm*, ed. G. E. Mitton (London, 1916), p. v.
26. Ibid. 113–14.
27. Baroness de T'Serclaes, *Flanders and Other Fields: Memoirs of the Baroness de T'Serclaes, M.M.* (London, 1964), 67.
28. Helen Zenna Smith [Evadne Price], *Not So Quiet . . . Stepdaughters of War* (1930; London, 1988), 13.
29. De T'Serclaes, *Flanders and Other Fields*, 41.
30. Olive Schreiner, 'Women and War', *Woman at Home*, 66 (Jan. 1915), 558.
31. The most striking example, perhaps, is Ford Madox Ford's *Parade's End* (1924–8); see also Henri Barbusse, *Under Fire* (1916), Erich Maria Remarque, *All Quiet on the Western Front* (1929), and Robert Graves, *Good-bye to All That* (1929).
32. De T'Serclaes, *Flanders and Other Fields*, 22.
33. Ibid. 48.
34. Rebecca West, *The Return of the Soldier* (1918; London, 1980), 37.
35. Excellent overviews are provided by Tylee, *The Great War and Women's Consciousness*, and Ouditt, *Fighting Forces, Writing Women.*
36. Modernism's relation to its own history, and especially to the war, requires further attention. See Stan Smith, *The Origins of Modernism* (Hemel Hempstead, 1994), esp. ch. 7; Hynes, *A War Imagined*; and Trudi Tate's study of modernism and the Great War (Manchester, forthcoming). For a different view, see J. M. Winter, *Sites of Memory, Sites of Mourning: The Great War in European Cultural History* (Cambridge, 1995).
37. *The Letters of Edith Wharton*, ed. R. W. B. Lewis and Nancy Lewis (London, 1988), 329–32. Wharton wrote a curiously unsympathetic story about people who helped refugees during the war, 'The Refugees', in *Certain People* (1930); repr. in Trudi Tate (ed.), *Women, Men, and the Great War* (Manchester, 1995).
38. Pam Thurschwell, '"That Imperial Stomach is no Seat for Ladies": Jamesian Ghosts, World War I, and the Politics of Identification', Objects of Modernism Conference, University of Southampton, July 1995. For Wharton's letters about the front, see *The Letters of Edith Wharton*, 348–56.

1

Mrs Humphry Ward and the First Casualty of War

HELEN SMALL

> As he sat there thinking, he began in an absent-minded way to look at his evening paper. He read the news on the front page, then turned to the inner sheets. His eye fell on these words printed at the head of the column next to the leading article:
>
> 'To the Women of the Empire. Thoughts in War-Time. By Pearl Bellairs.' Underneath in brackets: 'The first of a series of inspiring and patriotic articles by Miss Bellairs, the well-known novelist.'
>
> Dick groaned in agony...
>
> 'Inspiring and patriotic': those were feeble words in which to describe Pearl's shrilly raucous chauvinism. And the style! Christ!... She was a public danger. It was all too frightful.
>
> (Aldous Huxley, 'Farcical History of Richard Greenow')

ALDOUS Huxley's 'Farcical History of Richard Greenow' (1920) is a satirical account of the life and death of a young Englishman in the first two decades of the twentieth century. Dick Greenow's outstanding academic promise first becomes evident at preparatory school when he devours all three volumes of Mrs Humphry Ward's *Robert Elsmere* ('No length or incomprehensibility could put him off'). After studying at Aesop College (Eton), Dick goes on to read Classics at Canteloup College, Oxford, where he becomes a leading light of the Fabian Society. But at Oxford, a strange psychological disorder, first apparent at Aesop, begins to take over his life. Dick develops a split personality: by day he remains an uncompromising left-wing intellectual, labouring painstakingly at a *New Synthetic Philosophy*; but by night he metamorphoses into 'Pearl Bellairs', doyenne of *Hildebrand's Home*

Weekly and author of numerous works of romantic fiction with titles like *Heartsease Fitroy: The Story of a Young Girl* and *Daisy's Voyage to Cythera.* Dick manages to keep his hermaphroditic psyche a secret from even his closest friends, and after leaving college he lives rather comfortably on the profits of Pearl's 'indefatigable pen'; but, when war breaks out in 1914, Pearl begins to make larger and larger inroads on his life. Dick's politics are firmly pacifist. He organizes an anti-conscription campaign, and spends his days travelling the country, speech-making to 'impossible Christian sects' and braving the fists of drunken patriots. Pearl, however, has become 'a hungry tigress', devoting all her literary energies to government propaganda, composing stirring recruitment songs, and urging the women of England to give their all in the country's hour of need. When Dick dies, halfway through the war, it is not on the battlefields of France but in a London asylum. His left hand flails wildly and his voice yells in protest, but his right hand belongs to Pearl, and he expires scribbling her beastly-Hun propaganda: 'No peace with the Hun until he is crushed and humiliated. Self-respecting Britons will refuse to shake a Hunnish hand for many a long year after the war. No more German waiters . . .'.[1]

The 'Farcical History of Richard Greenow' is a heavy-handed satire against Huxley's famous novelist aunt Mrs Humphry Ward. Given the warmth of relations between them,[2] it is a surprising attack by Huxley, and one he probably regretted. Mary Ward died in March 1920, with a copy of 'Richard Greenow' on her bedside table,[3] and, though she enjoyed a joke, it is hard not to imagine that she was hurt by her nephew's public show of wit at her expense. (At her funeral, Huxley wept openly, the tears pouring down his cheeks.[4]) On a first reading, 'Richard Greenow' has all the hallmarks of a classic generational confrontation: the young man at the start of his literary career flinging his dissent in the face of the Victorian matriarch, rejecting her heavy moral seriousness, her incorrigible sentimentalism, and—above all—her apparently unshakeable faith in the regenerative power of a just war. But on closer inspection, the ironies of Huxley's story are rather more complicated. If Mary Ward's patriotic sentimentalism is under fire, so too is the young radical's desire to dissociate himself from war. Much to his own distress, Huxley's severely impaired sight debarred him from active service. In his journals he recorded the humiliation of being obliged to queue for yet another medical along with the 'half-wits, syphilitics . . . goitrous cretins, [and] rheumatic lepers'.[5] Despite his close association with the Garsington circle (he spent part of the war chopping timber for Lady Ottoline Morrell until a splinter almost took out his good eye), pacifism is not well represented in 'Richard Greenow'. The men and women who join the campaign against conscription do so with 'not the faintest interest in the welfare of humanity at large' being 'wholly absorbed in the salvation of their own souls and in keeping their consciences clear from the faintest trace of blood-guiltiness'.[6] Richard Greenow jots down one last tentative insight before he lapses into delirium: 'World will always be hell. Cap. or Lab., Engl. or Germ.—all beasts', but principled detachment may be a luxury the country cannot afford in wartime. 'Selfish intellect. Perhaps Pearl Bellairs better.'[7]

Huxley's absurdist caricature offers a usefully complex opening for a consideration of Mrs Humphry Ward's war propaganda and fiction. Patriotic fervour is an easy target for satire, and Mary Ward's attitude to the Great War was nothing if not patriotic; but Huxley's story leaves its hero and its reader with an uncomfortable awareness that—temporarily, at least—war may change the criteria for literary judgement. There are good literary reasons for not valuing Mary Ward's *Missing* as highly as Virginia Woolf's *Mrs Dalloway*, or her *Towards the Goal* as highly as *Three Guineas*. But, unlike Woolf, Ward wrote for a wartime audience, and she was convinced that what the public needed in 1914–19 was not high art. 'I have just finished a book,' she wrote to Aldous's brother Julian in April 1918, 'and am beginning another—as usual! . . . Literature is an honourable profession, and I am no ways ashamed of it—as a profession. And indeed I feel that novels have a special function nowadays—when one sees the great demand for them as a *délassement* and refreshment. I wish with all my heart I could write a detective—or mystery—novel! That is what the wounded and the tired love.'[8] Ward's sense that a wartime readership has different needs from the same readership in peacetime seems to have been borne out by her own subsequent reputation as a war writer. Between 1916 and 1919, Mary Ward was one of the most visible and successful writers in Britain;[9] but almost as soon as hostilities ended, her version of the war was displaced by that of younger writers whose approach was generally more critical, more ironic, and above all more 'modernist'.[10] To some extent her propaganda and late novels found a home within that large and historically under-considered category of 'middle-brow fiction' which, as Rosa Bracco has demonstrated, preserved a more respectful memory of the war than the bitter disenchantment which Paul Fussell took to be the dominant note of British post-war literature.[11] Yet even there she was rapidly eclipsed by such younger writers as J. B. Priestley, Ernest Raymond, R. C. Sherriff, and May Sinclair.

In literary terms, Mary Ward's persistently low repute as a war writer is understandable. Her own sense that the primary concern of the war novelist should be to provide relaxation for the battle-weary reader is better supported by her own books than the letter to Huxley might suggest. These are not demanding, or (in the main) aesthetically ambitious works; they are pick-up- and put-downable—ideal reading for tired nurses, munitions workers, and land-girls. Yet there is something faintly disingenuous about her emphasis on '*délassement* and refreshment', because, even at their most undemanding, the novels never allow the reader to forget the consuming importance of the war effort. Their subject-matter may be far removed from the front, but their tone is almost always proselytizing and their language is the language of moral conflict: fighting for one's ideals, defending one's principles, shoring up the psyche against cowardice and feebleness. As one of the leading literary figures conscripted into Britain's propaganda effort during the early years of the Great War, Mary Ward raises acutely the question of where 'literature' stops and 'propaganda' begins. In this chapter, I want to pursue the implications of the generic distinction between her writing for the War Propaganda Bureau and her writing of 'war novels'. I shall be arguing that, unflagging though her endorsement of Britain's role in the war was, she was also troubled by a sense of the aesthetic and ethical cost of her own passionate militarism—a concern which is strictly suppressed in her writing for the government, but which is allowed greater rein within the novels. As her letter to Huxley indicates, in her more self-conscious moments no one knew better than Mary Ward that writing in wartime is writing under siege.

Even given the low standing of propaganda as a literary genre, the neglect of Mary Ward within recent accounts of British writers of the First World War is, on the face of it, extraordinary. When the war began she was 63 years old and had published eighteen novels, plus a considerable body of short fiction, criticism, biography, and occasional journalism. In the 1880s she had established herself as the most successful woman novelist of her generation; in 1914, though strongly identified with the Victorian old guard, she was still a name to be conjured with. For most fiction readers her reputation remained indissociable from her first great literary success, *Robert Elsmere* (1888). Her writing never lost the high moral seriousness of that early work but, from the 1890s onward, financial pressures obliged her to write more and more rapidly and the quality of her work undeniably suffered. By 1910, although Mary Ward remained a significant figure on the British literary scene, the audience for her new books had dropped away sharply. Even in America, where her public remained more loyal than in Britain, she could no longer command the sales—or the publishers' fees—that had once come so easily. Huxley was one of her kinder satirists. Vanessa Bell summed up the view of most of the Bloomsbury set when she wrote to her sister, Virginia Woolf, in exasperation after reading Ward's memoirs: 'What is the peculiar mixture of commonplace banality, snobbishness, arrivism and boastfulness which makes her hit the bull's eye of British middle-class taste with such amazing skill each time? It's really fascinating, taken in small doses.'[12]

By 1914 Mary Ward's novels may have been a joke among the smart young set, but her skills as a writer, organizer, and public speaker were still very much in demand around the country. In 1897 she had founded the Passmore Edwards Settlement, a centre for working-class adult education and recreation which soon became famous for its pioneering provision of child-care. By 1902 it was providing day care for 1,200 children, and its work with handicapped children had become a model for other centres. Mary Ward remained closely involved with the Settlement's activities, raising vital funds for it, until her death.[13] She also attracted a great deal of more ambivalent publicity in the years immediately before the war when she became the leading figure in the organized opposition to women's suffrage. She presented the manifesto to the first meeting of the Anti-Suffrage League in 1908, and for the next four years she was their most visible campaigner. Between 1909 and 1912 she spoke at meetings all over the country, arguing vigorously that politics—especially international politics—should remain the preserve of the men who had made the empire what it was and who alone could be called upon to defend it, in the last resort, by force of arms.[14] The anti-suffrage campaign earned her debts of gratitude in high places; but the work was exhausting and her own heavy involvement in politics was clearly difficult to square with the principles she was avowing. The personal cost was sometimes high. In the late 1870s she had played a key role in the foundation of Somerville Hall, Oxford. In 1909, angered by her anti-suffrage work, the college broke with her completely.[15]

As John Sutherland argues, war was a release for Mary Ward. When Theodore Roosevelt wrote to her in December 1915, asking for her help in persuading America to change its policy of neutrality, the opportunity came as 'a bolt from the blue. But it was also a powerful tonic.'[16] Roosevelt had been enraged by the sinking of the *Lusitania* on 7 May, and was increasingly concerned that Britain's side of the war was not being put with sufficient force or justice to the American people. He felt (flatteringly) that she would be just the person to sway public opinion in his country, and he proposed a series of articles on Britain's conduct of the war, to be syndicated in American newspapers. Mary Ward expressed herself 'much puzzled and surprised', but she promptly contacted Wellington House—the headquarters of the new War Propaganda Bureau—and arranged to see the director, Charles Masterman, and the head of the American division, Sir Gilbert Parker. The government had by this stage clamped down firmly on celebrity tours of the front, particularly by women (there had been a few widely publicized incidents in 1914, in which society ladies in search of adventure had inveigled their way past the Belgian border guards and made their way to the British bases[17]). Masterman and Parker clearly felt that an exception could be made for Mrs Ward. They arranged for her to visit the principal munitions works in the north of England, to view the British fleet in the Firth of Forth, and, on three separate occasions, to tour the Allied bases in France, with her daughter Dorothy in attendance.

Mary Ward was adept at using her personal contacts to gain direct access to parliamentarians, civil servants, and top-brass military officials, quizzing them earnestly for any information

Fig. 1. Mary Ward with her daughter Dorothy and officer escort on one of her trips to the front. Reproduced by kind permission of the Trustees of the Imperial War Museum, London

that they might contribute to her 'little book' (A. J. Balfour, Margot Asquith, and Admiral Jellicoe were among those accosted). On her trips to France, she was granted privileges which must have made the professional journalists livid. Generals wined and dined her within earshot of the German guns; officers were commandeered to provide chauffeured tours of the war zone, always at a safe distance from the bombs, but still within sight and sound of the action.[18] While not the first or the only woman writer to visit the front from England (Katherine Mansfield, May Sinclair, and Edith Wharton were all there before her), she was the only one to do so with the backing of the government and the co-operation of the military. As a result, she had, for a woman, what was probably a unique education in the official conduct of the war. Among fiction writers, perhaps only H. G. Wells and Gilbert Parker were better equipped to defend Britain's role in the European conflict.

England's Effort—a collection of the first series of 'letters to an America friend'—was published in 1916, and went through four editions in that year. Roosevelt was not named at this stage, but the English editions carried a preface by an old friend of the Wards, Lord Rosebery (then vice-president of the Central Committee for National Patriotic Organizations[19]) and the American editions were introduced by the former American ambassador to Britain, Joseph H. Choate. *The Times* was predictably rapturous;[20] but the less partisan *Bookman* also hailed *England's Effort* as the ablest vindication to date of Britain's conduct during the first two years of the war, and the *Daily Telegraph* welcomed it as 'the best antidote to depression we have yet encountered'.[21] It was rapidly translated into French, Italian, Dutch, Swedish, Russian, Japanese, and German (according to Mary Ward, it received that most unlikely of accolades, a 'long and very civil review' in the *Preussische Jahrbücher*).[22] Janet Trevelyan (Ward's daughter and biographer) recorded that when America entered the war in 1917, 'it was reported by many Americans, with every accent of conviction, that but for *England's Effort* and the public opinion that it stirred, President Wilson might have delayed still longer'.[23] Whether or not it can claim to have influenced the course of history quite so directly, *England's Effort* was successful enough to warrant two sequels: *Towards the Goal* (1917) and *Fields of Victory* (1919). Mary Ward's literary contribution to the war effort did not end there. Between 1914 and 1920, despite chronic ill health, she published eight novels, various pieces of journalism, and a substantial volume of autobiographical reflections—an impressive output, by any standards.

Why has Mary Ward received so little serious attention from literary historians of the First World War? John Sutherland's recent biography has done a great deal to put her back on the literary map, and his account of her wartime activities draws for the first time substantially on her unpublished notebooks and on Dorothy Ward's diaries. But with that important exception, Mary Ward's late fiction and propaganda have attracted only sporadic, specialist interest.[24] Her neglect is most obvious among the numerous wide-ranging surveys of women's war writing published over the last fifteen years. At the very best she can now hope to be enlisted along with Jessie Pope as the most obvious example to hand of a pro-war woman writer. Claire M. Tylee gives her a few glancing references in *The Great War and Women's Consciousness,* grouping her together with Mrs Belloc Lowndes and Beatrice Harraden (a comparison she would almost certainly have found highly insulting[25]) as one of those 'women over 50 . . . [who] seem to have held the high Victorian belief that war would revitalise a society in danger of decadence'.[26]

Mary Ward's low standing in recent years has to be ascribed in part to her reputation as the leading campaigner against women's suffrage. Certain kinds of pro-war activity have long been recognized as 'compatible' with feminist history. Emmeline Pankhurst and her daughter Christabel famously put aside their suffragette banners for the duration of the conflict and urged their followers to devote themselves to the greater struggle, even changing the name of the *Suffragette* magazine to *Britannia.* But feminist writing about the Great War tends now to be more interested in women's resistance to militarism than in their cooperation with the war effort.[27] Revisionist historians and literary critics have been rightly concerned to expand the definition of war to include not only the trenches but the whole culture which sustains and justifies militarism. Mrs Humphry Ward's insistence on putting 'our boys at the front' first, her evident belief that, however important women's contribution was to the war effort, it paled in relation to the great drama going on in France, and her prominence within the Anti-Suffrage League have combined to make her an unpalatable figure for feminism.[28]

The historical connections between the suffrage issue and the Great War have been extensively written about in recent years.[29] Jane Marcus, for example, has argued influentially that the images of women used to promote the war effort between 1914 and 1918 indicate a strong backlash against the claims of the suffrage campaigners in the decade before. Resisting Sandra Gilbert's desire to see the posters of smiling VADs and land-workers as evidence of women's liberation during the Great War, she claims that the peculiarly insistent portrayal of women in the roles of mothers and nurses is evidence that war propagandists 'had to work particularly hard to erase the powerful new images created by women for women at the height of the [suffrage] movement'.[30] Given that Mary Ward learnt many of her skills as a war propagandist in the course of her work for the Anti-Suffrage League, one would expect that her war writing would be neatly contained within this model of First World War propaganda as a counter-feminist genre. Certainly, it would be possible to construct a very conservative picture of the trilogy of letters to America. In *England's Effort* and its sequels, Ward repeatedly links the themes of war and gender in ways which are determinedly (though not unsubtly) resistant to women's liberation. Her interest in the principle of labour 'dilution' is a case in point. 'Dilution' was the name given to the process by which work hitherto considered 'skilled' was broken down into various components, some of which could be designated unskilled and allotted to women, while others remained the preserve of skilled men. As a concept, dilution was attractive to Mary Ward, because it offered a model of changing relations between the sexes which was, to all intents and purposes, only a more discriminating means of distinguishing between male and female capabilities. Dilution allowed her to enthuse about the emergence of the 'new woman' in wartime without having to fear the eradication of 'the old needs and sweetnesses'.[31] In this and other instances, war seems to have provided Mary Ward with a welcome opportunity to update and, at the same time, reinforce her views on the woman question.

That said, Mary Ward's thinking about the war was neither as crudely patriotic nor as 'anti-feminist' as its current low standing in the canon of First World War women's writing would suggest. The need for women's labour was far less contentious for her than some of the other subjects she was called upon to address in her writing for the War Propaganda Bureau. Much more sensitive, especially in light of her views on the suffrage issue, was the question of women's right to have a say in the conduct of the war when they were not going to be called upon to give their lives. Mary Ward's propaganda work required her to become a public authority on Britain's response to the war, and in the process, she became more closely identified with the government than any other woman—a position clearly at odds with her avowed belief that politics was a male domain. More problematically yet, *speaking* on behalf of the government as often as not meant remaining silent on behalf of the government. Like any other commentator on the progress of the conflict in France, Mary Ward was required to subject her articles to the Censor for clearance. Not surprisingly, issues of speaking and not speaking become highly charged in her propaganda and her fiction, with complex repercussions for her thinking about gender. In what follows, I want to look closely at the thematics of censorship in Mary Ward's propagandist trilogy and in the two novels most directly concerned with the war, *Missing* (1916) and *Harvest* (written 1918, published 1920). What did it mean to her to be a woman writing about war, when, by her own definition, war was a man's subject? How did she respond in her propaganda to the ethical implications of censorship in a war which she strongly believed was being fought in defence of Truth? More importantly, from a literary point of view, how did questions of silence and censorship figure in her fiction, where she could reflect more freely on the nature of truth and falsehood in wartime, knowing that she was no longer so directly under the eye of the Censor?

Senator Hiram Johnson's observation that 'When war is declared, Truth is the first casualty'[32] would have had a mixed hearing from Mary Ward. Manipulation of public opinion by the state was something she associated very firmly with the enemy, and a scrupulous regard for truth was, for her, synonymous with Englishness. Few things angered her more about Germany's conduct in the early days of the conflict than the signing of a pro-war manifesto by ninety-three senior German academics—an act she saw as a fundamental betrayal of intellectual honesty. In the preface to the German edition of *England's Effort*, she took on the role of external examiner with a vengeance:

We held [German professors] to be servants of truth, incapable of acquiescence in a tyrannous lie. We held them also to be scholars, incapable therefore of falsifying facts and ignoring documents in their own interest. But in that astonishing manifesto . . . those very men who had taught Europe to respect evidence and to deal scrupulously with documents, when it was a question of Classical antiquity, or early Christianity, now, when it was a question of justifying the crime of their country, threw evidence and documents to the winds. How many of those who signed the professorial manifesto had ever read the British White Paper, and the French Yellow Book . . . ?[33]

German reports that a Zeppelin raid on the north of England had destroyed the Liverpool docks and left English industry in ruins excited similar patriotic scorn soon after she began work on *England's Effort*: 'We may suppose I think that the *Hamburger Nachrichten* has something of the same kind of standing in Germany as the *Liverpool Daily Post*, or the *Newcastle Chronicle* has in this country. Can one conceive either of these English papers romancing in the same way?'[34] Much of this is the familiar rhetoric of First World War propaganda: Germany seen as a war machine, its *Kultur* exposed as a lie.[35] Unlike many propagandists, however, Mary Ward was not interested in disseminating atrocity stories about German mutilations of women and children; whereas she was keenly interested in the more abstract questions of truth-telling and credibility in wartime. Here, gullibility to propaganda becomes a symptom of the degeneration of the German character. No British citizen could be so easily gulled: 'Our sense of humour, if nothing else, prevents.'[36]

Mary Ward's disdain for any defence of the war that could not support itself with meticulous regard for 'the facts' helps to explain the extraordinary care that went into researching her war reports. Her talent was for popularizing information about England's war effort, seasoning a barrage of information with her novelist's talent for realistic 'eyewitness' description. The bare facts were interwoven with, and seasoned by, autobiography. Impassioned defence of Britain's increase in munitions production, of the readiness of the country's fleet, and the valour of its armed forces, was given the stamp of authenticity by personal observation: 'two months of strenuous looking and thinking, of conversation with soldiers and sailors and munition-workers, of long days spent in the great supply-bases across the channel' had, she claimed, allowed her to 'realize'

England's effort 'more vividly than ever before'.[37] The vigorous insistence that she has 'been there' also enables Mary Ward to avoid some of the appearance of mere assertion, casting her writing instead as an exercise in research which has happily enabled her to reaffirm the already known. In the face of American doubt and enemy propaganda, she can confirm the unimpeachable integrity of the English: the valour of 'our boys' (evident in their cheerfulness on the ship over to France, and their frantic eagerness to be back in the fray); the commitment of civilians to the war effort (proven most impressively to her in the munitions works); and the particular contribution of women, whose willingness to take on previously male areas of employment had freed so many men for the front.

Given the level at which censorship was operating by 1916, however, her desire to deliver a full and honest account of Britain's response to German aggression was always going to be compromised. Mary Ward was co-opted into the propaganda business at a time when the British government was still in the throes of determining the proper limits of public information during wartime. Fleet Street—under the formidable leadership of Lord Northcliffe, proprietor of *The Times* and the *Daily Mail*—had been agitating against undue muzzling of the press ever since the war began.[38] By 1916 some concessions to the journalists had been made. There were now five official correspondents from the front, as well as a military 'Eye Witness' (soon to be joined by a second) whose job it was to feed information to the press, via the War Office. All were heavily circumscribed in what they could say. Any accurate information about troop movements, any details about units and battalions likely to yield such information, would be censored. Inaccurate reporting, on the other hand, might get through: 'the Press Bureau never guaranteed the accuracy of the reports it approved, and was not averse to creating mischief for German intelligence'.[39]

On the face of it, Mary Ward was allowed extraordinary privileges for a non-professional journalist. But one of her prime attractions for Wellington House was undoubtedly her willingness to submit her writing unquestioningly to the Censor's pen. 'Some day, perhaps,' she mused in *A Writer's Recollections* (1918), 'when peace has loosened our tongues, and abolished that very necessary person the Censor, there will be something more to be written.'[40] For the duration, however, she was fully content to write something less. Surprisingly, the War Office seems not to have worried about the contents of the personal notebooks she (or rather Dorothy) carried everywhere with her in France, no doubt in the knowledge that she was accompanied wherever she went, and that whatever she wrote for public consumption would be looked over by the Censor. The notebooks are packed with statistics. Many of them are insignificant, in that they were taken from *The Times* or from *Hansard* and were therefore already in the public domain. On a few occasions, however, she did gain access to sensitive information. In Étaples in February 1916 she was privy to extensive details about the size, the organization, and the methods of the training-camp; on her second visit in March 1917, she learned from a conversation with Colonel Plomer[41] that the sand-dunes behind the camp concealed an enormous ammunition dump begun in December 1916: '*Very secret*', she noted carefully.[42] When it came to the more brutal aspects of the war, however, there was no need to enjoin her discretion. The military bases in France arranged tours of the hospitals, and this seems to have been the least palatable part of the whole business for her.[43] She admired the nurses, but her taste was for the 'idea' of war, not for the reality of mutilation and death. She was pleased when one general informed her (quite untruthfully) that she had been 'nearer to the fighting than any woman has been in this war—not even a nurse has been so close';[44] and delighted when a colonel teased her for being 'bloodthirsty'.[45] Judging from her brief, distressed notes on the men she saw in the army hospitals, Brigadier-General John Charteris was nearer the truth when he recorded her visit to GHQ in his diary for 1916: '*March* 4. We have had our first lady visitor . . . Mrs Humphry Ward and her daughter have arrived on a more or less official visit. . . . I gave Mrs Ward dinner at the Press château. She is altogether charming, but I am afraid too gentle-hearted to bear the sight of some of the cruelties of war.'[46]

In a cartoon published in the popular penny journal *The Passing Show* in 1915, David Wilson gave sharp expression to the growing unhappiness about the government clamp-down on war reporters, and, in so doing, drew an explicit link between censorship and gender. His sketch for the cover of the 23 October issue shows an unhappy woman bound tightly to a post with heavy rope. She is standing on a quill pen, and a halo around

Fig. 2. David Wilson, 'Another Atrocity', cover illustration of *The Passing Show*, 23 October 1915. Reproduced by kind permission of the Syndics of Cambridge University Library

her head bears the inscription 'THE PRESS'. In the foreground stands the villain, 'THE CENSOR', depicted as a slick and sinister gentleman stroking his chin and carrying an enormous (presumably blue) pencil. The caption below reads 'Another Atrocity'. Much of the effectiveness of Wilson's cartoon for first viewers must have lain in its silent quotation of similar scenes from government propaganda, in which the barbarous Hun threatened the women of Belgium. By implication, Britain's censorship laws were becoming as threatening to democratic free speech as the enemy the country was supposedly fighting.

Mary Ward would have emphatically disagreed with David Wilson's view of the government's proceedings. It was a matter of pride for her (surprising in a novelist) that the language of her propaganda works was not so much her own as the filtered language of the men on the front. As she put it in *Fields of Victory*, 'I am of course quoting not any opinion of my own, to which I have no right, but what I have gathered from those responsible men who were in the forefront of the fighting.'[47] The diction of Mary Ward's propaganda—and, in a lesser degree, of the novels—has dated. Reading her enthusiastic defence of the 'spendid chaps who are winning the war', it would be easy to assume that even then she was merely striking the false note of the civilian propagandist, protected by virtue of her gender and her temperament from seeing the worst. 'Splendid', as John Sutherland notes, is her catchword. The politicians are always 'charming', the generals and senior officers are unfailingly 'courteous', the 'keenness and dash' of the English soldiers are without equal. This was not the language of the average Tommy in the trenches, but it was in tune with the kinds of pronouncement found repeatedly among the official memoirs and publications of the officers she was mixing with. Haig, for instance, sent the British forces into battle in April 1918 with a message of praise for 'the splendid resistance offered by all ranks of our Army under the most trying circumstances'.[48]

Much of the logic behind Mary Ward's willing abandonment of her own authority as a propagandist lay in her expressed belief that such writing was an act of war: 'I simply felt,' she wrote to her daughter, 'that money or no money, strength or fatigue, I was under orders and must go on.'[49] But the metaphors to which she most often had resort were more feminine. An awareness of gender was as central to her perception of the restrictions on freedom of speech in wartime as it was to David Wilson, but where he saw the government's exercise of control over writers as a form of violence, she was prepared to see a form of flirtation, even romance. Her response to the War Office's initial decision in January 1916 that she might go to France, but 'could not be allowed to go into the War Zone—or St Omer'[50] is a case in point. Undeterred, she presented herself at Eccleston Square on the following Thursday and enjoyed a thoroughly satisfactory meeting with Sir Edward Grey,[51] Sir Arthur Nicolson,[52] and Lord Robert Cecil[53] (she was in her element among so many titles). Sir Edward was 'very kind and cordial', Lord Robert was 'so attractive with his broad brow, & open courteous look'—and all three were agreed that the articles must be written, and that she should have what she asked for: 'a great deal of help'. She quickly persuaded this genial audience that a visit to France was essential if the articles were to have 'life and colour'. When Lord Robert suggested that she might also like to have 'a look at the Fleet', she was coy: 'I said that I had not ventured to suggest it, but that of course anything that gave picturesqueness and novelty—i.e. a woman being allowed to visit the Fleet—would help the articles.'[54] The 'feminine' note of gratitude for a show of trust from the men in power, the willingness to wait for them to pronounce, the sense that submission to orders might constitute a kind of dalliance with power, come through repeatedly in her propaganda. The language of romance permeates her account of her time in France, continually providing a softened focus on the cruelties of war. In the midst of so much death, romance held the promise of a hereafter. Perhaps this is partly why she was so struck to hear of the number of liaisons between British soldiers and French girls: 'how [the average Tommy] communicates with the French maidens with whom he walks out in the Base towns where he is temporarily quartered no one knows—Their talk is a new language known only to themselves. But there is no mischief, & there will be many marriages after the war.'[55] Shortly afterwards, on a separate leaf of the notebook, she scribbled an allusion to another, more famous English–French romance: 'O fair Katharine, if you will love me soundly with your French heart, I will be glad to hear you confess it brokenly with your English tongue.'[56] The lines are unglossed in Mary Ward's notebook, and she chose not to use them in her propaganda, perhaps with an awareness that their message was not without ambivalence.

In her writing for the War Propaganda Bureau, Mary Ward was an unshakeable defender of the government's right to decide where the boundaries of free speech must lie in wartime. Her fiction, however, returned repeatedly, almost obsessively, to the ethics of censorship and silence. In very different ways, the novels, particularly *Missing* (1917) and *Harvest* (1920), keep provoking the question which her propaganda had so carefully avoided: what are the moral implications of withholding the truth from others in a war supposedly being fought to uphold principles of honesty, integrity, and justice? Doesn't pro-war writing which refuses to acknowledge the limits of its own honesty court the same charge she had laid against the German press: that of 'romancing' the war?

A culpable failure to speak the truth is at the heart of the first novel in which Mary Ward directly addressed the subject of the war. *Missing* is the story of two sisters, Nelly Sarratt and Bridget Cookson. Bridget, austere, sour, and resenting her humble lot in life, cannot easily forgive her sister's uncharacteristically 'wilful' marriage to 'a young subaltern with only £250 p.a. besides his pay, when, with her prettiness, she might have married a wealthy man—and learned to love him in time'.[57] When the novel opens, George Sarratt is coming to the end of a long leave in England, convalescing from a wound sustained at the Battle of Ypres. Bridget's hostility to him on the grounds of poverty is exacerbated by a lack of sympathy for his passionate belief in the war. Staying on in the Lake District after George has returned to his regiment in France, she does her best to encourage a friendship between Nelly and the local squire, Sir William Farrell—a man whose charm, wealth, and station are far more satisfactory to Bridget's tastes. When George is reported missing after the Battle of the Somme, ambitions which have long lain half-formed in her mind emerge as real possibilities. She accepts the use of Farrell's house when Nelly breaks down under the strain of not knowing whether her lover is dead or alive; and—in the teeth of strong resistance from Nelly—takes every opportunity to leave her alone with Sir William. As the months wear on, Nelly's resistance begins to fail, not because she has stopped loving her husband, but because she cannot bear her emotional isolation: 'to live without being loved, to tear herself away from those who wished to love her—for that she had proved too weak. She knew it, and was not unconscious of a certain moral defeat; as she looked out upon all the strenous and splendid things that women were doing in the war' (195). That slight semi-colon carries more than its usual weight, in a novel where recognition of what other women are 'doing in the war' continually operates as a check on the indulgence of private feeling.

Just as Nelly seems to be turning towards Sir William for comfort, Bridget receives a letter from a doctor in France informing her that he believes he has identified her brother-in-law, alive in a military hospital. Rather than risk raising Mrs Sarratt's hopes unnecessarily, he asks Bridget to come to France and confirm George's identity. Bridget fabricates an excuse, and makes the trip across the Channel without her sister's knowledge. It is, indeed, George, but unconscious and slowly dying. Only a flicker of the eyelids indicates that he may have heard his sister-in-law whisper his name. Bridget tersely informs the doctor that there has been a mistake and returns home to England accompanied by a description which gives the reader no room to doubt that this woman has internalized the enemy: 'A dull sense of something irrevocable,—something horrible,—overshadowed her. But the "will to conquer" in her was as iron; and, as in the Prussian conscience, left no room for pity or remorse' (239). Moral Prussianism is, unsurprisingly, defeated in *Missing*: Bridget's crime is uncovered in time to allow Nelly and George a final three weeks together. But the novel is, significantly, more interested in exploring Nelly's conscience than in dealing out justice to her sister. Brought face to face with the moral cowardice that almost led her to betray George while he lay dying of his wounds in France, Nelly discovers reserves of character she did not know she possessed. After his death, she signs up for VAD work and finds a salve for her conscience in throwing herself into the war effort. For the persistently romantic reader, there remains the hope of a marriage to Sir William sometime in the future, but only when Nelly can be sure she has conquered her own weakness.

Bridget Cookson's failure to speak the truth after her visit to the war zone is evidently wrong—but, as the novel's relative lack of interest in her indicates, the ethics of telling or not telling what one knows are more complicated in *Missing* than the central incident would suggest. There are other situations, just as closely bound up with the war, in which refusing to speak the truth is not a crime but a positive virtue. When George Sarratt holds Nelly in his arms at the start of the novel and prepares to leave her, 'all sorts of images' flit through his mind 'of which he would not have told her for all the world—horrible facts of bloody war. In eight months, he had seen plenty of them' (17). Writing to George from England, Nelly deliberately censors all reference to her own depression: 'Nelly Sarratt slept little, and wrote every day to her George, letters of which long sections were often destroyed when written, condemned for lack of cheerfulness' (111). The difference between these silences and Bridget's calculated concealment of the truth gradually assumes the force of something approaching a definition of love in *Missing*. Near the end of *England's Effort*, Mary Ward describes a visit to a British convalescent camp in France where the 'skill and pity and devotion poured out upon this terrible human need' by the doctors, nurses, and VADs impressed her more than any other message the place could convey:

> After all, one tremblingly asks oneself, in spite of the appalling facts of wounds, and death, and violence, in which the human world is now steeped, is it yet *possible*, is it yet *true*, that the ultimate thing—the final power behind the veil—to which at least this vast linked spectacle of suffering and tenderness, here in this great camp, testifies—is *not* Force, but Love? (129)

Suffering, in *England's Effort*, is the veil behind which the truth of Love can be, if not directly seen, then at least intimated. The key terms are the same in *Missing*, but the logic is, significantly, reversed: suffering becomes, for George contemplating his return to the front, and for Nelly in her grief after the Battle of the Somme, the truth hidden behind the veil of Love. Lest this be thought to constitute a moral dilemma, *Missing* has an answer: nothing is hidden from a lover's eyes. George has no need to speak of what he has seen because the truth is 'graven on his young face'. When he is reported missing, Nelly, in her anguish, becomes prey to 'a series of dreams, almost always concerned with the war. . . . the trenches, always the trenches; those hideous broken woods of the Somme front, where the blasted soil has sucked the best life-blood of England; those labyrinthine diggings and delvings in a tortured earth . . . and the last crashing horror of the bomb, in some hell-darkness at the end of all . . .' (198–9). Such empathy leaves nothing to be said, because it knows the truth without being told. The 'veil' between Truth and Suffering becomes, rather, a hall of mirrors, in which Truth can only ever reflect itself back unchallenged.

It is one mark of the difference between Ward's propaganda and her fiction that *Missing* does, at least briefly, declare itself uncertain whether a lover's knowledge is to be desired or repudiated in wartime: is Nelly's capacity to envisage the trenches by the sheer force of her love part of the capacity for human sympathy that England is fighting to save, or a symptom of the 'softness' that Nelly must learn to purge from her character? The question is only allowed a brief airing. In the end, Wordsworthian Romanticism comes to the rescue of Mudiean romance. Watching Nelly and Sir William conversing amid the daffodils by the shores of Grasmere, his patriotic maiden aunt initially doubts whether there is a future for romance between them, but in her 'heart of hearts' she knows there will be.

Though Ward's next novel, *The War and Elizabeth* (1918), has less to say about the ethical problems attaching to silence and censorship in wartime, it does contribute importantly to an awareness of the changing role romance played in her defence of the war. In *The War and Elizabeth* love and the war go hand in hand, but with considerable difficulty along the way, as Elizabeth's growing affection for her cussedly anti-war employer, Squire Mannering, eventually reforms him into a saddened but wiser patriot. The novel has been somewhat generously described as Ward's attempt at symbolism.[58] Certainly, it invests heavily in the symbolic potential of classical mythology, no doubt with Gilbert Murray's yoking of classical scholarship and propaganda in mind. But whereas Murray presented his Oxford students and his wider readership with meticulous reinterpretations of Thucydides in the light of the current European conflict,[59] Ward seems rather to be treating classical allusion as an escape from modernity.[60] Perhaps because she was conscious of writing at a 'supremely critical moment in the War'[61] the novel's direction is more propagandist than *Missing* and it is considerably less willing to interrogate the terms in which it chooses to defend the war. This was the novel she chose to present to Douglas Haig when they met near Montreuil on her third trip to France, in January 1919 ('I gave him "Elizabeth" & he asked me to write my name in it. I wrote "To F.M. Sir D.H. with the thanks of an Englishwoman"').[62] One wonders what he thought of it. For all its unimpeachable commitment to celebrating the way in which English men and women at home were helping to win the war, the romantic promise of future happiness comes too late to hold this novel together. There is a strongly elegiac tone to *The War and Elizabeth,* which may well explain its failure to achieve the popular success of *Missing,* and which also marks it as a turning-point of sorts—or, perhaps more accurately, as a dead-end in Ward's use of the romance genre as a framework for her view of the war. For a more troubled and artistically ambitious return to the question of truth in wartime it is necessary to go to the last of Ward's novels, *Harvest,* begun during the final months of the war, and finished on New Year's Eve 1918.

Arnold Bennett got to the core of what many readers found irritating in the typical heroine of a Mary Ward novel. 'I have invented a destiny for Mrs Humphry Ward's heroines,' he confessed, in one of his most viciously witty pieces of literary journalism, written shortly before the war:

> They ought to be caught, with their lawful male protectors, in the siege of a great city by a foreign army. Their lawful male protectors ought, before sallying forth on a forlorn hope, to provide them with a revolver as a last refuge from the brutal and licentious soldiery. And when things come to a crisis, in order to be concluded in our next, the revolvers ought to prove to be unloaded. I admit that this invention of mine is odious, and quite un-English, and such as would never occur to a right-minded subscriber to Mudies. But it illustrates the mood caused in me by witnessing the antics of those harrowing dolls.[63]

As Bennett's 'un-English' fantasy implies, most of Mary Ward's heroines are carefully protected from any direct experience of the brutalities of life. At the worst, their men fail them morally. Physical violence rarely comes their way, and licentiousness is an unknown quantity. All this makes *Harvest* an unexpected departure from Mary Ward's normal repertoire. *Harvest* is her most 'modern' work in terms of its frank interest in sexual desire; as John Sutherland notes, it is also her most extended analysis of violent crime (at certain points it comes close to fulfilling Bennett's fantasy of what 'ought to happen' to Mrs Ward's heroines). And, though it alludes continually to romance, and invites its reader to approach it in those terms, *Harvest* is at odds with the romance genre almost from the start.

The novel tells the story of a young woman, Rachel Henderson, and her friend Janet Leighton. In the last summer of the war, Rachel buys a farm and the two young women set about managing it according to the latest scientific methods. The local farmers are predictably distrustful of these city girls with their new-fangled certificates in agriculture, but slowly the confidence of the old guard is won. On a visit to an American forestry battalion in the area, Rachel meets and falls in love with a young American commander, Captain Ellesborough. Ellesborough comes from an old Unitarian New England family who have imbued in him 'a strict and even severe standard in sexual morals',[64] and, as the relationship develops, it becomes gradually apparent that Rachel has a past to hide from his stern eyes. When the sinister and consumptive figure of Roger Delaney turns up, and takes to lurking outside the farmhouse at night, he is thought by the locals to be the ghost of a murdered man. In fact, Roger is Rachel's Canadian ex-husband, divorced by her after his drunken negligence ended in the death of their only child. Initially this unwelcome figure from the past wants only money, but Rachel has more reason to worry when another old acquaintance turns up and threatens to reveal that she was guilty of adultery. Faced with two potential blackmailers threatening to expose her to her lover as a divorcée and an adulteress, Rachel confesses everything to Janet and is persuaded that the only morally justifiable course is to tell the whole truth to Ellesborough. On Armistice Day, Rachel sends him a full account of her former life. That night, he comes to the farmhouse, his eyes burning 'with ardent, protecting love'. As he takes Rachel in his arms for what seems set to be a happy ending, Roger Delaney shoots his ex-wife through the window. 'Of such acts', Ward reflects 'there is no explanation. They are part of that black seed in human nature which is born with a man, and flowers in due time, and through devious stages, in such a deed as that which destroyed Rachel Henderson' (284).

The rhetorical flourish allows Mary Ward to bow out with something like aplomb, but the plot is rather more interesting than the ostensible moral here. The 'black seed in human nature' is a patently inadequate answer to the novel's perplexed examination of women's relationship to male violence or, more specifically, its interest in the extent of women's obligation to tell the 'whole truth' about their knowledge of that violence. Rachel sets out on her new life determined to put behind her a past she does not wish to admit as hers. She resists the burden of her name,[65] refusing to mourn, but she ends her life having recognized that to lie about the past is to become its slave. So far so pat. But when Rachel tells the truth, she dies at the hands of the man she has supposedly conquered with her honesty. How far the taint of adultery made Rachel an unsalvageable heroine for Ward is a moot point. There are strong overtones of high-Victorian moralism in the novel's presentation of her death as a kind of triumph and release ('Had it been, after all, "deliverance" for Rachel from this troublesome world . . . ?'; 283). Setting *Harvest* alongside the propagandist trilogy and the earlier war novels, however, it seems more accurate to describe the presentation of Rachel Henderson's death as an attempt by Ward to salvage a romantic interpretation of the Great War, at a time when the full extent of its horror was still becoming apparent. *Harvest* ends with the truth unable to withstand violence, and to that extent it is arguably a more 'honest' response to the war than anything else Mary Ward wrote. But in its claim to tragedy, its insistence that this doomed woman, like a latter-day Juliet, dies upon a kiss, Ward's final novel is defiantly sentimental. *Harvest* does not, in the end, abandon a romantic vision of the war. Rather, it finds a way of romancing the death of romance, and of softening its own recognition of the vulnerability of truth.

It would be difficult to extrapolate a general account of women's pro-war writing from the example of Mary Ward. Her engagement with the conflict of 1914–18 was shaped by a unique set of opportunities and influences: she had, for a woman, an extraordinary degree of access to government and military officials, she could draw on extensive experience not only as a novelist but as a journalist, and, not least, she held to her conviction that the most valuable thing she could offer a wartime reading public was a morally uplifting romance. More than many writers, she demands to be addressed on her own terms, and it is odd that she should so frequently have been enlisted—and dismissed—as a 'type' of the pro-war woman. It would be easy, on the other hand, to discount Mary Ward's view of the war with the complaint Doris Lessing once made against

George Eliot: 'there is a great deal she does not understand because she is moral'.[66] Certainly, Mary Ward was a moralist but, like George Eliot (who helped to inspire a love of literature in the 19-year-old Mary when they met in 1870), she believed in the obligation of writers to keep questioning the extent to which any ideal conception of 'truth' could stand up to the pressure of private and public circumstance. It is symptomatic of her conception of what the First World War required from her personally that such questioning occurred less openly in her published writing after 1914. For the latter-day reader, likely to be more critical than she was of the arguments used to justify Britain's engagement in the First World War, there may be some consolation in the knowledge that, occasionally, her private notebooks tell a different story. After their visit to the hospital base, her officer escort at Étaples in February 1917 took her to see some live bomb practice. They clambered to the top of a slope and watched from the crest, while a young soldier hurled three time bombs into a group of dummy figures in a sand-pit twenty yards away: 'he throws—we crouch behind the parapet of sand bags—a few seconds, then a fierce report. We rise. One of the dummy figures half-wrecked—only a few fragments of the bomb surviving. One thinks of it descending in a group of men—& one remembers the huge hospitals behind us—'. The thought struck home: 'War', she noted, 'begins to seem to me more & more horrible and intolerable—.'[67] But she omitted the sentiment from *Towards the Goal*, substituting for it that question to which *Harvest* had given such an ambiguous answer: 'is it yet *possible*, is it yet *true*, that the ultimate thing—the final power behind the veil . . . is not Force, but Love?'

NOTES

1. Aldous Huxley, 'Farcical History of Richard Greenow', in Huxley, *Limbo* (London, 1923), 113.
2. See Enid Huws Jones, *Mrs Humphry Ward* (London, 1973), 163.
3. Ibid. 164.
4. Sybille Bedford, *Aldous Huxley: A Biography*, 2 vols. (London, 1974), i. 108.
5. Ibid. 83.
6. 'Richard Greenow', 72.
7. Ibid. 110–11.

8. Janet Penrose Trevelyan, *The Life of Mrs Humphry Ward* (London, 1923), 290.
9. Between 1914 and 1918 sales of her novels averaged 35,000 copies per volume. H. G. Wells, at the height of his career, managed only 15,000. See Harold Orel, *Popular Fiction in England, 1914–1918* (Hemel Hempstead, 1982), 49.
10. For Woolf's current status as the paradigmatic woman writer about war, see particularly Mark Hussey (ed.), *Virginia Woolf and War: Fiction, Reality and Myth* (Syracuse, NY, 1991).
11. Rosa Bracco, *Merchants of Hope: British Middlebrow Writers of the First World War, 1919–39* (Oxford, 1993).
12. Vanessa Bell, Letter to Virginia Woolf, *c.* 19 Dec. 1918; quoted in Frances Spalding, *Vanessa Bell* (1983; London, 1994), 166. For other attacks on Ward, see John Sutherland, *Mrs Humphry Ward: Eminent Victorian, Pre-eminent Edwardian* (Oxford, 1991), 201. Also Rebecca West, 'The Gospel according to Mrs Humphry Ward', *Freewoman*, 15 Feb. 1912; H. G. Wells, 'The Novels of Mr. George Gissing', *Contemporary Review*, Aug. 1897; and, more recently, Hugh Kenner, *The Pound Era* (London, 1971), 8, deploring Ward's 'British so-cultured nullity'.
13. See Sutherland, *Mrs Humphry Ward*, ch. 18, and his pamphlet *The Mary Ward Centre 1890–1990*, privately produced (n.d.), sold in aid of the Mary Ward Centre.
14. On the connections between the anti-suffragists' arguments and the campaign against women's admission to the military services, see Jenny Gould, 'Women's Military Services in First World War Britain', in M. R. Higonnet, Jane Jenson, Sonya Michel, and Margaret C. Weitz (eds.), *Behind the Lines: Gender and the Two World Wars* (New Haven, 1987), 117.
15. Sutherland, *Mrs Humphry Ward*, 299–306.
16. Ibid. 350–1. And see *The Letters of Theodore Roosevelt*, ed. Elting E. Morison *et al.*, 8 vols. (Cambridge, Mass., 1951–4), viii. 998–9.
17. See 'GSO' [Sir Frank Fox], *GHQ (Montreuil-sur-Mer)* (London, 1920), 58–65.
18. On official tours of the front, see E. S. Turner, *Dear Old Blighty* (London, 1980), 48–51.
19. One of the numerous 'fronts' for the War Propaganda Bureau. See C. Haste, *Keep the Home Fires Burning: Propaganda in the First World War* (London, 1977), 41.
20. Humphry Ward was *The Times*'s art critic.
21. Reviews extracted in an advertisement for *England's Effort*, printed at the back of Mrs Humphry Ward, *Towards the Goal* (London, 1917).
22. Ibid. 2; Françoise Rives, 'Une romancière victorienne face à la Grande Guerre: Mrs Humphry Ward de 1914 à 1918', *Caliban*, 19 (1982), 65; Sutherland, *Mrs Humphry Ward*, 354.
23. Trevelyan, *Mrs Humphry Ward*, 281. For evidence of the continuing force of this claim, see Jean Elshtain, *Women and War* (Brighton, 1987), 112 n.
24. See Rives, 'Une romancière victorienne'; J. E. Sait, '"A Strange New Consciousness": Mrs Humphry Ward and the Great War', *AUMLA* 69 (1988), 98–132; George Otte, 'Mrs Humphry Ward, the Great War, and the Historical Loom', *Clio*, 19 (1990), 271–84.
25. Beatrice Harraden (1864–1936) was the author of numerous works of sentimental and sub-Gothic fiction. Her novel *The Fowler* (1899) caused

a minor stir for its depiction of 'a violent sexual predator who violates women's minds and bodies'. She was one of the leaders of the WSPU and of the Women Writers' League. Marie Adelaide Belloc Lowndes (1868–1947) was not 'over 50' until the very end of the war. She was the daughter of the feminist editor Bessie Raynor Parkes and a prolific novelist, best known for her Jack-the-Ripper-inspired thriller *The Lodger* (1913). See John Sutherland, *The Longman Companion to Victorian Fiction* (London, 1988), 280, and Anne Crawford *et al.* (eds.), *The Europa Biographical Dictionary of British Women* (London, 1983), 190, 263.

26. Claire M. Tylee, *The Great War and Women's Consciousness: Images of Militarism and Womanhood in Women's Writings, 1914–64* (Basingstoke, 1990), 104. Sandra Gilbert and Susan Gubar give Ward only fractionally more room in *No Man's Land: The Place of the Woman Writer in the Twentieth Century*, ii: *Sexchanges* (New Haven, 1989), 127, 274–5, 283, 295–6, 305. She is not mentioned at all in Dorothy Goldman's collection of essays on women writers of the First World War *Women and World War I: The Written Response* (Basingstoke, 1993). Similarly, Ward is barely mentioned in Nicola Beauman, *A Very Great Profession: The Women's Novel, 1914–1939* (London, 1983), and is omitted altogether from Mary Cadogan and Patricia Craig, *Women and Children First: The Fiction of Two World Wars* (London, 1978). And she has fared no better in more general accounts of First World War fiction such as Orel, *Popular Fiction in England*, George Parfitt, *Fiction of the First World War* (London, 1988), and John Onions, *English Fiction and Drama of the Great War, 1918–1939* (Basingstoke, 1990).
27. e.g. Anne Wiltshire, *Most Dangerous Women: Feminist Peace Campaigners of the First World War* (London, 1985); M. R. Higonnet and P. L.-R. Higonnet, 'The Double Helix', in Higonnet *et al.* (eds.), *Behind the Lines*, 31–47 (esp. pp. 46–7); Catherine Marshall, C. K. Ogden, and Mary Sargant Florence, *Militarism versus Feminism*, ed. Margaret Kamester and Jo Vellacott (London, 1987); and Carol J. Adams, 'Feminism, the Great War, and Modern Vegetarianism', in Helen M. Cooper, Adrienne Auslander Munich, and Susan Merrill Squier (eds.), *Arms and the Woman: War, Gender, and Literary Representation* (Chapel Hill, NC, 1989), 244–67. Jane Marcus makes the point most prescriptively: 'Women's history asks that we look not only at war texts but at those particular fictions in which suffrage and the war overlap and intermix' ('Corpus/Corps/Corpse: Writing the Body in/at War', ibid. 132).
28. She falls within none of the four categories Joan W. Scott lists as the established models for understanding women's relationship to the Great War. See 'Rewriting History', in Higonnet *et al.* (eds.), *Behind the Lines*, 23–5.
29. See particularly 'The Women and Men of 1914', in Cooper *et al.* (eds.), *Arms and the Woman*, 97–123; Sandra Gilbert, 'Soldier's Heart: Literary Men, Literary Women, and the Great War', *Signs*, 8/3 (1983), 422–50, rev. and repr. in (amongst others), Gilbert and Gubar, *No Man's Land*; Jane Marcus, 'The Asylums of Antaeus: Women, War, and Madness—Is there a Feminist Fetishism?' in H. Aram Veeser (ed.), *The New Historicism* (London, 1990).
30. Marcus, 'The Asylums of Antaeus', 140–1.
31. Mrs Humphry Ward, *Missing* (London, 1917), 342. See also *England's Effort: Six Letters to an American Friend* (London, 1916), 61–73, 77–8.

32. Variously attributed to Hiram Johnson, Arthur Ponsonby, Rudyard Kipling, and John Bright, the origin of the phrase is probably Dr Johnson, *The Idler*, 30 (11 Nov. 1758).
33. Quoted in Trevelyan, *Mrs Humphry Ward*, 265.
34. Honn notebook 34. Mary Ward toned this passage down considerably for publication. See *England's Effort*, 39–40.
35. See Daniel Pick, *War Machine: The Rationalisation of Slaughter in the Modern Age* (New Haven, 1993), ch. 11 (esp. p. 154). For similar propagandist insistence on the British government's refusal to hide or distort even the harshest facts of war, see H. G. Wells, *The War that Will End War* (London, 1914), 12.
36. Ward, *England's Effort*, 40.
37. Ibid. 8.
38. See Haste, *Keep the Home Fires Burning*, 30–7; and John Terraine, *Impacts of War 1914 and 1918* (London, 1970), 55–63.
39. Haste, *Keep the Home Fires Burning*, 32.
40. Mrs Humphry Ward, *A Writer's Recollections* (London, 1918), 372.
41. William Henry Plomer, CMG (1861–1937).
42. Honn notebook 39.
43. 'Col. Graham Thompson—asking what I would like to do & see at Etaples —Very anxious to show me as much as possible, but has made out a long hospital programme which I beg him to modify' (Honn notebook 34).
44. A hotly contested distinction. See e.g. Barbara McLaren, *Women of the War* (London, 1917).
45. Honn notebook 35. She repeats the conversation in *England's Effort*, 140.
46. Brigadier-General John Charteris, CMG, DSO, *At G.H.Q.* (London, 1931), 139–40; see also p. 201 on her second visit. By the time he came to report on the likelihood of a third visit, he was a little less effusive: '*October* 11. A letter from Mrs Humphry Ward . . . wanting to come out here again to get more material, chiefly for a popular explanation of the terms of peace. A little premature, and I am asking her to come out next spring' (pp. 259–60).
47. Mrs Humphry Ward, *Fields of Victory* (London, 1919), 51. See also *England's Effort*, 109, where she asks her reader to 'Suppose a British officer is speaking . . .'.
48. Haig, 'To all Ranks of the British Forces', 11 Apr. 1918, quoted in Charteris, *At G.H.Q.*, 302.
49. Trevelyan, *The Life of Mrs Humphry Ward*, 271.
50. Honn notebook 34.
51. Lord Grey was then Foreign Secretary; the Wards bought their country-house from him in 1892.
52. Sir Arthur Nicolson was Under-Secretary of State for Foreign Affairs 1910–16.
53. Lord Robert Cecil, Viscount Cecil of Chelwood, was Parliamentary Under-Secretary for Foreign Affairs 1915–18, and Minister of Blockade 1916–18; later a key figure in the drafting of the Covenant of the League of Nations.
54. Honn notebook 34.
55. Ibid.
56. Ibid., quoting Shakespeare, *Henry V*, V. ii. 104–6.
57. Ward, *Missing*, 7.

58. See Esther Marian Greenwell-Smith, *Mrs Humphry Ward* (Boston, 1980), 123; and, more cautiously, Sait, 'A Strange New Consciousness', 118.
59. See particularly his Creighton lecture, 'Aristophanes and the War Party' (1918), repr. in Gilbert Murray, *Essays and Addresses* (London, 1921), 31–55.
60. See Sait, 'A Strange New Consciousness', 117–20 for discussion.
61. Mrs Humphry Ward, *The War and Elizabeth* (London, 1918), foreword.
62. Honn notebook 39.
63. Arnold Bennett, 'Mrs Humphry Ward's Heroines', in his *Books and Persons: Being Comments on a Past Epoch, 1908–1911* (London, 1917), 52; first pub. in *New Age*, under the pseudonym 'Jacob Tonson'.
64. Mrs Humphry Ward, *Harvest* (London, 1920), 64.
65. The allusion is to the account of the massacre of the innocents in *Matthew* 2: 1.
66. Preface to *The Golden Notebook*, new edn. (London, 1972), p. x.
67. Honn notebook 34.

2

Payments and Face Values: Edith Wharton's *A Son at the Front*

MARY CONDÉ

ALL war novels must cope to a certain extent with the notion of payment: is war worth it? Ernest Hemingway's novel *Fiesta* (or *The Sun Also Rises*, 1927), a novel about the effects of the First World War, chronicles the narrator's gradual despairing abandonment of the concept of fair payment for anything. This is only an extreme example of the disillusionment and dissatisfaction expressed in American First World War fiction that had been exacerbated by America's late entry into the war, itself the subject of intensive and misleading propaganda. This late entry had forced into foreign armies young writers anxious to buy their fictional material at a fair price: Hemingway enlisted as an ambulance-driver on the Italian front, Cummings and Dos Passos as ambulance-drivers on the French front, and Faulkner as a cadet in the Royal Canadian Air Force.

Edith Wharton, by contrast, had already permanently abandoned the United States for Europe by 1911. She was allowed privileged access to French battlefields, as her documentary account *Fighting France* (1915) and her novel *The Marne* (1918) demonstrate, and her exceptionally valuable war work, especially with refugee children, was recognized when she received the Croix de la Légion d'honneur, rarely awarded to women. She might seem, then, to have had an insider's advantage in conveying the sense of alienation also apparent in the work of her male American contemporaries and her female contemporary Willa Cather, author of *One of Ours* (1922), who altogether lacked her specialist knowledge.

Yet Wharton's major work about the war was greeted as mistimed and misplaced. Louis Auchincloss wrote in 1961 that reading *A Son at the Front* gave one the feeling of taking an old enlistment poster out of an attic trunk.[1] Even the contemporary reviews of 1923 found it anachronistic. J. B. Priestley surmised that the novel had arrived at the wrong moment, 'and has been produced either too late in the day or too early'.[2] But most reviewers were decisive in their verdict that it was simply too late. John Macy of the *Nation* said bluntly, 'Her story is out of date',[3] the *New York Tribune* thought that 'If this were the year 1915, or even 1917, instead of the year 1923, Mrs. Wharton's novel might not seem so profitless an endeavor',[4] the *Bookman* called it 'a belated essay in propaganda',[5] and the *New Republic* opened its review with a wry allusion to Wharton's short story 'Souls Belated': 'Like a soul belated comes Mrs. Wharton with her novel of the War.'[6] The *New York Evening Post* reviewer said that 'The book gives me an odd sense of belatedness, both as to matter and manner. Why go back to all this business of the war, so painful to experience, so wearisome to remember? It was an unpleasant and even harrowing affair for most sons at the front and most parents back home; but merciful time has already dimmed that unhappiness.'[7] The *Saturday Review* thought the opposite: merciful time had not already dimmed that unhappiness, and so *A Son at the Front* jarred because 'It labours, with an effect of almost incredible obtuseness, the emotions that are still fresh and dreadful in the living hearts of men.'[8] Some reviewers agreed with Priestley's speculation that the novel might be not so much belated as too early. The *Independent*, which declared that publication in 1923 was 'like lugging in an old nightmare or else carrying on a rather futile bit of propaganda for France', thought that it would have been 'understandable' had Wharton waited: 'novelists for years and years to come are sure to find treasure in the World War'.[9] The *Times Literary Supplement* concluded: 'A war novel may be thought dull, unnecessary, at this time; but the pendulum swings back; and when the world is better adjusted, this book will be seen to have its permanent value among the minor documents of the war.'[10]

Appropriately enough, *A Son at the Front* opens not only with a supremely ill-timed gesture, as Campton tears a page off the calendar to hasten the advent of 31 July 1914, but with a reference to the vagaries of critical fashion. Wharton explains that three years earlier Campton had shot to fame through a portrait of his son George, even though it seemed to him 'exactly in the line of the unnoticed things he had been showing before, though perhaps nearer to what he was always trying for, because of the exceptional interest of his subject. But to the public he had appeared to take a new turn; or perhaps some critic had suddenly found the right phrase for him; or, that season, people wanted a new painter to talk about.'[11] Campton fails to understand the significance of the date, and fails to understand the reason for his sudden success, and it is on his failures of understanding that the whole novel turns.

Penelope Vita-Finzi remarks of a group of odious self-seekers in *A Son at the Front* that 'Edith Wharton presents them with some savagery while ostensibly retaining Campton's impartial point of view'[12] but it is rather that Campton is rarely anything but savage, and never anything but partial, especially to his own point of view. Judith L. Sensibar, in a brilliantly suggestive essay '"Behind the Lines" in Edith Wharton's *A Son at the Front*: Re-writing a Masculinist Tradition', has argued that Campton is blind to his incestuous, homoerotic desire for his son George, and unlike Whitman, from whom Wharton takes her epigraph ('Something veil'd and abstracted is often a part of the manners of these beings'), is unable to make use of his fantasy life in his art.[13] However, there is no evidence that Campton does not make use of his fantasy life unconsciously: it may be precisely the reason why it is a portrait of George that has catapulted him to fame. In this case, 'the exceptional interest of his subject', on the surface merely an amusing allusion to the extent to which Campton dotes on his son, has an ironic resonance. Whether or not the portrait does express Campton's homoerotic love, it presumably has a multiplicity of meanings for its viewers, just as George himself, an essentially enigmatic figure, has within the novel.

Wharton wrote to her friend Margaret Terry Chanler that 'Of course, from the novelist's point of view, the thing that interested me was the love of the ill-assorted quartette for their boy, & the gradual understanding between the two men.'[14] The 'quartette' presumably comprises Campton, George's mother Julia, her second husband Anderson Brant, and the woman George wants to marry, Mrs Talkett. But George is also adored by the elderly female Adele Anthony and the young male Benny Upsher, so that a number of loves, parental, sexual, comradely, in a number of uneasy combinations, focus on him. Inseparable from a love of George seems to be a sense of guilt and embarrassment. The least embarrassed is Madge Talkett, despite the fact that her love for George is adulterous, if unconsummated; but Benny Upsher's face, when he comes to Campton's studio to find George, is 'a mask of crimson' (89). Anderson Brant, George's stepfather, offers to buy George's portrait 'furtively one day at dusk' (20), and Adele tells Campton later that she saw Brant looking at this portrait in the Luxembourg and that he 'turned as red as a beet' (99).

Adele, who was obviously in the Luxembourg for the same purpose, is as besotted with George as Campton himself; she tells him, 'My dear, if you were to cut me open, George's name would run out of every vein' (181). She is reminiscent of Kipling's Mary Postgate, who stretches her lean arms towards the sky as her idol, the young and rather obnoxious pilot Wynn, flies past;[15] when George first leaves Paris, Adele comes to the Gare du Nord for 'a glimpse of her hero', and when Campton tells her repentantly that neither he nor George had seen her, she jerks back, 'No, but I saw—distinctly. That was all I went for' (84). Her surname, Anthony, does suggest an admixture of the masculine, and, again like Mary Postgate, she is candidly belligerent, but Campton's apostrophe of her as 'You gallant old chap you!' (273) misses altogether Adele's obvious sexual yearnings for George. Campton's own love for his son is explicitly compared with his youthful ardour for women (7), and he treats him as one might a fickle mistress, attempting to decode George's every utterance, and going through his possessions while he is asleep (44–5). The most straightforward of emotions for George is Julia's maternal love, in which Wharton is least interested, and Campton's own diagnosis is that Brant loves George much more deeply. There is, then, a strong suggestion of something illicit about George as an object of love, not necessarily linked to a suggestion of the homoerotic. Wharton's purpose in this is to make George a focus not only for love, but for guilt, so that he can provoke, in the most extravagant terms, the emotions inevitably experienced by non-combatants in wartime. To contemplate George, for his many ardent admirers, is to contemplate one's own shortcomings, and to indulge in futile yearnings for a closer involvement.

One of the overriding themes of *A Son at the Front* is that of the payment of dues. When Campton determines to save George 'from the consequences of his parents' stupid blunder' (66), the blunder he is thinking of is George's birth in France, which renders him liable for French military service. The younger generation's payment for the mistakes of their elders is redressed in the novel by Wharton's concentration on the anguish suffered by those at home.

'At home' is, however, a loaded phrase in connection with a character like Campton, an American who lives in France; Wharton remarked in *A Backward Glance* that her characters always appeared to her with their names, which were never fundamentally unsuitable,[16] and Campton, who lives in a bare studio with hardly any possessions, has the air of constantly camping out. When he reveals to his old French friend Paul Dastrey that he will try to get George discharged from the army, Dastrey replies without any rancour, 'My dear old Campton, I perfectly understand a foreigner's taking that view' (12). Campton is especially dislocated from any sense of home since he does not live with his adored son, sees little of his former wife Julia, has no other family in France, and enjoys no sexual relationship. Dastrey, in fact, is one of his few friends of either sex. Campton is not happy in this state: 'His misfortune had been that he could neither get on easily with people nor live without them; could never wholly isolate himself in his art, nor yet resign himself to any permanent human communion that left it out, or, worse still, dragged it in irrelevantly' (34–5). Like most of Wharton's male protagonists, he is an isolated, impotent figure, and he is uneasily conscious of his social ineptitude. His need for a stick and 'his lame awkward stride' (7) additionally afford him an excuse not to join in any kind of war work, even though Paul Dastrey, who is also lame, works near the front for the Red Cross (110).

One aspect of Wharton's theme of payment is her exposure of Campton's meanness about his art and his money: he tells himself that he cannot spare any money since it was his duty to save it for George, and that he cannot offer blank canvases for auction as some English painters are doing because that would force him into having to paint 'unpaintable' people and turning out work which would injure his reputation and reduce his sales after the war. Wharton offers this information without any authorial comment, and adds, it seems as an afterthought: 'So far, Campton had not been troubled by many appeals for help, but that was probably because he had kept out of sight, and thrown into the fire the letters of the few ladies who had begged a sketch for their sales, or his name for their committees' (111). He refuses help even to Boylston, a friend of George's, and remembers afterwards, mortified, that his nervous clinking of a bunch of keys in his trouser-pocket must have sounded like money (113). But of course Campton, through his painting and even through his mere reputation as a painter, does hold the keys to money. It is ironic that this is the first occasion on which he feels uneasy about what he thinks is George's acquiescence in taking an office job away from the front, and his lack of desire to 'be in it'. With all his small circle about him busy in some way with the war effort, Campton is at great pains not to 'be in it'; we are told of the word *act* that 'No verb in the language terrified him as much' (119).

This deliberate turning away from the life of the community does not prevent Campton from indulging in self-pity about his lack of any real home: when he sees the Fortin-Lescluze family group just before their son goes to war he feels a pang of envy, and reflects 'for the thousandth time, how frail a screen of activity divided him from depths of loneliness he dared not sound' (58–9). It seems to Campton admirably French that at a time of crisis the family square should re-form apparently undamaged, Fortin's dalliance with the Javanese dancer completely forgotten; and French families in the novel are consistently depicted as enduring, resilient units. The implication is that Campton has paid his dues neither as a family man nor as a member of the community, and therefore does not deserve to feel anything more elevating than envy and self-pity.

Adele Anthony is the most acerbic in pointing out to Campton that he has not paid his dues as a husband and father, that it was Anderson Brant who blew George's nose and paid for his dentist and doctor. Brant, then, has paid for George in love, in attention, and in money. But, as Adele concedes, if Campton had done so, he could never have become a great artist (100). Now that Campton has reaped the reward in money and reputation for his neglect of George—a reward he claims to value only for George's sake (215)—he wants, effectively, to buy George back from the Brants again, ignoring the fact that George has become what he is (for example, a lover of books) through access to the Brants' money. Since Campton has, he feels, earned his title to George so arduously through wasting what he calls 'precious years' on 'stupid faces', he is less inclined to let George pay the price for French citizenship in military service, eventually admitting to himself that he would have felt the same passionate reluctance had the country been America: 'That his boy should survive—survive at any price—that had been all he cared for or sought to achieve' (157).

Just as Campton is an extreme example of a non-combatant, so George is an extreme example of what Whitman called the 'veil'd and abstracted' in the soldier, in that he practises an elaborate deception on his parents, pretending that he is in a safe desk-job when he is actually at the front, a deception only revealed to Campton well over half-way through the novel: book 3 opens with the abrupt revelation that Campton is speeding through France with George's stepfather 'to the spot of earth where his son lay dying' (227). Even without this deception, George would be a bizarrely enigmatic character. He conceals his love for the brainless and beautiful Mrs Talkett over a long period, and even after it has been revealed, does not express it with any conviction: 'She's a pretty creature,' he comments casually to his father (267), and says breezily to her husband, 'Remember me to Madge.' Campton is astonished by this behaviour and can only cope with it by classifying it as 'modern' behaviour: '"Remember me to Madge!" That was the way in which the modern young man spoke of his beloved to his beloved's proprietor' (276). When Talkett leaves the room, George says of him, 'Poor devil! He's torn to pieces with it,' and Campton is at first startled by what appears to be his son's frank reference to his adulterous affair. But George is speaking of Talkett's indecision over how to react to the war, and the affair does not exist. It emerges that though George had wanted one, he had changed his mind when the war made him long for permanence. Mrs Talkett, meanwhile, having held out against an affair, now resists divorce, even appealing to Campton to persuade George to be satisfied with adultery. But Brant advises Campton that Mrs Talkett should be encouraged to seem to waver, since that will give George a motive for staying in Paris rather than returning to the front. George, however, although he realizes that she will never divorce Talkett, pretends to believe that she will in order to avoid sleeping with her, since, as he says to Campton, 'My dear old Dad—don't you guess? She's come to care for me awfully; if we'd gone all the lengths she wanted, and then I'd got killed, there would have been nothing on earth left for her' (328). This analysis hardly seems to square with the vain and shallow Madge Talkett we meet, and the whole situation is rendered farcical, and indeed tiresome, by its elements of calculation and miscalculation. Part of its tiresomeness depends on George's smug acknowledgement of his own supreme value, as in his letter to Adele, archly signed, 'Your George the First—and Last (or I'll know why)' (182). This very letter is in itself annoying as constituting part of the elaborate subterfuge practised by George: he sends Adele, who knows he is at the front, this kind of bland letter as a front for his real letters, so that if his parents ask to see Adele's letters they will be satisfied that George is still safe. Although the reader may enjoy picking up the clues that tell us that George really is a son at the front, as Julia imagines she is falsely claiming (188), like the clues that tell us of George's liaison with Mrs Talkett, or of his inevitable death, it is, finally, an irritant that he cannot simply declare himself as soldier, just as he cannot simply declare himself as lover.

Little can be gleaned of George's nature from the way in which Madge Talkett is presented in the novel, although her name perhaps suggests that her magic for George resides precisely in her voluble chatter. His friend Boylston remarks of her that 'she's got a talking face, poor little thing; and not much gift of restraint' (334). We might discount Campton's chagrin at discovering that the mysterious beauty of George's face had concealed a secret as 'commonplace' as Madge (258) on the various grounds of pique at being kept out of the secret, jealousy of Madge, and a general conviction that no woman could be good enough for his boy. But even before he had realized that George loved Madge Talkett, she had struck him as essentially evanescent, partly because she is clearly intended as a representative of 'a world that has lost its moorings', as Margaret B. McDowell calls the Paris of the novel.[17] She is 'a fashion-plate torn from its page and helplessly blown about the world' (74), a 'little will-o'-the wisp' (199), and one of those beings who seems to be made out of their surrounding reflections, 'as if they had been born of a tricky grouping of looking-glasses, and would vanish if it were changed' (195). This last is a description of the technique of the whole novel, which leads Campton to meditate of his beloved son, 'Who was "George?" What did the name represent?' (345), as if he were himself reading *A Son at the Front,* and might supply the answer that 'George' represents a soldier-knight who is set apart from ordinary mortals. (Campton 'reads' even George's sleep as 'an impenetrable veil' and decides that 'The sleep of ordinary men was not like that'; 345.)

Campton is at the same time the writer of *A Son at the Front* in the sense that the epigrammatic introductions of many of the characters, for example, are obviously his. It is clearly Campton who sees Mr Talkett as 'a kindly young man with eyeglasses and glossy hair, who roamed about straightening the furniture, like a gentlemanly detective watching the presents at a wedding' (197), even though it is Edith Wharton who knows that the presents, including Mrs Talkett, do need watching. Mr Talkett, although he does eventually enlist, remains an essentially flat character, with his docile echoing of his wife's phrases, unlike Anderson Brant, who at first appears equally comic and uxorious. We first see Brant through Campton's eyes 'advancing at a sort of mincing trot across the pompous garlands of the Savonnerie carpet' (19), and are told that 'he reminded Campton of a dry perpendicular insect in protective tints; and the fancy was encouraged by his cautious manner, and the way he had of peering over his glasses as if they were part of his armour. His feet were small and pointed, and seemed to be made of patent leather; and shaking hands with him was like clasping a bunch of twigs' (20). This contemptuous, dismissive view conceals from Campton, but not from us, the similarities between the two men, confirmed by their complicity in uniting against Julia's misunderstanding of George's likely reaction to their machinations (22). For Campton, of course, the burning difference between them is that Brant is a millionaire, and has thus, in his terms, unfairly bought George, but Brant, apart from his adoration of George, shares Campton's awkwardness, vulnerability, and loneliness. The real difference is that Brant exhibits throughout the novel a nobility and delicacy completely foreign to Campton's nature. Although Wharton wrote to Margaret Terry Chanler that she was interested in 'the gradual understanding between the two men', only in the closing paragraphs does Campton even begin to appreciate Brant's emotional generosity, which he repays by allowing Brant to pay for the monument to George (364).

The novel ends with the word 'began', and shows the artist once more at work, and on a project in which he is allowing Brant to share by financing it. This is positive enough. Nor can I agree with Judith Sensibar that this work is artistically unsatisfactory. She writes, 'And what of Campton's final portrait of George? It's a paradigmatic idealized image, a tomb image. And it's a copy. His imagination is stuck like a needle on a scratched record as it replays the first image we saw him draw, a sketch that's a copy of a famous painter's tomb image of his son.'[18] But the first image we see Campton draw merely reminds him of the story of Signorelli sketching his dead son, since he realizes that George asleep looks as if he were dead (46–7). Nor does Campton work from only one image of George. The last sentence of the novel reads, 'He pulled out all the sketches of his son from the old portfolio, spread them before him on the table, and began' (365). What is more, Campton is working in a new medium. A painter, he is now designing a monument in marble. The penultimate sentence of the novel reads, 'He had always had a fancy for modelling—had always had lumps of clay lying about within reach,' which could be taken to mean that Campton had always had the fact of mortality available to him, but had never utilized it until now.

The difficulty with the ending lies in its emotional muddle, in that it rests on what Cynthia Griffin Wolff calls Campton's 'sense of success' at realizing that he has had George inextricably debarred from anyone else. Since this realization depends on George's death, Wolff feels that Wharton has 'shamefully pulled away from the question . . . of living people'.[19] Wolff adds in a footnote: 'It was, we must remember, Wharton's novel: she could have chosen to let the son live. But that would have required her to confront Campton's quandary head-on. Probably the fictional decision to have George die is a sign of her desire to finesse the problem.'[20] Campton's quandary, as Wolff sees it, is 'How much must an artist rob from everyday actuality to feed his art? Too much for any other sustained and draining emotional tie?'[21] This quandary has been neatly expressed in Adele Anthony's perception that Campton needed to neglect George as a father to become a great artist, 'the great John Campton: the *real* John Campton you were meant to be' (100). What the whole novel is telling us is that Campton has no real notion of a sustained and draining emotional tie. It is thus fitting that he should end it by beginning on a dead son's monument whose artistic excellence is not in question. Wharton could not possibly have chosen to let George live, since her story is essentially one of loss: Campton loses the son he has never really known. His son is not at home with him, nor has ever been at home with him. Even after George has been identified as a son at the front, fighting a war of which Campton is almost entirely ignorant, he never reveals to his father anything of either its horrors or its comradeship. It may be argued that Wharton would have been very unwise to have attempted the former, but it could be surmised that she could have attempted something of the latter. Percy Lubbock in his *Portrait of Edith Wharton* recalls that she was allowed 'a memorable vision of life at the front, the long entrenched and immobilized front of those years, through repeated visits to posts along the whole of the French line; and it was here in the freedom and jollity, the confident cheer, the amused give-and-take which received and welcomed her, that she enjoyed her chance'.[22]

The difficulty with the novel's ending, then, is not that Campton's realization that George has belonged to him in a way denied to anyone else depends on George's death, but that it is a totally false realization put into his head by Boylston, who is not only famous for his tact, but who is also in the process of persuading Campton to design George's monument (355–6). Apart from the fact that no human being can own another in the way Campton would like to own George, George is a particularly slippery customer, eluding the grasp even of Mrs Talkett, who behaves on her last appearance like a parody of Campton, with his obsession with payment, exclaiming bitterly, 'I've never in my life been happy enough to be so unhappy!' (360–1). It is this bitter exclamation, astonishingly enough, which persuades him that Boylston was right in asserting that his possession of George had excluded everyone else. However, it is not in the least astonishing that Campton's selfish glee in this should lead him to pity Julia and Brant as less able to manage grief than himself, since it is an aspect of the same spiteful possessiveness which makes him twit Adele Anthony with never having had a child (184) and sneer at Brant for wanting to pay handsomely for his stepson's monument (364).

We are provided with another parody of Campton in Mme Olida, the Spanish girl for whom Campton had deserted his wife and son, now reincarnated as an immensely fat fortune-teller who dotes on her (obviously worthless) son. She considers him as 'beautiful as a god' (332) and, like Campton, declares that 'The money I earn is for my boy!' She is even a parody of the artist in Campton, continuing: 'That gives me the strength to invent a new lie every morning' (337). Yet this wry commentary on Campton's own ethos seems to coexist with Wharton's endorsement of her protagonist at his own face value. Campton both succeeds, and does not succeed, both realizes the truth and remains utterly blind to it. Wharton cannot decide whether to present her non-combatant as suffering in as serious and as important a way as a soldier,[23] or to present him as battening on the reality of a soldier's life and death to produce his own self-serving fantasies.

Charles Scribner, the publisher of *A Son at the Front*, observed rather endearingly that 'I might wish that the story was not so exactly a war novel (as clearly indicated by its title).'[24] Scribner foresaw that the sales would only be moderate, because of the belatedness of the subject, and perhaps hoped that Wharton might provide another title which would not give the game away so disastrously. But how 'exactly' is *A Son at the Front* a war novel? Wharton does touch briefly on the horrors of war in the story of another devoted father, Fortin-Lescluze, who is forced, without warning and in vain, to amputate both of his own son's legs (103). She touches briefly on its corruption in the analogy which Campton perceives between the machinations of Mayhew's party to gain control of the war-charity funds, and Germany's manœuvring the world into war (318). She touches briefly on the way in which war corrupts language in a passage which anticipates Frederick Henry's famous reflections on the words 'glory', 'honour', and 'courage' in *A Farewell to Arms* (1929): Dastrey says of 'honour' and 'honourable' that the meaning has 'evaporated out of lots of our old words, as if the general smash-up had broken their stoppers' (161).

Yet Elizabeth Ammons has claimed that, despite the radical impact of the war on Wharton, 'it was not in her fiction about the war that its significance was felt'.[25] It is rather, however, that in *A Son at the Front* Wharton ponders the significance of the non-combatant rather than that of the soldier. George's elaborate deception is presumably intended more as an exaggerated version of the distance between those in action and those waiting at home than as a convincing plot device. His constant and rather irritating smiling, and his calm acceptance of the adoration of those around him, express Wharton's conviction that ultimately, however painful or even fatal involvement may be, it is a less complex and bitter fate to take part than to be an outsider. This conviction explains Wharton's ambivalent attitude to Campton as simultaneously a failure and a success, and her choice of his role as, specifically, a portrait-painter. Lev Raphael, in his excellent account of Campton as a 'prisoner of shame', seizes on this as an ironic example of Campton's entrapment: 'The man who in effect abandoned a marriage to paint and bed a passing Spanish beauty, this man of impulse, has become a society portraitist!'[26] Although his studio is hung with 'tattered tapestries with their huge heroes and kings' (109), it is Campton's distasteful life-work to depict the fashionable and rich; one of the reasons that it is George's portrait which propels him to fame is presumably that in his 'jealous worship of his son' (211) he at last has a huge hero for his subject, inspiring the 'communicative warmth' and 'magic light' of the painting (50–1).

Campton is simultaneously a failure and a success as a painter not only because his commercial success implies a failure of integrity, but because it depends on his skill in reading faces,[27] a skill which is both specialized and severely limited. He can read the changes in George's face which his own art has recorded (50), but utterly fails to read the two-facedness of George's behaviour, taking him at face value for a civilian when he is actually a soldier. Campton's professional reaction to the war is to reflect, 'What a modeller of faces a great war must be!' (88), but he is adept at noting this modelling only in terms of art: Mme de Dolmetsch has become 'some haloed nun from an Umbrian triptych' (130), his ex-wife Julia 'some mortified Jansenist nun from one of Philippe de Champaigne's canvases' (255). The difference between a professional and an emotional response to a face is well expressed in the incident of the sentinel who asks Brant and Campton for their pass, and grumbles doubtfully as he looks from their faces to their unrecognizable photographs. Brant is about to attempt a bribe when Campton says simply, 'My son's dying at the front. Can't you see it when you look at me?' (233). Campton depends here on a reading of a face of which he is incapable, although he does grasp that one must pay one's way in wartime not through coin but through suffering.

In his own reactions to faces of grief Campton reveals a fear and hostility which are chilling. It is through his eyes that we see the effects of the loss of Benny Upsher: the tears which rain down Mme de Dolmetsch's face wash off the paint like mud in a shower; Mayhew's complacent face goes to pieces as if it had been painted with vitriol (175); Mme Olida's tears for her son make dark streaks through her purplish powder (333); Adele tells Campton at one point that Julia is powdering her nose because 'she has an idea that if you see she's been crying you'll be awfully angry' (71). Campton's fear and hostility here are surely due to his unwilling, perhaps unconscious, identification of himself with all four of these grieving people, who have reacted with varying kinds of dishonesty to the prospect of making a sacrifice for the war. But in two parallel scenes of grief depicting Mme Lebel's bereavement, first of her son and then of her grandson, Wharton combines a 'painterly' response from Campton and his own consciousness of his role as outsider to confer heroic status on Mme Lebel, treated throughout the novel as a type of French stoicism. Each scene is a tableau: the prostrated old woman, the abandoned sewing, the fatal letter lying nearby, clearly viewed, and even constructed, with a painter's eye (159, 321). Campton here frankly acknowledges his own inadequacy. As he watches George comfort Mme Lebel, he says to himself, 'These two are closer to each other than George and I, because they've both seen the horror face to face. He knows what to say to her ever so much better than he knows what to say to his mother or me' (322). Mme Lebel, although a non-combatant, is accorded this kind of tragic dignity and knowledge not merely because she is bereaved but because she is French, and France has chosen to fight.

As George dies, America enters the war, and it is this that bursts the 'healing springs' of sorrow for Campton, and sends him back to work (354). Throughout the novel Campton has withheld payment from France, his adopted country if not his home, or has mishandled payment. He tries to deny France his son, giving her instead a picture of him—but only so that he may cheat Brant of it (51). He gives the dying Frenchman René Davril another picture of George, when what Davril needed was Campton's approbation of his own art (128). America's entry into the war of course has no logical connection with either George or Campton, and it is this lack of logical connection which makes the ending of the novel muddled and unclear: psychologically, however, Wharton uses George's death as the final payment which buys America's participation, her movement out of the shadow of the non-combatant. Hence in the last pages of the novel, despite all his failures of understanding and generosity, Campton, in Wharton's eyes at least, can share the tragic stature of Mme Lebel, or France. It is not necessary, Wharton implicitly argues, for such a terrible payment to be made willingly, or knowingly, for it to be heroic: Mme Lebel's own last words are, 'I don't understand any more, do you?' (322).

Campton does actually reflect at one point, after George is first wounded, that he, with his two languages, might get himself sent on a propaganda mission to America (295). This is, in effect, the way that Wharton tries to use George in the novel, and it is, to a large extent, the reason that *A Son at the Front* was somewhat testily regarded as belated propaganda by so many of its contemporary reviewers. The difficulty with Wharton's argument that America should have come into the war much earlier is not only that the argument itself comes too late, but that it is based on a situation which is very specific to the novel: German atrocities are only briefly, and rather colourlessly, mentioned, except for a single incident involving Mme Lebel's granddaughter (107–8), which achieves importance because Mme Lebel works for Campton, and because he knows and respects her. Wharton is less concerned with what reprisals Germany deserves than with what America owes France. But she tries to demonstrate this through two Americans, Campton and his son, who are exceptional cases in that they live in France. Campton, additionally, has worked and gained his reputation in France, and derives enormous pleasure from the beauty of Paris, described in some of the novel's most powerful and moving passages, and initially taken by Campton as the beauty of an invulnerable city (48–9). Wharton explicitly widens her scope beyond Campton and George at a moment when Campton, wrestling with his conscience about his son's return to the front, thinks:

> An Idea: that was what France, ever since she had existed, had always been in the story of civilisation; a luminous point about which striving

visions and purposes could rally. And in that sense she had been as much Campton's spiritual home as Dastrey's; to thinkers, artists, to all creators, she had always been a second country. If France went, western civilisation went with her; and then all they had believed in and been guided by would perish. (314)

The difficulty with this argument is not only that it too is belated, coming as it does almost at the end of the novel, but that France does not seem to have offered Campton much solace in the way of a 'spiritual home', since he is condemned to portrait-painting, which he despises, and is lonely, thwarted, and unhappy, and, above all, unable to recognize the real links of care and responsibility which bind father to son, or, until the last minute, which bind citizen to country. Wharton tries to depict Campton simultaneously as an American dislocated and emotionally adrift because he is a foreigner in France, and as an American who owes France everything. All of the 'ill-assorted quartette', indeed, who love 'their boy' are Americans, and it is only Mrs Talkett, the most insubstantial character of them all, who goes back to America. One of the reasons that George has both a father and stepfather is presumably so that Campton and Brant can represent American art and American banking respectively, but Wharton does not investigate the commercial links between France and America except in so far as the Brants' 'expensive and irreproachable' Paris drawing-room (14) has been bought with American money. The Brants have only a financial and social interest in art: Brant has unknowingly bought a fake Reynolds, which he regards as an investment (301). That Wharton endows Brant with the tragic nobility she denies Campton, although Brant never consents in any sense to George's participation in the war, underscores her proposition that it is artists above all who owe France a living, but at the same time it undercuts the force of her appeal for the bonds between France and America. The propagandist element in *A Son at the Front*, which Wharton's early reviewers so much deprecated, sits uneasily with her subtle and complex delineation of individuals, and her unravelling of the rivalries provoked by thwarted love.

Wharton is, finally, over-ambitious in her attempts to combine a particular tussle over a beloved object with more general reflections on the necessary unknowability of a soldier by civilians, and on the historical debt owed to an embattled France by artists and thinkers. By filtering the events of the novel through the eyes of an artist who has fostered his professional life at the expense of his private life, who is seduced by face values, and who refuses to recognize the inexorable logic of his own philosophy of payment, Wharton has produced an extraordinary, though flawed, document of struggle, deception, and loss.

NOTES

1. Louis Auchincloss, *Edith Wharton* (Minneapolis, 1961), 27.
2. J. B. Priestley, 'Fiction', *London Mercury*, 9 (Nov. 1923), 102–3; repr. in Tuttleton, 351.
3. John Macy, 'The American Spirit', *Nation*, 117 (10 Oct. 1923), 398–9; repr. in James W. Tuttleton, Kristin O. Lauer, and Margaret P. Murray (eds.), *Edith Wharton: The Contemporary Reviews* (Cambridge, 1992) (referred to hereafter as 'Tuttleton'), 340.
4. Burton Rascoe, Review of *A Son at the Front, New York Tribune*, 9 Sept. 1923, 17–18; repr. in Tuttleton, 331.
5. Review of *A Son at the Front, Bookman*, 65 (Oct. 1923), 46; repr. in Tuttleton, 344.
6. Robert Morss Lovett, Review of *A Son at the Front, New Republic*, 36 (19 Sept. 1932), 105; repr. in Tuttleton, 331.
7. H. W. Boynton, 'The Incidence of War', *New York Evening Post*, Literary Review, 22 Sept. 1923, 61; repr. in Tuttleton, 335.
8. Gerald Gould, 'New Fiction', *Saturday Review*, 136 (6 Oct. 1923), 390; repr. in Tuttleton, 338.
9. H. De W. F., 'Mrs. Wharton Struggles with Masculinity', *Independent*, 111 (13 Oct. 1923), 157–8; repr. in Tuttleton, 341.
10. 'New Novels: *A Son at the Front*', *Times Literary Supplement*, 20 Sept. 1923, 618; repr. in Tuttleton, 334.
11. Edith Wharton, *A Son at the Front* (London, 1923), 3–4.
12. Penelope Vita-Finzi, *Edith Wharton and the Art of Fiction* (New York, 1990), 125.
13. Judith L. Sensibar, '"Behind the Lines" in Edith Wharton's *A Son at the Front*: Re-writing a Masculinist Tradition', in Katherine Joslin and Alan Price (eds.), *Wretched Exotic: Essays on Edith Wharton in Europe* (New York, 1993).
14. Letter to Margaret Terry Chanler, 1 Oct. 1923; repr. in *The Letters of Edith Wharton*, ed. R. W. B. Lewis and Nancy Lewis (London, 1988), 471.
15. Rudyard Kipling, 'Mary Postgate', *A Diversity of Creatures* (London, 1917), 425.
16. Edith Wharton, *A Backward Glance: An Autobiography* (1934; London, 1993), 132.
17. Margaret B. McDowell, *Edith Wharton* (Boston, 1976), 112.
18. Sensibar, 'Behind the Lines', 251.
19. Cynthia Griffin Wolff, *A Feast of Words: The Triumph of Edith Wharton* (New York, 1977), 350–1.

20. Ibid. 436.
21. Ibid. 351.
22. Percy Lubbock, *Portrait of Edith Wharton* (London, 1947), 122.
23. Only Brant, not Campton, is compared with 'a civilian under fire' (214).
24. Millicent Bell, *Edith Wharton and Henry James: The Story of their Friendship* (New York, 1965), 339.
25. Elizabeth Ammons, *Edith Wharton's Argument with America* (Athens, GA, 1980), 129.
26. Lev Raphael, *Edith Wharton's Prisoners of Shame: A New Perspective on her Neglected Fiction*, intro. Cynthia Griffin Wolff (London, 1991), 188.
27. The word 'faces' is used obsessively throughout the novel.

3

'Contagious ecstasy': May Sinclair's War Journals

SUZANNE RAITT

IN Richard Aldington's 1929 *Death of a Hero*, George Winterbourne sees troops returning from leave and muses: 'These men were men ... They had been where no woman and no half-man had ever been, could endure to be.'[1] This notion that the front, where the 'real' business of war was carried out, was no place for a woman left many women feeling that they had no place in the war. Sandra Gilbert has suggested that women were liberated by the widespread absence of men from their domestic and working lives, although she does point out that as well as their 'sexual glee' women felt intense anxiety and guilt at having got what they wanted at so many men's expense.[2] But despite the government's efforts to recast the roles of mother, wife, and indeed of 'woman' in the mould of war,[3] women seem to have remained confused and uneasy, afraid of doing things wrong, but unsure how to do things right. For many women, especially older women who had no children to look after, and were beyond the age where they could be recruited for war service, the war heightened their feelings of uselessness. As Gilbert and Gubar see it, women felt curiously free, and so curiously unnecessary. Women like May Sinclair, already 51 when the war broke out, struggled to make a place for themselves in a world that was preoccupied with the vulnerability of young men, rather than of older women. Her war journals reveal in painful and awkward detail the shame of a middle-aged woman who sees in middle age her last chance at life. What kind of action could Sinclair undertake that would express and satisfy both her own greedy sense of herself as a woman, and the needs of a Europe at war? The war journals offer a unique opportunity to explore the perversity of her position, her refusal of political engagement in favour of an awkward and excessive immersion in what she saw as 'real life'. This chapter will suggest that femininity is repeatedly experienced and represented as shame at times of social and cultural crisis. For May Sinclair was over and over again ashamed of being herself, and we should value the war journals not only for what they can tell us about women's humiliation, but also for their images of women's resistance, their ungainly refusal to be made to feel stupid or unnecessary. All patriarchies do this, but patriarchies at war do it most of all, pouring financial, emotional, and cultural resources into the maintenance of military masculinity.

It was into a war-world of sexual confusion and anxiety, as well as of enormous violence and suffering, that May Sinclair ventured in September 1914, as a member of the Munro Ambulance Corps, which went out to the front under the sponsorship of the Belgian Red Cross. She stayed about two and a half weeks. While she was there, she kept daily notes in a 'Day Book', and after her return, wrote them up as a journal. Three fairly lengthy extracts from the journal were published in the *English Review* in 1915, and a full version appeared as *Journal of Impressions in Belgium* later in the same year.[4]

As the war developed, Sinclair was to experience at first hand the trauma of bereavement: three of her nephews were mobilized. Two died in 1915 aged respectively 34 and 25 (William, son of her eldest brother William who lived in Hull, and Harold, son of her brother Joseph, who had emigrated to Canada). The third, Harold Lumley, also one of William's children, in a POW camp during the war, was invalided out in 1918 at the age of 30, and collapsed with pneumonia, arriving at Sinclair's house in London and requiring devoted nursing for several months. These traumas do not seem to have lessened Sinclair's support for the war. Until the end of her writing career in the late 1920s, she continued to produce novels which explore its attractions: *Tasker Jevons* (1916), *The Tree of Heaven* (1917), *The Romantic* (1920), *Mr Waddington of Wyck* (1921), *Anne Severn and the Fieldings* (1922), *The Rector of Wyck* (1925), and *Far End* (1926). As this list indicates, May Sinclair was a prolific writer and by the beginning of the war a very well-known and wealthy novelist. Relatively little has been written about her, but her war writing is a crucial and idiosyncratic contribution to women's literature of war. As Laura Stempel Mumford points out, the absence of all political comment from any of Sinclair's war texts means that they can be read as justifications simply of the activity of war, and Rebecca West, in a contemporary review of the *Journal*, comments that 'one cannot imagine Miss Sinclair presuming to express an opinion upon international affairs. Yet by her mysterious subterranean methods she makes one ache for Belgium.'[5] It was the ache of war in which Sinclair was interested. She seems to have had remarkably little interest in the causes and the political justifications of Britain's entry into the First World War. What she cared about was war's psychology: the lure of danger, the revulsions of cowardice, the desire for power. Her support for the war seems to come not from her political awareness, but from her attraction to war's perversity. That attraction was a peculiarly feminine one, since she explored the psychology of those who were in some way excluded by the war (the pacifist in *The Tree of Heaven*, the pathological coward in *The Romantic*, women in all the war novels) from the point of view of one who was acutely conscious of her own exclusion as a highly-strung middle-aged woman. Yet she does not simply reiterate the complaint of countless women like Alix in Rose Macaulay's *Non-combatants and Others* (1916): 'it's jealousy that's demoralising me most. Jealousy of the people who can be *in* the beastly thing.'[6] Sinclair dwells on the ecstasy of war, on the pleasures fantasies of war can bring, on the contentment of the fighter. In Sinclair's novels there is no pain, no wounds, little disgust. The war in Sinclair's fiction is a perversely bodiless affair, as though Sinclair denied herself, or was denied, access to those male bodies which the war destroyed. It is the dynamics of this perversity that I shall explore in this chapter, and I shall be suggesting that Sinclair uncomfortably touched on one of the most awkward aspects of feminine consciousness: the association of humiliation with megalomania, and the vicarious sexualized enjoyment of masculine aggression. As Samuel Hynes says of the *Journal*, Sinclair was one of only a few women to convincingly represent the unpalatable 'reality of a woman's war'.[7]

From the first day Sinclair was outspoken in her support of the Great War. On 18 September 1914 twenty-five writers signed an 'Authors' Declaration' in *The Times*, stating that 'Great Britain could not without dishonour have refused to take part in the present war.'[8] Among the twenty-five were four women,

May Sinclair, Jane Ellen Harrison, Flora Annie Steel, and Mrs Humphry Ward. In an apparently unpublished paper, written during the war and called 'Influence of the War on "Life and Literature"', Sinclair, echoing Edmund Gosse's comment that the war would cleanse modern art of its decadent and degenerate tendencies,[9] wrote:

I do not think we are going to be interested any more in their erotics, or their sex-problems, or, primarily, in sex at all; because of the enormous widening of our range of motives and instincts and emotions. Some of these—the will to fight, the violent courage and violent honour of War, and the greatest of them all, Religion, are primitive instincts if you like; and all the primitive instincts hang together. We shall no longer be able to regard Love, for instance, as an isolated phenomenon, but we shall see it as it is, rooted and platted in with the rest, having no more colour or importance than it gains by the general heightening of emotional values all round.

For there is no doubt that these values were precisely what we were beginning to lose in 'life and literature', along with Religion, that is to say with our hold on Reality, before the War. Most of us—with the exception of one or two poets—were ceasing to live with any intensity, to believe with any conviction compatible with comfort, and to feel with any strength and sincerity. Yet we were all quite sincerely 'out for' reality without recognising it when we saw it and without any suspicion of its spiritual nature.

And Reality—naked, shining, intense Reality—more and not less of it, is, I believe, what we are going to get after the War.[10]

For Sinclair the war represented emotional stimulation and release. It demonstrated the closeness of sex, violence, and mysticism. Moreover, it proved that love did not simply watch the fighting, but was part of the fighting itself. Sex and the erotic were no longer recognizable as distinct in themselves, but were seen to be inseparable from aggression and a number of other primal drives. To fight was to love; to love was to fight. As we shall see, other works by Sinclair, particularly the *Journal*, suggest that she did indeed see the battlefield as an opportunity to acquire sexual knowledge. In the piece quoted above, however, she quickly veers away from such an image to concentrate on the received image of pre-war Britain as an apathetic and dissociated society. She falls back on the vagueness of abstraction, 'Reality', to describe her sense of the war's consequences. In spite of its imprecision, such a phrasing emphasizes the sense that she—and perhaps more than she—had before the war that they were not really living, that this was not life. As she wrote to St John Adcock, in a letter of 28 February 1915 that was probably intended as a covering note for her unpublished piece: 'personally, I feel as if I had never lived, with any intensity, before I went out to [the war] in the autumn'. The limits of her vision are indicated, though, by the preceding sentence of the letter: 'most of these things, at this stage, resolve themselves into what we feel personally about the War'. Much of the time she seems to have been unable to see beyond her own personal experience. The war was her romance: it gave her access, for the first time in her life, to a world of violence in which men and women mingled freely in an atmosphere of heightened awareness. The war becomes her answer to those wider questions which she so rarely asks. As she says in an article for the magazine *Woman at Home*, '[the war] came to us when we needed it most, as an opportune postponement if not the end of our internal dissensions—the struggle between Unionists and Nationalists, between Capital and Labour, between the Suffragettes and the Government, between Man and Woman'.[11] For Sinclair the final pair seems to have been the most important.

As an untrained woman, May Sinclair was an unlikely person to find herself on the battlefield so soon after the outbreak of war. Her sense of war as a marginalizing force emerges strongly from the repeated portrayals, in her fiction, of people who for reasons of age and health are unable to enlist. 'Red Tape', for example, which appeared in the women's newspaper *Queen* in November 1914, describes a middle-aged pair, male employer and female secretary, who race one another to get out to the war first. They are 'sleepless with ecstasy' at the thought of being near the fighting, and as Starkey, the employer, trains at a base camp, Miss Delacheroy becomes increasingly frustrated at her repeated failures of her Red Cross nursing exams.[12] Her (undeclared) fixation on Starkey is indistinguishable from her impatience to be in the thick of military activities: 'she saw [the war] as one immense, encompassing sheet of shells and bullets that converged on Mr Starkey in the middle of it. It was there, in the middle of it, that she desired to be.'[13] Miss Delacheroy is excited by the idea of danger: it provokes and fulfils desire. This is true also of the character Khaki, in the story of that name, first published in the *English Review* in September 1913, and describing Khaki's unexpected enlistment in the Boer War: '"He was in love, *all the time*," she said. "He was in love with honour. He was in love with danger."'[14] Khaki's death redeems his ridiculous life and indicates that he had passions of which none of his friends had been aware. The war *expresses* him as no other love would have done, and for Miss Delacheroy too, the war is the man she loves. It offers her intimacy with him, a shared passion, a mutual intoxication. It is significant that 'Khaki' was written some time before the outbreak of the First World War. The war must indeed have come as the grotesque answer to May Sinclair's dreams, and her psychical investment in the idea of war meant that when it came, she welcomed it and longed to experience it.

But 'Red Tape' does not end happily. Fired with excitement because she has finally passed her exams, Miss Delacheroy runs down the stairs in the Red Cross building, trips and sprains her ankle. Surprisingly, Starkey is on hand, in the middle of teaching a First Aid class. The two, astonished to see one another, confess that neither will actually see any action: both have separately been told that since they are over 40 the War Office has little use for them. The tone of the story's ending is ambiguous, neither melancholy nor jubilant. The relationship between Starkey and Miss Delacheroy is unresolved; the war has faded into the background. We are left simply with the stark and unglamorous fact of age and the recalcitrance of death. It is as hard for Sinclair to experience and re-create disappointment as it is for the patriotic mother in *The Tree of Heaven* (1917) to 'realize' the Boer War: 'the forms were grey and insubstantial; it was all flat and grey like the pictures in the illustrated papers; the very blood of it ran grey'.[15] But the blood in her family does run grey: her youngest son is at first refused because of his heart condition, and her husband, over 35, is refused because of his age: 'he said bitter things about "red tape", and declared that if that was the way things were going to be managed it was a bad look-out for the country'.[16] The family are humiliated not just by these events but also by their son Michael's initial unwillingness to enlist: the war brings shame as well as, eventually, pride.

Miss Delacheroy is humiliated by her inability to pass her nursing exams, and Starkey only makes it worse by continually pretending that he is about to leave for Belgium. Her shame is a sexual shame: about being a woman, about not being as good as a man, and, implicitly, about her sexual rejection by Starkey and his cruel teasing of her. May Sinclair's own experience of the war was somewhat different. She managed to bypass the red tape that would have kept her away from the front because she had money. There had been no money in her family: her father was a shipowner who went bankrupt when she was about 8 years old, and for much of her adult life Sinclair lived with her mother in some poverty, undertaking dreary translations from German to support them both. But by the beginning of the war she was a bestseller: *The Divine Fire* (1904) was the first of many of her books to sell thousands, particularly in the United States. In 1914 she was an independently wealthy woman whose money gave her a sense of power and who was determined not to be sidelined. Yet her own accounts of her three weeks in Belgium show her undergoing both sexual and social humiliation, exactly because of her anxiety, like Miss Delacheroy's, to be in the thick of things. The accounts she wrote of her time with the Munro Corps are, as Rebecca West pointed out, records of 'humiliations',[17] and through Sinclair's arch and often awkward prose we can read a sensitive and poignant account of the embarrassment of middle age for women, of female superfluity. It is not enough to dismiss her journals, as Claire Tylee does, as 'narcissistic and myopic'.[18] Through the pictures of wounded and dying young men trails the spectre of a small and opinionated woman whose difficulty is that she is not yet dead. In the end she would be tricked into going back to Britain, and then prevented from ever returning to the front. Her disappointment manifests itself as a kind of obstinate bafflement: 'all that I know is that I love it and that I have left it. And that I want to go back.'[19] As we shall see, it was this stubborn refusal to recognize humiliation that got her out there in the first place, and kept her there in the face of much irritation and disapproval. It was presumably this resistance to feelings of disappointment or shame that prevented her from bringing 'Red Tape' to a satisfactory close. Beyond the end of the story are two people surplus to requirements left to live out their lives away from the place where they are certain life is really happening.

The Munro Corps was remarkable for many things, apart from numbering among its members an argumentative and apparently useless middle-aged woman. Its Commandant, Dr Hector

Munro, like many others who wished to put together ambulance and other units, had had to jump through many hoops to get the Corps out to Belgium in the first place. Women in particular were viewed with suspicion: Mrs St Clair Stobart, who had founded the Women's Convoy Corps in 1907, was not sent out to the Balkan war in 1912 because the British Red Cross refused to accept any women, even those who were already trained, as Mrs St Clair Stobart's were, along Royal Army Medical Corps lines.[20] At the beginning of the 1914–18 war, the British War Office was still very resistant to the idea of women. It refused to authorize the Scottish Women's Hospital Units, founded by Elsie Inglis in 1914, and Flora Murray and Louisa Garrett Anderson's Women's Hospital Corps, which went to Paris in September 1914 under the auspices of the French Red Cross.[21] Munro's Corps included an unusually large number of women. As the Baroness de T'Serclaes, one of his original recruits, commented: 'the founder and leader of the corps, Dr Hector Munro, was an eccentric Scottish specialist, one of whose primary objects seemed to be leadership of a feminist crusade, for he was far keener on women's rights than most of the women he recruited'.[22] When the war correspondent Philip Gibbs encountered the Munro Corps shortly after Sinclair's departure, he noticed with surprise the number of women in it:

> They did not seem to me at first sight the type of woman to be useful on a battlefield or in a field-hospital. I should have expected them to faint at the sight of blood, and to swoon at the bursting of a shell. Some of them were at least too pretty, I thought, to play about in fields of war among men and horses smashed to pulp. It was only later that I saw their usefulness and marvelled at the spiritual courage of these young women, who seemed not only careless of shell-fire but almost unconscious of its menace, and who, with more nervous strength than that of many men, gave first-aid to the wounded without shuddering at sights of agony which might turn a strong man sick.[23]

It was this sort of attitude that men like Munro and women like the Baroness de T'Serclaes, who later became famous as one of the Heroines of Pervyse, had to face. She describes the attitude of the other women in the party (including May Sinclair) when she and Mairi Chisholm arrived at Victoria Station in knickerbocker khaki suits: 'the others were slightly scandalized—one could see it in their furtive glances . . . It was difficult for these gentle ladies, who wore correct costumes and picture hats, to think there could really be any need for stepping right outside the conventional lines, at all events until they got to the war zone.'[24] Applying for permission to set up an Advanced Dressing Station just behind the front lines, the Baroness was told by the Admiral that as a woman she would not 'stand the strain'. She told him that 'because I was a woman I could stand strain and hardship (I nearly asked him if he had ever heard of child-birth)'.[25] But all the same there may have been something in Philip Gibbs's comments. Munro, mistrustful of officialdom, did not want trained nurses. He was anxious to attract young women who were adaptable and adventurous. In the end he took only four of his 200 applicants, and of those four, only one, Mrs Knocker (who would become the Baroness), was a trained nurse.[26]

Munro was a doctor, psychotherapist, and one of the directors of the newly incorporated Medico-Psychological Clinic, of which May Sinclair was a founder-member.[27] Several of the women with whom he worked commented on his comic appearance, his disorganization, and his charm. Baroness de T'Serclaes describes him as 'a likeable man and a brilliant impresario, but wonderfully vague in matters of detail, and in appearance the very essence of the absent-minded professor'.[28] However, she was unimpressed with his carelessness, and left the Munro Corps to set up her own operation in Pervyse soon after May Sinclair's departure. Sinclair seems to have been more susceptible. In an entry in the manuscript version of the journal, which was not included in the printed book, she notes that Munro is 'not only a psychologist & psychotherapist, but a "psychic", & he has the "psychic"'s uncanny power over certain people (they are generally women)'. In the published *Journal* she attributes her departure to the front to his challenging her fear during an intimate dinner at her house: 'it is as if he said, "Of course, if you're *afraid*"—(haven't I told him that I *am* afraid?). The gage is thrown down on the scullery floor. I pick it up. And that is why I am here on this singular adventure.'[29] Munro would have been aware that in January 1914 Sinclair had invested the considerable sum of £500 in the clinic. He knew that she had money; he knew also that she was keen on women's rights, and had written several articles and pamphlets in support of the suffrage movement.[30] He must have imagined that she would be keen to support a feminist venture, not to mention the added incentives of her own excitement about the war and her prior connection with Munro through the clinic. Since the corps was unable to secure official backing until the last minute (Sinclair notes that they were rejected by the War Office, the Admiralty, and the British, American, and French Red Cross),[31] they were in desperate need of money, and all four women recruits paid their own way (Baroness de T'Serclaes records that Mairi Chisholm, a fanatical motor-cyclist, sold her motor bike to raise funds).[32] There was a further financial emergency even after the corps had finally secured the support of the Belgian legation and was reorganizing itself as a commission of inquiry into the condition of Belgian refugees.[33] In a passage omitted from the published journal, Sinclair notes that 'our Treasurer, three days before the Corps had arranged to start for Belgium, had started for America, leaving all our funds safely locked up in his private account at his bank' (fo. 3).

Given this kind of pressure, it is very unlikely that May Sinclair would *not* have made some financial contribution. Habitually self-effacing but eager to help others with loans and gifts, it is not surprising that her journals do not mention the fact or the degree of her support. But Marie Belloc Lowndes in her autobiography suggests that the ambulance corps was originally Sinclair's idea:

> There must have been an extraordinarily noble streak in this remarkable writer. . . . She went on writing books, all more or less successful, until the outbreak of war in 1914. She then, with her savings, started an ambulance, putting in charge of it a brilliant medical man who, she felt, had not had his chance in life. She must have left this man completely free to select his staff, and herself occupied, in the little party which accompanied him, a post which she called that of 'the scribe'.[34]

It is also hard to believe that Munro would have allowed Sinclair to join the party unless he was dependent on her financial support. It was unclear even to Sinclair exactly what her role in the corps would be: 'they've called me the Secretary and Reporter, which sounds very fine, and I am to keep the accounts (Heaven help them!) and write the Commandant's reports, and toss off articles for the daily papers, to make a little money for the Corps'.[35] But, as Sinclair herself notes, she knew nothing of accounting, and was not a trained journalist or reporter. In the end she sent virtually nothing back to Britain, and Munro and the others seem to have gone out of their way to prevent her from seeing any action. The Baroness de T'Serclaes did not understand what she was doing there:

She was a very intellectual, highly strung woman who managed to survive only for a few weeks before the horrors of war overcame her and she was sent home. Her functions were not entirely clear: I think she was to act as secretary to Dr Munro, although she could only have had the effect of making his own confusion slightly worse, and there was an idea that she might help to swell the corps' tiny finances by writing articles for the Press about its work.[36]

Sinclair was superfluous not only to the war effort itself, but to the unit to which she belonged as well. Only money could buy her the proximity to war that she so desperately craved, but money could not buy her youth or expertise.

Near the end of the *Journal* she reveals that she felt like a 'large and useless parcel which the Commandant had brought with him in sheer absence of mind, and was now anxious to lose or otherwise get rid of'.[37] This feeling has been accumulating throughout the journal as Sinclair fights to be allowed to go with the ambulances to pick up wounded. Twice she describes being physically removed from the footboards of vehicles as she clings on in her anxiety to go with them. The tone of her descriptions is at once ashamed, defiant, and accusatory:

Mrs Torrence [Baroness de T'Serclaes] got on to the ambulance beside the driver, Janet jumped up on to one step and I on to the other, while the Commandant came up, trying to look stern, and told me to get down.

I hung on all the tighter.

And then—

What happened then was so ignominious, so sickening, that, if I were not sworn to the utmost possible realism in this record, I should suppress it in the interests of human dignity.

Mrs Torrence, having the advantage of me in weight, height, muscle and position, got up and tried to push me off the step. As she did this she said: 'You can't come. You'll take up the place of a wounded man.'

And I found myself standing in the village street, while the car rushed out of it, with Janet clinging on to the hood, like a little sailor to his shrouds.[38]

Throughout the unpublished journal, and from marginal comments in G. A. MacDougall's copy of the published *Journal*,[39] we know that Sinclair regarded the Baroness and Munro as the main obstacles to her full participation in the war. Despite her characteristic timidity, the intensity of her desire to put herself in danger pushed her to defiance and exposed her to ridicule. During the corps' retreat from Belgium after the fall of Antwerp in October 1914, Sinclair, obsessed with a wounded man who had been left behind, tried desperately to return to Ghent with Miss Ashley-Smith, a nurse who also turned back at Ecloo. The chauffeurs refused to drive them, so Miss Ashley-Smith boarded a train which arrived unexpectedly. 'I got on too, to go with her, and the Chaplain, who is abominably strong, put his arms round my waist and pulled me off. I have never ceased to wish that I had hung on to that train.'[40] The *Journal* is studded with curious little vignettes such as these, which attempt to demonstrate the injustice of Sinclair's treatment as well as her courage and her desire not to betray the wounded man whom she had nursed the night before.

But what kind of a courage is this? Did Sinclair at 51 really allow herself to be bundled around in this way? Miss Ashley-Smith denied it, writing next to this passage in the margin of her own copy of the *Journal*: 'Dear me! I never saw this happen!' and adding at the end of the sentence in which Sinclair expresses her wish that she had hung on: 'Thank the Lord she didn't She said she wd come if I waited till she got her 2 suitcases!!' Elsewhere in her copy Miss Ashley-Smith does pay tribute to Sinclair's considerateness, for example in arranging to take Miss Ashley-Smith and her wounded out of Ghent with them (262), and in spite of her evident impatience with the whole Munro Corps she does not on the whole single Sinclair out for adverse comment. It seems likely then that Sinclair's description of being hauled off the train is at least an exaggeration, as though she is trying all the time to find images for her own frustration and also to avoid responsibility for her lack of success either as war correspondent or as nurse. Miss Ashley-Smith's comment about the suitcases reveals Sinclair's basic lack of understanding of the real dangers and urgency of war. Sinclair was not used to taking communities into account, working and living alone apart from a maid. By the time she went to Belgium she had lost any sense of collectivity or public responsibility, and episodes like this read like embarrassing exposures not only of naïvety but also of arrogance. Why should she return to Ghent, a town on the verge of invasion? As an untrained woman whose only experience of nursing had been markedly unsuccessful,[41] she would have been no earthly use. In a letter to Hugh Walpole written two years after her return from Belgium she seems to recognize the awkwardness of her position: 'I'm not at all sure that *my* duty wasn't to stop at home lest I sd. get ill & become a nuisance' (4 March 1916). Her intense desire to be at the centre of things overcame the sobriety of analyses such as these.

The *Journal* repeatedly describes Sinclair's compulsive attraction to danger. As they approach Ghent for the first time they become aware of the presence of troops.

> A curious excitement comes to you. I suppose it is excitement, though it doesn't feel like it. You have been drunk, very slightly drunk with the speed of the car. But now you are sober. Your heart beats quietly, steadily, but with a little creeping mounting thrill in the beat. The sensation is distinctly pleasurable. You say to yourself, 'It is coming. Now—or the next minute—perhaps at the end of the road.' You have one moment of regret. 'After all, it would be a pity if it came too soon, before we'd even begun our job.' But the thrill, mounting steadily, overtakes the regret. It is only a little thrill, so far (for you don't really believe that there is any danger), but you can imagine that thing growing, growing steadily, till it becomes ecstasy. Not that you imagine anything at the moment. At the moment you are no longer an observing, reflecting being; you have ceased to be aware of yourself; you exist only in that quiet, steady thrill that is so unlike any excitement that you have ever known.[42]

It is immediately obvious that for Sinclair, the war is an experience of *sensation.* The highly sexualized terms of her description, extending even to the fear of 'coming' too soon, indicate at once the extent of her sexual investment in the war, but also her inability to realize the war as an experience that might be *other than* sexual. As she gives herself up to feelings, she fails to realize the potential danger she is in, and the passage as a whole disavows the sensations it describes with its repeated use of 'you' to mean 'I'. The war seems to offer an opportunity to experience sexual excitement without the guilt of sexual responsibility. May Sinclair's fierce sense of individualism (in *The Tree of Heaven* she writes with horror about the 'collective soul' of both the suffrage movement and the war[43]) dissolves into the ecstasy of passivity. For it is her body, her own capacity to 'thrill', not her mind, which acts. Elsewhere she describes going to the war in terms that are reminiscent of conventional descriptions of falling in love, with the conventional wisdom, too, that nobody can help it: 'it is as if something had been looking for you, waiting for you, from all eternity out here; something that you have been looking for; and, when you are getting near, it begins calling to you; it draws your heart out to it all day long'.[44] The sensations of war were an obsession, almost a monomania, for Sinclair.

Her romance with war had all the thrill, the aggression, and the humiliation of an illicit affair. She notes in the *Journal* that she cannot tell Munro what she really wants, which is to go out and search for wounded under shell-fire.[45] Such a desire, she knows, is perverse and unjustifiable; indeed her presence in the war zone is perverse and unjustifiable. This sense of transgression only adds to the thrill.

> It is with the game of war as it was with the game of football I used to play with my big brothers in the garden. The women may play it if they're fit enough, up to a certain point, very much as I played football in the garden. The big brothers let their little sister kick off; they let her run away with the ball; they stood back and let her make goal after goal; but when it came to the scrimmage they took hold of her and gently but firmly moved her to one side. If she persisted she became an infernal nuisance. And if those big brothers over there only knew what I was after they would make arrangements for my immediate removal from the seat of war.[46]

Sinclair knows that she is there under false pretences, and that her real reason for being there is illicit and impossible to own up to. She carries the secret of her desire around with her. Safety becomes 'intolerable',[47] as she describes in a poem that was written for a 1914 anthology:

> They go: and our shining, beckoning danger goes with them,
> And our joy in the harvests that we gathered
> in at nightfall in the fields;
> And like an unloved hand laid on a beating heart
> Our safety weighs us down.[48]

To be in danger is to be in love, to respond. Safety merely slows the sluggish body.

Sinclair's 'joy' in the wounded men she did manage on occasion to save is expressed as a form of love. In Lokeren she is dispatched with a stretcher to pick up a man with a wound in his back. 'I loved him. I do not think it is possible to love, to adore any creature more than I loved and adored that clumsy, ugly Flamand. He was my first wounded man.'[49] This is a kind of displaced defloration, and the description of the man's wound only intensifies the sexual tone: 'a wound like a red pit below his shoulder-blades'.[50] It is passages such as these, including the lines from the poem I quoted earlier, which make Sinclair's work so hard to read and even harder to interpret. For although there is love of a kind in descriptions like these (and Sinclair at one point attempts to carry the Flamand's stretcher herself, impatient with the stretcher-bearers' speed),[51] there is very little pity or compassion. Sinclair is moved much more evidently to pity the unwounded refugees who huddle together in their thousands in the Palais des fêtes.[52] Wounds and blood, and even the thought of a battlefield, move her rather to a sado-masochistic exaltation which is profoundly alienating and disturbing. She alternates between an image of herself as all-powerful (saving lives, arguing with Munro, and forcing him to apologize; journal MS, fo. 92*a*), and an image of herself as a useless and humiliated child. Both images are aggressive, distorted by Sinclair's rage at being rejected by a world, a war, and a man. Both moods betray too the narcissism and the exaggerated self-deprecation of someone who is unrequitedly in love. Certainly from the excised passages of the journal we can see that she was sexually attracted to Hector Munro. Her anger with Munro for going under shellfire with Lady Dorothie Fielding ('Ursula Dearmer' in the *Journal*) seems to derive as much from sexual jealousy as from concern for Lady Dorothie's safety, and the unpublished manuscript reveals a more stormy and more intimate relationship between Sinclair and Munro than is described in the *Journal*. In the published *Journal*, 'the sight of the Commandant [Munro]' reminds Sinclair that she has all the funds of the ambulance corps in her belt upstairs, and that if it retreats and leaves her behind, as Munro has threatened, it will not get very far. In the unpublished version, it is 'the sight of Lady Ursula and the C.' (fo. 88) which distresses her, and when Munro reiterates that she may be left behind, the following response is described in the unpublished but not in the published version: 'I am absurd enough to feel the tight, agonising grip of pain, such as a creature might feel if it found itself betrayed' (fo. 89). As far as Sinclair was concerned, Munro persuaded her to come, and in the manuscript she blames him for her bad treatment and for her inadequacy: 'it has turned out exactly as I thought it would when I told the Commandant that I sd. be no earthly use to him or his ambulance' (fo. 77*a*). She came at his invitation and now he has spurned her, preferring to work with the younger women in the unit (Lady Dorothie, like Sinclair, was untrained). As Marie Belloc Lowndes writes of Munro's refusal to allow Sinclair to return to Belgium: 'though I do not think [Sinclair] was in love with [Munro], this treacherous conduct on his part in a sense broke her heart'.[53] Both Sinclair's companion in later years, Florence Bartrop, and Sinclair's niece, Wilda McNeile, wrote that she was 'not fond' of Munro, and she had few dealings with him socially after the war was over.[54]

Perhaps then it was love that made her bold. She evidently agreed to follow Munro to the war against her own instincts, and was paralysed by fear for weeks before their departure.

> And for five weeks, ever since I knew that I must certainly go out with this expedition, I had been living in black funk; in shameful and appalling terror. Every night before I went to sleep I saw an interminable spectacle of horrors: trunks without heads, heads without trunks, limbs tangled in intestines, corpses by every roadside, murders, mutilations, my friends shot dead before my eyes.[55]

As we have seen (and as she herself points out), the proximity of danger and the actual sight of wounded men provoke very different feelings in her from those she had expected: 'others may have known the agony and the fear and sordid filth and horror and the waste, but [those who have been converted to the war] know nothing but the clean and fiery passion and the contagious ecstasy of war'.[56] It is as though having passed through the 'dark night' (one of Sinclair's subsequent titles) of fear the convert is released into a brave new world of pleasure and faith.[57]

As we have seen, May Sinclair made her own war experiences the basis of a number of subsequent novels. The novel that was closest to Sinclair's own experience, *The Romantic* (1920), reproduces many of the events described in the journal, even down to the names of the villages. It tells the story of John Conway and his lover Charlotte Redhead, who have an intense but platonic relationship. Conway is passionately eager to go out to the front, but when they get there, Charlotte, who is his chauffeur, gradually realizes that he is a pathological coward who more than once leaves wounded men, and even Charlotte herself, behind because he is too afraid to stay with them. Finally John is shot in the back by the servant of someone he refused to help. McClane (obviously Munro), the psychotherapist leader of another ambulance corps stationed in the same hotel as John and Charlotte, explains to Charlotte that John was 'an out and out degenerate' whose masculinity was disturbed and incomplete:

> He jumped at everything that helped him to get compensation, to get power. He jumped at your feeling for him because it gave him power. He jumped at the war because the thrill he got out of it gave him the sense of power. He sucked manhood out of you. He sucked it out of everything—out of blood and wounds. . . . He'd have been faithful to you for ever, Charlotte, if you hadn't found him out.[58]

John has previously told Charlotte that the reason he has turned against her is disgust at her evident desire for him: 'anybody can see. It's in your face. In your eyes and mouth. You can't hide your lust.'[59] John's cowardice is linked to his fear of women, 'like a raw open wound in his mind'.[60] His excitement at the prospect of war comes from the same source as his terror, and both are signs of a gender that is unachieved. As McClane explains it, John's life is driven by the desire for and fear of masculinity. His humiliation brings out his sadism and is somehow linked to the masochism of his desire to go to the front in the first place.

How does this presentation of cowardice link with Sinclair's own experience and with her sense of the war's significance? Although she repeatedly states in the *Journal* that her fear disappeared as soon as she reached the front, G. A. MacDougall believed otherwise. She wrote on page 307 of her copy of the *Journal*: 'they panicked the whole lot of them—there was no danger for a few days' and 'they had no orders to leave Ghent when they did it was sheer funk (*sic*)'. In a heated correspondence after the first publication of extracts from the journal, of which MacDougall's side is lost, Sinclair implies that MacDougall has suggested she was a coward: 'as for the vile motive you have seen fit to credit me with—how could I put "the cowardice and panic or whatever it was" on to you?' (n.d. [1915]). Accusations of cowardice fly back and forth, and in other of her novels Sinclair demonstrates a preoccupation with the question of what cowardice actually is (Colin, in *Anne Severn and the Fieldings*

(1922), develops shell-shock exactly because he is determined not to be a coward, and enlists despite his doctor's warning that his nervous system isn't up to it). Sinclair's representation of John Conway is an attempt to define cowardice, to explore the psychology of fear and its relation with ecstasy. Men who are frightened are not really men, and Anne Severn's nursing of Colin is a reconstruction of his masculinity. 'You've made a man of him again,' says Colin's brother.[61]

For Sinclair, as for Elaine Showalter in her book *The Female Malady*, men's fear in the Great War is both cause and symptom of a crisis of masculinity.[62] But, and this is a question neither Showalter nor Gilbert and Gubar ever ask, what is the geography of women's fear? How does it relate to their desire, to sexual and aggressive arousal? How does it relate to women's sense of their own lack of agency in both military and civil society? Sinclair has no answers. But she has at least asked the questions, questions which, in an era that assumed women would only go to the front because they wished to help their men or their country, were rarely asked and even more rarely listened to. Sinclair was angry and ashamed but determined to brave it out. It might be stretching a point to suggest that such awkwardness is a basic condition of many women's lives, but it certainly is one answer to Freud's famous question 'What do women want?' Perhaps like Sinclair they want a femininity that is neither sidelined nor ridiculed; they want a sexuality that is neither embarrassing nor frustrated; and they want a public persona that is built on more than money. The question that is at the centre of Sinclair's war journals is how to develop an authentically feminine agency at an age when you are no longer perceived as sexually pliant and fully a woman. The awkward pride of Sinclair's attempt to develop such an agency should not be undervalued, for it throws light on one of the most occluded and repressed experiences of our own society: women's shame at their own superfluity.

NOTES

1. Richard Aldington, *Death of a Hero* (Garden City, NY, 1929), 263.
2. Sandra Gilbert and Susan Gubar, 'Soldier's Heart: Literary Men, Literary Women, and the Great War', in *No Man's Land: The Place of the Woman Writer in the Twentieth Century*, ii: *Sexchanges* (New Haven, 1989), 264.

3. See e.g. the 'Little Mother's' letter, 'A Mother's Answer to a "Common Soldier"', which was widely circulated for propaganda purposes, and reproduced in Robert Graves, *Goodbye to All That* (1929; Harmondsworth, 1960), 188–91, and A. E. Foringer's poster *The Greatest Mother in the World* (1918), repr. in Claire M. Tylee, *The Great War and Women's Consciousness: Images of Militarism and Womanhood in Women's Writings, 1914–64* (London, 1990), pl. 6.
4. The extracts appeared in *English Review*, 20 (1915), 168–83, 313–14, 468–76. The full version was *Journal of Impressions in Belgium* (London, 1915). The original Day Book, and the full-length MS version of the published journal, which contains many passages that were cut before publication, are both in the Department of Special Collections, Van Pelt Library, University of Pennsylvania. Most of May Sinclair's unpublished papers are in this archive. References in the text which do not give publication details are to papers held here.
5. Laura Stempel Mumford, 'May Sinclair's *The Tree of Heaven*: The Vortex of Feminism, the Community of War', in Helen M. Cooper, Adrienne Auslander Munich, and Susan Merrill Squier (eds.), *Arms and the Woman: War, Gender and Literary Representation* (Chapel Hill, NC, 1989), 175; Rebecca West, 'Miss Sinclair's Genius', in Jane Marcus (ed.), *The Young Rebecca: Writings of Rebecca West 1911–1917* (London, 1982), 304–7, 305–6.
6. Rose Macaulay, *Non-combatants and Others* (London, 1916), 222.
7. Samuel Hynes, *A War Imagined: The First World War and English Culture* (London, 1990), 95.
8. Ibid. 27.
9. Gosse's comment is quoted ibid. 13.
10. 'Influence of the War on "Life and Literature"', 1–2.
11. May Sinclair, 'Women's Sacrifices for the War', *Woman at Home*, 67 (Feb. 1915), 11.
12. May Sinclair, 'Red Tape', *Queen: The Lady's Newspaper* (14 Nov. 1914), 802–3, 802; repr. in Trudi Tate (ed.), *Women, Men, and the Great War* (Manchester, 1995).
13. Ibid. 802.
14. May Sinclair, 'Khaki', repr. in *Tales Told by Simpson* (London, 1930), 21.
15. May Sinclair, *The Tree of Heaven* (London, 1917), 67.
16. Ibid. 258.
17. West, 'Miss Sinclair's Genius', 305.
18. Tylee, *The Great War and Women's Consciousness*, 30.
19. Sinclair, *Journal*, 332.
20. David Mitchell, *Women on the Warpath: The Story of the Women of the First World War* (London, 1966), 152–3.
21. Ibid. 178–88.
22. Baroness de T'Serclaes, *Flanders and Other Fields: Memoirs of the Baroness de T'Serclaes* (London, 1964), 37.
23. Philip Gibbs, *The Soul of the War* (London, 1915), 173.
24. *The Cellar-House of Pervyse: A Tale of Uncommon Things from the Journals and Letters of the Baroness de T'Serclaes and Mairi Chisholm*, ed. G. E. Mitton (London, 1916), 1–2.
25. Baroness de T'Serclaes, *Flanders and Other Fields*, 63.
26. Mitchell, *Women on the Warpath*, 126.
27. For further information about the Medico-Psychological Clinic, see Theophilus E. M. Boll, 'May Sinclair and the Medico-Psychological Clinic

of London', *Proceedings of the American Philosophical Society*, 106 (1962), 310–26.

28. Baroness de T'Serclaes, *Flanders and Other Fields*, 37.
29. Sinclair, *Journal*, 17.
30. See e.g. May Sinclair, 'Message', *Votes for Women*, 1 (1908), 79; 'How it Strikes a Mere Novelist', *Votes for Women*, 2 (1908), 211; *Feminism* (London, 1912); and 'Women's Sacrifices for the War'.
31. Sinclair, *Journal*, 1–2.
32. Baroness de T'Serclaes, *Flanders and Other Fields*, 37.
33. Sinclair, *Journal*, 3.
34. Marie Belloc Lowndes, *A Passing World* (London, 1948), 196.
35. Sinclair, *Journal*, 4.
36. Baroness de T'Serclaes, *Flanders and Other Fields*, 37–8.
37. Sinclair, *Journal*, 324.
38. Ibid. 247–8.
39. The copy of *Journal of Impressions in Belgium* at the Imperial War Museum contains the marginal annotations of G. A. McDougall (née Ashley-Smith), a British nurse who was working with war-wounded at St Peter's convent in Ghent. Sinclair made arrangements for her to join the Munro party when it became necessary to leave Ghent.
40. Sinclair, *Journal*, 300.
41. See ibid. 250–9.
42. Ibid. 13–14.
43. See references to the 'collective soul' of the feminist movement, and the 'collective war-spirit', in Sinclair, *The Tree of Heaven*, 110, 330.
44. Sinclair, *Journal*, 79–80.
45. Ibid. 104.
46. Ibid. 122.
47. Ibid. 288.
48. May Sinclair, 'Field Ambulance in Retreat: Via Dolorosa, Via Sacra', first pub. in Hall Caine (ed.), *King Albert's Book* (London, 1914); repr. in Catherine Reilly (ed.), *Scars upon my Heart: Women's Poetry and Verse of the First World War* (London, 1981), 98.
49. Sinclair, *Journal*, 196.
50. Ibid.
51. Ibid. 197.
52. Ibid. 61–9.
53. Belloc Lowndes, *A Passing World*, 197.
54. See Wilda McNeile to T. E. M. Boll, 24 June 1959, and Florence Bartrop to T. E. M. Boll, 3 Mar. 1960, both in the University of Pennsylvania archive.
55. Sinclair, *Journal*, 8.
56. Ibid. 182.
57. May Sinclair, *The Dark Night* (London, 1924).
58. May Sinclair, *The Romantic* (London, 1920), 245.
59. Ibid. 214.
60. Ibid. 162.
61. May Sinclair, *Anne Severn and the Fieldings* (London, 1922), 139.
62. For an analysis of this issue, see Elaine Showalter, 'Male Hysteria: W. H. R. Rivers and the Lessons of Shell Shock', in *The Female Malady: Women, Madness and English Culture, 1830–1980* (London, 1985), 167–94.

4

'A great purifier': The Great War in Women's Romances and Memoirs 1914–1918

Jane Potter

Romance and memoir are by far the most common forms used by women writers during the First World War.[1] Most of the authors are unknown to us now. The works themselves are not 'great literature', but they are of literary and historical interest for what they say about the place of women in, and their attitudes towards, the Great War.

The texts I shall examine in this chapter all share a common theme: that of the transformative power of war. They also share the eugenic anxieties about physical, mental, and spiritual deterioration which emerged in Britain towards the end of the nineteenth century. If society was suffering from a 'degenerative' disease, 'a falling-off from original purity, a reversion to less complex forms of structure',[2] then war was a means of regeneration and purification. It was a eugenic *good.* The 'conservative polemic of popular fiction'[3] had a number of 'unfit' targets. Among them were exotic and erotic artistic tastes such as highbrow art, aestheticism, and art nouveau. A further threat to both women and men was the suffrage movement. It was blamed for de-sexing women, encouraging them to become pseudo-men, and causing them to lose all touch with their 'feminine' natures. Such were the ideas that abounded in the press and in various sections of society.

That there was actually a cohesive set of values is what Samuel Hynes calls the 'myth' of the years preceding the Great War. 'The arguments in this polemical war were various, and by no means consistent with each other: the attackers shared only a general sense of who their enemies were.'[4] The modern age

Fig. 3. Jacket from Berta Ruck, *Khaki and Kisses* (© the estate of Berta Ruck; Hutchinson: London, 1915)

came to be seen as the 'spirit of peacetime triviality, which war's seriousness had refuted and dispersed'.[5] In this way, the war was viewed as a cleanser and a purifier, and was used to justify the warnings of Germany's evil intentions.

Four writers are discussed in this chapter: the romance writers Berta Ruck and Ruby M. Ayres, and the memoirists Kate Finzi and Olive Dent.[6] Berta Ruck's collection of short stories entitled *Khaki and Kisses* (1915) exploits the narrative and didactic possibilities of the Great War. A heart dominates the centre of the paperback's khaki-coloured cover. Inside the heart is an illustration of a blonde woman in a powder-blue dress holding a pink rose. She is held in the embrace of a dark-haired man in uniform. It is an image that is, even today in romance novels, touted as the fantasy of every woman—a tall, dark, and handsome, manly man (manly by virtue of his soldier uniform).

The opening tale in this 'series of delightful love stories', 'Infant in Arms', depicts the transformation of 'She' from flippant coquette to serious lady, and 'He' from feeble artist to heroic soldier. Obsessive concerns about degenerate youth permeate the story, particularly in relation to the 'hero'. Neither character is given a specific name other than 'He' or 'She', as if to reinforce the idea that they could be any man or woman in Britain at the time—any middle- or upper-class man or woman, that is. The first part opens at a party in June 1914, a glittering scene of 'men and women in fantastic costumes—Harlequins, Nautch-girls, Vorticist Princesses, Futurist Follies, Caliphs à la Bakst'.

'She' is dressed as Nijinsky's Spectre de la Rose, 'He' as a Black Panther. Under the decadent, modern influences, seemly behaviour is flung aside. Even more shocking is the charade of sexual activity in which She is the dominant partner, despite the implications of their costumes, almost forcing the movements and relishing them. In what might seen as an attempt on his part to 'make an honest woman' out of her, He proposes marriage, shyly, with reticence, in a pleading fashion. She refuses even to 'care a little', saying she will eventually marry, not for love and commitment, but 'for frocks and a setting, and that sort of thing'. She has a rebellious, cold modernity with more concern for show and glamour than affection as 'they walk up and down; black, grace-ful, free-limbed, silhouette against the frieze of the sighing willows and the star-spangled sky, leaving a trail of cigarette smoke (hers) and a deep-voiced mutter of appeal (his) upon the breeze'.[7] The romantic beauty of their shadows and the summer evening are set against the inversion of their personalities: she smokes, he appeals. To her, He is not a man, but an infant in arms, feeble, and 'predictable', which she claims is 'fatal' to a woman's opinion of a man. 'A girl can't want to marry a man when she knows she knows much more than he does! Sorry. Sorry for myself too. It would be more amusing for me if I weren't too wide-awake, too spoilt, too sophisticated to fall in love! But I am' (10). While there is meant to be a sense of scorn for her spoilt sophistication, it is He that is most culpable. If he were only a man, strong-willed, assertive, dominant, and not taken in by the insipidity of the avant-garde, She would not feel so spoilt. The modernist world has encouraged men to be shades of Wildeian aesthetes, as it has encouraged an unnatural interest in sex and sophistication in women.

But before such nonsense can take hold of these people, the war begins. The story then switches to the spring of 1915, and a better London has bloomed as a result, showing what England is really made of: 'London's gayest finery of lilac and laburnum seems put on in special honour of the khaki boys that throng her streets; London's sons preparing for the Front, or returning, snatching a few days' leave from the trenches. For the soil of slackness that produced those gay and bizarre blossoms of decadence has not proved so deep after all; there was British bed-rock beneath it!' (11). The artificial decoration of the summer party is transformed into a scene of natural goodness. The blossoms of decadence seem limp in comparison to the solid, gritty elements of soil and bedrock, with all the sexual implications that might be there for the country's 'manhood'.

Transformed, too, is our heroine. We see her on her way to hospital, this time not in teasing 'Nijinsky rig' but in a sensible 'long, belted coat'. He, in hospital, is also different. Gone is the Black Panther costume as he lies under a 'black panther rug', drained, but (of course) still handsome: 'He was a dilettante sculptor once, but looks a thorough soldier now. He answered the Call to Arms at the beginning of the War; gained his commission and lost his leg at Ypres' (12). She looks at him 'and her heart swells with pride for him. It sinks with shame for herself. And she had thought herself so much wiser, so much better than the infatuated boy at who she laughed—What folly! . . . A new thrill runs through her. She had thought herself "sophisticated" out of that. But again she thrills, glowing and shy at the thought of what had left her flippant and indifferent last year. Can it be that this War, which has cut all life in half for our nation, has worked another miracle in her?' (15). She is put in her place, but she 'thrills' at it. The war is seen as a miracle, as something positive, even when—and perhaps because—it has 'cut all life in half'. She sees his wounding as a cause for rejoicing because it proves that he is not an insipid artist; he risked his life in a manly pursuit for the good of the empire and the nation.

He has, is seems, become manly in another way. Whereas before he only appealed for a kiss, Ruck records that there is 'an uneasy movement under the panther rug'. We are left to speculate what this might be, but the sexual implications are clear. Such masculine stirrings cause him to think that she is just feeling sorry for him, and she must convince him otherwise: 'The radiant, kneeling girl beside him laughs and sobs together. "Oh, can't you understand that this has made everything different? You're just twice as much of a man, now that you'll have to get on with one leg, as you were when you were dancing and fooling about on two! As for me, I'm not even a woman unless you'll help make me one"' (15). Ruck's theme is clear: the social order and future of the nation are based upon men as defenders and women as yielding, mothering partners. War has transformed this couple. Before, 'He' was parading, 'fooling about' as a man, wearing a pelt, masquerading as a warlike brave animal; now, because he has been a soldier and sacrificed a limb, he does not have to dress up. The bedrock as there all the time. 'She', too, has been purified, not only of a flippant outlook, but of an unseemly, teasing sexuality. She is still fashionable, but sensible.

Yet there are many contradictions here. Whilst the war may have purified them, their roles have not really changed very much. The loss of his leg means that, in some ways, He is still the infant in arms of the title. She is still the dominant partner physically. She is mother to his infantilized state. But, as Ruck seems to want to make clear, she surrenders her sophistication, and 'wide-awake' outlook to his guidance. He will make her a woman, so in one sense, *she* becomes the infant in arms. They each have a master–child role to play.

The same idea is even more blatantly expounded in Ruck's story 'Wanted—A Master'. The title, again, plays a dual role: to whom does it refer? Is it the dog named Sydney owned by a soldier going to the front, or is it the heroine, also named Sydney, who answers the advertisement to look after the pet? Both have masculine-sounding names, but they are spelt in the feminine way; both human and animal are female, but have the guise, through their actions, of aggressive males. Sydney Ellerton, the heroine, was once 'aggressive' and every man was her enemy, for she had been 'the most uncompromising Militant Suffragette who ever embittered the life of a policeman—or of a politician'. In time of war, however, 'it all seemed very long ago and trivial now. In these days Sydney grudged every penny of the money that she had once thrown recklessly away on subscriptions to The Cause, and on petroleum and pamphlets and other inflammatory propaganda, for now her small independent income was being stretched to the uttermost to help a Belgian orphan' (205). The suffragette becomes reformed and in her way as a single woman she performs a mothering role by sponsoring a child. The war has clarified her values, shown her the error of her aggressive ways and her political pretensions. Ruck's romance becomes another propaganda tract, this time against votes for women.

Amazed that Sydney Ellerton is a woman, the dog's owner recognizes her from a suffragette rally where she berated him on his pre-war occupation as an MP opposed to the female franchise. Sydney also admits that she was the activist who set his house on fire, burning it to the ground. He takes this information with amazing composure, forgiving her, and commenting that the house had nothing of value in it: 'This war seems to show one which are the things one really does care about—which are things that count.' Sydney has realized this as well, but as she renounces her militant past, calling it 'criminally silly', and adding that 'it was wrong even to try and merge the difference between women's work—and yours', she does not actually blame women but men:

All those lady-like young men who used to sit about on lawns and settees, prattling about Art and Socialism, and Russian Opera and Politics, what had they done to deserve the Franchise? What had they, in short, done? Nothing! except make girls with healthy brains and healthy instincts into Suffragettes,' declared Sydney, only half-laughing. 'How could one help despising them—as they were? It was those slackers who made us lose all sense of proportion. But now these same people are working as Territorials and enlisting as Kitchener's men and making brilliant charges, as the London Scottish, and one feels so different about them!

'It's taken war, and the sight of man doing a man's old job as a woman's protector, to put all these things in the right places.' (210)

That is what Ruck means when she alludes to the 'old' values and the 'natural' roles of men and women: men are soldiers, and made to protect women, and women are meant to keep their homes warm, and their love alive. Women must pick up the pieces by adopting male behaviour, but it is unnatural for them to do so. This challenges the arguments made by Gilbert and Gubar where they suggest that women desired, and revelled in, a gender inversion.[8] For Ruck and other female writers, men have particular characteristics, women have theirs, and the state of the nation and the future is best served by each preserving their natural roles. Rather than being a sensible endeavour, the fight for the vote is actually a reaction against feminized men. The war, which combatants and rescue workers alike describe as chaos, is actually a stabilizing force for the real chaos at home where gender roles have been almost irrevocably reversed. It has put things back in their 'natural' places.

Slackers, evil Germans, and the soldier's sweetheart are common characters in Ruck's other tales in this edition. She continued to write similar love stories with telling titles: *The Bridge of Kisses* (1917) and *The Land-Girl's Love Story* (1918), both published in years when the scale of the slaughter was generally known. As many propagandists have done before her, Ruck does not question this reality, but uses it to justify the cause. *Khaki and Kisses* cannot be claimed to be just light reading. It is a didactic work and a strong piece of propaganda for the war effort directed specifically at women.

While publishers catered to the public demand, research into the propaganda activities of government-sponsored Wellington House, in the early years of the war, reveals that commercial publishing houses were paid five guineas for the use of their imprint on works designed to influence public opinion.[9] In this way, works by various authors attached to Wellington House would appear to offer a private, unofficial viewpoint. The works produced were mainly pamphlets by well-known writers and intellectuals, and although it is highly unlikely that Ruck had anything to do with Wellington House, it is interesting to note

Fig. 4. Jacket from Ruby M. Ayres, *Richard Chatterton, V.C.* (Hodder and Stoughton: London, 1915; reprinted by permission of the Peters Fraser & Dunlop Group Ltd.)

that such an association between the government propaganda machine and established publishing firms did exist. These facts put the didactic themes of Ruck's stories into a new perspective.

Her sentiments are not simply her own, but part of a larger effort to reinforce popular support for the war. They also dictate an acceptable behaviour for women counter to the trends of feminism, pacifism, the avant-garde, and the intellectual that could undermine the war effort. Behaviour like that of Ruck's heroines frees men to do their task of fighting, extols their masculinity, and rules out of order any questions concerning the 'why' of the war.

A romance novel which tries to communicate a sense of the battlefield as it deals with a man's transformation by it is Ruby M. Ayres's *Richard Chatterton, V.C.* (1915). The title is surely meant to call to mind the 'marvellous boy' poet Thomas Chatterton, who died young, and thereby to add to the sense of a doomed but romantic youth to the novel. The cover illustration shows a uniformed man crouching, alert in no man's land, the sky above him alight with shell-fire. Over the picture is written: 'A laggard in love, a laggard in war. What did they give him his manhood for?', lines adapted from Lady Heron's Song about young Lochinvar in Walter Scott's *Marmion.* In Ayres's novel, 'manhood' includes the hero's maturity, in terms of age and sexuality, and ideas of virility, bravery, boldness, fortitude, strength, and heroism. Richard Chatterton's 'gift' of manhood is wasted. He does not demonstrate virility and action. He is idle, slow, lazy.

Throughout the novel, Chatterton attempts to throw off his derisive nickname 'laggard' with all its implications, especially potent in wartime, of slacker, coward, and effete layabout. He is an example of the lazy gentry when the story opens, spending his days at his club, dozing and disturbed only by the marching of recruits in the street. The members of the club and Sonia, his fiancée, begin to berate him for his failure to enlist. His valet, Carter, is anxious to join the ranks, and has a recruiting poster ('Will they ever come?') pinned to his bedroom wall 'surmounted by a row of little flags'.[10] Sonia echoes Ruck's heroines (and quite a number of war posters) in her enthusiasm for the war and in her complaint 'Oh, if I were only a man! [. . .] Because if I were I shouldn't be here dressed up like a doll—idle, useless! Because if I were I shouldn't have to stay at home and let others go out and fight for me. Oh, how can they be content not to help—all those men who might so easily go?' (30). Chatterton, surely, is her prime target. Her 'bitter disappointment and disillusion' which 'had beaten down her love' for Chatterton is also representative: 'he was a laggard—a weakling, content to stay at home while others cheerfully offered their lives in the sacred cause of freedom' (28).

Sonia's romanticism, however, does not go unchecked. Lady Merriman, her guardian, is realistic and insightful—'she'd worship any man who came back wounded or disabled'—and checks Sonia's enthusiasm as 'stuff and nonsense', saying: 'Take it from me, my dear, that mothers and sweethearts don't give a fig for the country when they hear that their sons and lovers have been butchered by those German savages' (28). While Lady Merriman has something to say about empty and idealistic patriotism, she expresses the prevalent belief shared by Ruck and by writers of invasion literature that the Germans are evil.

Another character tempers Sonia's enthusiasm when she exclaims: 'I don't find the War at all depressing . . . It's the most wonderful, greatest thing that's ever happened in all the world, I should think. I'm never tired of hearing about it and reading about it.' Mr Courtney, a young friend just returned from the front, tells her: 'You wait until you've lost a friend or some one out there [. . .] That'll make all the difference, Sonia. There doesn't seem anything very grand or wonderful about it when some one you've known all your life is finished off by a German bullet or killed by a gun' (126). Ayres, a woman and a noncombatant, exhibits an awareness of the war and the fighting which is usually assumed to be unavailable to the imagination of the home front. It is possible that Courtney's speech comes right out of her direct experience with a returned soldier. Newspapers, letters, and first-hand accounts from men on leave certainly did give those at home some sense of the horrors of the war. But, for many like Ruck, and even the seemingly more enlightened Ayres, awareness did not necessarily go hand-in-hand with pacifism, and their characters reflect this.

Sonia, disgusted with Chatterton, breaks off her engagement with him, becomes attached to his friend Montague, and, like the fair Ellen, she nearly marries this 'dastard'. Montague had been lamed in a motoring accident, so is unable to enlist. While his disability is the result of manly activity, and allows him honourable exemption from fighting, it is not given the same status as the injury incurred by Ruck's hero in 'Infant in Arms', which results from the manly pursuit of war and the defence of empire. There is a hierarchy of disability. Montague has a 'picturesque lameness', not a heroic one. He begins as a sympathetic figure, but ends up the antagonist.

Chatterton finally enlists, unbeknownst to Sonia. Once in uniform as a Tommy (he refuses to wait for a commission), he is a changed man. Like Ruck's transformed feeble artist, the donning of the soldier's uniform is the donning/dawning of manhood.

> Where had his manhood been all these weeks that he had not rushed to do his bit in the fight against murder and militarism? He felt himself the veriest pigmy of a man, a coward of giant proportions. No wonder Sonia has despised him [. . .]
>
> After all, there was still something glorious in life, even though it were shorn of love; something glorious in the knowledge that he was at last one of the hundreds of thousands of men rushing out to swell that thin brown line of khaki which was all that would ultimately stand between Germany and the freedom of the Channel.
>
> With a new pride and confidence in himself, Richard Chatterton squared his shoulders and lifted his head. They had called him a laggard—they had laughed at him, well, he would show them [. . .]
>
> The fighting instinct had struggled uppermost at last through the enveloping slackness and inertia born of long years of indolence, and as eager and loyal a soldier as ever drew a sword in defence of King and Country walked proudly through London's dimly lit streets in the person of Richard Chatterton. (99)

In the pigmy-versus-giant comparison, Chatterton is both a little, stunted man and a larger-than-life coward. Both images are derisory. Also, the reference to pigmies intimates savagery and regression. He has somehow reverted to a lesser state of development in the imperial eye that sees the white race as superior to those in 'primitive' societies. The language of empire, degeneration, and myth all come into play.

Chatterton is transformed from a fop into a man when he dons the khaki uniform. He becomes a man of action at the front. War, here, as in Ruck, strips away the false surface to reveal the 'bedrock'. The metaphors of surface and depth are potent for they attest to the belief, or the hope, that underneath frivolous exteriors there lies a serious interior that will be drawn out in time of crisis. Dross gives way to quality. Chatterton's heroism also reinforces the bravery of the British army as a whole. Standing for eight hours in the liquid mud of the trenches, he 'had seen men dropping all around him—seen broken limbs and shattered bodies, witnessed the bravery with which Englishmen can bear away.' *Their* manhood is also proved.

Chatterton's gallantry is described in detail in the novel's main action scene. Ayres's description of battle is vivid and dramatic. While the dead and the dying are described, and the scale of death is represented, the scenes are not meant to repulse, but to reinforce the hero's amazing actions. The Germans are seen as giant vermin, supernaturally strong, and the 'earth seemed to breed those swarming, grey-clad figures'. Compared with the mud-stained and exhausted British troops, they seem 'as fresh to-day as when they started' (273), a warning that the enemy will not be easily overcome.

In contrast to the pestilential Germans, the Tommy is above reproach. He goes out fighting: 'Shouting, swearing, even singing snatches of song, they leapt the parapets of the trenches and rushed forward.' Tommy also goes down fighting: 'Men were dropping like flies around him as he ran; some falling with a laugh, and using their last drop of vitality to struggle to their feet again; some went down without even a moan, and lay where they had fallen, shapeless, huddled masses, their khaki uniforms one with brown, riddled earth' (268). Not surprisingly, Chatterton's heroism goes beyond this fearlessness in the face of death. He rescues not one, but two men from no man's land while under fire, and after being repeatedly wounded. The laggard truly becomes the man of action, for, thinking that Sonia has married Montague (she has not; Carter was misled by that 'dastard'), Chatterton is spurred on to reckless, do-or-die action:

> A sort of mad exuberance seized Chatterton. The blood was hammering in his veins. As he ran he shouted and yelled with the rest. It was like hell let loose. Fear was forgotten—left behind with the mud and death in the trenches [. . .]
>
> At one time even the thought of bayoneting a man had turned Chatterton sick, but now each time a grey-clad figure went down before him the exuberance grew in his veins. . . .
>
> This was vengeance; this was the wiping out a little of the heavy score of the earlier days of the war; he was striking a blow for England, and each blow went home [. . .] (276)

Angry at Montague and Sonia, as well as the Germans, Richard feels a 'primitive savagery [...] rush through his veins'. This regression is acceptable because it is harnessed to defeat the enemy of England. It is important that Ayres stresses vengeance, not just blind violent aggression. Chatterton is not like the Germans who instigated the war. He is a defender, an agent of a kind of divine retribution, and feels an 'exuberance' as each of his bayonet thrusts strike the enemy. The word 'home' not only indicates the lethal, physical stab to the enemy, but also reinforces the sense that the blow, the fighting, is for the 'home' of England.

Chatterton runs through 'shrapnel falling like rain' to save Carter and a young lieutenant. This young officer 'lost his cap, and his fair, curly hair looked almost like a girl's in the mingled glare of grey dawn light and gunfire. . . . Something in the boyish excitement of his shaven face reminded Chatterton of Sonia a little.' The sexual ambiguity, and the hint of homoeroticism, is quickly rejected by Ayres and her manly character, with: 'Actually there was no resemblance, but his brain was a ferment of pain and madness, and in such a mood a sentimental streak of moonlight on the floor of a barn would have made him think of the woman he loved' (277). There is to be no suggestion that he is anything other than heterosexual. The feelings of attraction to this boyish figure and the degeneracy they recall are countermanded by Chatterton's thoughts of a woman, Sonia, and by the statement that in this deadly environment he is half-mad—in such a state that any romantic image like moonlight would recall his beloved. He loves men in comradeship, in the brotherhood men feel in war, but he does not love them sexually. Thus, his exploits on the battlefield are to leave no doubt about his masculinity and heroism. Ayres attempts to re-create a more realistic sense of battle by describing broken limbs, a 'dead boyish face', a 'death-spattered field', and the 'groans and prayers of the wounded and dying'. It is not a sanitized picture, but a hellish scene that reinforces Chatterton's superhuman effort which is exciting and melodramatic, and confirms his worthiness to be called a hero.

He is ultimately awarded the VC and, after a lengthy convalescence, he survives with little worse than a limp—a 'picturesque lameness'—a wound in a 'mentionable place' in the words of Sassoon, for Sonia to enthuse over.[11] Chatterton earns the noble epithet of Scott's hero: 'So faithful in love, and so dauntless in war, | There never was a knight like the young Lochinvar.' By invoking the romantic world of Walter Scott, and the ideals upon which much of his work is based, Ayres aligns her novel with the chivalric tradition and suggests to her readers that Chatterton is the latest in that line of heroes, and that the Great War, the agent of his transformation from laggard to modern knight, is itself part of that legacy of noble conflict.

Transformation is also a major theme in memoirs. These first-hand accounts by women on active service are numerous.[12] Kate Finzi's *Eighteen Months in the War Zone* (1916) and Olive Dent's *A V.A.D. in France* (1917) may serve as examples. While they had a different perspective, both Finzi and Dent share the view propounded by their fiction-writing counterparts that war is a great purifier.

Kate Finzi, 'fresh from the statutory discipline of the wards of a London hospital' and three years of nursing training, went out to France in October 1914. Her *Eighteen Months in the War Zone* contains an introduction by Major-General Sir Alfred Turner, praising the nurses that 'softened the horrors of War to our soldiers, who ministered aid to them when they were stricken by wounds or diseases, and mitigated their tortures'.[13] He states that the 'women of England showed what they were made of—a phrase which echoes Ruck's sentiments and calls upon all the other imagery of bedrock and natural attributes so often invoked. War, again, 'brings out the best' in people.

The Major-General's praise for women is coupled with a vehement attack on the Germans, who are the embodiment of evil, and he asserts that Finzi's account, in a 'plain, unvarnished style [is] a terrible and graphic picture of the horrors of war' (p. xv). Finzi does not write, according to the Major-General, like an emotional woman, but like a man, a soldier, without flowery sentiment, just the plain facts. This is somehow meant to give credence to her account—the starker it reads, the more realistic and truthful it is. He validates this woman's account of a man's war: she is a qualified observer and her views can be trusted.

She begins her account with a condemnation of the evil Hun, repeating stories of German atrocities that were becoming increasingly familiar to those in England through the Bryce Report and pamphlets such as 'The Truth about German Atrocities' (1915). Like Ayres, she too is convinced of German military prowess: 'surely we are pitted against a foe so strong in physique and so brave and cunning, that many years of strenuous training and thrift will be required to fit the united races to withstand the onslaught' (10). Such an assertion about the country's unreadiness is a reminder of the fears engendered by the Boer War, when it was discovered that half the male population was unfit for military service. Finzi condemns this unpreparedness, but she deals most frankly with problems in her own profession. She is scathing about VADs who wear the same uniforms as qualified nurses. She asks, 'for what are a number of first-aid lectures or stretcher-drills as compared with the real hospital training? It is ridiculous to imagine that V.A.D.s with their theoretical experience, are competent to run hospitals themselves' (51). She says it would not be difficult 'to sift the wheat from the chaff, the seekers after sensation from the genuine workers. There is no romance in the work of the hospital, no jaunts to the battlefields bearing cups of water to the dying, no soothing of pillows and holding the hands of patients; but ten to twelve hours each day occupied in the accomplishment of tasks so menial that one would hesitate to ask a servant to perform them' (52). She is, in some respects, addressing an audience used to servants, a privileged class of women imagining themselves as Florence Nightingales of the western front. She is trying to dissuade the 'daughters of educated men', as Virginia Woolf called them,[14] from coming to France in pursuit of excitement.

Thus, Finzi does not mince words in describing her experiences as a nurse. For her, patriotism comes not out of some romantic vision of wiping a fevered brow, but in recognizing the brutality waged upon the British soldier. She is depressed by 'the fact that half of the people are quite content to let others do their jobs whilst they look on with an amused smile and reap the benefit of the shortage of men' (93). She longs to see such shirkers—presumably men and women—'well strafed', and was probably a firm exponent of the 1916 Conscription Act: 'Why, after all, should our beautiful island be left with the unfit, the loafers, the "funks" as fathers for the future generations? In every other country the army is representative, not of the pick of the land, but of the average male population. We, however, seem bent on committing race suicide' (94). Like Berta Ruck in her stories, Finzi is articulating here the obsession with the perceived degeneration of the country, and aligns herself with eugenicist theories of race development.[15] Those who answered 'the Call' were the bedrock of Britain; even those who were on the fringe of the avant-garde or who were initially laggards eventually came to their senses. They were not entirely lost. But, in Finzi's perception, there are still those who are unrepentantly degenerate, who feel no duty to volunteer their services to their country.

Finzi's memoir, then, is not simply a recollection of her time in France, but an indictment of all those at home who have both an unrealistic view of the war and a complacent attitude to the cause. Yet, for all her admonition about the idealistic war-worker, her account nevertheless expresses the view that she and others like her are part of a special generation in history, banded in 'one great unity of purpose' (200). Memories of the dead haunt her, and she finds herself in a privileged position: 'They are gone. I alone am left to tell the tale' (205). Echoing the messenger in the Book of Job ('I only am escaped to tell thee'), and like Edmund Blunden and Robert Graves, she feels compelled to tell her story, to 'go over the ground again'. That she seems more intent on telling the story of the suffering of the men than she does about telling her own suffering and feelings is clear, but in telling about the men, she does tell about herself—as a woman in this war. Along with male memoirists, Finzi too follows in the tradition of the heroic-age poet who, as Jon Stallworthy argues, 'was not primarily a warrior. His function was to ensure that his friends did not die unsung. He must escape that he might tell; bear witness.'[16] Finzi bears witness for both the male soldier and the female nurse in her rhetorical questions to the reader:

> Have you seen the men as they come down from the Front during the first mad months, primitive, demented, at their last gasp, ready to face death in any form rather than the hellish uncertainty they had just left? Have you heard the groans of the wounded, seen arms rotting off and legs smashed to pieces, and dressed black gaping holes in young boys' sides? Have you seen faces blown beyond recognition—faces eyeless, noseless, jawless, and heads that were only half heads?
>
> [. . .] have you heard them live through their battles again in their slumber or under anaesthetic? [. . .] Have you removed clothes and boots from helpless limbs caked on with seven weeks mud and overrun with vermin? Have you seen forever nameless enemy corpses washed and carried out to the mortuary, and enemy though they were, because of their youth, wished that you could tell their mothers you had done your best?

> When you have seen this [. . .] you will know what modern warfare means.
>
> Yet is it all something one would not have missed, although no sane person would face it a second time; for, as an American said recently: 'Those who have not participated in this war will be forever lacking something which is not to be recaptured later'. (227)

Echoing the lines from *Henry V* about the men who 'will think themselves accursed they were not here' on St Crispin's Day,[17] Finzi aligns herself with a special generation. She does not mince words; the images are horrific and brutal. They do not lead her to the anger of Owen and Sassoon which was directed at the 'old men' who ran the war. Rather, her experiences reinforce her resolve to defeat Germany, while her compassion for the young enemy soldiers still leads her to wish 'that you could tell their mothers you had done your best'. Finzi demonstrates that women did know 'what modern warfare means', and, that they also wanted to communicate this knowledge to civilians at home. That she does not condemn the cause aligns her with the government propaganda campaign; yet, while she is pro-British, she is not pro-war. She has seen too much suffering to want to see it happen again. But, precisely because so many have suffered, the war must be brought to a noble conclusion with the complete defeat of Germany, the cause of all the horror.

Finzi shares with her male witnesses the sense of alienation from those at home. For Graves and Blunden, the home front was filled with blood-lust,[18] but Finzi perceives a complacency, an indifference to what is happening in France. What is, of course, important to note here is that Graves and Blunden produced their memoirs in a post-war world, where time and the political and indeed literary climate gave them the opportunity and the mandate to speak more openly and critically, with reflection and even embellishment. But Graves, Blunden, and Finzi share a discomfiture with the experience of going home, and with the attitudes of those they find there. Finzi describes her speech before a community meeting in Cumberland. The audience wants to hear great tales of heroism, of her risking her life with daily shell-fire and the Hun close at hand: 'What they want are descriptions of weeping gas victims and death-bed scenes (that in reality are far better forgotten—if it is possible) and incidents of such as a youthful convalescent sapper confided to me recently—of the man who, though his head was blown clean off at midday, was found to be convulsingly clawing at the earth with fingers that seemed yet alive at sundown!' (149). Of course, to the readers of this memoir, she communicates some of the very things she derides the Cumberland audience for wanting to know. Yet she stresses that the real heroism is not in such atrocious and horrific tales. For nurses, the greatest and most difficult feature of life at the base was 'maintaining continual cheerfulness in the face of odds like bursting boilers . . . the dullness of buttering endless loaves . . . the dreadful monotony' (149).

Finzi is critical of the home front, but blames the government for keeping it in ignorance. Her position is made clear when she aligns herself with the Northcliffe press. People at home are 'utterly oblivious' to the seriousness of the shell campaign, she writes, despite warnings in Northcliffe's *Daily Mail*, which Finzi calls 'the only organ strong enough to bring the truth before the public and combat the weaknesses of a desultory government' (146). Northcliffe was often at odds with Wellington House over their cautious and restricted release of information about the events in France. She asserts in the epilogue to her diary that she intends to 'make good to those at home the silence enforced by a rigorous censor' (259) after the war, but how she would have done so outside its constraints can only be conjectured.

Another nurse who recorded her role in the Great War and its effect upon her was Olive Dent. *A VAD in France* (1917) conveys the same sense of patriotic duty, but her tone is more jovial than that of Finzi. By the time of its publication, excerpts from her memoir had already been serialized in the *Daily Mail* and some provincial papers. Again, we have a Northcliffe connection, and an indication right from the start of the alignment of Dent's views. She dedicates her book 'to all those brave Boys whom it has been my privilege and pleasure to Nurse'. This statement characterizes the whole tone of the memoir: the gratefulness for service, the undying admiration for the 'boys', and the sense of duty in a Great Cause.

Like Ayres's heroine Sonia, Dent is caught up in the idea of 'fire, slaughter, dripping bayonet, shrieking shell', and laments her gender: 'For the first time in a happy, even life one felt bitterly resentful of one's sex. Defence was the only consideration in the popular mind in those early August days. And defence was a man's job, and I, unfortunately, was a woman.'[19] The weapons and danger of war are mentioned with an excitement that does not take in their true nature and which recalls the romantic sentiments that Finzi berates. When she and her VAD colleagues arrive at their camp in France, they receive a 'chilly reception from the night superintendent nurse' (29). The camp sister (in language Finzi might have used) 'lucidly and emphatically explained to us that she had no idea what "people were thinking about to send girls such as we, girls who had not come from any training school"' (29). Characteristic of her faith in the cause of the war and in the powers that asserted this, Dent counters the nurse's complaint with her expression of confidence that the government 'knew what it was doing' when it sent them.

Eventually, she records, the VADs got on well with the nursing sisters, and put up with the sparse living conditions and the gruelling schedules. The daughter of the educated man, used to a comfortable life, is also 'an adaptable girl', she says, who 'soon learns to overcome such minor difficulties' (36) as no hot water, no taps, no sinks, no fires, and no gas-stoves. Dent records her daily routine: the early morning work consisting of making beds, dusting twenty-four lockers, taking twenty-four temperatures, and tidying the wards. Then there is a snack lunch, a change of apron and the giving of medicines, inhalations, applying fomentations, eusol dressing, two or three doses of castor oil, cleaning a linen cupboard, and the distribution of the boys' dinner. The afternoon brings more medicines, the washing of patients, and the making of beds before she goes off-duty at 5 p.m. This is the monotony of routine mentioned by Finzi.

Dent also records her experiences of night-nursing 'with its tense anxieties, its straining vigilance, its many sorrows' (270). She says her initial perception that it would be 'dull' 'was in the days before the war, when I had no acquaintance with ghastly wounds which require dressing every two hours . . . when cerebral hernia, tracheotomy, trephine, colotomy, laprotomy, and the evil-smelling gas gangrene were comparative rarities' (278). While her perceptions of the reality of war-nursing change, her perceptions about the meaning of the war alter very little, except, perhaps, to strengthen her resolve about it, a resolve inseparable from her devotion to the 'boys'. Dent, Finzi, and other women played down their personal achievement in characteristic self-effacing form, concentrating on the quiet suffering of the men they cared for. It represents both the sacrifice of those who answered 'the Call', and a condemnation of those who shirked duty.

Dent does not dwell on graphic descriptions of wounds but neither does she avoid such things as foul-smelling gangrene, blue-purple trench-feet, and amputated limbs. While giving testimony to the suffering of the men, they also illustrate this once-pampered woman's ability to endure the sight and the smell of such unpleasant realities for the sake of Britain: 'ours is a country worth fighting for, worth dying for, worth being maimed for. A funny thing—love of one's native land' (136).

She is in no doubt about the rightness of the cause. One nurse, she records, is, and cries out: 'What a useless wastage of human life! . . . a useless waste!' (337). As if not only to answer that particular nurse's cry, but, by extension, those of her readers who perhaps harboured or expressed such thoughts, Dent records a colleague's passionate reply:

> How can the gift of those lives be called a 'useless waste'? Is it a waste for the men to fight, to suffer, and to die for all that they hold dear—their liberty, their ideals, and their loved ones? [. . .]
>
> To-day's stories of fighting, told to us red-hot from the lips of the boys who have lived them, those stories and the many little incidents we have all witnessed, have shown up that, while war may be a great wastage, it is also a great purifier. It has brought out valour indescribable, self-sacrifice unforgettable, patience and magnificent endurance untellable. And are these nothing worth? [. . .]
>
> There may be brutality, bestiality, fiendish recklessness, devilish remorselessness, anguishing mutilation and destruction in war, but to-day I have met fortitude, devotion, self-abnegation, that has brought with it an atmosphere of sanctity, of holiness.
>
> I am too tired to sleep, too tired to do anything but lie . . . too tired to shut out of sight and mind the passionate appeal of dying eyes and the low faint whisper of 'Sister, am I going to die?'
>
> But, oh, how glad I am to have lived through this day! With the stinging acute pain of all its experiences raw on me. I say it has been a privilege to undergo these sensations. For the pain will pass, since all pain ultimately dies, but what will endure for ever is the memory of the nobility, the grandeur, the approach to divinity we have all seen. It has made better women of us all; it has brought knowledge to our understanding, life to our ideals, light to our soul. (337)

The image of purification both sanctifies the horrific, ghastly images of wounds and the dying, lifting them to the level of the divine, and, as in the novels of Ayres and Ruck, wipes clean all trace of degeneracy and deviance, not just in men, but in women also. They are no longer idle, useless, dolls, but agents of healing. They gain knowledge normally forbidden to them of men's bodies and their functions, but because it is gained in the cause of war, and in relation to their caring, feminine role, such knowledge is transformative for the better. They are awakened from an innocent but useless state to a noble and active one, a kind of all-encompassing motherhood, in the service of the nation and its ideals of freedom. However much, today, we may view their vision as clouded by patriotic rhetoric, Finzi, Dent, and other women viewed their enlightenment and transformation as real and valuable in their very sincere wish to save lives.

The works examined in this chapter see the war as an almost spiritual event. While the romantic novels may validate the worst accusations of male combatants, the memoirs provide more contradictory, if not complicated, pictures of women's experience of the war. They do not gloss over wounds or extreme mental and physical distress. Their feelings about the war are by no means confined to the abstract ideals of glory, honour, and love of country, but these are the ideals that they fall back upon, in light of all they have witnessed. They use them to convince both the wartime readers and themselves that the suffering of the men has not been in vain. Because of either the Censor, or their own inability or unwillingness to question, or a combination of both, these women, in the end, presented to the public a clear-sighted and determined vision, much-needed or desired, in a war that was increasingly seen as an aimless 'waste'. Like other women of their time, and afterwards, Dent and Finzi were compelled to 'tell the tale'. Cyril Falls asserts that 'The Great War has resulted in the spilling of floods of ink as well as of blood.'[20] This applies as much to the ink of women as to that of men.

NOTES

1. Claire M. Tylee's bibliography in *The Great War and Women's Consciousness: Images of Militarism and Womanhood in Women's Writings, 1914–64* (Basingstoke, 1990) provides an excellent listing, by year, of primary sources, and is a helpful starting-point for locating forgotten works by women.
2. David Trotter, *The English Novel in History 1895–1920* (London, 1993), 111.

3. Ibid. 118.
4. Samuel Hynes, *A War Imagined: The First World War and English Culture* (London, 1990), 59.
5. Ibid.
6. Berta Ruck (b. 1878) was the daughter of a Welsh army colonel. She studied art at the Slade and at Colorossi's in Paris before turning her hand to writing in about 1913. In her long lifetime—she died at age 100—she published over 150 books. (*Who Was Who 1971–1981*, vii (London, 1981).)

   Ruby M. Ayres (b. 1883) wrote fairy stories as a child, then at 25 began writing fiction. By the time she began to publish her novels in 1915, she had written stories for almost every newspaper and periodical in the country. She died in 1955. (*Who Was Who 1951–1960*, v (London, 1967).)

   Kate Finzi, a trained nurse when the war began, served in France until ill health forced her to return to England. Little other personal information is known about her. (Kate Finzi, *Eighteen Months in the War Zone* (London, 1916).)

   Olive Dent, the youngest daughter of the publisher J. M. Dent, lost her two brothers in the war—one at Gallipoli and the other at Neuve Chapelle. Her sister Muriel was a munitions worker. (J. M. Dent, *The Memoirs of J. M. Dent: 1849–1926* (London, 1928).)
7. Berta Ruck, *Khaki and Kisses* (London, 1915), 9.
8. Sandra Gilbert and Susan Gubar, 'Soldier's Heart: Literary Men, Literary Women, and the Great War', in *No Man's Land: The Place of the Woman Writer in the Twentieth Century*, ii: *Sexchanges* (New Haven, 1989).
9. Hodder & Stoughton, Methuen, Blackwood, John Murray, T. Fisher Unwin, and Macmillan were among the publishers most often employed (Peter Buitenhuis, *The Great War of Words: Literature as Propaganda 1914–18 and After* (London, 1989), 15.)
10. Ruby M. Ayres, *Richard Chatterton, V.C.* (London, 1915), 20.
11. Siegfried Sassoon, 'The Glory of Women', in *The Oxford Book of War Poetry*, ed. Jon Stallworthy (Oxford, 1984), 178.
12. I estimate that at least fifty were published between 1914 and 1919. Approximately fifteen of these are not listed in Tylee, *The Great War and Women's Consciousness.*
13. Finzi, *Eighteen Months in the War Zone*, p. xviii.
14. Virginia Woolf, *Three Guineas* (London, 1992), 207.
15. Daniel Pick, *Faces of Degeneration: A European Disorder*, c.*1848*–c.*1918* (London, 1989), 195–9.
16. Jon Stallworthy, 'Survivors' Songs in Welsh Poetry', Annual Gwyn Jones Lecture, University College, Cardiff (1981), 6.
17. William Shakespeare, *Henry V*, IV. iii. 64–5.
18. Edmund Blunden, *Undertones of War* (London, 1928), 223; Robert Graves, *Goodbye to all That* (1929; London, 1985), 199.
19. Olive Dent, *A V.A.D. in France* (London, 1917), 14.
20. Cyril Falls, *War Books: An Annotated Bibliography of Books about the Great War* (London, 1989), p. xiii.

5
The Dissidence of Vernon Lee: *Satan the Waster* and the Will to Believe

GILLIAN BEER

VERNON Lee (Violet Paget) is cited most often now as the thinker who brought the concept 'empathy' into Anglo-Saxon understanding. This is a rather odd fate for the irascible, outspoken, brilliantly critical Lee, whose political non-conformity and lesbian sexuality set her at odds with British society. Yet it has a certain justice when applied to her writing which, alongside its sunny evocation of place and incident, also stirs 'the needs and impulses, the uncatalogued passions not manifested directly in outer behaviour to our neighbours, and which, if guessed at by those neighbours, are guessed only in so far as already familiar to them in their own hidden selves.'[1]

Vernon Lee had a very long writing career and she made full use of the time. Her books date from 1880 to 1932. They range across philosophy, fiction, evocations of place, musical theory and reception, moral and immoral essays, ghost stories, aesthetics, and feminist argument. A recurrent theme is the persistence and the dangers of the will-to-believe. Her writing career before the First World War was very successful, though she was never afraid of controversy as her early novel *Miss Brown* (1884) demonstrates as clearly as her ambitious critique of contrasted intellectual movements *Vital Lies* (1912).

Things changed, however, during the war itself. 'The greatest tragedies, dear Clio, being founded on error, are never without an element of the grotesque. But this ludicrous side always escapes those who take part in them' (22–3). Satan is speaking to the Muse of History in Vernon Lee's *Satan the Waster*. In this extraordinary work Lee makes sure that 'this ludicrous side' is borne in upon the wincing reader. Satan is glib; Lee is not. But her satirical *Ballet of the Nations*, first published in 1915 and later placed at the centre of *Satan*, is to jar on the reader with its apparent insouciance. It avoids individual scenes of horror in close-up, but the sweeping arc of its display shifts blithely between fireworks and poison gas: 'For the Ballet of the Nations, when Satan gets it up regardless of expense, is an unsurpassed spectacle of transformations such as must be witnessed to be believed in' (50, 52). 'Death's Dance' can continue 'regardless of the condition of the dancers':

> yet dance they did, chopping and slashing, blinding each other with squirts of blood and pellets of human flesh. And as they appeared and disappeared in the moving wreaths of fiery smoke, they lost more and more of their original shape, becoming, in the fitful light, terrible uncertain forms, armless, legless, recognizable for human only by their irreproachable Heads, which they carried stiff and high even while crawling and staggering along, lying in wait, and leaping and rearing and butting as do fighting animals.

Clio writes and recites this hellish scene, while behind her speech the voice of Heroism sings bars of 'Tipperary' and 'with great solemnity Haydn's "Gott erhalte unseren Kaiser"'. Sometimes Clio writes at the dictation of Satan, sometimes on her own account: 'Since you should know that, although politicians say the contrary, Nations can never die outright' (51).

History here is implicated in falsification and disaster. She is the scribe of Satan. Yet she is also the admonitory recorder. By having the figure of the allegorical woman, writing, on stage throughout her 'ballet' or 'pantomime', Vernon Lee places herself too on the exposed stage of history. The *Ballet* (occupying about twenty-five pages) appeared in 1915. The work's later enlarged version—Introduction, Prologue in Hell, The Ballet of the Nations, Epilogue, Notes to the Prologue, and Notes to the Ballet of the Nations—runs to 300 pages and was published as *Satan the Waster* in 1920.

It is a work that raises the question: who is licensed to write, and especially to write satire in wartime? When satire comes from the trenches it sickens and convinces, as in the work of Sassoon. Soldiers writing have a blood-boltered authority. But a non-combatant woman, a writer on aesthetics, what does she here? That issue has been raised again very recently by the Irish poet Eavan Boland. She has recounted how, though the question of who may write about the troubles in Ireland is never quite confronted, still as she began to write she knew well that (whoever this figure was) it was not she, a Dublin housewife in the suburbs. Her latest collection of poems, responding to that implicit exclusion, is entitled *In a Time of Violence* (1994).

With Lee's *Satan* we are confronting a work that is beyond the *pale*: outside the palisade of nationality, patriotism, community, even humanitarianism. How to read its outrage? What value to accord it? Does it repudiate connection or produce new meanings for empathy? In recent influential writing on the First World War Lee's work has simply been ignored: Paul Fussell's *The Great War and Modern Memory* nowhere mentions her; nor, more surprisingly, does Daniel Pick in his excellent *War Machine.*[2] Yet George Bernard Shaw, reviewing *Satan the Waster* in *The Nation* in 1920, wrote that 'Vernon Lee, as her dated notes to this book prove, has never been wrong once since the war began'; 'by sheer intellectual force, training, knowledge, and character, [she] kept her head when Europe was a mere lunatic asylum.'

What makes this all the more extraordinary, Shaw remarks, is that Vernon Lee is an Englishwoman:

> And remember, Vernon Lee is an Englishwoman. Had she been Irish, like me, there would have been nothing to her dispassionateness: the three devastated streets of Louvain would have been balanced (not to say overbalanced) by the three hundred devastated acres of Dublin; and 'the broken treaty' would have meant for her the treaty of Limerick. No wonder I had a comparatively mild attack of war fever. But Vernon Lee is English of the English, and yet held her intellectual own throughout.[3]

Vernon Lee does not 'fit'. The *Ballet* resulted in many broken friendships. Her contemporaries were not likely to be reassured by the support of Shaw, himself a brazen sceptic from the other island 'Ireland'. More recent commentators have passed over her awkward presence in silence, and her intervention has been excluded from 'modern memory'.

Satan the Waster, the work central to my argument, is generically mixed, calling in then very recent technological changes such as film and gramophone and splicing them with neo-classical and current references. Intriguingly, Lee uses the intellectual weapons identified with the preparation for war in order to resist and repudiate war and its effects. In *Why War?* Jacqueline Rose comments: 'If truth is destroyed by war, truth as abstraction on the other hand is identified by several psychoanalytic writers as one of the determinants of war. According to a note on strategy that Clausewitz wrote in 1809, more than twenty years before *On War*, abstraction kills—it is a "dry skeleton" or "dead form" (the destructive element here is not the invasive reality, but the constricting suffocating theory of war)'[4].

Lee uses abstractions as figures in *Satan*; masque-like presences called 'Greed, Loyalty, Discipline, Comradeship, Jealousy, Chivalry, Egotism, Bullying, Science, Organisation, Ennui, Discipline, Self-interest, Fear' form the corps-de-ballet. Being a play for performance these abstractions bear the bodies of people, the *corps de ballet*. They decompose conceptions such as patriotism. And they decompose. Death is the Ballet Master: 'seen at first only from the back, a long, lank figure in loose black evening clothes (long tailcoat) with a long, pianist's head of hair round a shiny bald patch. . . . But it is only when he turns full round that we become aware that he is a skeleton, and that the grey head of hair surmounts a grinning skull' (32). The genre of *Satan the Waster* does not quite correspond to any other work, though it is perhaps closest to Thomas Hardy's *The Dynasts* and Bernard Shaw's *Back to Methuselah*. Or even, to take a greater European example, Goethe's *Faust*. And, as I shall suggest, it has its effects in Virginia Woolf's pageants of history.

In this chapter I place the *Ballet of the Nations* and *Satan the Waster* in relation to Lee's controversy with militant suffragists, her resistance to then current theories of the crowd, and her attempt to analyse human needs and their transformations, sometimes in relation to Freud.[5]

Vernon Lee's reputation as the cleverest woman in Europe was not unearned. Indeed, the specification 'woman' was an important defence against her. Part of what made her threatening to the literary élite was that, if let loose, she might turn out to be the cleverest *man* in Europe too. Her frank lesbianism, or, in the language of the time, 'inversion', opened the door between male and female intellectuals dangerously wide. Her presence was felt as threatening to a good many among the intellectual male establishment of the time. Henry James thought her in 1893 'dangerous and uncanny as she is intelligent which is saying a great deal'. Like George Eliot, she was a Renaissance woman; unlike George Eliot, however, she was no sybil. She was waspish, angry, and with more relish for critique than sympathy.

Suffragism and Pacificism

Vernon Lee's vehement advocacy of pacificism brought her into conflict with many of her feminist friends and associates before the First World War began. The composer Ethel Smyth urged Lee to set out her objections to militant action and charged her with accepting too slow a pace for reform. With her usual exuberant wit Smyth needles Lee by setting her alongside those ordinary sluggards quick to see absurdity and slow to approve strong innovation of any kind:

> My dear Vernon I quite understand that you or anyone sh. disapprove of militancy just as I understand the public disliking Wagner at first or the Jews thinking the expedition to Jerusalem a great mistake—I think a very forward policy is for those who see the evils you want to set right as I see them—i.e. as I should look on terribly primitive sanitary arrangements in a village towards which cholera is advancing. Do anything but acquiesce—for if you do acquiesce you deserve to go and will go to hell.[6]

Vernon Lee would not relish being set among the philistines or the assimilated, since she flared out always as one in opposition to the timid bourgeoisie. Smyth figures herself here as doctor, or simply sanitary worker, taking the first fundamental precautions against disaster. The letter continues:

> I think though that two facts escape your attention. First of all it is nearly 70 years since Mill pronounced the vote to be nothing less than a necessity—& nearly 50 years since women have been working for it (a great waste of time & energy, tho' I don't forget the educative value of these years in the Desert). We can't help there now being (which state of things Mill foresaw) 5 million women working outside the home for starvation wages—without the tool men have found essential to bettering their own conditions & which we can't take from them. The longer they have it & *the women haven't*, the more the women get pushed down into prostitution, the more the race deteriorates through disease & through the terrible burden put upon the mothers' backs.

Without the vote, Smyth argues, women are without power as wage-earners, as physical beings, and through their sickness and exploitation the future withers. Women are *wasted*: either through endlessly prolonged struggle for their rights—nearly fifty years since women have been working for it, a great waste of time and energy—or 'through the terrible burden put upon the mothers' backs'. Wasted here has the sense both of set aside and of consumed.

Smyth's letter goes on to instance child-abuse, the perpetrators let off 'scot-free'. Perhaps here she calls back to Vernon Lee's mind the concerns of Lee's own early novel *Miss Brown* (1884), where the heroine's commitment is transformed from aesthetics to social activism by what she sees of incest among the poor. To Smyth, then, the campaign for the vote embraced the whole range of experience and, without it, energies that should be creative are consumed away. Vernon Lee's response was, evidently, to argue that there was 'no hurry', other crises in Europe being more important. In a letter dated 24 January 1913 Ethel Smyth invites Vernon Lee to contribute an open letter to the *Suffragette.* She is, she says, willing to accept disagreement 'But . . . *I want to see it formulated.*' Vernon Lee did not accept the invitation. She did, however, contribute forcefully to attempts to ward off the coming of war. For example, Olive Schreiner congratulates her in 1913 on 'your fine little letter in "The Nation" . . . One has to live through a long war as I have, & *amid* its horrors to know how unmixed an evil it is. Its brutalizing results are often worse than the war.'[7] And just after the war began Lee unmasked in the New York *Nation* the implications of an article by H. G. Wells in the *Daily Chronicle* in which he urged the Americans to cut off supplies to Germany. He cast the argument in terms of war *matériel*; she countered that the real message was 'Let America use and show her neutrality by starving Germany.'[8]

Vernon Lee, living until the war in Florence away from the site of British feminist struggle, is a thorn in the side of her friends who are committed militant suffragettes—the more so since they recognize that she is willing to 'force the pace', as Smyth writes, on questions that do immediately engage her. Vernon Lee's demurrals cannot grasp the oddity of causes and effects, of propinquities, that those in the thick of the experience know. Her long-standing friend Mona Taylor, a friend also of Smyth and active in militant feminism, writes to her in the winter of 1911–12: 'But none of these things will convince you dear Vernon that to have proved to the Public that the Police cannot protect Jewellers shops has brought the Vote within sight. Of course this is absolutely "illogical"—but fact.'[9] That same 'illogic' took another twist in the public mind, producing a different affective leap. Some argued that the deep disturbances produced in public order and social relations by the suffragettes were lowering the inhibition against violence, and hence contributing to a willingness to countenance war. Lee, along with many who were her political enemies, seems to have feared something like this. For her, pacificism was the dominant commitment, and actions that eroded resistance to international violence could not be countenanced. In *The Pre-war Mind in Britain: An Historical Review* (1928) Caroline Playne, an admirer of Vernon Lee's work, quotes H. G. Wells on 'the spinning straws' of 1913–14: 'The arson of the suffragettes, the bellicose antics of the Unionist leaders in Ulster, General Gough's Curragh meeting, were all part of the same relaxation of bonds that launched the grey-clad hosts of Germany into Belgium.'[10] Wells implicates feminists in the oncoming of 'grey-clad hosts' by apposition, but he is suggesting a more insidious affinity: the crossing of bounds, national, cultural, or simply the bounding assumptions of others, is levelled with invasion.

H. G. Wells becomes a principal opponent in the commentary to *Satan the Waster*. Playne, however, is in sympathy with the suffragist movement, yet her analysis accepts the links between militant suffragism and militarism: 'all this constituted a state of mind which easily rebounded later on to the primitive combative war-spirit . . . The women's methods were an exaltation of primitive emotional passion, although the objective was the clearance of ancient prejudice, and the assertion of social rights which circumstances quite justified' (294). Playne, with the advantage of hindsight, blames women's movements before the war both for their invoking of primitive passions and for their ineffectiveness.

To Smyth before the war, precisely the unexpectedness and impossibility of controlling violence from a guerrilla army of women is what gives hope of success. She sends Lee a jubilant (undated) postcard: 'The shops in my streets are boarded up, & shelters put up everywhere at dusk. No one knows who will be the next victim. No more wholesale imprisonment of women —& then peace for a while! This can't go on—you can't stop guerilla war-fare—The thing will become a scandal & that's what we want.' Smyth sees the end-stop as *embarrassment* for the government: 'scandal'. Precisely the taken-for-granted passivity and powerlessness of women is what now gives zest to their incursions. Smyth's occasional skittishness is part of the campaign. The government is being made fools of by 'foolish women'. This is meta-war, not its actuality. The whole is framed by the assumption that the government can eventually be shamed. That is, rather than there being a 'relaxation of bonds', the government is believed finally to share the same fundamental social and national values as the suffragettes. Smyth had not yet spent time in Holloway jail when she wrote thus.

But perhaps that assurance of communality, as well as the waste of women's energies in pursuing what should long ago have been granted them, did drain energy necessary to oppose the war before its outbreak. Playne quotes the resolution of a meeting called by women's organizations on the evening of 4 August 1914:

> Whatever the result, the conflict will leave mankind the poorer, will set back civilization, and will be a powerful check to the amelioration of the conditions of the masses of people on which the real welfare of nations depends.

She comments:

> In this terrible hour, when the outbreak of war in Europe is pending, it is accepted as inevitable, and a fine band of women, having a clear 'death-bed' vision of what is involved, hurries to pick up crumbs of comfort in coming to the assistance of prospective victims. This is a notable example of the impotence of the neurotic mind of groups, which is, like the neurotic individual, oblivious of existing realities. (382–3)

Playne does not explain what the women *could* have done among, as she acknowledges, 'decisions which women have no direct power to shape'. Her argument is part of the discussion of the 'group-mind' already advanced in her book *Neuroses of the Nations* (1925).[11] And that work draws on a longer controversy among psychologists derived from William McDougall, author of *The Group Mind* (1920), *Body and Mind* (1913), and the immensely influential *An Introduction to Social Psychology*, orginally published in 1908 and in its sixteenth edition in 1921.[12] In that controversy, as I shall later illustrate, Vernon

Lee set herself in opposition to any anthropomorphic entity called 'the nation'.

Vernon Lee, living in the midst of Europe and carrying on correspondence with many people in French and German as well as English, is less sanguine than her English friends like Smyth about the possibility of containing violence for directed ends. The city of Florence may sound an aesthete's paradise, but Vernon Lee was there much more in the thick of European tensions than were her friends in England. For example, during her long correspondence with the philosopher Richard Semon from Munich he speaks of the resurgence of 'die alten Raubtierinstinkte der Menschen' (the ancient predatory instincts of mankind) and argues that this predatoriness is present equally in all the nations of Europe, to say nothing of the United States: '*Keine* der europaïschen Kulturnationen mit Einschluss der U.S.A. Yankees ist ubrigent in dieser Beziehung besser als die anderere'[13] ('In this respect, *none* of the European civilized nations, including the US Yankees, is, incidentally, any better than the others'). Like Semon, Lee argued that the *simple* may be both primal and dangerous 'biological memory (what Semon calls the *Mnemic principle*), reproducing simple combinations' (*Satan*, 233).[14]

Instincts of the Herd

While Vernon Lee was writing the copious notes and essay-commentaries for *Satan the Waster* she read W. Trotter, *Instincts of the Herd in Peace and War* (1916).[15] Trotter's influential arguments were first presented in two essays in the *Sociological Review* in 1908 and 1909 and then rewritten, amplified, and altered during the First World War, in 1915. Lee's own copy is inscribed 1917 with a pencilled note 'Read. Aug 1918'. It is very heavily annotated most of the way through. Lee writes wry, witty, sometime outraged comments, not only alongside the text in the margin but sometimes in loops round and round the printed page —which allows her to get more of a say in reply to Trotter and entoils him satisfactorily. At the front of the book, pencilled over end-paper, title-page, and all possible spaces, she writes a six-page critique of what she sees as Trotter's inflexible organicism.

Above all she resists the totalizing views of Trotter and his mentor McDougall: where he emphasizes the single herd, the tribe, the war machine, the hive, she insists on multiple and diverse subgroups that range and recompose themselves according to differing needs and interests:

The members of a nation, i.e. the classes and individuals do not co-operate and compete in time of peace with reference *to the nation* but with reference to their trade, locality etc. A bee makes honey for the hive; but a workman makes *goods* for *anyone*, for consumption or barter. Similarly a man of science does not add to a *national* stock but to an international one; a financier deals with international *wealth* etc.[16]

Instead of one coherent unit ('the nation', 'the hive') she emphasizes what we might now describe as multiple subject positions and the shifting amalgams produced. In *Satan* she emphasizes that even patriotism is a cluster of interests and 'virtues' not contained within the country. Always, she opposes the idea of autonomy and emphasizes the permeability of inside and outside, whether the example be the community, the nation, or the body.

She is suspicious, too, of Trotter's praise of Freud and of Freud's tendency to produce 'entities'. Part of her annotation reads:

Freud's (mistaken) treatment of instincts as if irreducible, indissoluble wholes, moreover as eternally so, instead of analysing them into elements wh. can or could be re-grouped leads to a kind of mythological view of a 'desire' as an individual specified entity. A kind of ghost in the dream and attribute of a given moment, a ghost eternally haunting an underworld whence it emerges under disguises.

A little earlier she pencils in a comment on Freud: 'His mind is mythopoeic, analogical, *mediaeval* in its methods.'[17] Of course, despite her scepticism and her spry resistance, she works in *Satan the Waster* with just such analogical ghostly figures and transfigurations. And indeed in her published notes to that text she acknowledges how close her own discussion of delusion runs to Freudian thought on projection. One of the first aspects of Freud's thought to attract her was his analysis of fantasy and of wishes.[18]

We allege impersonal reasons; we point to outer and alien explanations. We say: *it is, implying by it* the character of our neighbours, the peculiarity of circumstances, the laws of thought, the constitution of the Universe; when if we told, if we could tell, the truth, we should say: *I want, I need, I wish, I feel*... And to the endless protean Delusions... we add a crowning self-delusion: that of believing that we have no such feelings, passions, impulses, and needs, or that they happen to be in abeyance at the moment of speaking. (*Satan*, 142)

The sentence is immediately followed by a footnote in which she says that the Freudians' 'insistence on hidden springs of our thought and action is, to my view, their great gift to psychology'. But, she claims, 'these obscure psychological phenomena have their explanation in something more primordial than sex'.

What is that 'more primordial' source or condition? Here Lee's work in aesthetics and acoustics informs her political analysis as well as her psychology. She resists any approximation between the single organism and the community or species. Instead she argues that rather than equivalences there are 'obscure, changing yet undying, feelings, primordial and protean, like those marine creatures which are round or oblong, transparent or opaque, single individual or colony, parent or split-off offspring, plant or animal, turn about' (*Satan*, 141). She thus finds herself at odds with a powerful intellectual movement of the time, that of 'crowd mentality'.[19] That work was based to a large extent on the recapitulation theory of post-Darwinian evolution, in which a homology was supposed between the development of the individual and the development of the class or species. Lee was cautious, and caustic, about any attempts to move analogy into homology.

Certain ideas matter intensely to Lee throughout her career and draw together apparently disparate concerns, such as music, feminism, psychology. One such idea is that there are no stable entities but rather combinations of diverse impulses. 'The *Self* is... a highly variable and perpetually varying spiritual (for I know you hate the words *psychological* and *subjective*) complex.'[20] The other idea is that process and rhythm are the primordial condition; they are also, in her argument, the synchronic means to experience. 'Expansion and rest' (142) are the primary inner needs. But change (not stability) is the key to understanding. 'The importance of the notion of evolution and all it has brought with it, lies largely in its teaching us to think thus genetically, which means thinking in terms not of stability, but of change' (*Satan*, 178). In her 1901 annotations to Henry Rutgers Marshall's *Pain, Pleasure, and Aesthetics* (1894) she comments:

'since we must substitute *processes* for *entities* (images) so also we may have to substitute for the old picture of the printed page left ("registered") in consciousness, a *movement* originally set up in the act of first perception, and repeated with variations, in every subsequent re-perception or reminiscence'.[21] The idea is framed here in terms of aesthetics. It raises for her as her career proceeds profound questions about the efficacy and extent of rationality: 'To the genetic psychologist the laws of logic are but the traces compacted and made regular by the repeated pressure of millions and more generations of Man's fulfilled or disappointed expectations.' Repeated impressions 'have grouped themselves into what he thinks of as "things" and "repeated experience of his own reactions to such impressions . . . have grouped themselves into the necessities and incompatibilities, the inclusions and exclusions, the superposed systems of what is called rational inference'.[22]

Lee's usual intricate account, cautioning, waylaying, evading conclusion, makes it hard to guess whether the process she is describing feels heavy or light. Are these the effortless motions of consciousness ('process', 'movement') or the cumbersome need for a whole historical continuum in which to experience any single thought?

Accreting Satan

The actual composition and putting together of *Satan the Waster* shows this dilemma at work in her own creativity. Like *The Dunciad* it sometimes seems a work that requires what it attacks. And, like Pope's poem, it becomes ornamented, encrusted, weighed down, by its own satirical apparatus as it goes from phase to phase. As with all satire the tension between attack and mimesis is difficult. Miming those you oppose may produce an identity with them. And not for nothing was Vernon Lee the person who introduced into the Anglo-Saxon world the term and concept of 'empathy' or *Einfühlung*. She is not a great one for sympathizing, but the inhabiting and enacting of another, poised on the edge of mimicry but taking also the risk of identity, suits her well. Indeed, in one of her most self-revealing notes she observes with compunction her own dilemma in the war community; this particular note is headed 'Einfühlung!'

There is a contrast between my state and that of my fellow-pacificists, so far as I know them. They are not isolated like myself in war-atmosphere, but rather segregated in their own clique. They seem to see the war-feeling entirely from outside 'Oh, it's so odious', or 'Oh, it's so unjust', or 'Oh it's so childish'. With me there's no such condemnation; rather an overwhelming sense, throughout all my antagonism, of the extraordinary *naturalness* and inevitableness of it all. It is not at all incomprehensible. On the contrary, I feel that it is I who am incomprehensible; I feel that it is I who must seem odious, unjust, childish, etc. etc.[23]

Complicated transactions are going on here. The empathic identification she makes with her ideological opponents also isolates her from her expected co-operative group, other pacifists. This may be as much a form of self-defence as of identification: it is not hard to see what a difficult ally Vernon Lee must have been. She is sharp-eyed about the notion of self and other, refusing to see them simply as opposed or autonomous zones—just as, in argumentation, she refuses polarized arguments.

Satire, with its limber multiplicity of positioning, is in accord with Lee's ideological insistence on process, change, and unstable amalgam. It also, let it be said, chimes in with her extremely high opinion of her own powers, placing her as the unwelcome but authoritative source of interpretation. And to that end, she makes a self-aware and challenging identification: with the devil, weary of hypocrisy. The whole project may well have begun as a psychic reply to a more virtuous communal enterprise.

In 1915 Vernon Lee contributed to a collection of essays edited by Charles Roden Buxton, *Towards a Lasting Settlement.*[24] It included essays by, among others, G. Lowes Dickinson, J. A. Hobson, Maude Royden, and Philip Snowden, MP. Snowden, in particular, argues that the war will have been fought in vain if it does not lead to increasing openness in diplomacy and negotiation: 'if it has not taught the working classes of Europe the paramount necessity of publicity in foreign affairs'. Snowden points out the class warfare disguised by national warfare: 'of the thirty-seven attachés successful in the civil service competition between 1908 and 1913 twenty-five had been to Eton, and only one had not been at either Oxford or Cambridge'. Class and gender together mean that there is an excruciatingly narrow range for consultation: no women, no workers, scarcely any even of the bourgeoisie. Snowden argues that democracy 'is not military but pacific';[25] Lee, in her essay on 'The Democratic Principle and International Relations', argues that democracy itself is 'not a set of present institutions but a *tendency*' (210).

In that same year, in some contrast to this sober volume, Vernon Lee published *The Ballet of the Nations*, described on the title-page as 'A Present-Day Morality by Vernon Lee with a Pictorial Commentary by Maxwell Arnfield'. The book is beautifully framed and decorated by orange patterned borders and by pictures that show women, children, men in a *mélange* of classical, medieval, and modern costumes, or naked. Members of the crowd crouch, flee, mask, do obeisance, converse, become puppets, never quite slaughter on stage. The illustrations are at once light-hearted and menacing, always in motion. The play is a masque with Virtues, Passions, and Muses, but it is set in a London square which is, at the same time, 'The World; a Theatre of Varieties, Lessee and Manager, SATAN'. It ends with the nations dancing Death's ballet, invisibly according to Lee's strict instructions: 'The stage upon the stage must be turned in such a manner that nothing beyond the footlights, the Orchestra and auditorium shall be visible to the real spectators, only the changing illumination . . . Similarly . . . none of the music must be audible, except the voice and drum of Heroism. Anything beyond this would necessarily be hideous, besides drowning or interrupting the dialogue' (*Satan*, 57). So the whole play, which Lee seems at least to have hoped might be performed, is accompanied by mute music and voided dance. The final dance figure is revenge, the *revanche* which in dance is turn and turn about, without fixed conclusion.

In its original form the *Ballet* opens: 'For a quarter or so of a century, Death's celebrated Dances had gone rather out of fashion. Then, with the end of the proverbially *bourgeois* Victorian age, there set in a revival of taste, and therefore of this higher form of tragic art, combining, as it does, the truest classical tradition with the romantic attractions of the best Middle Ages.'

The burden of Satan's assertion in the ballet is that he is the *waster*: wasting virtues, bodies, sacrifice emotional and physical, without renewal or recompense. Not compost, but detritus is the outcome: what Satan calls 'sheer loss'. Satan's companion the Ballet Master Death gives some bleak gleams of possible change. Death's other name is Horror and he is at the opposite pole from Great Natural Death, 'twin of Sleep and Sister-Brother of Love'. Along with all the other Passions that constitute the Orchestra of Patriotism appear for the first time Science and Organization. Science is a woman: 'the lady, if one may call her such . . . uncompromisingly literal and modern'. Are they, Death wonders, 'Spies in the service of life and Progress?' Maybe not, the outcome suggests.

The jarring of genre and topic is both perturbing and precious. The ironies of the play discountenance the reader, or speaker, because it is impossible to set them apart, or in a stable relation. It is striking that Lee insisted that the play was to be spoken aloud by any reader, whether or not it was acted. By doing so she implicated the voice, the body, of any one approaching the text. Demur we may, but not evade its violence. For it is a violent text, trouncing the reader as well as making her or him a partisan of its excoriating insights.

The notes take up the whole second half of the volume. Her literary adviser Mr Edward Garnett, she firmly explains, has warned her they are *de trop* and may 'be voted a bore' (p. ix). Few readers are likely to disagree entirely with Garnett, yet the notes also act as a deepening meditation on much that would seem trifling, even pert, in the play alone. Lee explains that these are essays provoked by shared and solitary reactions to European experience, and that they are addressed to the young and to those who come after. Instead of writing as in the past of *Hortus Vitae*, the garden of life, now she must investigate the garden of war, which 'has its spiritual, I will not say *flowers*, nor even *fruits*, but just vegetation, of thoughts' (p. ix).

Mona Taylor, who had deplored Vernon Lee's reluctance to involve herself in militant feminism, wrote her several letters about *Satan the Waster* in the early 1920s. In one we may hear insinuated the contrast between the direct self-sacrifice of the suffragette activists and Vernon Lee's hauteur:

> Receiving Satan stopped me [writing a letter] for a time till I had read it, and though I knew a great deal of it already it is not a book you can bolt. I still find it interesting and thought-compelling—and I still do not agree with your wholesale denunciation of selfsacrifice as waste and folly in itself. To my mind though it is often—perhaps more often than not—needless or a mistake 'waster', the impulse that prompts it is to me in 9 cases out of 10, beautiful. And its reverse, selfishness, is ugly, even hideous. On that point we vitally differ.[26]

Vernon Lee is indeed 'selfish', or implacable, in her determination that she has a right and duty to speak, all the more because she is, as she puts it, *not in* the war. Rather than feeling her position undermined by her physical withdrawal, she argues that this allows her to observe the degree to which all the nations are implicated. In her *Ballet* Satan demonstrates that all the virtues active in war are corrupt and corrupting:

> But I will not forestall my Ballet. Except to tell you that one of its main themes, its *Leit-Motivs*, as Wagnerians say, is my dealing with just such virtue: the sweet and ardent loyalty of noble lads, lest dear comrades should have died in vain; loyalty also which makes the bereaved mother send her last son that his dead elder brothers may not feel forsaken. That is virtue, you will not deny. (12)

'Idealism, Love of Adventure, Pity and Indignation, above all, Heroism' are the players in Satan's Orchestra and '*Patriotism* is the collective name of the whole orchestra whom I train for these performances.' When we consider that the *Ballet* appeared in 1915 and the whole of *Satan* was written before the Armistice, save for one or two final notes, the degree of Vernon Lee's fortitude becomes clear. Her writing was courageous in the extreme; to some it seemed venomous. Another feminist friend of hers, Helen Swanwick, wrote in 1930 (or is it 1920?):

> Some weeks ago your publisher was so good as to send me '*Satan the Waster*' and I read it slowly and meditatively and recalled how you used to read the 'Ballet' during those awful years and how few people understood the bitter and tragic meaning of your satire.[27]

And there is a note of a more complex regret, that includes remorse and anger, in another letter from Mona Taylor, sent in the summer of 1922:

> You always thought that I and all of us felt opposed to you when you were here during the war. But it was not so so far as Margery and I were concerned. Au fond I of course agreed with your principles and hatred of all war as wicked and wasteful.
>
> All that you and I differed in [*added*: it was a difference of policy not of principle] was your wish to stop the War, and your wish to make peace by negotiation.—and my belief that it was necessary to the future good of the world to fight it out—and also my other appalling conviction that the longer the war went on the more effectually would

it cure the world of war. You were right in saying it would ruin Europe —Victors as well as vanquished. It has, and *so much the better for the future.* Every day I see that more and more

yours Mary

Vernon Lee may well have gasped at this letter: had *Satan* communicated nothing? What Mona Taylor calls policy to Lee was principle, and was, moreover, the principle on which she had spent so much effort during the war years of writing, resistance, and exclusion from friendship. Bleak indeed.

Mona Taylor's underlined phrase is suggestive but on the face of it baffling in relation to the preceding paragraphs. *So much the better for the future.* Here, Taylor takes a radical leap away from the past that makes Lee seem positively laggardly. And that may be the incentive: the letter has the energy of resentment in it, a resentment that drives back into the pre-war history of suffragism and Vernon Lee's aloofness then. Taylor hopes for cleansing and a fresh start. There is change afoot: 'Well' she wrote in the earlier (?1920) letter quoted: 'American women have got the vote and I have a fixed belief that women are on the side of no more War and of no rows. German women have the vote, they can well be trusted in this and International Labour will act, or threaten to "act", against war so I feel hopeful.' Some of that hopefulness has ebbed in her second letter, but it is the bellows of her exasperation. Her desire to throw Europe overboard seems to be a longing to be done with the past.

In section III of the Introduction to *Satan* Vernon Lee acknowledges that 'even in its earliest fragmentary published version, it has offended some of the people I can least endure offending'. She sets out eloquently their objections, italicizing the passage for prominence. The second half reads:

'*We who loathe war are making war against those who believe that war is not a crime. This*' (said my friends or seemed to be saying), '*this is how we feel towards this war in which we participate with horror but with deliberate choice. and* YOU, *in this shallow satire of yours, represent this struggle between Good and Evil, this trial of strength between Justice and Injustice, as a mere collective world-cataclysm for which all are equally responsible or rather irresponsible; you dare to represent it as a mere involuntary, aimless, senseless dance of Death, in which all the Nations, with little to choose between them, join hands in imbecile, abominable obedience to Satan's fiddling. Is this*' (so ends the spoken or unspoken protest of my warlike friends), '*Is this, CAN this really be, your meaning?*'

IV

It is. . . .

Grave, impenitent, Vernon Lee confronts her accusers. It is, of course, a heroic stance, a problem of rhetoric for one who had in the *Ballet* displayed the figure of Heroism as blind, sacrificial, and devoted to Satan. Here, she dramatizes in herself an awakened heroism the cost of which is isolation: 'aloofness', even (worst of all) triviality. Her satire chooses modes of representation that are 'shallow', preoccupied with surface, that refuse the metaphors of profundity or 'depth': masques, ballets, personifications, cinematograph screens, discs whose scratched surfaces produce sounds. Outmoded and up-to-the-minute means of representing mingle: all produce action at a distance; none show suffering directly. Her satire filters out both suffering and compassion. It is deliberately thin and motley, though complicated enough.

To have dared to represent communal suffering and death as absurd was violence enough against the temper of the times. But to justify it in longer retrospect was both adamant and reckless: chilling and admirable. It is, therefore, not surprising, if depressing, that the work seems to have suffered a degree of censorship. One friend, the novelist Margaret Skelton, wrote to her that: 'Our Public Library in Woolwich contains an almost complete collection of your writings . . . "Satan" is not there however. I saw the review by Shaw in the Nation, and got it for myself.'[28]

But despite its absence from public libraries *Satan the Waster* did have its effects, most immediately in the work of other women. Margaret Skelton acknowledges that 'It gave me many ideas for my own book', her widely reviewed novel *Below the Watchtowers* (1926). Caroline Playne makes a direct comparison with Shaw, citing passages from each for comparison: 'Whilst Bernard Shaw's plays are often representations of effects of neurosis [she cites particularly *Heartbreak House*] Vernon Lee's war drama, *Satan—the Waster* analyses spiritual ravages, insanities, the soul's "uncatalogued poisons." After following the course of the war's advent, we may well agree with her profounder analyses.'[29] And in *Neuroses of the Nations*, published three years earlier, Playne cites *Satan the Waster* and quotes Lee directly. In her copy Vernon Lee congratulates herself in the margin: 'Good V L !'.

Sexuality and Rhythm: Sources of Survival

Vernon Lee read and annotated with enthusiasm a book by William Morrison Patterson that chimed in with her own long-held aesthetic interests. Patterson's study *The Rhythm of Prose: An Experimental Investigation of Individual Difference in the Sense of Rhythm* (1916) suggests that the balancing of rhythmic patterns in language is similar to 'the way we enjoy a single act of body balance'.[30] She queries 'Is it similar?' She is excited by his distinction between poetry and prose: language is prose 'so long as syncopation and substitution predominate over coincidence between the accented syllables'. In her instructions to the reader at the outset of *Satan the Waster* she announces: 'The whole of this drama is intended to be read, and especially read out loud, as prose.' Even where passages scan, she asserts, 'whatever rhythmical elements have been intentionally introduced, should be merely felt as an indefinable quality, so to speak a *timbre*, of what is in other respects ordinary speech'.

That insistence on *ordinary speech* and on reading out loud is the pre-condition to understanding what most compels her and what, to her mind, is more fundamental than sex. Lee, from early in her career to its end, conceives inner and outer as in a constant process of exchange controlled by interactive rhythmic motions. When she reads Wilhelm Wundt's *Lectures on Human and Animal Psychology* in 1894, she writes 'suggestive' beside a passage on photochemical processes: 'Such processes play an important part in organic nature; *e.g.*, in the breathing of the green portions of plants and in the production of the colours of flowers. Now a chemical process, even if it is comparatively soon over, always requires a considerably longer time for its completion than does a simple transmission of motion.'[31]

Later, when Wundt discusses 'rhythmical sense-excitation' she remarks: 'But rhythm is not merely expectation and realisation but a special balance of action. A–A *is not* rhythm ABBA or AABB is.'[32] Rhythm becomes in her thought the fundamental form of action. So the scrapping of music, the constant interruption and faulture in *Satan*, is part of the demonic collapse she is there figuring.

Intriguingly, Vernon Lee finds most difficult to stomach in Freud precisely that example where rhythm and sexuality in his analysis first come together: the baby sucking at the breast. She comments in an annotation to Trotter: 'According to his disciple Pfister, Freud actually pushes things so far as to derive alimentary pleasure for the *sucking* baby from the sexual instinct . . . he then treats it as the *origin* of all Desire. His mind is mythopoeic, analogical, *mediaeval* in its methods.'[33] William McDougall uses this same example in an attempt to refute Freud: 'who would explain the direction of the sex impulses of man towards woman by the assumption that the male infant derives sexual pleasure from the act of sucking at his mother's breast. It is, I submit, a sufficient refutation of this view to ask—How, then, does the sex instinct of woman become directed towards man. How explain the fact that homosexuality is not the rule in women?'[34] How indeed? The question, of course, is not one that Freud ignored, though his arguments have not satisfied many women. For Vernon Lee as a lesbian the question had particular valency. To her, 'a child is a neuter'. Reading Charlotte Perkins Gilman on *The Home: Its Work and Influence* (1903) she is delighted by Gilman's attack on the social formation of girls and home-bound women and sidelines Gilman's passage on forced gender distinctions: 'As if we feared that there might be some mistake, that she was not really a girl but would grow up a boy if we looked the other way, we diligently strove to enforce and increase her femininity by every possible means.'[35] Vernon Lee remarks beside she 'would grow up a boy if we looked the other way': 'As some small girls undoubtedly hope.'

Lee is troubled by Freud's view that all jealousy 'has been sexual'; in an annotation to Trotter she adds revealingly concerning the taboo against explaining sex to children:

> surely the sex jealousy of the adult would not exist where the sexual act was still impossible? A child is a neuter: perhaps the taboo might originate in the wish to prolong neutrality; it could not arise *during* neutrality from any such fear. Surely the Taboo must be referable to other origins—perhaps to revealing that the elder is not different. Parents don't like alluding to their weaknesses.[36]

'The wish to prolong neutrality' is Vernon Lee's too. Well aware that objectivity is self-delusion, she yet seeks a privileged place for her analysis: her distance not only from English solidarity but from the ordinary gender divisions gives her, she seems to hope, some shelf from which honestly to survey the chaos of Europe crumbling.

But that 'neutrality' will not countenance self-deception or the deception of others. It is not the equivalent of autonomy, or wholeness or even reserve. Some of her harshest comments are reserved for those who deceive children and so contort sex relations. Such lies undermine the growth into adulthood. McDougall declares himself against a Freudian analysis of childhood and for censorship:

> even a full insight into the psychology of sex is highly dangerous. Surely the boy should know only part of the facts! Surely it is permissible to lead him to believe that all women are more or less as we would have them be in an ideal world, and to allow men to appear to him as rather better in these respects than they actually are! The tree of knowledge cannot be robbed of its dangers, though it be draped in the driest of scientific jargon.[37]

Vernon Lee sidelines this passage and writes large 'Vile Lies!'

In *Satan the Waster* Satan denies that he has planted or can control the 'Tree of Knowledge', also called the 'Tree of Good and Evil': 'They are the same. . . . Why that Tree's planting means my doom, however long postponed by my manifold arts.'[38]

> I've bled its sap; stripped off its bark and sered its roots and branches with frost and fire; urged Man to cut it down, lest it should prove a upas and strangle all his children in its growth. I've borrowed all Jove's official lightnings to blast it. I have seen it parch and wither, branch drop off after branch, crop mildew after crop. But alas! only to note with anguish new blossoms and ever unexpected shoots.

The Tree has been planted neither by God nor by Satan but by '*Man* and Man's wife, Woman'. Knowledge, in Lee's mindset, is not to be confounded with belief any more than it is with power. Very late in her life she moved her thought towards a refined materialism which can find room both for Freud and for new technologies of rhythmic exploration: 'In my present more developed (perhaps a little owing to my bête noire Freud!) ways of thought, it strikes me that many—almost all—of our supposed beliefs are emotional states, indeed bodily conditions, movements, urges, attitudes, which some magically fine instrument might show and measure, as our deepest seated organs are shown by the radiographer through *les parois* of our body.'[39]

In the Epilogue, probably now the most readable part of the work, she tries out new kinds of representation and rhythm, combining the 'cinematograph screen' with 'a large gramophone'. They 'work in concert after a preliminary wheeze and clatter and a corresponding flicker and blur' (*Satan*, 64). The ironic promise is that we are to be shown 'real Reality' and the 'Real Ones'. First interiors and exteriors roll across the screen showing figures 'mainly masculine, elderly, often bald, and not always very dignified', 'occasional significant gestures accompanied by insignificant words'. The scenes are garbled, endless, resistant to interpretation. To be understood they must be caricatured. Satan announces: 'I will, to please you, transform Reality, which seems to have no point, into bare Caricature, which *has*' (66, 67). A series of 'pre-war scenes' rolls by in a kind of pageant. 'The gramophone wheezes,' we are repeatedly told.

Did Virginia Woolf hark back to memories of *Satan* for the pageant in *Between the Acts* with its wheezing gramophone, its mirrors? And did she half-recall the *Ballet* for the climactic scene in *Orlando*, where Orlando changes, with much accompaniment from neo-classical personifications like those in Lee's ballet, from a man into a woman? It is tempting to think so, particularly as Vernon Lee personally represented the double life of gender, the man-woman woman-man, for more than one generation of women writers. Perhaps, too, when Woolf sought a means of representing the First World War in *To the Lighthouse*, the narrativeless, personification-haunted 'Time Passes' section owes something to Lee's stylized ballet-satire on slaughter.

While reading *Satan* it is sometimes tempting to see the harshest irony of all as one that Vernon Lee did not plan. 'My sacrifice is sheer loss: and the offering to my essential godhead, is *waste*,' Satan tells the Muse of history, Clio (14). *Satan the Waster* is wasted: all its commitment to honesty, its play, its wit, its tussle with language, its experiment with genre. The desolate aloofness of its insight makes it almost unreadable. So too does its length: the way each sentence unfurls in an effort to track the processes of the thought with which it was written, the traps its syntax lays for the writer. Normalcy for Lee is the great delusion, and in that she is almost certainly correct. How she fears to acquiesce, to miss the delusion curled beneath the verb or couched in the ordinary relations of subject and object. Strenuous, impassioned, wary, the whole work runs counter to her more frequent lapidary style. Its manners move among epigram, fustion, and an empathy as chilly as it is total.

That is one reaction to my reading of it. Yet I have read it and admired it, even laughed aloud, writhed too. So have others, as this chapter has shown. Vernon Lee does not share Satan's final problem: she is never bored. Nor is her writing boring; but it is *exigéant* to the last degree. This was the period of such exacting masterpieces, of course. Indeed, Logan Pearsall Smith writes to her in 1922 in terms not unlike those that other of her friends used about *Satan the Waster*: 'What really weighs most on us here, is that terrible ominous & enormous book, Joyce's "Ulysses", but this you in Florence will be spared. Here many of my neighbours have become exhausted, ill and old with whitened hair, in their awful efforts to read it through; but I have wisely got a doctor's certificate saying that I am to be spared this undertaking.' He does not mention *Satan.* But Lee's work too is worth the risk of some white hairs. Its meaning was not exhausted with the First World War. It made a claim that needs still to be made: a claim for passionate analysis undeterred by clan loyalties, however virtuous the clan. Only thus, she argues, will conflict be understood, even possibly halted. She lays bare through argument, abstraction, and drama those cravings whose 'lack of open recognition merely establishes their paramount tyranny; they are oligarchies and dynasties without a name, divinities without a temple, yet forever receiving a hidden sacrifice of common sense and truth' (*Satan,* 142–3).

NOTES

1. *Satan the Waster: A Philosophic War Trilogy with Notes and Introduction* (London, 1920), 142.
2. Paul Fussell, *The Great War and Modern Memory* (Oxford, 1975); Daniel Pick, *War Machine: The Rationalisation of Slaughter in the Modern Age* (New Haven, 1993).
3. George Bernard Shaw, 'A Political Contrast' (the contrast is with Lloyd George), *The Nation,* 18 Sept. 1920, 758, 760. The review occupies two full-column pages.
4. Jacqueline Rose, *Why War?—Psychoanalysis, Politics and the Return to Melanie Klein* (Oxford, 1993), 24.
5. Vernon Lee has fortunately left a good deal of evidence through which one can pursue these questions. Apart from her published essays such as *Vital Lies* there is a wealth of unpublished material. Sixteen cases of

letters to her, stretching across a very long span of her life, are now in the possession of Somerville College, Oxford, and I am grateful to have had the opportunity to begin exploring the collection. Much remains to be done with this material. The Somerville collection has no letters *from* Vernon Lee. More of Lee's papers are in the library of Colne College, Maine. I hope to explore these later. Around 350 of Vernon Lee's books, many with numerous annotations by Lee herself, are now at the British Institute in Florence. The works are in English, French, German, and Italian, and many are heavily annotated by Lee herself so that when, for example, we read Nietzsche here, it is Nietzsche in debate with Lee. The annotations are always in the language of the European text she is reading at the time. I am grateful to the Librarian and the Director of the British Institute for making the collection available to me, allowing me to quote Vernon Lee's annotations, and for their hospitality.

6. From Ethyl Smyth, Hotel Kumner, Vienna, 15 Dec. [?1912], Somerville College, Oxford, Vernon Lee Papers, Box 13. I am grateful to the Principal and Fellows of Somerville for permission to quote from these letters and for their hospitality.
7. Somerville College, Vernon Lee Papers, Box 13.
8. Quoted in Peter Gunn, *Vernon Lee: Violet Paget, 1856–1935* (London, 1964), 204.
9. Mon. 25 [?winter 1911–12], Somerville College, Vernon Lee Papers, Box 13.
10. Caroline Playne, *The Pre-war Mind in Britain: An Historical Review* (London, 1928), 420. The book is in Vernon Lee's library.
11. Caroline Playne, *Neuroses of the Nations* (London, 1925).
12. The 1921 edition is that in the Vernon Lee library. This seems belated for a first reading, and the comparative paucity of annotation suggests that she had read it before.
13. Letter 7, 6 Oct. 1911, Somerville College, Vernon Lee Papers, Box 13. The correspondence throughout 1911–13 is preoccupied with the European political situation.
14. Five volumes of Semon's work (some of them translations) are in the Vernon Lee library. Here she is referring to his *Die Mnemischen Empfindungen* (Leipzig, 1909) and *Die Mneme* (Leipzig, 1911).
15. W. Trotter, *Instincts of the Herd in Peace and War* (London, 1916).
16. A passage from Vernon Lee's long critique pencilled into the front of the book.
17. Annotations to Trotter, *Instincts of the Herd in Peace and War*, 79, 73.
18. Her library includes, for example, Edwin Holt, *The Freudian Wish and its Place in Ethics* (London, 1915), published at the time she was developing the *Ballet* into *Satan the Waster*.
19. Among books that bear on these questions the following are heavily annotated in her library: James Baldwin, *Mental Development in the Child and the Race* (London, 1903); William McDougall, *Psychology: The Study of Behaviour* (London, n.d.); G. F. Nicolai, *The Biology of War* (London, 1919); J. Novicow, *Les Luttes entre sociétés humaines* (Paris, 1910); Playne, *Neuroses of the Nations*; Trotter, *Instincts of the Herd in Peace and War*; Wilhelm Wundt, *Grundriss der Psychologie* (Leipzig, 1909).
20. *Satan*, 'Self-Sacrifice', 192.
21. Henry Rutgers Marshall, *Pain, Pleasure and Aesthetics: An Essay Concerning*

the Psychology of Pain and Pleasure, with Special Reference to Aesthetics (London, 1894). Lee records that she finished reading 'Nov 11 1901'. Annotation to p. 192.

22. *Satan*, 'The Continuum', dated Apr. 1918, 178–9.
23. Quoted from unpublished notes entitled 'Myself' in Gunn, *Vernon Lee*, 206. The entry was made on 5 Sept. 1916 at Adel, the house outside Leeds where she lived for much of the war.
24. Charles Roden Buxton, *Towards a Lasting Settlement* (London, 1915).
25. Lee's essay runs 203–16.
26. 21 Aug. [?1920], Somerville College, Vernon Lee Papers, Box 13.
27. 4 June 1930, Somerville College, Vernon Lee Papers, Box 13.
28. 2 Jan. 1927, Somerville College, Vernon Lee Papers, Box 13. Margaret Skelton described in this letter the fate of her own anti-war novel *Below the Watchtowers* (1926), praised in the middlebrow press, ignored or sneered at in those papers she thought her natural allies. Skelton's novel is a powerful and immediate account of the love between an Englishwoman and a German doctor torn apart by the war. The last section, describing events in 'Gunton' during the war, is full of chilling testimony to the behaviour of people in fear.
29. Playne, *The Pre-war Mind*, 333–4.
30. William Morrison Patterson, *The Rhythm of Prose: An Experimental Investigation of Individual Difference in the Sense of Rhythm* (New York, 1916), 83.
31. Wilhelm Wundt, *Lectures on Human and Animal Psychology* (London, 1894), 110–11.
32. Annotation to Wundt, *Lectures*, 377.
33. Annotation to Trotter, *Instincts of the Herd in Peace and War*, 73.
34. McDougall, *Psychology*, 198. Vernon Lee's copy is much annotated.
35. Charlotte Perkins Gilman [Stetson], *The Home: Its Work and Influence* (New York, 1903), annotation to p. 259.
36. Annotation to Trotter, *Instincts of the Herd in Peace and War*, 84–5. See her comments on p. 90, where she differs from Trotter's interpretation of Freud.
37. McDougall, *Psychology*, 420–1.
38. *Satan*, Prologue, 17.
39. Unpub. notes, July 1933, quoted in Gunn, *Vernon Lee*, 230.

6

The Grotesque and the Great War in *To the Lighthouse*

TRACY HARGREAVES

IN *Realities of War* (1920) Philip Gibbs recalled Field Marshal Haig's derision of the newly appointed war journalists: 'I think I understand very well what you gentlemen want,' he said. 'You want to get hold of little stories of heroism and so forth and to write them up in a bright way to make good reading for Mary Ann in the kitchen and the man in the street.'[1] Gibbs was among the government-appointed journalists who from 1915 were to send to the home front, subject to censorship, 'authentic' records of life on the western front. Haig's comment is, in some ways, more telling than the 'colourless phrases of the newspapers',[2] as Virginia Woolf described them. Not only does his misgiving betray anxieties about protecting a form of fellowship (only 'those who were there' could really 'know' the war), it also raises questions about what constitutes authentic reportage which, in this case, threatens a specific construction of masculinity. The battlefield, according to Jung, was the *natural* place for men to resolve conflict: women, on the other hand, resolved their antagonisms in psychic conflict.[3] Haig's apprehension that militarism could be transcribed into suitable reading-material for Mary Ann (popular slang for homosexual) in the kitchen and the non-combatant on the street registers an anxiety about feminizing and, *ipso facto*, perverting a narrative that, he implies, was more appropriately the healthy boy's own story. Yet developments in the technology of the war machine forced a reconsideration of how sexual difference was organized: the conservation and preservation of particular ways of organizing and maintaining difference were under threat. The First World War is usually seen as marking a divisive point in twentieth-century history and culture, one that marks the entry into modernity. If the only defining experience of that moment can be the experience of 'those who were there' (creating, as Claire Tylee has argued, a cult of the 'Two Nations'[4]), then women are placed outside an arena that organized cultural and modern understanding.

In the introduction to his 1930 war booklist, Edmund Blunden wrote that it would be 'inevitably a long time before a real account of the war could make its way to light'. 'Real' or defining accounts in 1930 included Brigadier-General Aspinall-Oglander's *History of the Great War Based on Official Documents Military Operations: Gallipoli* (1929); H. W. Fawcett and G. W. W. Hooper's *The Fighting at Jutland: The Personal Experiences of Sixty Officers and Men of the British Fleet* (1921); Sir Ian Hamilton's *Gallipoli Diary* (1924); Grand Admiral Von Tirpitz's *My Memoirs* (1919); Sir C. V. F. Townsend's *My Campaign in Mesopotamia* (1920)—and so on. 'My Memoirs', 'My Campaign' indicate that such autobiography can also work as a legitimizing narrative, securing narratives of war as a masculine treatise. Yet, Katherine Mansfield's mandate for post-war literature: 'the novel can't just leave the war out', points to shifting meanings for war where military action is perceived as a necessary lacuna in the new post-war narrative: 'I don't want (God forbid!) mobilisation and the violation of Belgium.'[5] This signals a development in narrating war experience: if, as Mansfield argued, literature must account for war, not by recounting militarism but by recognizing a profound shift in values, how, formally and thematically, will this shift be conceptualized and defined? If (masculine) presence legitimizes narratives of war, then might it not be possible to argue that absence from the organized sites of conflict consolidates an inauthentic sense of post-war cultural subjectivity for women? As late as 1937, after publication of *The Years*, Woolf still felt able to write to Stephen Spender, 'I couldnt bring in the Front as you say partly because fighting isn't within my experience as a woman.'[6]

Writing what you know had been a mainstay of Woolf's writing praxis as early as 1906, when she told Madge Vaughan: 'Only it seems to me better to write of the things that I do feel, than to dabble in things I frankly dont understand in the least.'[7] When she came to write the 1914, 1917, and 1918 chapters of *The Years*, she turned to her most private narratives to furnish material for that most public of events: 'To freshen my memory of the war, I read some old diaries.'[8] But what is most personal is what is also most significant and, in the process of this research, her vision of war is dimmed rather than freshened, and the appeal of private remembrance supplants an attempt at a more public-spirited sense of responsibility—the war that Woolf feels obliged to remember is, actually, just as easily forgotten—'I've forgotten to say that peace was signed . . . I've forgotten the account I was going to write . . .'[9] 'Old Virginia', she reproached herself in 1921, 'will be ashamed to think what a chatterbox she was, always talking about people, never about politics.'[10] The war that she wants to claim a cultural and personal stake in is also one that she problematically reproduces as a site from which she is ignorant and excluded, raising, as well as a set of ideological difficulties, a crisis in narrative confidence. Her response to the 'preposterous masculine fiction'[11] of the war was to imagine it as narrative and to gain mastery by dismissal: 'One ought to say something about Peace day I suppose, though whether its worth taking a new nib for that purpose I dont know.'[12] Woolf both invokes and denies the 'reality' of the war of book-lists like Blunden's, organized around the principle that stories of men in battle provide the only true account. But, as she oscillates, Woolf's narratives also reconstruct war as an unstable category, and the ramifications of this instability are radically significant, since everyone could be 'in' the war. The technological developments of the war machine meant that the home front was also susceptible to bombardment and war could no longer be seen as an unproblematically propagandist showcase for the heroic defence of the defenceless. The often stagnant nature of trench warfare was superseded by the way in which 'war' was also constantly relocated, and 'war' began to extend its territorial boundaries in effect, in language, and in experience.

Apart from *The Years, To the Lighthouse* (1927) is Woolf's only other text which engages with the period preceding, including, and following the First World War. *To the Lighthouse* marks the limits of Woolf's engagement with an often intensely personal vision set in the context of the then unprecedented historical, political, and social consequences of the First World War. The text is often seen as an elegiac reconstruction of Woolf's childhood summers in Cornwall and a nostalgic recollection of her parents, in particular her mother, Julia Stephen. But *To the Lighthouse* incorporates the First World War in its often haunting middle section, 'Time Passes'. A decade separates the first and third sections, narratives characterized by postponement and closure, in which a group of people do not go to the lighthouse and the artist Lily Briscoe does not complete her painting. In the third section, ten years later, the trip to the lighthouse is made and, simultaneously, the picture is completed, culminating in Lily's cathartic moment of vision. In between these moments of postponement and closure, during the war, Mrs Ramsay dies, and so too do her eldest children, Andrew and Prue (in battle and in childbirth). Mrs McNab, an elderly woman who lives locally, saves the Ramsay house from complete ruin by repairing years of rot and neglect. The most perfunctory elements of plot are the profoundest symbols of this text.

An intricate series of connections links the artist Lily Briscoe with the 'caretaker' Mrs McNab, and Mrs McNab with Mrs Ramsay. The connection between these very different women is important because it enabled Woolf to engage with personal recollection and artistic belief as part of a defining account of the 'preposterous masculine fiction' of the First World War. Woolf's narrative makes a tacit connection, then, between the dynamics of the family and the patriarchal state by posing a relationship between the Ramsays and Lily's painting and then recasting these relations in the lyric 'Time Passes' in the war-time and post-war actions of Mrs McNab.

The extant holograph version of 'Time Passes' reveals that Woolf was actually ambivalent about Mrs McNab, who was, in revision, transmuted into an ambling, grinning idiot. I want to focus, to some extent, on the holograph version of Mrs McNab, not only because Woolf found this section the most difficult to write, but because 'Time Passes' originally comprised a more explicit, if intricate, condensation of images of the First World War with the compositional difficulties of Lily's painting and the personal difficulties experienced by Lily in her relationship with the Ramsays. In holograph, 'Time Passes' offers a comment on the almost insurmountable difficulties not just of writing a war narrative, but of representing how women negotiated cultural representations of war. The paradoxical bind at the heart of Woolf's post-war writing is expressed here: war cannot be represented in art: 'The black snout interfered with the whole composition. Was there no composition at all then?'[13] And at the same time it cannot be ignored: 'Equally benignant & sublime, she contemplated his misery, she condoned his meanness, she acquiesced in his torture.'[14]

Two old women cleaning a house and saving it from irreparable ruin was, then, how Woolf imagined and allegorized the carnage of the First World War and the renaissance of post-war Europe. 'Time Passes' is a splendidly, if not shamelessly, understated title for the 1914–18 years. In it, Woolf revises an enduring ideology which assumed a new intensity during the war years —the 'cult of motherhood'—or, the assertion of the maternal as the cultural role for women. *To the Lighthouse* abounds with mothers, from the placatory Mrs Ramsay to the slatternly Mrs McNab. Maternity is the root of an impossible identification (Lily's desire to be one with Mrs Ramsay) and Woolf also produces an interesting corollary: maternity and the battlefield are fatal in the respective instances of the beautiful Prue and the brilliant Andrew Ramsay, who both die during the First World War. After the war, clearly, there will be no more Mr and Mrs Ramsays. If human character changed 'on or about December 1910', the 1914–18 years completed the transformation.

Paul Fussell has argued that one of Lord Northcliffe's editorial strategies for writing about war was the 'shrewd use of domestic similes which anchored the novelties of modern war to the world of the familiar, the comfortable and the safe'.[15] This tactic was used and developed for uncomfortable rather than consoling effect by Woolf. In *Jacob's Room* (1922) Betty Flanders thinks that she can hear the guns in battle. Taking solace in what she believes is impossible, and diverting her thoughts from her combatant sons, she imagines instead that the guns are 'The nocturnal women . . . beating great carpets'.[16] The image takes on for her the status of a truth that substitutes women for combatant soldiers, carpet-beating for battle scene, as the unfamiliar is troped into familiarity, authenticating, in the process, Betty Flanders's grasp of events. It is as if, argue Sandra Gilbert and Susan Gubar, 'battle itself were a kind of gigantic housecleaning'.[17] Gigantic house-cleaning is, indeed, the imagined, or fantasized, site of conflict in *To the Lighthouse*, where the model of bountiful maternity, the consoling and pacifying Mrs Ramsay, is usurped by the Rabelaisian figure of the bawdy and chaotic Mrs McNab.

'Time Passes' marks both women's estrangement from *and* their involvement with (or in) the war years. Lily and the surviving Ramsays are quite unaware of what happens to the house (or the significant scene of action) when they are not there. In their place, Woolf moves two women, both mothers, to the heart of the action, as it were, as she gives them a central role and agency in the ravages of war-torn and post-war Europe. Mrs McNab and Mrs Bast, like Lily Briscoe, hold the memory of loss, but they are also responsible for restoration and reparation as they make do and mend the Ramsay house. If this implies the inscription of an unofficial history into an 'official' literary narrative, it is deeply equivocal, for Mrs Bast and Mrs McNab are depicted as a motley pair, travesties, even, of the consolation which is offered by Mrs Ramsay.

In the process of writing *To the Lighthouse,* Woolf had recorded in her diary the idea of 'a solitary woman musing [?] ... It is to be an endeavour at something mystic, spiritual; the thing that exists when we aren't there.'[18] It is Mrs McNab who holds the key to understanding 'a revelation more ~~profound~~, ~~but~~ confused, but more profound than any accorded to solitary watchers, pacers on the beach at midnight'.[19] Mrs McNab is Woolf's troubled and troubling saviour of post-war Europe. For, just as the outcome of the war looked uncertain at the beginning of 1918, so the Ramsay house stands tentatively on the verge of collapse. Through metaphors of maternity and militarism, Mrs McNab is the corroded mechanism of the workforce who can put the European house back into a semblance of order with her 'rusty and laborious birth'[20]—as makeshift and patchy as the 1919 Versailles Treaty. The young, the healthy, the brilliant, the beautiful cannot regenerate the post-war world (or so we would infer from the deaths of the embryonic Mr and Mrs Ramsay—the brilliant Andrew, the beautiful Prue). What Woolf finds most distasteful, but also most fascinating and enduring, is what saves the Ramsay house as the aged and the 'witless' renew the post-war world.

'We all seem to think the world will emerge out of the melting-pot into some strange new shape', argues Maynard in Rose Macaulay's *Non-combatants and Others*; 'optimists hope and believe it will be the shape they prefer, pessimists are almost sure it will be the one they can least approve.'[21] Into a post-war era searching for a re-evaluation of its moral and ethical structures, ambles Mrs McNab: 'As she lurched (for she rolled like a ship at sea) and leered (for her eyes fell on nothing directly, but with a sidelong glance that deprecated the scorn and anger of the world—she was witless, she knew it), as she clutched the banisters and hauled herself upstairs and rolled from room to room, she sang.'[22] The debauched and wanton Mrs McNab is the possessor (just) of a 'sidelong leer which slipped and turned aside even from her own face'.[23] In the holograph, she 'had been drunk in her day, & of her six children, two, it was said, were not by her husband; she had lived, she had loved, in short'.[24] Yet if she is the bringer of reparation, she is also the harbinger of destruction, the embodiment of the war years: '(for night and day, month and year ran shapelessly together) in idiot games, until it seemed as if the universe were battling and tumbling, in brute confusion and wanton lust aimlessly by itself.'[25] As Gayatri Spivak comments, 'The disappearance of reason and the confusion of sexuality are consistently linked . . .'.[26] In the holograph, the war years are presented as an even wilder bacchanalian orgy: 'Now it seemed ~~fiercely~~ battling for no reason, then at peace; now mounting in lust or conquest one upon another, so that they seemed to until it seemed as if the universe were ~~filled from~~ earth to sky ~~with~~ was full of shapes mounting one on top of another, battling & tumbling—~~& the~~ now swiftness, now stagnant, but always in a ~~wild~~ brute ~~commotion~~ confusion.'[27] If Mrs McNab is the incarnation of the new civilization, she is presumably Rose Macaulay's strange new shape emerging from the melting-pot and deserving disapproval. At any rate, Virginia Woolf appears to be corroborating Leonard Woolf's view of post-war life and the, for him, almost synonymous collapse of civilization: 'by 1918 one had unconsciously accepted a perpetual public menace and darkness and had admitted into the privacy of one's mind or soul an iron fatalistic acquiescence in insecurity and barbarism'.[28]

Although the 1919 campaign medals bore the inscription 'The Great War Fought for Civilization', there was a belief (popular with Bloomsbury) that, rather than upholding it, the war heralded the collapse of civilization. Leonard Woolf includes seven references to civilization in the first three pages of his account of the outbreak of war in 1914.[29] Clive Bell's *Civilization,* dedicated to Virginia Woolf and published in 1928, argued for the necessary existence of a 'slave class': 'Complete human equality', argues Bell, 'is compatible only with complete savagery.'[30] John Maynard Keynes declared: 'Never in the lifetime of men now living has the universal element in the soul of man burnt so dimly.'[31] When asked why he wasn't fighting for civilization, Lytton Strachey took it upon himself to be its personification: 'I am the civilization for which you are fighting . . .' runs the possibly apocryphal story.[32] Freud counteracted wryly that 'our mortification and our painful disillusionment on account of the uncivilized behaviour of our fellow citizens during this war were unjustified. They were based on an illusion to which we had given way. In reality our fellow-citizens had not sunk so low as we feared, because they had never risen so high as we believed.'[33]

In mythology, Antaeus built a temple to his father from the skulls of his enemies. If civilization is built upon the bloody triumphs of masculinity in the celebration of paternal authority, what is Woolf doing with Mrs McNab and the collapse and resurrection of civilization? And what does Mrs McNab have to do with Woolf's post-war interest in different narrative forms of cultural representation?

Woolf's ambivalence towards the working class is well known —even a cursory look through her diaries reveals a panoply of conflicting feelings of culpability, sympathy, and alienation as she both laments and celebrates working people as 'other'. Her scorn for the popular responses to the beginning and the end of the war found its way into 'Time Passes' with her representation of Mrs McNab. At the beginning of the war, Woolf revealed to Duncan Grant her distaste for, and refusal to identify with, the populace: 'One might have thought in peace time that they were harmless, if stupid: but now that they have been roused they seem full of the most violent and filthy passions.'[34] At the end of the war, Woolf wrote in her diary that 'the peace at any rate is over; though the poor deluded servants are spending their day out on a bus to see the decorations. I was right: it is a servant's peace.'[35] Woolf's invidious private responses reveal a horror at the scale of the ominous and cheerful reactions to war and peace. Yet part of her distaste with what she saw as the sordidity of the celebrations is that she cannot entirely extricate herself from the rank and file: they all share the same alienation from the organized arena of conflict, and this alienation is a point that troubles Woolf. Although her distaste settles on class difference, her anger is actually directed towards political officialdom: 'But I don't know—it seems to me a servant's festival; something got up to pacify & placate "the people"'.[36] What is irritating for Woolf is not just the complicity 'the people' showed towards participating in the infantilizing peacetime celebrations, but the sheer inappropriateness of how the end of the four-year débâcle was marked. Her alienation from the returned soldiers reveals a kind of shame at the organized celebrations in 1919: 'It was a melancholy thing to see the soldiers at the Star & Garter with their backs to us, smoking cigarettes & waiting for the noise to be over. We were children to be amused.'[37] At this moment, she is clearly not to be distinguished from 'the people', and at this moment, too, she registers a feeling of complicit guilt and inadequacy. Into an earlier attempt at a 'concise historic style' in her diary, she reflects on the impact of wartime shortages—only one butcher's shop open, and empty boxes displayed in shop windows.[38] Into this account, too, creeps the rhetoric of war—shops are 'beseiged' and they 'parade' their goods. As it stands, her record of privation (no chocolates, the expense of flowers, only one bun for tea) seems to reveal a selfish and deeply unsympathetic engagement with either the domestic shortages which war inevitably brings, or, indeed, with the horrors of trench warfare. But this account, reconsidered in *To the Lighthouse,* also furnishes an attempt to understand what war means to those who have no understanding of its politics and strategies:

> How Mrs. McNab, of all people, had come to tolerate & to forgive, who shall say—Mrs. McNab . . . whose existence was ignored who was nothing but a mat for kings & kaisers to tread on, who would indeed stand patiently in the streets to see the kings go riding by, & whose sugar & tea were ~~now cut cut down by their passions &~~ reduced at their command, passes ~~any sort of an that of the~~ understanding.[39]

There is a pathos about this champion of the heads of state—those who both rely on *and* ignore her obscure existence. Yet Woolf distinguishes the humble significances of political and social practice from other forms of cultural representation, and this distinction leads to an ambivalent account of Mrs McNab.

We know that as Mrs McNab leers and lurches round the Ramsay house, she sings. In the holograph, her song was once a 'sprightly dance song' which becomes an elegy. This lament becomes, in the revised text, an old music-hall song. Privately, Woolf confessed to a discomfort with the music-hall: 'for surely we could have risen higher'.[40] In this diary entry, she discloses a dislike and an inability to understand the 'low grade . . . queer

English humour' that she encounters, but she does recognize what is for her a form of cultural conflict: what she finds debased she also marks as a form for celebration, something that is quintessentially English: 'you can't help feeling it's the real thing, as in Athens one might have felt that poetry was'. In the holograph of 'Time Passes', the music-hall song becomes a primeval, semiotic burble which resists meaning within symbolic discourse, but in the published text, Mrs McNab, the 'voice of witlessness', is also the thief of meaning as Woolf turns the 'care-taking' woman into the root of a, for her, post-war cultural conflict. For Mrs McNab also shadows problems of representation and a breakdown of traditional forms of hegemony.

Mrs McNab, the narrator argues, holds the key to a mystic understanding of war, an understanding keener than that of the solitary watchers on the beach invoked in the narrative. Solitary watchers pace the beach on two occasions. The first of these occasions is when Nancy, one of the elder Ramsay children, acts as chaperon to one of the Ramsay guests, Minta Doyle. Nancy, as if anticipating the war, plays God over a rock-pool, bringing 'darkness and desolation . . . to millions of ignorant and innocent creatures'.[41] Rounding a corner, she is outraged to see Paul Rayley (another of the guests) and Minta Doyle kissing. For her, and for Andrew Ramsay, this heralds an uncomfortable recognition of an accession to sexual identity: 'All the same it irritated Andrew that Nancy should be a woman, and Nancy that Andrew should be a man . . . '.[42] Panic ensues when Minta realizes that she has lost her grandmother's brooch, and instantly everyone adopts their appropriate role: Andrew and Paul become 'manly' and Minta sobs. It is Lily's fantasy that she, not Paul, will find the missing brooch, that, wandering on the beach at dawn, she will triumph 'and thus herself be included among the sailors and adventurers'.[43] With an uncharacteristic show of emotion, Lily offers to help—an offer which is casually (and cruelly) rejected, 'as if he had said, Throw yourself over the cliff if you like, I don't care.'[44] Perceiving herself as being outside the rituals and celebrations of sexual attraction, Lily comes to a realization: 'she need not marry, thank Heaven: she need not undergo that degradation. She was saved from that dilution. She would move the tree rather more to the middle.'[45] Moving the tree to the middle throws into relief Lily's preoccupation with the structural problems of her painting, with all its semantic complexities. It is at the end of the dinner that Andrew, Prue, and Lily pace the beach at midnight and, on their return, echoing Sir Edward Grey's famous remark 'The lamps are going out all over Europe'.[46] They usher in the war: 'One by one the lamps were all extinguished' and 'So with the lamps all put out'.[47] Lily, feeling herself poignantly outside, but also absolved from Mrs Ramsay's social engineering, turns to the compositional difficulties of her painting. Mrs McNab, as we will see, harmonizes these disparate elements.

In the holograph of 'Time Passes' Lily's dream of harmony with Mrs Ramsay ('Could loving, as people called it, make her and Mrs Ramsay one?') is reconsidered in the context of the advent of war:

> As for the watchers, the preachers, ~~the souls who who had~~ those spirits who, in sleep, had left their bodies, & dreamed of some communion, of grasping the hand of a sharer, & completing, down on the beach, ~~the~~ from the sky or sea the cliff, ~~or the~~ the ~~fu~~ fullness that was incomplete, the vision that asked for ratification, either they had been woken from their dreams by that prodigious cannonading which had made the wine glasses tinkle in the cupboard, or that intrusion—that black snout—that purple foaming stain—had so gravely ~~interfered~~ damaged the composition of the picture that ~~w~~ they had fled. They had gone in despair. They had dashed the mirror to the ground. They saw nothing more. They stumbled & strove now, blindly, pulling their feet out of the mud & stamping them further in. Let the wind blow, let the poppy seed itself, & the carnation mate with the cabbage.[48]

In the holograph, the war intrudes on the subject of Lily's painting:

> This intrusion into a scene ~~which was~~ otherwise calculated to stir the most sublime reflections & lead to the most comforting conclusions stayed their pacing. If that snout ~~out in~~ thrusting itself up ~~in the~~ there ~~expressed the desire wish to~~ meant death, & starvation, & pain, it was difficult to abolish its significance, & to continue, ~~walking by the sea, to adm marvel at the~~ as one walked to marvel at the ~~completeness, & at the roundness, &~~ rounded completeness of ~~human~~ existence.[49]

The subject of Lily's painting—Mrs Ramsay reading to James—is just such a scene 'calculated to stir the most sublime reflections'. Just as Lily is about to criticize Mrs Ramsay, William Bankes's rapturous contemplation of Mrs Ramsay and James 'made it entirely unnecessary for her to speak . . . For him to gaze as Lily saw him gazing at Mrs Ramsay was a rapture, equivalent, Lily felt, to the loves of dozens of young men.'[50] The moment of intrusion which destroys this sublime scene and insistently threatens the execution of the painting is the 'thrusting snout'—Mr Ramsay's arrival. His arrival is also the occasion of an arresting moment of fecundity for Mrs Ramsay:

Mrs. Ramsay, who had been sitting loosely, folding her son in her arm, braced herself, and, half turning, seemed to raise herself with an effort, and at once to pour erect into the air a rain of energy, a column of spray, looking at the same time animated and alive as if all her energies were being fused into force, burning and illuminating (quietly though she sat, taking up her stocking again), and into this delicious fecundity, this fountain and spray of life, the fatal sterility of the male plunged itself, like a beak of brass, barren and bare.[51]

As Mrs Ramsay comforts her husband, James's antipathy towards his father is aroused as the Oedipal drama is played out:

Flashing her needles, confident, upright, she created drawing-room and kitchen, set them all aglow; bade him take his ease there, go in and out, enjoy himself. She laughed, she knitted. Standing between her knees, very stiff, James felt all her strength flaring up to be drunk and quenched by the beak of brass, the arid scimitar of the male, which smote mercilessly, again and again, demanding sympathy.[52]

James's hatred of his father and his affections for his mother are mapped out through the dynamics of his Oedipal attachment to his mother. Mrs Ramsay remains the sexual centre of the triangular relationship as she soothes her husband: 'If he put implicit faith in her, nothing should hurt him; however deep he buried himself or climbed high.'[53] His implied sexual satisfaction leads to a regression to a pre-Oedipal polymorphous pleasure, however, since he is 'filled with her words, like a child who drops off satisfied'.[54] Yet words are precisely *absent* from the polymorphous pleasures of the infant: pleasure circulates exclusively around the body and its drives, not around the symbolic order of language. Mr Ramsay is the child who drops off satisfied; it is the phallic James who remains 'stiff between her knees'. The collapse of paternal authority is, here, complete. 'All human relations have shifted,' argued Woolf in 'Character in Fiction'; 'those between masters and servants, husbands and wives, parents and children.'[55] These relationships are precisely the ones examined by Woolf in the course of the text. Our sympathy is, with no small degree of irony, invoked: the narrator's sardonic engagement with Mr Ramsay's aggrandizing fantasies place him as a man of heroic integrity, a stalwart, 'dead at his post, the fine figure of a soldier'.[56] The meaning of his bravery finds its resolution in chivalry: our hero removes his armour and pays homage to his wife and son. Mr Ramsay's fantasy is, however, abruptly dashed: 'his son hated him'—and the chivalric romance as family romance collapses. Although the pre-war setting assumes something of a teleological overview in relation to the 1914–18 years, the heroic defence of the defenceless is seen, even here, as an anachronism. Mr Ramsay's reverie is supplanted by his ostensible infantilization as the phallic beak of brass is overwhelmed by the 'delicious fecundity' of Mrs Ramsay. The collapse of paternal authority results from the failure of an imagined form of heroism and the collapse of particular constructions of male and female identity.

Mrs Ramsay, at this moment, is both phallic *and* vaginal, which is in accordance with the condition of James's Oedipal attachment: the assumption that there is no genital difference between himself and his mother. The end of the Oedipal drama for the boy is marked, argues Freud, by the recognition of genital difference as the boy sees that his mother is 'castrated', thereby ending an identification with her. Such a scene of recognition seems hardly necessary given the fecund, self-fertilizing mother who reinvigorates her husband by making his 'barrenness . . . fertile'. And how is this achieved? By making 'all the rooms of the house . . . full of life—the drawing-room; behind the drawing-room the kitchen; above the kitchen the bedrooms; and beyond them the nurseries; they must be furnished, they must be filled with life'.[57] Implicit is the relationship between sterile, impotent masculinity and the barren post-war landscape which women reinvigorate: for Mrs Ramsay in her domestic triumphs surely prefigures Mrs McNab in hers.

Mrs McNab's work of restoration in fact destroys the hybrid result of wild abandonment (the self-seeding poppy, the carnation mating with the cabbage) in her 'rusted laborious birth'[58] energized by (what else?) the rhetoric of war. With a 'magnificent conquest' and 'partial ~~conq triump c~~ triumph' she and Mrs Bast save the house from irreparable ruin. On the lawn, Mrs Bast's son, Fred/George, stops to pause only when 'there was only one square ~~army of~~ of thick waving grass yet to be demolished on the lawn'. Fred/George himself 'advanced like the sweep of an invincible army over the ~~insugr~~ insurgents rioting ~~before~~& wary in their tumult . . . ~~b~~ up the bank & over the lawn & ~~so~~ laid them flat'.[59] As George vigorously scythes for victory, Mrs Bast and Mrs McNab bring peace in their massive act of maternal generativity. And so the house is saved as peace is restored to Europe. Yet, in the margin of the holograph, as Mrs McNab and Mrs Bast 'stayed the corruption & the rot', Woolf wrote: 'ask them what the war had been about—did they know?'[60] Prophetic and mystical knowledge conveyed through the broken syllables of a song is one way of inscribing women and knowledge into the war years, but to infer that Mrs McNab and Mrs Bast would not know what the war was 'about' is to place them historically, socially, and politically outside the discourses that inscribe the boundaries and actions of the war as the battleground of soldiers and politicians. Mrs McNab is, after all, still the doormat of Kaiser and King. In the revised text, Mrs McNab does know what the war means, if she does not know what it had been about: 'every one had lost someone these years. Prices had gone up shamefully, and didn't come down again neither. . . . Things were better then than now.'[61] What still matters, five years after the end of the war in *Mrs Dalloway* (1927), is that it is never over for people like 'Mrs. Foxcroft at the Embassy last night eating her heart out because that nice boy was killed . . . or Lady Bexborough who opened a bazaar, they said with the telegram in her hand, John her favourite killed . . .'.[62] It is precisely this kind of story that Haig had perceived as a threat to the 'official' histories of the war that were being written as Woolf was writing this text (see Blunden's war book-list). The text retains a characteristic ambivalence, as it invites a recognition of loss and the financial hardship experienced during (and after) the war years, even as it is recognizes the master narrative of officialdom (what the war had 'truly been about').

The representation of inchoate female identity in relation to the war years was something that Woolf interrogated and negotiated consistently, if not insistently, for much of her writing life. During the 1930s she was interested in what she saw as a mutually exclusive, though enticing, opposition: something that she called the life of fact and the life of vision. Female identity and the imminence of violent conflict were related in 'Professions for Women', an essay that is at the heart of *The Years* and *Three Guineas.* Woolf's inspiration for a project in which she wanted to explore 'the sexual life of women' emerged from a speech which, before its revisions, incorporated into images of militarism images of women's professional advance; murder (albeit symbolic) to facilitate self-expression (and self-defence); and impotence as a result of inexperience and the threat of swaggering sexuality in the work of writers like D. H. Lawrence, who render the woman writer 'shrivelled and distorted'.[63]

Ethel Smyth, who is omitted from the revised version, is: 'of the race of pioneers . . . one of the ice breakers, the gun runners, the window smashers. The armoured tanks, who climbed the rough ground, drew the enemies fire, and left behind her a pathway—not yet smoothed and metalled road—but still a pathway for those who come after her.'[64] With the landscape, machinery, and technology of the First World War incorporated into the feminist struggle for recognition and validation, Woolf does manage to negotiate fact as vision. She utilizes the iconography of the war to foreground a feminist struggle. What Woolf is doing with Mrs McNab is more ambivalent, but it is deeply embedded in her notion of character in fiction and issues of representation, from Mrs Brown in theory ('for Mrs. Brown is eternal; Mrs. Brown is human nature'[65]) to Mrs McNab in practice. Mrs McNab is more the index of Woolf's concern with a genealogy of writing and the advent of the modern in its various cultural representations than with either a mockery or a glorification of working people.

I share Hermione Lee's reservations about some critical assessments of Mrs McNab which cast her and Mrs Bast as 'translations of a temporary antiphallogocentric discourse, awaiting the time when the charwoman herself will write fiction'.[66] The difficulty with such criticism is that it takes for its lead Woolf's own problematic relation to what she felt she could not authentically engage with or reproduce—and so, it fantasizes. Woolf's concern is not so much with the charwoman who will write fiction as the charwoman who is character in fiction, character with 'the power to make you think not merely of it itself, but of all sorts of things through its eyes—of religion, of love, of war, of peace, of family life, of balls in county towns, moonrises, the immortality of the human soul'.[67]

'Ultimately,' argues Michèle Barrett, 'she prefers the romantic voice of the eternal artist to the political voice of the artist as propagandist.'[68] Woolf teases out some politics only to cover up what she stirs up under the blanket of 'the vision'. Yet, the vision, as we learn from the climax of *To the Lighthouse,* is the thing that will never be seen, and the things that we cannot see are, also, the things most palpable to Woolf. As she wrote to Stephen Spender on the difficulties of reproducing war imaginatively and from the basis of personal recollection: 'Its the thing we do in the dark that is more real.'[69] Woolf raises the spectre of social responsibility and politics, but she is ultimately more concerned to make this spectre work as part of her writing praxis, hence the ambiguity of the representation of Mrs McNab. Socially, Woolf feels distaste for her; artistically, Mrs McNab symbolizes what is at the heart of literary representation and possibility—Mrs McNab is inchoate, fluid, mutable, chaotic, and insistent. When Lily catches a glimpse of her as she is again struggling with the structural difficulties of her painting, the appearance of Mrs McNab contributes to what Lily thinks of as 'some common feeling which held the whole together'.[70]

In her final, unfinished piece, 'Anon', Woolf returned to a figure she had invoked in *A Room of One's Own* (1929). 'Anon', she had ventured to suggest in this text, represented a lost history of female representation: like the voice of Mrs McNab, Anon also refuses to be stifled—Anon is 'the common voice singing out of doors'.[71] Woolf's own self-appointed task was to inscribe women into both history and a literary tradition. She did this with the 'infinitely obscure lives that remain to be recorded' and which Mary Beton, in *A Room of One's Own,* hopes will be recorded in Mary Carmichael's work. The 'infinitely obscure lives' represented the future of women's writing: 'from the women at the street corners with their arms akimbo, and the rings embedded in their fat swollen fingers, talking with a gesticulation like the swing of Shakespeare's words; or from the violet-sellers and match-sellers and old crones stationed under doorways'.[72] In Woolf's writing, the figures with arms akimbo, the violet-sellers, and old crones are both unsettling but also affirmative, sometimes mystical figures, from the 'old blind woman' singing from 'the depths of her gay wild heart—her sinful, tanned heart'[73] to the old woman singing about the memory of 'some primeval May'[74] who fertilizes the post-war barren cityscape of the Euston Road, to the leering and lurching Mrs McNab and the violet-selling beggar in *The Years*, who shocks the middle-class Martin Pargiter: 'She had no nose; her face was seamed with white patches; there were red rims for nostrils. She had no nose.'[75] All of these women are fixtures of the city; they are encountered as part of the daily occurrences of people's lives. But they are also testimony to how Woolf believed the writer must engage with the reader: 'by putting before him something which he recognises, which therefore stimulates his imagination, and makes him willing to co-operate in the far more difficult business of intimacy'.[76]

In a review of a poem, 'The Village Wife's Lament', written just before the end of the war, Woolf criticizes the poet, Maurice Hewlett, for his inability to provide a convincing account of a woman's grief at the death of her husband, killed in action, and after that, the death of her infant son. Woolf's criticism was that the poem conveyed 'not so much . . . the thoughts and laments of the woman herself, as the words of a very sympathetic spectator who is doing his best to express what he supposes must be there beneath the silence and at the heart of the tears'.[77] For Woolf, this is game-playing merely, and such textual transvestism will not do. An articulate man writing about the inarticulate grief of a woman was doomed to fail. Silence, wrote Woolf, would have been better, for 'Perhaps it is the coarseness—the quality that is the most difficult of all for the educated to come by—that is lacking.'[78] But this is not a value-judgement: it is celebration: 'By coarseness we mean something as far removed from vulgarity as can be. We mean something vehement, full-throated, carrying down in its rush sticks and stones and fragments of human nature pell-mell.'[79]

NOTES

1. Philip Gibbs, *Realities of War* (London, 1920), 24.
2. 'Two Soldier Poets', *Times Literary Supplement*, 11 July 1918; repr. in Virginia Woolf, *Essays 1912–1918*, ed. Andrew McNeillie, ii (London, 1987), 269–70.
3. C. G. Jung, 'Woman in Europe' (1927), repr. in *Aspects of the Feminine* (London, 1982), 56.
4. *The Great War and Women's Consciousness: Images of Militarism and Womanhood in Women's Writing, 1914–64* (Basingstoke, 1990), 128–9.

5. 10 Nov. 1919, in *The Letters of Katherine Mansfield*; cited in Samuel Hynes, *A War Imagined: The First World War and English Culture* (London, 1990), 269.
6. 30 Apr. 1937, in *Letters*, ed. Nigel Nicolson and Joanne Trautmann, vi (1936–41) (London, 1980), 122.
7. June (?) 1906, in *Letters*, i (1888–1912) (London, 1975), 227.
8. 17 Dec. 1933, *Diary*, ed. Anne Olivier Bell, iv (1931–5) (Harmondsworth, 1983), 193. See also *Diary*, i (1915–19) (Harmondsworth, 1979), 6 Dec. 1917, 3 Jan. 1918, which is a probable source for the raid scene in the 1917 chapter, and 8 Mar. 1918.
9. 12 July 1919, *Diary*, i. 291.
10. 18 Feb. 1921, *Diary*, ii (1920–4) (Harmondsworth, 1981), 92.
11. V. W. to Margaret Llewellyn Davies, 23 Jan. 1916, in *Letters*, ii (1912–22) (London, 1976), 76.
12. 19 July 1919, *Diary*, i. 292.
13. *To the Lighthouse: The Original Holograph Draft*, ed. Susan Dick (London, 1983), 222.
14. Ibid.
15. Paul Fussell, *The Great War and Modern Memory* (Oxford, 1977), 88. Lord Northcliffe was the proprietor of *The Times.*
16. *Jacob's Room* (1922; London, 1990), 172.
17. Sandra Gilbert and Susan Gubar, *No Man's Land: the Place of the Woman Writer in the Twentieth Century*, ii: *Sexchanges* (New Haven, 1989), 315.
18. 30 Oct. 1926, *Diary*, iii (1925–30) (Harmondsworth, 1980), 114.
19. *Holograph Draft*, 216.
20. *To the Lighthouse* (1927; London, 1990), 133.
21. Rose Macaulay, *Non-Combatants and Others* (London, 1916), 152–3.
22. *To the Lighthouse*, 124.
23. Ibid. 125.
24. *Holograph Draft*, 214.
25. *To the Lighthouse*, 128.
26. Gayatri Chakravorty Spivak, 'Unmaking and Making in *To the Lighthouse*', in her *In Other Worlds: Essays in Cultural Politics* (New York, 1987), 38.
27. *Holograph Draft*, 223.
28. Leonard Woolf, *Downhill all the Way 1919–1939* (Oxford, 1980), 191.
29. Leonard Woolf, *Beginning Again* (Oxford, 1980), 103–5.
30. Clive Bell, *Civilization* (London, 1928), 205.
31. John Maynard Keynes, *The Economic Consequences of the Peace* (London, 1919), 279.
32. Cited in Hynes, *A War Imagined*, 244.
33. Sigmund Freud, 'Thoughts for the Time on War and Death' (1915), in *The Standard Edition of the Complete Psychological Works of Sigmund Freud*, xiv (London, 1914–16), 285.
34. 15 Nov. 1915, in *Letters*, ii. 71.
35. 24 July 1919, *Diary*, i. 294.
36. 19 July 1919, *Diary*, i. 292.
37. 20 July 1919, *Diary*, i. 294.
38. 5 Jan. 1918, *Diary*, i. 100.
39. *Holograph Draft*, 214.
40. 1 May 1918, *Diary*, i. 144.
41. *To the Lighthouse*, 70.

42. Ibid. 71.
43. Ibid. 94.
44. Ibid. 95.
45. Ibid.
46. Sir Edward Grey, *Twenty Five Years 1892–1916* (1925), cited in Hynes, *A War Imagined*, 3.
47. *To the Lighthouse*, 119.
48. *Holograph Draft*, 227–8.
49. Ibid. 222.
50. *To the Lighthouse*, 44.
51. Ibid. 34.
52. Ibid. 35.
53. Ibid.
54. Ibid.
55. 'Character in Fiction', *Criterion*, July 1924; repr. in *Essays*, iii (London, 1988), 422.
56. *To the Lighthouse*, 33.
57. Ibid. 35.
58. *Holograph Draft*, 229.
59. Ibid. 232.
60. Ibid. 229.
61. *To the Lighthouse*, 130.
62. *Mrs Dalloway* (1925; Oxford, 1992), 5.
63. 'Professions for Women', repr. in *The Pargiters*, ed. Mitchell Leaska (London, 1978), p. xxxix.
64. Ibid. p. xxvii.
65. 'Character in Fiction', 430.
66. Hermione Lee, 'Virginia Woolf and Offence', in John Batchelor (ed.), *The Art of Literary Biography* (Oxford, 1995), 133. Lee is citing Jane Marcus.
67. 'Character in Fiction', 426.
68. Michèle Barrett, *Virginia Woolf: Women and Writing* (London, 1979), 22.
69. V. W. to Stephen Spender, 30 Apr. 1937, in *Letters*, vi. 122.
70. *To the Lighthouse*, 183.
71. 'Anon', repr. in Bonnie Kime Scott (ed.), *The Gender of Modernism* (Bloomington, Ind., 1990), 692–3.
72. *A Room of One's Own* (London, 1977), 85.
73. *Jacob's Room*, 61.
74. *Mrs Dalloway*, 71.
75. *The Years* (1937; London, 1990), 206.
76. 'Character in Fiction', 431.
77. 'War in the Village', Review, *Times Literary Supplement*, 12 Sept. 1918; repr. in *Essays*, ii. 293.
78. Ibid.
79. Ibid.

7

'It goes on happening': Frances Bellerby and the Great War

NATHALIE BLONDEL

> Oh yes, the war: the inseverable bond between all men, women and children (yes, and children—I am not muddling my dates) whose lives it broke; like having had the same operation as someone you meet casually—what a bond! The Wonderful Great War That Came To A Bad End with the Peace That Passeth Understanding.
>
> (Frances Bellerby, 'Ex-Service')

THE 'Wonderful Great War' of 1914–18 haunts the work of the neglected English writer Frances Bellerby (1899–1973). Not trench warfare as experienced by soldiers at the front, but the effects of war on civilians and ex-soldiers who survive in England. In narratives which are set before, during, and after the war, Frances Bellerby depicts the ordinary daily activities of life for the middle classes in English towns and villages—school, work, attending church, socializing, going on holiday. Parochial the settings may be; the writing is not. For what makes Frances Bellerby's fiction distinctive and compelling is the way it shows how this fragile interwoven cloth of respectable English life sometimes veils but often cannot protect the bereaved fathers, mothers, sisters, wives, children, friends, and ex-soldiers whose lives have been broken by their sense of loss. People live double lives: they interact with the living whilst dwelling in memories of the dead.

As Frances Bellerby's work illustrates, the results of this 'double-exposure' vary from one character to another. In *Hath the Rain a Father?*, one of the two novels I shall be discussing, the protagonist, Elizabeth Gray, has a vision of her cousin Julian, who has been killed in the war. It is momentary and takes place some years after his death: 'As she approached the broken gate in the top hedge she raised her eyes, and saw Julian waiting there.'[1] This deadpan statement is followed by a break in the narrative, yet this epiphanic apparition is enough to sustain Elizabeth for the next few years. By contrast, her father, the Revd Oliver Gray, is increasingly obsessed by what he sees as the senseless war-death of his son Roger, and he withdraws more and more into his memories until eventually he dies. That the war killed people as effectively with grief as with bayonets and bombs is a fact repeatedly highlighted by Frances Bellerby's narratives. The war may not always be in the foreground, but as this chapter will show, its effects are insidious and immanent.

'There is a Spirit in the Fire,' writes Frances Bellerby in an early essay, 'Fires', explaining:

> I am not referring to Fire the element, which Man and Beast from all time have known to be spiritual; but I mean the Fire built of coal and wood which, from our controlling grates, gives us warmth, company, comfort. Tidy, economical folk who hanker after electric and gas fires, need read no further; their darlings are full of common sense indeed, and—as with so many people given to that plenitude—have no heart. To make all clear—I am now writing of Fires, in grates, and with hearts.[2]

The combination of confident assertiveness, humorous tone, and an interest in the preternatural is characteristic of Frances Bellerby's writing. Often, she explores the strange and the uncanny, which, like the Spirit in the Fire:

> is . . . thus; flickering firelight can play cruel tricks upon human senses. It can, for instance, turn the face of another in the room with you to a horrible skeleton face . . . you shut your eyes in terror, and open them to find nothing unusual; but in a moment the unsteady light plays upon the face from which you cannot now keep your eyes . . . again you are looking upon a grinning skull . . . There is no crueller trick than this: in *that* deep armchair, just where & how it always used to be, is the shadowed figure of one who can never come again . . . so real appears the quiet, resting figure, that you lean forward, half-hoping, half-believing . . . but the chair is empty, & the firelight dies down subdued, as though ashamed of having hurt you so cruelly. There is a Spirit in the Fire, a terrible, torturing Spirit; who, knowing more about you than anyone else knows, can wound so much the more deeply.[3]

Unlike other writers in this collection, such as May Sinclair and Mary Butts, who shared their era's fascination with the occult and the supernatural, Frances Bellerby never made a study of these other dimensions. Instead, the ghosts which appear in her fictions, her 'shadowed figures', are always people who have died and therefore 'who can never come again', except in this ethereal form.

Since Frances Bellerby is probably the least well-known writer to appear in this volume, a few biographical details may be helpful, especially as they are, in some respects, typical of women of her generation and her class. Anyone wishing for a more detailed account should read the late Robert Gittings's insightful biographical introduction to the 1986 edition of Frances Bellerby's *Selected Poems.*

Born in south Bristol as Mary Eirene Frances Parker[4] on 29 August 1899, Frances Bellerby (as she later became) grew up in the poor area of Crew's Hole where her father was the vicar of the parish church of St Aidan's. Her mother was a nurse who gave up her job to bring up the children and help run the parish. Frances Bellerby had one sibling, an elder brother Jack, born in 1896, to whom she was extremely close. She attended Mortimer House School in Clifton and was a much-liked and outstanding pupil. Her early outspoken pantheistic beliefs, however, led her into some trouble: 'it distressed me, for I adored school', she conceded sixty years later. 'But it made no fragment of difference to my Pantheism.'[5] This assertion shows how early Frances Bellerby acquired her own vision of the world—a vision which remained unaltered all her life.

As soon as the First World War broke out her brother joined the Coldstream Guards as a private, pretending to be 22 when he was only 18. The following year, on 8 August 1915, he was blown up in France. 'Never mourn the deathless dead,' opens '1915',[6] the final version of a poem Frances Bellerby published in response to Jack's death, a death which is all too representative of soldiers of the 'Wonderful Great War That Came To A Bad End with the Peace That Passeth Understanding', as the narrator wryly terms it in 'Ex-Service'.[7] In 1970 she wrote that, far from diminishing, the experience of his death '*goes on happening*',[8] and her writing reflects the way in which the past does not disappear but remains in the minds of those who remember, who cannot help but remember. Thus she dedicated her 1970 *Selected Poems* 'To the brief but everlasting life of my brother'.

This sense of the persistence of the dead goes some way towards explaining why the Great War and the subsequent Long

Week-End form the focus of so much of her fiction. Fifteen years old when the war broke out, Frances Bellerby saw many of her generation die before they reached adulthood. Rereading the 1914 and 1915 Oxford anthologies of poetry when they were reissued in the 1960s, she commented on how they made 'such sorrowful reading now. Some were dead before the 1915 publication . . . [and the editor] in the Foreword to the 1914 collection, speaks of it as being a year of promise.'[9]

'Once the world had belonged to himself . . . and his contemporaries, for a short time; a very short time,' until it was 'cut off as with a sweeping scythe', muses Dan in 'Walking along a Frieze', one of her characters who was 'lucky' enough to come back from the war.[10] This story goes on to explore the fracture in outlook the experience of war created between those who fought and the succeeding generation. As with many of Frances Bellerby's stories, the plot of 'Walking along a Frieze' is simple—in this case a walking-tour in England undertaken by two friends. Yet, increasingly the older war veteran Dan is driven to fits of fury towards the younger Mark, whom he feels has no understanding of the psychological scars caused by the war. At one point, when Dan is unable to sleep because of nightmares of war, he looks over at Mark's peaceful sleeping face: 'Plenty of things you don't even know could exist, young Mark, young cock-of-the-walk-of-life,' thinks Dan, adding angrily:

> If I tried to tell you about them you'd smile oh so gently and change the subject oh so tactfully. Bad for the old buffer to think about such things. Morbid. *Morbid*! As though life weren't utterly morbid! But you wouldn't know that. You don't know much. What if I showed you young James, who would have played for England? What if I pointed him out, hanging screaming on barbed wire? You'd not hear or see. You'd not believe he was the finest three-quarters for his age that had been known—You wouldn't believe either that Gerald would be known the world over as a poet by now, if he weren't in the mental home where he's been since he was about your age. You wouldn't believe. Poor chap, you'd say. Poor chap—It's *you* who are twenty-one now, the world's *your* toy now, my friends and I are less than ghosts—[11]

'Less than ghosts'—Dan's negative self-characterization of having even less reality and presence than an ethereal phantom—demonstrates survivors' feelings of frustration at the invisibility and incommunicability of the experience of war for those who had never been there; after all, like most women, Frances

Bellerby never went to the front. Dan's sense of injustice is so great that he almost strangles Mark, but recovers himself just in time and Mark is never aware how close he came to being yet another victim of war. Dan is only one of Frances Bellerby's many characters who no longer understands the world he now lives in; in 'The Yard Door Rattles', a story set in the 1920s, the father of a dead war-hero spends many evenings alone musing on how 'war was insane waste' and how his 'boy's brief life seemed far distant, and to have been lived in a different phase of the world's being'.[12]

Jack Parker's death led to the break-up of what had been an extremely close-knit family: Mrs Parker had a nervous breakdown and committed suicide in 1932. As a result Frances Bellerby felt a sense of estrangement from her father, who died in 1954. Her marriage in 1929 to John Rotherford Bellerby, who would later become a noted economist, was not a happy one and they finally separated permanently in the summer of 1940 when she went to live in Plash Mill, a secluded cottage on Bodmin Moor in Cornwall. Whilst she had made up poetry from the age of 3 or 4, she was unable to write any poems during her marriage and confided to her journal that these had been '12 lost years'.[13]

Quite apart from her personal loss (she outlived all her family by more than twenty years), Frances Bellerby suffered from three severe physical handicaps. An accident in 1935 led to a spinal injury which debilitated her for most of her life. In 1950 she discovered that she had cancer in both breasts and underwent excruciating X-ray therapy followed by an operation in 1951. 'Did you know I was condemned to death (cancer) in 1951? Left Plash Mill on a stretcher in an ambulance. Never saw it again,' she wrote over twenty years later.[14] For when she left hospital she moved for a time to Clearbrook on the southern edge of Dartmoor and then to Goveton, near Kingsbridge, in south Devon, where she remained until her death. She felt at the time that she had died and been reborn like Lazarus, the name she gave to a poem which presented this experience. Indeed several of her stories, e.g. 'Soft and Fair' and 'Walking from Harley Street', are centred on acutely and often terminally ill women.

In the autumn of 1957, when all her family had been dead for some years, Frances Bellerby started to write her autobiography. Over the next eight years she worked at this 'life' but eventually gave up because of the pain it caused her: 'It draws blood at every touch. Can I live through it?'[15] she asked herself in 1965. Three years later she explained to a friend that fear of insanity prevented her from completing the work. The harrowing nature of this journey into her past is reflected in the original title she gave to the project: 'A pebble in the pocket on which the hand automatically closes in moments of stress or in abeyance'.[16] In a sense there was no need for Frances Bellerby to publish her autobiography—all the information and experience which she could bear to write about had already been distilled into her fiction.

In 1957, just before beginning her autobiography, Frances Bellerby was diagnosed as having intermittent claudication, a condition which causes cramplike pains and weakness in all the limbs. In 1972 the cancer returned and she eventually died from this on 30 July 1975. The poet Charles Causley, who had championed her work since the 1940s, wrote in her obituary in *The Times* a few days later, 'The death . . . of Frances Bellerby . . . has robbed contemporary poetry [and prose, I would claim] of a unique and distinguished voice,' adding: 'To read her, is to be in the presence of a true original.'[17]

Whilst these later years were isolated and painful, Frances Bellerby remained extraordinarily productive: most of her fiction was published in this period and received favourable reviews, as did her volumes of poetry. Several of her stories were included in O'Brien's annual *Best Short Stories* collections.[18] Perusal of her correspondence and interviews shows that she read a great deal and kept in touch with what happened in the world, albeit at a distance, and, as in her youth, her poems and stories continued to be published in magazines and anthologies such as *Orion*, *Unicorn*, and *New English Weekly*, *One and All: A Selection of Stories from Cornwall* (1951), and *The Chatto Book of Modern Poetry 1915–1955* (1956), edited by Cecil Day Lewis and John Lehmann. Despite the often extreme pain that she felt, she never lost her sense of humour. 'By the way,' she once wrote to a friend, 'I never forget Katherine Mansfield's phrase of description of what life feels like sometimes—"eating ashes with a fish-fork"!'[19] Indeed, 'never forgetting' seems to have been Frances Bellerby's gift and curse: she could read through a long poem once or twice before going to sleep and remember it perfectly the next day; yet it is also the reason that she lived and relived her past life with such intensity.

If the name of Frances Bellerby is remembered today, it is for her poetry. She saw herself primarily as a poet, and several volumes of her finely wrought and powerful poetry were published during her lifetime and after her death. Surprisingly, however, none of her powerful poems is included in Catherine Reilly's *Scars upon my Heart: Women's Poetry and Verse of the First World War.*[20] Whilst I shall refer to several of her poems, this chapter will focus on her prose narratives, for, as the poet Jeremy Hooker argues, 'Frances Bellerby brought as much rigour and passion to the art of the short story as she brought to the poem.'[21] I would add that this applies to all of her prose. 'I do indeed love words,' Frances Bellerby once declared, with the tribute: 'my mother was an impassioned dictionary-reader—that's how I grew up.'[22] Yet her relationship to language is by no means a simple or easy one: 'words distort experience, yes,' she acknowledged in a letter to her friend Bill Cotterell, adding: 'But words *are* experience—what one does with them, & what they do with one.'[23]

Regrettably, most of Frances Bellerby's prose has never been reprinted. The only text which is currently in print is the volume of *Selected Stories* published by Enitharmon Press in 1986; indeed the Enitharmon Press (and its editor at the time, Alan Clodd) is the only publisher to have recognized the importance of Frances Bellerby's work in recent years. This selection, chosen and introduced by Jeremy Hooker, includes seventeen stories from the three volumes of short stories which were published during her lifetime: *Come to an End and Other Stories* (1939), *The Acorn and the Cup with Other Stories* (1948), and *A Breathless Child and Other Stories* (1952). In addition to these works I shall refer to Frances Bellerby's earliest publication, *Perhaps?* (1927), a collection of fifteen essays and stories, and two of her novels: *The Unspoiled* (1928) and *Hath the Rain a Father?* (1946). These make up the majority of her fictional works—a more complete bibliography lies at the end of this chapter.

Though most of Frances Bellerby's fiction was not published until the Second World War and after, the Great War informs most of her narratives. Rather than offering a close analysis of specific texts, I shall consider some of the myriad ways the war is evoked and invoked across her work. For to read Frances Bellerby's work is to acquire a kind of kaleidoscopic view of the war: how stable and safe England seemed before it; the impact of its outbreak on everyone, adults and children, those who fought at the front, but equally those who stayed 'at home'; its consequences both physical and mental for the 'survivors'; to the extent, even, in 'The Carol', of having a dead soldier ghost-narrate the story of his brief return to his childhood bedroom. Her stories consider the implications of human mortality—the very different ways the dead are remembered or cast out by the living, as the bereaved bear the invisible burden of death-in-life. This gives a number of her characters an air of not being wholly alive as, for example, Richard Gail in the story 'A Breathless Child'.

This twenty-page narrative is set just after the First World War and centres on Ursula, an extremely gifted and intelligent 9-year-old who has severe physical handicaps as the result of an accident, yet whose literary talents and sensitivity are recognized by Miss Moon, her governess. Ursula has a grown-up brother Charles, who was at war when the accident happened, and whilst he takes Ursula out for tea occasionally, it is clear that he finds it difficult to deal with her physical problems. One afternoon Richard Gail, a friend of Charles, takes Ursula to a exhibition of contemporary paintings. All that Charles tells Miss Moon about Richard Gail is that he has had 'a bad time in the war, of course',[24] and although this poet and critic is perfectly charming and well-mannered, there is something about him which troubles the observant Miss Moon, who, as the narrator tells us, is '"sensible" . . . in the true meaning of that often abused word' (*SS* 133). Whilst it is only later in the story that we are told what Gail's 'bad time' involved (which I shall reveal below), we learn how it is affecting him from Miss Moon's Austenian sensibility. For when 'this truly sensible woman . . . turned her *wide, reverent, intelligent, singularly clear,* gaze . . . upon Richard' (my emphases):

> suddenly, almost with the effect of falling through a curtain, she became aware of the extraordinary graveness of Richard's rather sunken nearly colourless dark eyes; for an instant, she was dismayed, and quite bewildered, and it occurred to her that his eyes seemed to be actually watching, and listening to, something else, all the time he talked, and listened, and ate. 'Why, he isn't *real*!' thought Miss Moon. And in that moment of blank astonishment her mind seemed to her to rear back violently, as though, frisking along through a buttercup field, it had come suddenly to the edge of a gaping black hole. Sensibly, she set her mind to a sober walk around that black hole. (*SS* 133)[25]

Frances Bellerby's use of metaphor is striking. Simple yet stark images occur throughout her work and result in her stories being surprising in ways which can be exciting, distressing, and, at times, disconcerting, as you can never be quite sure which way they will turn. To a certain extent her writing acts as a kind of remembrancer pointing both to the experiences of the 1914–18 war but, more than this, to the unpredictability of life which is true far beyond the context of any wartime. Frances Bellerby described herself as a 'sacramentalist rather than a symbolist'[26] and there is a transcendental quality in her writing which makes it both reflective of her period and still relevant today. 'The only sure thing about the Future is that it contains surprises,'[27] we are told in her first novel, *The Unspoiled*, and this belief is one Frances Bellerby returns to repeatedly: in 'Pre-war', a story included in her first collection of stories in 1939, we are told that 'Life had suddenly become a stranger' for the two children because 'for three days their mother had been shut away from them in her bedroom' (*SS* 17). In fact she is just ill, but the break this creates in the normalizing routines of childhood lead the children to consider for the first time what mortality might mean. With her typically ironic humour, Frances Bellerby has the children climb to the top of the house where the older child fixes a tin soldier to the roof and scratches in their initials and the date, '1/1/11'. Whilst he does this ostensibly for other children to find 'long after we've gone', it is clear that the date is not random and that (with a little rearrangement of numbers) Frances Bellerby is also referring obliquely to the Great War and the date of the armistice: 11/11 (*SS* 20).

The Acorn and the Cup with Other Stories, published almost ten years later, includes 'My Brother Martin', which opens with the same preoccupation about the unpredictability of experience:

> They say you can get used to anything. But it would be absurd to assert that you can get used to life. Talk about life, read about it, learn the consolation of analysing it; but if you let yourself imagine you have become used to it, you are a poor fool and a severe shock is coming your way. Sooner or later, there you'll be, gasping and crying: 'Why it's impossible! It can't be! Why, only the other day! . . .[28]

It is a story of a few pages in which the narrator describes the shock of hearing of his brother Martin's sudden death. This is not a war death; yet the narrator's sense of Martin's simultaneous presence and absence leads him to conclude: 'a jet of words soar up in my mind, words I have read in a story by a man called Richard Wright, and it seems to me that I see the words, and read them, and say them, and hear them said, and also that I think them: *The doomed living and the dead that never dies.*'[29] Here the estrangement of the bereaved from the world of the living is imaged through their estrangement from language itself. The narrator can speak his grief only mediated by the words of another. We could perhaps see ghosts themselves as a kind of quotation: bodies that stray into our time and space from another world, like phrases out of context. When asked in an interview whether she wrote 'to give pleasure? To communicate?', Frances Bellerby replied: 'Not to give pleasure. . . . To communicate, yes; but not primarily. The attempt to communicate comes when the first draft is finished. And if communication is achieved—the relief is tremendous, like morphia after pain.'[30] Frances Bellerby's reference to morphia is not merely a metaphorical one, for, as I have explained, she wrote from a position of experience of repeated serious illness. 'Why on earth does one write? Self-justification? Or a wild attempt at it?' declares one of her characters. Frances Bellerby has no answer, but goes on to describe the process of writing as 'the one occupation which can be done in hospitals, in damp dilapidated "furnished cottages", in attic "flatlets", in Lyons tea-shops, in waiting-rooms, in grimy bed-sitting-rooms dark as night the twenty-four hours through—Oh, charming places in which to put pen to paper, in which to open one's self out as a vessel for the spirit to pour through!'[31]

During and after the First World War, the practice of double-exposure developed in the late nineteenth century was used to create photographs in which dead soldiers were superimposed on the portraits of living relatives as a sign of their continued presence in the minds of the bereaved. Frances Bellerby's fiction creates literary equivalents to these photographs by showing the ways in which memories of the dead 'cruelly, teasingly, vividly' continue to affect the living (*TU* 38). This is often achieved through the depiction of closely observed details—thus, as mentioned above, in *Hath the Rain a Father?* the Revd Oliver Gray is broken by his son's death in the war. In the nervous collapse which precedes his death, it is not his eyes, nor his face, which show Mrs Gray how much he is suffering; rather: 'Hands, thought his wife, can wear no mask. Oliver's hands had shown his struggle and growing exhaustion for years, to her; so much more consistently than his face' (*HRF* 45).

At times in Frances Bellerby's work, as in her poem '1915' and also in the short story 'The Acorn and the Cup', the dead become deathless, as temporal experiences become part of some larger pattern. Frances Bellerby's visionary sense was with her as a young child: 'I am Welsh on my mother's side. It is a powerful streak in my blood,'[32] she once wrote, commenting elsewhere how 'archetypal memories do play an influential part . . . more so perhaps in people of Celtic blood'[33] (a conviction that led to an interest in Laurens van der Post's work). The pantheism for which she was chastised at school led to moments of revelation. 'At 16,' she explained in a postscript to a letter in 1973, 'I once saw in the March stars above the Netball Court at school, my brother's young life and death and my life and death and all Life and Death—beautiful, calm and perfect for ever.'[34] A month later she referred again to the 'faint stars above the Netball Court', explaining that 'It is by this and other such experiences throughout life; that I live.'[35] Not surprisingly, Frances Bellerby was very interested in Blake's work, a passion she shared with the poet Kathleen Raine, with whom she corresponded about the magical power of language.

Frances Bellerby's unsentimental, sympathetic understanding of children and the effect of the war upon them is present in many of her narratives, several of which such as 'Pre-war', 'The Cut Finger', and 'Such an Experienced House', centre on children. Especially poignant is the story 'Winter Afternoon', which opens: 'Although the war was over, many of the children remained in the Evacuees' Hostel on the moorland road; they had, for a variety of reasons provided by life or by death, nowhere else to go' (*SS* 159). Whilst this opening might appear to be referring to Second World War evacuees, the story is set in the early 1920s and describes how three war orphans spend a few hours with a woman who gives them buns, pleased to have someone to talk to. When they ask about her own children she feels an unaccustomed sense of 'at-homeness' when talking about her son who died in the war: 'No need to choose words. They'd every one been chosen years and years ago, and here they were . . . she was moved by an emotion whose existence she had forgotten long ago, an emotion of such peace, gentle safety, and complete at-homeness, as she had neither experienced nor hoped to experience since that day in 1917 when War had splintered her brittle world' (*SS* 167).

'Time never mends,' declares Felicity, the middle-aged narrator of one of Frances Bellerby's longer short stories, 'The Green Cupboard', when relating the death of her uncle Paul, who was 'blown to pieces at dawn one summer's morning' during 'that war'. 'I am thankful, really,' she continues: 'to have learnt at least that one lesson so early in life, learnt it once and for all. It is, I may say, the one certainty which I have always carried with me. So at least one cruel false treacherous cliché has never had power to concern me' (*SS* 125). This categorical conviction that time never mends is part of Frances Bellerby's passionate attack on sentimental equivocations about loss of life. Its truth for her is bound up with her sense that memory works to confound any clear-cut boundaries between past and present—as a character in another story explains: 'One thinks: Twenty years ago, twenty years, what an age! But then suddenly it isn't anything at all, and the thing is happening again here and now, happening again and can never stop happening—there isn't any healing in time, none, none, because time, in the usual sense, doesn't exist. . . . If only time were real, if only twenty years meant anything at all . . .'(*SS* 129).

'The Green Cupboard' explores this idea of time's claustrophobia, of the impossibility of 'moving on'. It begins when a child named Janey makes Felicity see that a cupboard, which Felicity had seen as green, is in fact black. 'I lay back in my chair very still with astonishment and with the shock of my predicament,' declares Felicity. 'That cupboard had not been green for about forty years. Yet, until this very afternoon I had thought of it, and seen it, as green. Apple green. Why?' (*SS* 114). This self-questioning is characteristic of Frances Bellerby's writing, her desire to *understand* the way the mind can delude itself. Felicity continues:

> I faced the answer to that. Because of the passionate intensity of my desire to move life back to the time when the cupboard was still green. Yes, I saw clearly that the re-painting of that cupboard symbolised for me the changes which I had never, in spite of all pretence, ceased to blame and deplore. I had been at-home in life before the re-painting of the green cupboard. But ever since then I had been a homesick stranger. And there was something in my mind, something blind,

unreasoning, & desperate, which believed that if the cupboard were still green, life also would be still my home. And so, my mind had kept the cupboard green. And this fact, with the fact of my endless, unappeased, homesickness, the innocent and merry Janey yesterday brought crashing down upon me, destroying all my 'discipline' of the years. Today my conscious mind goes back, goes back. (*SS* 114–15)

What the narrator is doing here is exploring her mind's refusal to 'see' any change which would force her to recognize that she was no longer 'at-home in life'. Whilst the dislocation is initially produced by the break-up of her parents' marriage, it is actually what happens after that, the results of the First World War, which cause the 'discipline' of decades of misremembering. In the rest of the story the narrator 'goes back, goes back' over her painful past. Her name, Felicity (like 'Felix' and 'Felicity' in Mary Butts's *Armed with Madness* and *Death of Felicity Taverner*), is quite clearly ironic, in view of the traumatic events of her teenage years, just before, during, and after the First World War.

The green cupboard had been painted black after her father, an architect, had left her mother to live with his secretary. Standing in her father's study, it had contained all his work materials, including the green ink with which he drew the bushes on his plans, for which at that time Felicity 'had a passion' (*SS* 116). The significance of the original function and layout of this room was so great that though it was later used as a music-room, even as an adult she continued to remember it in its former appearance. Thus, as she explains: 'every time I opened the door a mental picture was newly obliterated by the new appearance of the room. Every time. I grew not to heed it at all, but it happened every time. And one of the changed unchanged things was the cupboard' (*SS* 120). Through her use of the symbolic green–black cupboard Frances Bellerby delineates the ways in which remembered and present-day experiences can overlap and become confused. 'The Green Cupboard' is a first-person narrative which self-consciously presents this 'changed unchanged' quality of existence.

The departure of Felicity's father to some extent frees Damaris Stubbs, her mother's friend. The 33-year-old daughter of an extremely conventional father, Damaris is typical of the spinsters who inhabit Bellerby's fictions. They have little or no freedom in late Victorian, Edwardian, and even inter-war England. Instead, like Harriet Frean and Mary Olivier, the eponymous protagonists of novels by May Sinclair, or Mary Jocelyn in F. M. Mayor's *The Rector's Daughter*, these women's outward lives are lived in accordance with and at the mercy of their parents' wishes. In the case of Damaris, this means refusing an invitation from Felicity's mother to accompany her to a classical concert. 'I'd rather', declares her father, 'see my daughter in her coffin than going about the streets as those fallen women do, their shameless heads uncovered' (*SS* 116). For to be a hatless woman, in his eyes, is equivalent to being a 'fallen' one, and Damaris cannot go. According to Felicity, Damaris must have carried out 'some really tremendous rebellion' to have spent so much time with Felicity's mother, Phil, after her father's departure, as a 'woman left by her husband would have been smeared with pitch for [Mr Stubbs]' (*SS* 120).

The eventual destinies of Phil and Damaris, whilst different, are themselves representative of their generation. Initially when Paul, Phil's much-loved younger brother, comes to live with Felicity and Phil, things improve greatly. (Like Damaris, Paul makes his entry into the story at the age of 33, and there is clearly a similarity between their sacrificial slaughter and Christ's.) But then the Great War happens and Paul is killed. As a result Phil becomes insane (as do the governess and Mrs Waring after Jack and Lawrence are killed in 'The Governess') and Damaris, who was pregnant with Paul's child, dies of a miscarriage. Not surprisingly, one of the facts which Felicity is belatedly forced to face is the silence which was cast at that time and since over both her mother's insanity and Damaris's death. Indeed the chilling account of Damaris's death implies a great deal about the fate of some women at that time:

> Her parents had not known that she was pregnant. . . . had she shouted the news in their ears they would either have fallen dead or simply have heard no sound. But Damaris had taken no chances. Damaris had remained silent. And in silence she had died. I suppose her to have been in agony as she died, but she would not utter a cry that could disturb those two squat nightgowned sleepers in the other room, virtuous in their double-bed where the blasphemed flesh mouldered to its final foulness of death. (*SS* 126)

Since she was not a soldier at the front, Damaris's death passed unnoticed, and yet she was clearly as much a victim of the war as Paul.

Frances Bellerby's description of the early months of the First World War powerfully conveys both its initial lack of reality for Felicity, as for many English children, and the insouciance of Paul's attitude to joining up: 'The outbreak of the war meant nothing at all to me,' the older Felicity remembers:

> until horses were commandeered, in September. The farmer who passed through our edge of the town once a week delivering eggs and butter and vegetables told us about it. Then his horse, of whom I was fond, was taken. Paul's going was in sequence to the horse's. He gave his age as twenty-seven, 'to make sure of seeing some of the fun quickly,' and became a private in in the Coldstream Guards. When people at my school, hearing of his regiment, ejaculated: 'O, I say!' I became impressed myself. There weren't many other privates in our school list of Service relatives. There were no other Guardsmen. (*SS* 125)

Whilst Paul may have represented those men (and boys) who initially saw fighting as 'fun', Lawrence in 'The Governess', who is 15 in 1914, spends every night from then on whispering to himself '"Oh God, let it end before my turn comes, oh dear God, let it end before, for Jesus Christ His sake." Over and over and over again' (*SS* 140). After his death, his father, a vicar, considering such fear to be cowardice, is relieved to be able to indulge in lofty pronouncements about his son's bravery and 'Great Sacrifice'.

In *The Unspoiled*, the novel which Frances Bellerby dedicated to her mother, the Great War and its aftermath are also explored, particularly with regard to the contrasting roles ascribed to men and women. Most of this novel is set in England during and just after the war. Yet it starts with a brief chapter set in the pre-war period, and the apparently insignificant event described there actually encapsulates the divisive social conventions which are exacerbated by the death of so many young men during the war.

It is the summer of 1913. The twins Sylvia and Tony Drayton are the same age as the century. When they play a practical joke on a visitor Tony is caned. Sylvia wants the same punishment but her father refuses: 'If he caned Tony he ought to cane her, he *ought*—he *ought*. It wasn't fair' (*TU* 21). Whilst her brother agrees, he adds in apparent mitigation that:

> 'A man can't beat a girl; surely you know that, you freak!'
> 'Why not?'

'Oh I dunno. It just isn't done.'
'But it isn't fair!'
'Oh well, p'raps not.' (*TU* 22)

In fact, Sylvia's punishment is far worse than her brother's, as her father will not speak to her for the remaining two and a half days of her holiday. This distinction between a brief physical punishment and the (seemingly) long mental torture, which causes Sylvia to fall ill, prepares us for the disparity in their situations in 1917. Their father is killed in action and when the teenagers are sent home from their respective boarding-schools for the funeral, Tony announces that he is going to join up. 'Anyone would take me for nineteen at least' he declares (*TU* 43), and in the following exchange and description Frances Bellerby encapsulates the different life-paths of a boy and girl of this period. 'I tell you, Sylvia,' explains Tony,

> 'I can't stick Daddy's being killed, and my not even fighting—and it may all be over before I get out there if I wait another year. I'd never forgive myself—'
>
> Sylvia stared at her brother, and something leapt in her heart at his words, something furious, sorrowful, envious, admiring. He could sit there, looking straight before him into the dusking room, with his chin thrust out, and his eyes steady, and his voice level, quiet, determined, like a man's. He could do these things because he *was* a man, who could fix his gaze upon some far goal, and, having decided it to be worthy, never once glance at all he had to push ruthlessly aside on his way thither. But Tony might have to push Life itself aside—
>
> She turned to the window and saw the inky bears and crocodiles that the silhouettes of the great cedar made against the clear primrose western sky—and saw the gleam, like water, of the little road between the quiet hills, and the gleam, like clear gold, of a star peering over the straight black hill-top, high against the faintly blue sky—and saw, in the shadowy garden, the pale gleam, like white flowers at night, of two childish faces; the faces of little Tony and Sylvia who were playing quietly out there, in the summer twilight that had long been dead— (*TU* 44–5)

To be a man at this early stage of the war before conscription came into effect meant having the choice of action; women had no such choice. Nor is Frances Bellerby equivocating on the dangers of action, for Sylvia is well aware that Tony's fighting might result in his death, as indeed it does. She is left not only with her complicated tangle of emotions about him, but also with the fact that *she*, because she is a *woman*, can have no equivalent *active* response to her father's death. Instead she must stay behind. 'Thank goodness you can't go,' exclaims Tony. 'I shall at least know that you, and Mother and the Kid [their younger sister] will be safe' (*TU* 45). Tony does not want to have to worry about his sister; like the brothers, fathers, and uncles who went away to war, he wants to have her to fight *for*. By contrast, Sylvia's role in life is contained in the powerful evocation of the night sky and the memory of them both as children. She will remain as the bearer of memories of the dead. Choosing not to go to university, she had played the only part in the war effort available to her by training as a VAD as soon as she left school the following year. 'For a week she was almost content, spending her days chiefly in scrubbing floors and washing-up; too tired at night for anything but sleep' (*TU* 52). However, her brother then dies and Sylvia's real role begins: that of being with her mother. When Sylvia 'dared' to mention her desire to continue her hospital work, 'Mrs Drayton's eyes filled with tears. . . . "Must you go *too*?" she asked piteously. . . . "I shall be quite alone, then." She turned her head away and sighed, and Sylvia caught her murmured words—"the inevitable sacrifice of Motherhood—"' (*TU* 54). And so Sylvia must stay at home. Mrs Drayton's emotional blackmail is by no means unusual. As the narrator of 'The Governess' explains: 'So many parents were saying those . . . words to their daughters then!' (*SS* 142).

Quite apart from a sense of guilt at her mother's grief, Sylvia is trapped by the rigid conventionality of her Aunt Gladys, who comes to live with them. Gladys is shocked to see Sylvia 'sitting astride—hatless—with her hand on a young man's shoulder' when she is given a lift by her friend Peter on his 'motor-bicycle' (*TU* 107); shocked that her skirt is right up to her knees and her hair is bobbed in the modern manner; shocked that Sylvia uses the word 'bitch' in conversation with Peter, even though she was referring to a female dog, because 'the word had a bad meaning and soils the lips of a gentlewoman' (*TU* 110). When Sylvia's mother explains that 'Quite nice girls do these things now and nobody thinks anything of them,' Gladys can only retort indignantly: 'If these are the customs of to-day, give me the modest decent young woman of twenty years ago' (*TU* 108). No doubt many young women were constrained by similar suffocating rules of pre-war morality after the First World War.

Sylvia is saved from the stifling atmosphere by becoming a kennel-maid, in spite of her aunt's belief that 'no gentlewoman could possibly go in for Dog-Breeding' (*TU* 74). As in the story 'The Chestnut Colt' and the chapters in *Hath the Rain a Father?* where the protagonist, Elizabeth, goes to work for a vet, Frances Bellerby's descriptions of animals in *The Unspoiled* are characteristic of her attention to detail—she once complained of D. H. Lawrence's inaccuracy when describing a tortoise. Her love and sanctification of life extended to every living thing including plants and, quite apart from the care she took to present animals realistically and unsentimentally in her fiction, she also wrote passionate articles in their defence such as her essay exposing the practice of rabbit-gassing in Cornwall at that time. In her own life Frances Bellerby tended to the needs of a large variety of animals and birds and once declared that 'the R.S.P.B. is to my mind one of the most valuable organisations in the country'.[36] Human beings, especially children, are often compared to animals in her narratives and *Hath the Rain a Father?* includes a lengthy polemic on what Frances Bellerby terms the 'life-receptacle'. The speech is that of Julian, a young man who would have become a vet had the war not robbed him of his life, and it illustrates how Frances Bellerby's anti-war beliefs are bound up in an all-encompassing religious vision: 'The source of life is all the same,' he declares to his younger cousin Elizabeth:

> So how can Man dare to deny his kindred? When he tortures and destroys, it is his own brother to whom he does it. Perhaps he sometimes is bound to destroy, but he is a blasphemer if he does it without recognition of what it is he does, or to whom. . . . It is always blasphemy, for look—when you've caught a bird in your gin, little man, who is it you have struggling there in terror and anguish? Why, it's God. Of course it's God. Only Man could be such a fool—a low degraded fool, a blasphemer, a sinner against the Holy Ghost—as not to recognise his own brothers and sisters, not to recognise his own father, because he's let the God-spark die within him—and so now, when he beholds life in any other shape but his own he has but room for one idea: Exploit! Exploit! Or failing that, Kill! Kill. Man thinks he is made in the image of God. Who told him so? It is *Life* that is made in the image of God, in the thousand, million images of God. The whole of Life, not only animal life— . . . We knew all these things once, when Man was a purer simpler child, but by now he has forgotten more than he has learnt, and more important things. Now, poor fool, he sees no reason why he should not do as he pleases with the other animals, and with the whole

of creation if he can. For he believes that he is the only soul-possessor. He is a fool. If they, the others, have no soul, then neither has he. He stands or falls with them, his kindred. The source of life is one, and one life-receptacle cannot be informed by soul and another not thus informed, because all are informed by Life itself. (*HRF* 24–6)

The clearly propagandist language of Julian's speech suggests that it was not only pro-war campaigners who used this kind of rhetoric.

Like *The Unspoiled* (and indeed all her fiction), *Hath the Rain a Father*? is set in England. It opens in the summer of 1914 and ends in 1927. Many of the characters in this novel die: both of the young men, Julian and Roger, are killed in action; Roger's father, Oliver, has a nervous breakdown and eventually dies from his grief. His daughter, Elizabeth, unable to carry on with her studies, begins to work for a divorced vet, John King, taking part in his impassioned campaign against gin-trapping. However, he eventually seduces her and, whilst this upsets Elizabeth, it is the long-term physical and mental exhaustion brought on by the war and the continual strain of trying to live out her vision (handed on by Julian) of how the world should be that cause her death.

The writing is powerful, and the work sold well. Frances Bellerby achieves this through the way the characters *affect* one another, the way some sacred quality of life is passed on, despite death. Thus the 'brilliant eternal fortnight of Julian's visit . . . age-long and moment-brief' (*HRF* 22) just before the war remains for his younger cousin an unforgettable, 'deathless' experience and she lives on after his death in a kind of 'communion' with him. Something of the 'understanding' they shared is felt between herself and Mr Edwards, the vicar who stands in for her sick father. In spite of his somewhat ludicrous physical presence, Mr Edwards has a 'spiritual power' (*HRF* 46), the gift to make people feel at ease in his company. Mrs Oliver is greatly helped by his presence as she tries to deal not only with the pain of her husband and daughter, but also with her own grief. Like the bereaved mother in 'A Yard Door Rattles', who knows that 'this [ten years] not sleeping, nobody will ever know what it's been' (*SS* 47), Mrs Gray's sense of bereavement remains unspoken, existing only in her own memories. Her happiest time had been that of Roger's birth: 'There she had spent a time so happy that in retrospect the happiness seemed not actually possible. Not simply had *she* been so happy—the *time* had been.

Looking back, she saw it always as a little brilliantly-coloured square patch, caught right up out of the ordinary grey-blue stretch of Time: a patch not in Time, but not indisputably in Eternity' (*HRF* 48). Yet this quiet, joyful reminiscence inevitably turns to anguish as 'her conscious mind steadily, calmly, [tells] . . . her unconscious':

Listen! Listen, and don't forget again: that red-faced crumpled infant of whom you are thinking was your son Roger, who grew up, and is dead. He has been dead for years. . . . But nevertheless this unshakeable truth seemed no more tinged with possibility than did the brilliant happiness of that scrap of eternal-time. Less, perhaps; for she could see clearly the picture of that happiness, but Roger dead she could never picture. And yet how unaccountable this was! For by all accounts, her own included, that safely immobile infant in the firelit cot had years since, years since, shot right through life and out at the other end! Infant, Child, Adolescent, Soldier, Corpse. Like counting prune-stones . . . (*HRF* 49)

In *Between the Acts* (1941) Virginia Woolf uses an archaic version of the cherry/prune-stone rhyme—'Tinker, tailor, soldier, sailor, apothecary, ploughboy . . .'[37]—to portray a dual sense of the passing of time and its continuity. Frances Bellerby distorts the ordinary counting-game—Tinker, tailor, soldier, sailor, rich man, poor man, beggar man, thief—to point to the extent to which war ravages even innocent children's ditties.

The most ironic aspect of *Hath the Rain a Father?* comes at the very end of the novel, when Mr Edwards is tending Elizabeth's grave. He has a sudden vision in which he hears his 'own excited voice exclaiming':

War? Of course there will be no more war! Why, already, now in 1927, not so very late in time after all, we have seen the last big war! Yes, yes, we have learned our dreadful, bitter lesson, and the deaths of Jesus, of Roger, of Julian, of all those others, have been proved worth-while, have been proved to be the light of their lovely lives—for because of their death, there will never, never again—be—war! (*HRF* 222–3)

Yet it would seem that the 'dreadful, bitter lesson' of the First World War was not learnt; *Hath the Rain a Father?* was published after the Second World War in 1946.

Frances Bellerby's work deserves to be republished. Part of its power stems from its refusal to be merely clever; instead it is always concerned with the essential qualities of life which the senselessness of war threatens to destroy. If on occasion there are awkwardnesses, these are always the result of her taking risks. As this chapter has tried to convey, her writing is both of her time and somehow outside it. Rather than give answers, her narratives tell us to find our own individual ones: in 'The Acorn and the Cup' two people's interpretations of the same event are no less true for being contradictory. Frances Bellerby was concerned to write against what she saw as the damaging effects of hypocritical conventionality especially in a world which had been changed beyond recognition by the Great War. What she was writing against and within was the experience of a generation who had to carry about unforgettable memories like that held by Richard Gail in 'A Breathless Child'. For what was the 'bad time' he had during the war? It was not an event at the front but one that would have been experienced by that civilian majority, women, who could not fight. It is a trauma 'at home', in the England which men were fighting to save, that Richard Gail relives again and again; the memory of when, after an air raid, he

> stared steadily down, trained by practice, at the face of his young wife on the dawn-lit rubble. He noted carefully the excessive beauty and relaxation of the unmarred face, and its defencelessness which was the perfection of its defence. He marked how the body was completely hidden up to the breast under its curious counterpane, and how from that covering the right arm emerged in its memorably exquisite gesture to lie across the neck of the child who lay face downwards near his mother. And, oddly, he both knew, and was waiting to be told, the truth about that gesture. He knew that both arm and child's neck had been severed, but were held in position by the casual stones, and thus for a little while defied their experience. Yet he was waiting to be told all this, and so was obliged to stoop and raise that arm, feeling it, afresh, loosely come up in his hand, seeing the faceless head of their little son, released, roll away until checked in a hollow that might have been made for it . . . (*SS* 83)

NOTES

1. Frances Bellerby, *Hath the Rain a Father?* (London, 1946), 84. Subsequent references to this novel will be prefixed *HRF.* I wish to thank the following for their enthusiastic assistance with regard to this chapter: Dr Charles

Causley, literary executor of Frances Bellerby's estate; Alan Clodd, former editor of Enitharmon Press, who published a great deal of Frances Bellerby's work; David Cotterell for permission to quote from Frances Bellerby's letters to his father Bill Cotterell held at Exeter University Library; Clare Gittings for permission to quote from Robert Gittings's biography of Frances Bellerby and for her very generous gift of her father's Frances Bellerby papers for my perusal; and the library staff at Exeter University. I would also like to thank David Higham Associates for permission to study the Frances Bellerby papers at Exeter University Library and to quote from several of Frances Bellerby's works. My greatest thanks are due to Jeremy Hooker, who first introduced me to Frances Bellerby's work.

2. M. E. Frances Parker (Frances Bellerby), 'Fires', in *Perhaps?* (London, 1927), 15.
3. Ibid. 18.
4. *Perhaps?* (1927) and *The Unspoiled* (1928) were both published under this name.
5. Letter to Bill Cotterell, 29 Mar. [1973], University of Exeter Library, Bill Cotterell Archive. Subsequent references to letters by F. B. are from this Archive.
6. '1915', in Frances Bellerby, *Selected Poems*, ed. Anne Stevenson, with biographical intro., by Robert Gittings (London, 1986), 125.
7. 'Ex-Service', in Frances Bellerby, *Come to an End and Other Stories* (London, 1939), 79.
8. Letter to Marjorie Battcock, quoted by Robert Gittings in *Selected Poems*, ed. Stevenson, 37.
9. Letter to Bill Cotterell, 24 June [1973].
10. 'Walking along a Frieze', in *Come to an End*, 108.
11. Ibid. 117.
12. 'The Yard Door Rattles', in *Come to an End*, 166.
13. Quoted by Robert Gittings in *Selected Poems*, ed. Stevenson, 22.
14. Letter to Bill Cotterell, June [1973].
15. Quoted by Robert Gittings in *Selected Poems*, ed. Stevenson, 35.
16. Ibid. 34.
17. Charles Causley, 'Frances Bellerby', *The Times*, 7 Aug. 1975, 14g.
18. 'Early Summer', in *The Best British Short Stories 1937*, ed. Edward J. O'Brien (Boston, 1937); 'Come to an End', in *The Best British Short Stories 1938*, ed. Edward J. O'Brien (Boston, 1938); 'Sympathy', in *The Best British Short Stories 1940*, ed. Edward J. O'Brien (Boston, 1940).
19. Letter to Bill Cotterell, Oct.–Nov. [1973].
20. Catherine Reilly (ed.), *Scars upon my Heart: Women's Poetry and Verse of the First World War* (London, 1981). There is a biographical entry for Frances Bellerby in *Women's Poetry of the 1930s*, ed. Jane Dawson (London, 1996). Unfortunately none of her poems is reprinted.
21. Frances Bellerby, *Selected Stories*, edited and introduced by Jeremy Hooker (London, 1986) 8–9. References to stories included in Hooker's selection will be prefixed *SS.*
22. Letter to Bill Cotterell, [June–July 1973].
23. Letter to Bill Cotterell, June [1973].
24. 'A Breathless Child', in *Selected Stories*, 131.
25. F.B. repeatedly uses the metaphor of a curtain to refer to a lack of understanding, e.g. in 'Walking along a Frieze' (112) and 'The Yard Door Rattles' (171), both in *Come to an End.*

26. Letter to Bill Cotterell, 31 Mar. [1973].
27. M. E. Frances Parker [F. B.], *The Unspoiled* (London, 1928), 82. Subsequent references to this novel will be prefixed *TU*.
28. 'My Brother Martin', in Frances Bellerby, *The Acorn and the Cup with Other Stories* (London, 1948), 7.
29. Ibid. 12.
30. 'An Interview with Frances Bellerby', *Unicorn* (Winter 1960–1), 13.
31. 'Walking along a Frieze', in *Come to an End*, 106.
32. Letter to Bill Cotterell, [June–July 1973].
33. Letter to Bill Cotterell, 17 Mar. [1973].
34. Letter to Bill Cotterell, 19 Jan. [1973].
35. Letter to Bill Cotterell, 'Feb 17 or so' [1973].
36. Letter to Bill Cotterell, 1–2 Mar. [1973].
37. Virginia Woolf, *Between the Acts* (1941; London, 1992), 32.

Bibliography of Frances Bellerby's Writings

PARKER, M. E. Frances, *Perhaps?* (London, 1927).
—— *The Unspoiled* (London, 1928). (*TU*)
BELLERBY, MARY EIRENE FRANCES, *The Neighbours* (London, 1931).
——*Shadowy Bricks* (London, 1932).
BELLERBY, FRANCES, *Come to an End and Other Stories* (London, 1939).
—— *Plash Mill* (London, 1946).
—— *Hath the Rain a Father?* (London, 1946). (*HRF*)
—— *The Acorn and the Cup with Other Stories* (London, 1948).
——*The Brightening Cloud and Other Poems* (London, 1949).
—— *A Breathless Child and Other Stories* (London, 1952).
—— *The Stone Angel and the Stone Man* (Plymouth, 1958).
—— *The Stuttering Water and Other Poems* (Gillingham, 1970).
—— *Selected Poems*, chosen and introduced by Charles Causley (London, 1970).
—— *The First-Known and Other Poems* (London, 1975).
—— *Selected Poems*, ed. Anne Stevenson; with biographical intro. by Robert Gittings (London, 1986).
—— *Selected Stories*, edited and introduced by Jeremy Hooker (London, 1986). (*SS*)

8

'Still some obstinate emotion remains': Radclyffe Hall and the Meanings of Service

CLAIRE BUCK

'As a woman, I have no country. As a woman I want no country. As a woman my country is the whole world,' writes Virginia Woolf in *Three Guineas* (1938),[1] her exploration of the relationship of militarism and masculinity. Woolf's rejection of patriotic identification is assigned to 'the outsider', her figure for resistance to the 'tyranny of the patriarchal state' (160) and its corollary militarism. The Society of Outsiders which Woolf then proposes in *Three Guineas* stands as an influential model for a feminist politics based on marginality. Emerging out of an analysis of women's exclusion from the institutions of power, her formulation reinterprets the terms and effects of that exclusion as a source of critical and political strength.

Since Woolf, feminists with very different theoretical and political positions have embraced marginality. For example, Jane Marcus argues that feminist criticism 'will only flourish in the collective and in the wild. In captivity, in the rarefied hothouse atmosphere of current academic criticism, it may wither and die'.[2] Likewise, Bonnie Zimmerman quotes the lesbian novelist and critic Bertha Harris's view that the marginality of the lesbian, her status as 'that which has been unspeakable about women',[3] makes her a privileged figure of feminist resistance. Toril Moi in *Sexual/Textual Politics* yokes Woolf to a feminist post-structuralism on the basis of Kristeva's insistence on the structural function of women's marginality in the symbolic order. 'Woman is positioned as the limit to that order and therefore neither inside not outside, neither known nor unknown,'[4] both the support of that order and a threat to its stability.

The immediate textual context for Woolf's proclamation demands, however, a cautious assessment of women's relationship to nation and to patriotism and the difficulties or potential contradictions of a politics of margins. Woolf continues:

> And if, when reason has said its say, still some obstinate emotion remains, some love of England dropped into a child's ears by the cawing of rooks in an elm tree, by the splash of waves on a beach, or by English voices murmuring nursery rhymes, this drop of pure, if irrational, emotion she will make serve her to give to England first what she desires of peace and freedom for the whole world. (166)

The 'obstinate emotion' which remains, love of one's country, is rendered in terms of a nostalgic and poetic English pastoral instilled in childhood. Having no country doesn't free the woman from the vision of belonging, the memory of having once belonged or imagined oneself to have belonged. The counterside of the outsider's political rejection of nationalism and all that it stands for in the late 1930s is 'this drop of pure, if irrational, emotion' which Woolf is attempting to harness to a larger pacifist, internationalist, and rationalist politics. As such, this moment in *Three Guineas* signals Woolf's recognition of the inescapability of the 'irrational' in politics and a demand that we engage it and bind it to pacifism. However, the moment is also an impasse since Woolf's use of a language saturated with nostalgia cannot so easily escape the network of relationships between patriotism, militarism, and an Englishness construed in terms of pastoral elegy. The 'emotion' is caught up in a rhetoric central to the imaginary of patriotism and national identification despite her attempt to make it 'pure'.

The difficult relationship Woolf sets up between a politics of marginality and the inconvenient 'irrational' love of country, and in particular the problem of the languages available to the outsider to frame the terms of her belonging, offers a useful entry to Radclyffe Hall's work. It enables an examination of the relationship of the outsider to a rhetoric of service pervasive throughout Hall's writing, and suggests a new way of looking at those aspects of Hall's work which are frequently seen as most conservative and even laughable, such as her attachment to English upper-middle-class values. In particular, Woolf's difficulties with the identificatory pull of patriotism and its rhetoric suggest the importance of examining the ways in which gender and sexuality intersect with nation in the imagining of political identities. In a statement to her defence counsel in 1928 at the time of the novel's trial for obscenity, Hall said, 'When I wrote *The Well of Loneliness* I had in mind the good of the whole quite as much as the good of congenital inverts.'[5] Her purpose with regard to inversion was to persuade society that inverts should be helped 'to give of their best and thus contribute to the good of the whole'. Written in the inter-war years, Hall's fiction is preoccupied in a variety of ways with this theme of service to society. For example, *The Unlit Lamp* (1924) explores the futility of the Edwardian daughter's self-abnegating duty to her family, and *Adam's Breed* (1926) takes an Italian waiter as its main protagonist. Service is central to Hall's attempts to imagine a place on the inside, whether for the invert in *The Well of Loneliness* (1928) or the Italian immigrant in *Adam's Breed.*

In this context the First World War is necessarily privileged because the rhetoric of service to one's country is one of its key discourses, so that Hall can use the war to depict and explore its relationship to the figure of the outsider. But the source of this rhetoric's attraction is the same as its contradictions with respect to Hall's attempt to imagine a community which could include inverts. The war weds the ideal of service to the language of nationalism, thus offering a model for community and identity. However, its rhetoric makes hegemonic definitions of gender, sexuality, and race structural to the imagined unity of the nation, reproducing the hierarchies and exclusions such unity might be supposed to transcend. As Eric Hobsbawm comments in *The Invention of Tradition,* the imagined community and 'social cohesion' of the modern liberal nation-state is belied by its *de facto* inequalities so that 'some [are] encouraged to feel more equal than others'.[6]

With respect to Hall's primary instance of the outsider, the invert, the rhetoric of patriotism and service during the First World War did not in fact announce a society hospitable to lesbians, even 'at this moment of splendid national endeavour'.[7] Her contemporaries were fully aware of the opportunities which the war opened up for the mannish woman, and less than sanguine about its effects. Lady Londonderry, founder of the Women's Legion, wrote in her 1938 *Retrospect* that 'We had to contend with a section of "She-Men" who wished to be armed to the teeth and who would have looked quite absurd had they had their way'.[8] Similarly, Sharon Ouditt has shown how frequently women's First World War fiction attacks 'women who adopt a "masculinized" construction of leadership'[9] and treats overt lesbian sexuality as troubling women's effective war service by contrast with the inspiring homoeroticism which defines the experience of soldiers. Women's desire to enter the military and to don uniform provoked anxiety about those for whom the wearing of military uniform might signal an inappropriately eager assumption of masculinity which could only taint the 'true patriotism' of normal women. With the radical disturbance of traditional assumptions about women's capacities and their social and economic roles, the figure of the mannish woman was of particular significance. Rather than coming into her own as especially fitted in body and temperament to masculine work, the 'She-Man' is a figure who allows the reinscription of a proper femininity for women undertaking war work, designating as she does an improper usurpation of masculine roles.

Yet in the face of such hostility, of which Hall shows herself well aware, she attributes to the war a special emancipatory status for the female invert which is linked to the opportunities it provides for service. Thus, although a comparatively short episode in *Well of Loneliness*, the war gives Stephen the opportunity for heroism which wins her the Croix de Guerre; the physical scar which becomes a visible mark of her valour as well as an ineradicable mark of her difference; and, most significantly, the opportunity for sexual and romantic fulfilment with another woman. Narratively, the war comes at a crucial moment in the novel, following soon after Stephen has recognized that without sexual fulfilment she cannot succeed as a writer: 'I shall never be a great writer because of my maimed and insufferable body' (217). The war is therefore of considerable importance for what it makes possible in the novel. Its particular significance for Hall's representation of the invert can be gauged by its role in *Adam's Breed* where the main protagonist, Gian-Luca, is also an outsider, but on the grounds of race and nationality rather than gender or sexuality.

In *Adam's Breed* Hall makes no attempt to represent the war as reconfiguring the terms of identity for the outsider, other than to reiterate his alienation. Speaking of Italy's impending entry into the war, Gian-Luca reflects on his embittered feelings of exclusion: 'There is something in my blood tonight that tells me that my people will fight—but it will not make any difference to me; I am English in the eyes of the law.'[10] His uncertain nationality, divided between blood and law, is enough to bar Gian-Luca from the fulfilment promised by the call to serve his country. Because he is a bastard without an Italian father, his naturalization as an English subject separates him from his Italian people; while his Italian origins ironically define the terms of his service in the English army. He is drafted into the 'Army Service Corps' on the strength of his experience as a waiter and refused the entitlement to bear arms and potentially serve as a hero: 'but you're not an Englishman, are you? Aren't you an Italian or something' (200) is the response to his frustrated protests. The privilege of serving one's country as a hero is strictly determined by race and class, as well as gender and sexuality. While others may die for their country, Gian-Luca must fight all his battles 'with the peasants over chickens. A fine victory the capture of a couple of fowls, a splendid victory!' (222)

But Gian-Luca's bitterness is none the less a measure of the power of the discourse of patriotic service to underwrite identity even despite the novel's clarity about the hierarchies which nationalism mobilizes. The fact that the war produces the turning-point in Hall's narrative displays the extent to which national identification is the ground for meaningful service. Before the war, despite or perhaps because of his persistent 'sense of being just outside', afflicted by a 'queer empty feeling of having no real country and hence no real ties with those who had' (150), Gian-Luca's life was dedicated to the ideal of service, even though its object as a waiter is ludicrously inappropriate. Hall describes him as marked by 'that rarest of all gifts, the instinct for perfect service' (108). After the war he is unable to maintain his belief in the meaning of service as a waiter. The disparity between the two concepts of service which Hall juxtaposes in the novel, the service of an ideal and the service of physical and economic needs, is too great. Hall's solution is to make Gian-Luca the hero of a quest narrative which leads him to a recognition that the true meaning of service can only be found in religion.

Hall turns to Christianity to provide the model for universal brotherhood which will transcend the divisions of nation and class, allowing Gian-Luca to become the natural man alluded to in the novel's title. Stripped of his ideals and illusions, Gian-Luca embarks on a quasi-religious pilgrimage in the course of which he gives up all attachment to the material world. Hall reduces him to a hermit existence in the New Forest, where he becomes part of the 'simple, innocent life of the earth' (328), giving away his money and food to the Brothers and Sisters of the Road. Finally, he dies an ascetic death from exposure and starvation, a gesture which seems to symbolize his rejection of a lifetime's service to physical and material needs. It is the conversion experience at the moment of his death which initiates a new understanding of the meaning of service in religious terms. He becomes 'the servant of all that was helpless, even as God was their servant and their master' (345). The new understanding of service which Hall gives to her protagonist is predicated on self-abnegation and a willingness to take on the suffering of others, 'to suffer with God'. Death is then an apt resolution to Gian-Luca's problem with nationality and selfhood, since the possibility of belonging depends here on the giving up of self in service to others, by contrast with his earlier attempts to 'make [the world] serve him' (345). However, Hall refers this moment back to the question of nationalism by concluding the death scene with the words: 'And that was how Gian-Luca returned to his country after thirty-four years of exile' (346). Country is elevated beyond the restricted meaning of nation, whether England or Italy, and given the more inclusive connotations of an edenic nature guaranteed by God. Significant too is the restoration of the family to which Gian-Luca never belonged, through the double emphasis on a maternally connoted nature and the ultimate name of the Father. A narrow notion of national identity, predicated on exclusions, is replaced by the imagined communities of religion and nature to which everyone can belong.

In *Adam's Breed,* then, Hall demonstrates a clear understanding of the limitations as well as the power of nationalism as the grounds for identity. The difference between *Adam's Breed* and both *The Well* and the short story 'Miss Ogilvy Finds Herself' (1934) suggests therefore that there is a specificity to Hall's understanding of the invert's relationship to patriotism and the war. England's call to service addresses the homosexual Englishwoman in a way that it does not address the naturalized immigrant regardless of his gender. In common with her post-war generation, Hall defines the war in terms of an absolute break with the past. The war changes the position of inverts forever. However, Hall's interpretation of the break differs from the familiar construction of the war as making the replacement of an innocent and naïve idealism with a new and unwelcome maturity characterized by disillusion and irony in, for example, the writings of Vera Brittain. In Hall's writing, the invert's life in the pre-war period is one of frustration and discomfort because of her failure to conform to traditional expectations of femininity in either appearance or behaviour. The war therefore is welcome because it temporarily expands the possibilities for women. Post-war disillusion is the result of a return to pre-war conditions. The war itself remains wrapped in its aura of courageous acts and high achievement. The idea of a decisive break is a consequence of a new political consciousness. Thus, although inverts are persecuted by a post-war society for refusing 'to slink back and hide in their holes and corners' (*The Well*, 412) the war has given them a new self-consciousness as inverts: 'A battalion was formed in those terrible years that would never again be completely disbanded. War and death had given them a right to life, and life tasted sweet, very sweet to their palates' (*The Well*, 275). Here, we have the beginnings of a reverse discourse, a politicized sexual identity formed out of the materials of sexology and patriotism.[11] So, for example, in 'Miss Ogilvy Finds Herself' the invert's war work is described in terms of both nationalism and rights. 'Many another of [Miss Ogilvy's] kind was in London doing excellent work for the nation . . . asserting their right to serve, asserting their claim to attention.'[12]

Patriotism entitles inverts to a place in society, a 'claim to attention', and hence to the possibility of recognition and belonging. But this new consciousness is to be understood not only in terms of new roles and responsibilities. Hall demands recognition of the sexuality which defines that identity. Stephen is not simply a woman with a masculine body in *The Well*; she also desires women and is allowed, by Hall, a relationship which is only frustrated by social pressures. The sexual satisfactions of the relationship, although represented obliquely, are fully acknowledged by the novel. Similarly, the point of 'Miss Ogilvy Finds Herself' is the fantasy of sexual love which comes after the war and has been enabled by the experience of service at the front. But by Hall's own acknowledgement the invert's patriotism during the First World War did not make her sexuality any more acceptable to English society. What therefore are the mechanisms which link the invert's emerging identity to her war service?

'Miss Ogilvy Finds Herself' is the best vehicle for exploring the logic of Hall's attempts to forge a connection between the invert's sexuality and her identity as a citizen by means of service. The title itself underlines the journey of emancipation through self-discovery which the story charts. 'Miss Ogilvy' opens, however, with the end of the war and is concerned with the moment where the lesbian's 'right to serve' is once more denied by a world which 'will always forget an indebtedness which it thinks it expedient not to remember' (1447). To a certain extent Hall's project is memorial, her story prefaced with a note referring to 'the noble and selfless work done by hundreds of sexually inverted women during the Great War' (299), and motivated by post-war English society's determined rejection of the invert in her role as citizen, servant of her country, *and* sexual being. Sir Chartres Biron, the Chief Magistrate who presided over the trial of *The Well of Loneliness*, for example, attacked the novel for its depiction of 'a number of women of position and admirable character, who were engaged in driving ambulances in the course of the war' as 'addicted to this vice'.[13] Hall's picture of Miss Ogilvy is a poignant one in which, returning from the front, Miss Ogilvy in 'manly trench-boots and her forage-cap' is once more out of place and, although an occasion for pathos, a figure also of fun. The war itself has given her the opportunity to escape fifty-six years of claustrophobic domesticity with her mother and sisters by forming an ambulance unit. Miss Ogilvy's mannish qualities and physique are precisely fitted to the conditions of the war and to front-line service. She is described as having a 'tall, awkward body with its queer look of strength, its broad, flat bosom and thick legs and ankles' (1443). Her posture is a masculine straddle, 'as though she were still standing firm under fire while the wounded were placed in her ambulances' (1443). The focus of the story, however, is the disillusion which faces 'all the Miss Ogilvies back from the war' and the efforts of Hall's heroine to find a viable alternative to her now unendurable pre-war life of genteel spinsterly domesticity in Surrey. Hall is quite explicit about the precarious status of the liberation which the war permitted lesbians. At the front: 'Miss Ogilvy forgot the bad joke that Nature seemed to have played her . . . she lived in a kind of blissful illusion. She was competent, fearless, devoted and untiring. What then? Could any man hope to do better? She was nearly fifty-eight, yet she walked with a stride, and at times she even swaggered a little' (1447). The war gives her the experience of feeling in harmony with her work and her body, allowed to walk and swagger like a man, and, as Sandra Gilbert and Susan Gubar point out, it also grants her the knowledge that she is one among many, surprised by 'how many cropped heads had suddenly appeared as it were out of space' (1447).[14] But, this community of 'cropped heads' is gathered as much under the sign of nation as that of lesbian. And Hall is quite clear that this is a temporary illusion which must necessarily give way to the post-war reality of frustration and ridicule. 'Poor all the Miss Ogilvies back from the war with their tunics, their trench-boots, and their childish illusions!' (1447).

The second half of the story engineers a resolution to Miss Ogilvy's dilemma by means of an uncanny rediscovery of an earlier life as a stone-age man. In the flashback to this life she is able, as a man, to realize sexual fulfilment with a stone-age woman of exemplary femininity. With fulfilment comes death and Miss Ogilvy's body is found at the end of the story seated outside the cave which is the setting for the events of her previous life. Miss Ogilvy thus dies, as Ouditt writes, having 'found herself' even though 'the circumstances of her post-war world are not such that she could practise lesbianism openly. It can only be realised through a fantasy of the "pre-historic" self.'[15] Finding herself is, as Ouditt suggests, a question of Miss Ogilvy's sexuality so that the episode gives her the experience of herself as a sexual being which she does not achieve during the war, despite its momentous significance for her identity. But the decision to use a reincarnation motif turns the flashback into a myth of origins, offering the reader a clue to what determines the female invert's identity, as well as expressing her repressed sexuality. The prehistoric setting then has a central role in setting the terms for Miss Ogilvy's sexuality by invoking a concept of natural, primitive sexuality determined by instinct. Hall's stone-age man possesses only one word which must serve to express all the facets of his feelings for his woman. Otherwise, the lovers communicate in 'guttural sounds . . . meaningless save only to themselves' because their language is barely developed, 'a primitive tongue' (1454). Nature itself is similarly untrammelled by civilization, 'the air . . . cool and intensely still', is 'wonderfully pure . . . one might almost say young' (1452). And gender relations, familiar to readers of *The Well of Loneliness,* are ludicrously clichéd, offering the man as virile and aggressive protector of a domesticated and timid woman. The latter, anticipating her defloration, 'thought of the anxious virgin soil that was rent and sown to bring forth fruit in season, and she gave a quick little gasp of fear' (1456). The natural status of Miss Ogilvy's predecessor's masculine sexual aggressivity is inscribed as fully as his mate's reproductive destiny. Consummation is accompanied by the sounds of 'great birds, crying loudly' and 'love songs' bellowed by 'fierce wild aurochs' marking the lovers' closeness to a nature from which man has barely begun to separate himself. Only his tenderness and the ability to 'put by his weapon and his instinct for slaying' in order to make love to his woman make him 'lord of these creatures' and not one among them.

Miss Ogilvy's inversion is referred, therefore, to a model of natural sexuality as yet uncorrupted by civilization. But that sexuality is modelled on the masculine instinct. Ouditt in her discussion of the story leaves aside the gender reversal which turns Miss Ogilvy from repressed spinster to virile caveman, thereby implying that the gender reversal, like the prehistoric setting, is part of the alibi which makes the story possible, and even publishable. However, the extensive work which has been done on sexology in recent years suggests that masculinity also has a structural role in Hall's version of the female invert. Her reliance on the work of Havelock Ellis, in particular, roots Hall's ideas about female homosexuality in the idea of a congenital inversion of sexuality whereby a 'masculine' woman will exhibit 'an active sexuality which [Ellis] thought of as "male"'.[16] In, for example, *Sexual Inversion,* Ellis comments that by contrast with either heterosexual women or inverted men possessing 'a more or less feminine temperament', inverted women 'who may retain their feminine emotionality combined with some degree of infantile impulsiveness and masculine energy, present a favorable soil for the seeds of passional crime'.[17] Femininity and the infantile contribute the necessary irrationality and weakness of control here, but it is masculinity which links sexuality and aggression. Ellis also quotes Magnus Hirschfeld's view that 'the inverted woman is . . . more aggressive, more heroic, than either the heterosexual woman or the homosexual man'.[18] 'Her mannishness' may even tend to 'reckless brutality', according to Hirschfeld. Whilst not criminal, and in fact an example of the superior abilities believed by apologists to be characteristic of homosexuals of a higher social class, Miss Ogilvy is the pattern of the female homosexual of sexology with her masculine body and temperament, and Hall leaves the reader in no doubt that she is born with this predisposition. Miss Ogilvy insists, as a child, 'that her real name was William and not Wilhelmina' (1444). The paradox, then, on which the story rests, that Miss Ogilvy finds herself only as a man, is inherent to Hall's definitions of inverted sexuality as much as to the problems of representing sexual passion between women. It also suggests the connections between her war experiences and the liberation of her sexuality.

The war does more than allow Miss Ogilvy to escape a confining feminine domesticity; it also allows her a temporary identity as a man, more or less. Nature's 'bad joke' is that she has all the capacities and qualities of masculinity in the anatomical guise of a woman. During the war she has been able to forget this and, all too briefly, 'find herself'. Thus she gains access to the active, aggressive sexuality which is deemed to be the prerogative of the male. The war's significance is not just a question of the right employment. Hall's acceptance of a biological model of sexuality invokes a link between male sexuality and aggression characteristic of nineteenth-century scientific theory still influential in the twentieth century. Freud, for example, in *Three Essays on the Theory of Sexuality* (1905), wrote that 'The sexuality of most male human beings contains an element of aggressiveness—a desire to subjugate. The biological significance of it seems to lie in the need for over-coming the resistance of the sexual object by means other than the process of wooing.'[19] Somewhat later, in *Civilization and its Discontents* (1930), in a discussion of the requirement that aggression be sublimated and otherwise inhibited for the sake of civilization, the atrocities of the First World War are one of his reference-points for the vicissitudes of the process.[20] Similarly, the late Victorian radical journalist W. T. Stead, in *War against War in South Africa*, expresses a general concern with the relationship of masculine aggression to an overmastering sexual instinct in relation to the demands of war upon men, linking the primitive and the aggressive in his argument about the morality of the modern soldier: 'The progress of civilization is attested by the extent to which mankind is able to restrain the aboriginal savage who is let loose by a declaration of war within [a] continually narrowing limit.'[21] Hall herself makes the link between an instinctual primitive aggression, masculinity, and war explicit in 'Fraulein Schwarz', a short story published in the same collection as 'Miss Ogilvy Finds Herself'. Describing a young man enraged by news of the German invasion of Belgium she writes: 'there lurked an instinct that was very unregenerate and old—mild Mr. Pitt of the Y.M.C.A. was seeing red, as a long time ago some hairy-armed cave-man had done before him'.[22]

For Hall, therefore, the evolutionary and sexological discourses on which she relies already establish the link between war and sexuality, making masculinity, aggression, and a virile sexuality interchangeable terms. She can thus represent the experience and validation of the invert's masculinity in the war as leading to her realization of an active sexuality in the prehistoric scenario. However, the explanatory status of the flashback in 'Miss Ogilvy' also allows the qualities which enable Miss Ogilvy to fill a masculine role to be interpreted as the result of this earlier life as a man. This is important for Hall's attempt to forge a link between sexual and national identity. It locates Miss Ogilvy's sexuality, not as that which puts her at odds with society, but as the actual source of her civic virtue, her capacity to serve England.

The causalities which Hall establishes by means of this interrelationship between the flashback and its frame are contradictory, however. The prehistoric episode contains traces of an evolutionary discourse despite the alternative structure of repetition implied by the reincarnation motif. The reference to a primitive and as yet embryonic language is one example of the way in which a narrative of progress is structural to the story. But principally the temporalities of evolution are invoked by Miss Ogilvy's primitive persona's prescient understanding that his type, stone-age man, is about to be superseded by the new 'round-headed ones' whose bronze-age weapons are recognizable to both reader and hero as evolutionarily superior. These elements of an evolutionary narrative raise a whole series of questions about their relevance to Hall's story about the female invert's position in the post-war world. If this primitive man, on the verge of extinction, is Miss Ogilvy's earlier self, what implications does the story have for a vision of a future in which the invert can be accepted by her society as a full sexual being? What kind of forerunner is he? In part, the answer lies again within evolutionary theory and in its intersections with sexology.

Sexology's attribution of a tendency to moral and intellectual superiority in homosexuals is well known, the sublimation of 'gross physical manifestation[s]' of their sexuality translating into 'an ardor wholly unknown to the normally constituted individual' in 'the work of human service'.[23] Likewise, the concept of the individual in advance of its species is a necessary element within evolutionary theory. Hall's stone-age hero is such an individual. His recognition of his people's danger, and his uncanny access to Miss Ogilvy's era in which the sea will have encroached, making the spacious lands his people inhabit a tiny offshore island, constitute an advance in civilization which enables him to see beyond the limits of his own culture, conceiving the time of his peoples almost in the advanced terms of post-Darwinian nineteenth-century geology and anthropology. Miss Ogilvy's primitive predecessor has, therefore, the superior character and vision of Ellis's invert which ought in evolutionary terms to be the seed of human progress. As a result, Hall side-steps the danger that her mapping of homosexuality onto the primitive dovetails with late nineteenth-and early twentieth-century theories of sexual inversion as a form of degeneracy.

But, Miss Ogilvy, patterned on her ancestor, remains ambiguously placed as both heroic forerunner and tragically knowing victim of an inevitable process of extinction—an anachronistic 'survival'. The invert is either one who can 'contribute to the good of the whole' and to 'the future generations' or one who must die out as having outlived her time. Miss Ogilvy's death at the end of the story is not the only way in which Hall registers this latter perspective. During her life Miss Ogilvy is, as it were, shown her own death—the skull of a stone-age man killed by a bronze axe. For reasons which are, at that moment, obscure to both her and the reader, 'she was swept by another emotion that was even more strange and more devastating: such a grief as she had not conceived could exist; a terrible unassuageable grief, without hope, without respite, without palliation, so that with something akin to despair she touched the long gash in the skull' (1452). This inexplicable grief registers, of course, her connection to the pre-historic age which she is about to rediscover. The description of an unmasterable loss, 'unassuageable' and 'without hope' or 'respite', suggests that the object of her mourning is her people's extinction as much as her own death. Thus for the reader the war which will destroy his people has already happened when Miss Ogilvy's forerunner tells his lover about his stark vision of coming destruction. Even while the lover is addressed as 'happy small home of future generations', the story has already suggested that the battle is already lost and extinction an inevitable destiny.

Hall does offer some consolations. That the female invert can find any access to sexual and romantic fulfilment in literature at this period is an achievement, as the trial the following year of *The Well of Loneliness* shows. But also Hall somewhat turns the tables on a heterosexual world which will not accept her. Her stone-age man possesses a nobility which is denied to the round-headed ones who surpass him, so that his extinction is a tragedy for the human race as much as for the individual. Aggression, although central to the expression of Miss Ogilvy's sexuality in the flashback, is given by Hall as something to be mastered, rather as Herbert Spencer argues that competition and primitive traits are essential to the evolutionary struggle by which aboriginal man 'prepare[d] the earth for its future inhabitants' but in modern, civilized man are signs of primitive regression.[24] Her primitive hero divests himself of his aggression at the moment of sexual consummation, putting by 'his weapon and his instinct for slaying' and making himself 'defenceless with tenderness, thinking no longer of death but of life' (1457).[25] In accord with the demands of evolution the round-headed ones possess all the aggressive competitive qualities which will ensure their victory. It is those who usher in the future who paradoxically acquire the negative aspects of instinctual aggression while the stone-age man is all civilization. However, Hall's moral victory is a pyrrhic one, since her primitive protagonist's superior claim to civilization implies, once more, that the invert cannot both serve and be sexual. The links which Hall trades on between a natural sexuality, masculinity, and aggression mean that the mastery of instinct entails a renunciation of the very sexuality which she has used to define the female invert. And, despite the optimism of the story's title, Hall leaves her heroine with no time in which to be the self she finds. Miss Ogilvy is both ahead of her time, forerunner of a lesbian future for which the world is not ready, and yet she has also outlived her time, the 1914–18 war in which she could with other lesbians experience a sense of entitlement and belonging, 'doing excellent work for the nation'. Hall thus leaves unresolved the problem of how, if the war does represent such a complete break with the past, the female invert with her new expectations and demands can bring together national and sexual identities in the post-war world. She seeks to address this same question in *The Well of Loneliness* the following year, where the war again provides the link between citizenship and sexuality, but this time by means of the language of chivalry.

The war's significance in *The Well of Loneliness,* as with 'Miss Ogilvy Finds Herself', is explicitly tied to the question of service. It is introduced as one more instance of Stephen's search for an adequate occasion for the service which will provide a purpose to her life and a means of overcoming her situation as an exile and outlaw. This is a search which is shared too with a range of heterosexual outsiders in Hall's fiction, most strikingly in the case of Gian-Luca in *Adam's Breed.* Although Hall gives a largely ritual nod to the 'true meaning of war', its wasteful horror, that is, her real focus is on the opportunities for heroism and patriotism which it allows or seems to allow. Thus Hall's account of the war in *The Well* begins with a catalogue of service and sacrifice from which Stephen is excluded by virtue of either her gender or her inversion. As a woman she is not entitled to fight, and as an invert her nature doesn't fit her either to nurse or to make woman's ultimate sacrifice, to give up her sons to die for her country: 'She felt appalled at the realization of her own grotesqueness; she was nothing but a freak abandoned on a kind of no-man's-land at this moment of splendid national endeavour. England was calling her men into battle, her women to the bedsides of the wounded and dying, and between these two chivalrous, surging forces she, Stephen, might well be crushed out of existence' (271). Stephen shares, here, the emotions of other women who were excluded from fighting solely on the grounds of gender, expressed, for example, by Nora Bomford in 'Drafts', where 'Sex, nothing more ... Decides the biggest differences of all ... Why should men face the dark while women stay / To live and laugh and meet the sun each day.'[26] Hall's particular focus on inversion, however, blocks an identification with the feminism which Bomford is voicing, and makes Stephen's relationship to masculinity, rather than the relative capacities of each gender, the central issue. Hall's paradigm requires a fixed gender opposition which will allow the female homosexual's identification with masculine sexuality. Both Stephen and Miss Ogilvy are, in a sense, looking for a recognition of their masculinity rather than renegotiating increasingly anachronistic definitions of masculinity and femininity as were feminists like Brittain or Bomford. Thus, the terms of her identity demand that Stephen serve as a man so that the possibility of identification with England's 'national endeavour' depends on finding a place via her masculinity.

In order to negotiate the difficulties of finding such a place, in view of both the female invert's fundamental unacceptability and her gender, Hall turns to the language of chivalry. The way this works can be exemplified by looking at the novel's treatment of the heroic death of Stephen's rival Roger Antrim. Although Roger wins the VC posthumously, and achieves a heroic glamour which Stephen can never fully emulate, his death is not used to underline further Stephen's exclusion from English nationalism. Instead, Hall makes it the occasion of a reconciliation and the means towards a mode of belonging for Stephen. A problem with masculinity, its definition, and its relationship to anatomical sex is expressed through Stephen and Roger's rivalry both as children and later as competing lovers of Angela Crossby. Their necessary antagonism over who can be a man, and in Roger's case how secure he can be in his masculinity, is overcome by means of 'the immutable law of service': 'Roger—so lacking in understanding, so crude, so cruel and remorseless a bully—Roger had been changed in the twinkling of an eye into something superb because utterly selfless. Thus it was that the undying urge of mankind towards the ideal had come upon Roger' (292). Roger's patriotism is subsumed here by a higher law of which service to one's country is only an instance: 'By dying as he had died, Roger, all unknowing, had fulfilled the law that must be extended to enemy and friend alike—the immutable law of service' (293). This makes use of a familiar First World War motif in which national enmity could be put aside in the face of a common experience of the horror of modern warfare.[27] Moreover, Hall couches the event in the 'heroic idiom' of pre-war militarism appealing to a model of chivalric courtesy.

But Roger dies in order to save not an enemy but a 'friend', his own captain—a fundamentally patriotic act. Hall's appeal to a 'law that must be extended to enemy and friend alike' refers therefore not to Roger's role in the war but to his enmity with Stephen, which is transcended by means of his death. Thus, the 'eternal warfare' of the normal world against inverts is grafted onto a moment where the male soldier makes the supreme sacrifice for his country. The historically specific war with its appeal to national unity becomes a vehicle for superseding the divisions and enmities of this eternal war of sexuality.[28] At the same time, Hall turns patriotic service into a form of universal service in which the female invert can find a place. The basis of the 'immutable law' is that of self-sacrifice, the key heroic virtue which allows Stephen, in the course of the novel, to turn renunciation, the only virtue which society allows her as an invert, into the basis of service to her fellow inverts. Her own death, symbolized by the violent sacrifice of her own sexual desire and its fulfilment, becomes a guarantee of her own heroism and ultimately her entitlement to masculinity. She joins Roger, 'changed to something superb because utterly selfless', but also steals a march on him because in her case the sacrifice is 'knowing'. Thus, even though the Armistice turns Stephen back into an outsider, her appeal to a law of service beyond patriotism promises a larger community to which the female invert can belong, the price of belonging to this community being a self-sacrificing death, whether actual or symbolic.

This community, which transcends love of country and promises a universal brotherhood, does not, however, imply a transcendence of gender oppositions. I have already argued that Hall's definition of inversion requires a fixed and conventional gender opposition. Moreover, her project in *The Well of Loneliness* is to wrest from a heterosexual society recognition of the invert as a valuable and normal member of society. A humanist model in which difference is to be overcome can never deliver the sense of belonging which Stephen, with her 'curious craving for the normal' (213), seeks. The transformation which Hall engineers in the ideals of patriotic service therefore requires a reworking of masculinity if Stephen is to be included on the basis of her masculine identification. Roger once again exemplifies this process. Through his selfless death Roger changes from 'so crude, so cruel and remorseless a bully' into 'something superb'. Throughout the novel Hall describes him in terms of an aggressive, virile, and instinctual masculinity. His 'masculine instinct' is 'outraged' by Stephen's inversion, which threatens 'his right of possession' (184). In dying he is recast in terms of a chivalric heroism which is, in *The Well of Loneliness*, the type of true masculinity to which Stephen aspires. We can detect in this transformation Hall's attempt to wrestle with the consequences of her attachment to congenital theories of sexuality. Liberal theories of innate homosexuality claim a rightful place for the invert as a member of the human species on the grounds of nature. In *The Well of Loneliness* Stephen's right to be seen as part of nature becomes an insistent refrain. But the theory, among its many problems, leaves the female invert's masculinity as inferior to the man's since she lacks a male body. Hall herself describes this when she makes Stephen's dog discern 'in the man a more perfect thing, a more entirely fulfilling companion' (425). Nature in this way betrays both Stephen and Hall. The significance of Roger's heroic death lies therefore in the sublimation of an instinctual, natural masculinity into a highly civilized model of selfless honour, reminiscent of Stephen's father.

The terms in which Hall characterizes this revised version of masculinity are significant. Thus although Stephen possesses her masculinity by nature, it is not primarily signified as a primitive and aggressive virility. Despite the clear bodily marks of Stephen's virility, and her early, passionate desire to fight Roger Antrim, Hall insists on the transformation of instinctual and natural masculinity into the code of chivalric English manhood. When, for example, Stephen agrees to leave Morton rather than fight her mother's disapproval at her unnatural love for another woman, she 'found her manhood' (205), proving her superior strength by sacrificing that which is dearest, her home, and by giving way to the weakness of her feminine opponent. If what is sacrificed is Stephen's will, it is largely because the sacrifice signifies an overcoming of the instinctual aggressivity associated with masculinity. The overcoming of instinct is made explicit in the novel when Stephen is forced, after her father's death, to give up hunting because of her recognition of its essential barbarity. The fox, 'a crawling, bedraggled streak of red fur', is too obviously hounded like herself, and its painful death too reminiscent of Sir Phillip's, for her to take pleasure in its death. The nature of her renunciation is expressed through Stephen's horse, Rafferty, who becomes the bearer of a violent residue which is still linked to Stephen but no longer acknowledged as hers: 'a memory bequeathed him by some wild forbear . . . of fierce open nostrils and teeth bared in battle, of hooves that struck death with every sure blow, of a great untamed mane that streamed out like a banner, of the shrill and incredibly savage war-cry that accompanied that gallant banner' (125). The costs, a bodily pleasure and an instinctual aggressivity now overcome, bring a gain in spirit which will be the basis for her entry to a community of service at the end of the novel.[29]

However, Hall does not entirely leave nature and instinct behind. The intensity of Stephen's struggle to master herself in these moral battles becomes a mark of the virility of her instinct. Moreover, Hall attempts to invest chivalric masculinity with its own dividend of nature. Too much of the novel is predicated on her claim that the invert is born of nature to make a concept of acquired masculinity satisfactory. Thus manhood is not only earned in *The Well*, it is also inherited. Stephen's father, Sir Phillip, exemplifies the model gentleman. He catechizes Stephen: '"What is honour, my daughter?" . . . "You are honour," she said quite simply' (59). Hall uses Sir Phillip's social position to guarantee a non-instinctual masculinity by bequeathing it to Stephen as part of her inheritance.[30] Kinship here knits culture to nature. Hall writes:

> There was little of the true pioneer about Stephen. She belonged to the soil and the fruitfulness of Morton, to its pastures and paddocks, to its farms and its cattle, to its quiet and gentlemanly ordered traditions . . . do what they would they could never completely rid themselves of her nor she of them—they were one in their blood. (107)

The terms which define Stephen are drawn from a nationalist discourse which relates the power of traditions to 'soil' and 'blood'. She belongs 'by right of those past generations of Gordons . . . whose bodies had gone to the making of Stephen'. Thus, although Stephen earns her entitlement to manhood through the renunciation of instinctual aggression, the masculinity which she assumes is renaturalized by means of the language of nationalism. And it hardly needs saying that this is a specifically English nationalism, the 'pastures and paddocks . . . farms and cattle' calling up an English pastoral akin to Woolf's 'cawing of rooks in an elm tree'.

Stephen's fidelity to tradition leads inexorably, of course, to the renunciations which institute the narrative of invert as victim which, as Sonja Ruehl points out, has made Hall's later influence on definitions of lesbianism so problematic. Stephen's final sacrifice is, as critics have often noted, the pre-condition of her role as martyr and saviour, the one who 'like Christ . . . is crucified for her kind'.[31] By the end of the novel 'Stephen has taken on a religious duty, the task of interceding with society and with God on behalf of all inverts.'[32] Like Christ, she cries out in her suffering: 'Acknowledge us, oh God, before the whole world. Give us also the right to our existence!' (436). But, paradoxically, the move to a brotherhood of service beyond national divisions depends in *The Well* on the configuration of chivalric masculinity and English nationalism. Even while Hall lays claim to a higher community of brotherhood and service through sacrifice, her access to an enlarged ideal of service is dependent on her Englishness. Although Stephen is forced to give up Morton, 'cast . . . out of Eden', as Jean Radford puts it,[33] she is still what her country made her: 'do what they would they could never completely rid themselves of her nor she of them—they were one in blood' (107). The masculinity which defines her inversion is derived from, and guaranteed by, her English heritage, and the ideal of a more inclusive community transcending national and sexual enmities ultimately derives its identificatory power from nationalism and patriotism.

When Woolf refers an irrational and inconvenient love of England to a larger international context, she proposes a harmonious relationship whereby her female outsider 'will give to England first what she desires of peace and freedom for the whole world'. Her formulation is polemic rather than convincing. It is consistent with her claim that 'as a woman my country is the whole world'. 'What she desires of peace and freedom for the whole world' can only be safely given to England first if the world is her country. But this depends on Woolf's attempt to claim that her 'love of England' is pure. That is, it is an emotion which can be subordinated to the higher aims of international peace and freedom. The language which represents this 'drop of . . . irrational emotion' is saturated with Englishness.

The identificatory power of the passage is inseparable from the myth of English pastoral innocence. Thus, the equation Woolf asks us to make between the woman's exclusion from the privileges of national citizenship, 'as a woman I have no country', and her status as a citizen of the whole world, 'as a woman my country is the whole world', depends on the resources of nationalism even as it aspires to a higher international ideal. In view of Woolf's inability to leave behind the languages which invest nationalism with its identificatory power, Hall might be forgiven for her failure to imagine a mode of belonging for the invert which is not severely compromised by what Benedict Anderson calls the 'limited imaginings'[34] of nations. Instead Hall's construction of the invert in relation to the First World War exemplifies the difficulties of imagining identity, community, and service in terms other than those of the nation.

NOTES

1. Virginia Woolf, *Three Guineas* (New York, 1938), 166.
2. Jane Marcus, 'Storming the Toolshed', in Robyn Warhol and Diane Price Herndl (eds.), *Feminisms* (New Brunswick, 1991), 145.
3. Bonnie Zimmerman, 'What has never Been: An Overview of Lesbian Feminist Literary Criticism', in Warhol and Herndl (eds.), *Feminisms*, 127.
4. Toril Moi, *Sexual/Textual Politics* (London, 1985), 213.
5. Quoted in David Baker, *Our Three Selves* (London, 1985), 126.
6. Eric Hobsbawm, 'Introduction: Inventing Traditions', in Eric Hobsbawm and Terence Ranger (eds.), *The Invention of Tradition* (Cambridge, 1994), 10.
7. Radclyffe Hall, *The Well of Loneliness* (1928; London, 1981), 271.
8. Quoted in Jenny Gould, 'Women's Military Service in First World War Britain', in M. R. Higgonet, Jane Jenson, Sonya Michel, and Margaret C. Weitz (eds.), *Behind the Lines: Gender and the Two World Wars* (New Haven, 1987), 114.
9. Sharon Ouditt, *Fighting Forces, Writing Women: Identity and Ideology in the First World War* (London, 1994), 25.
10. Radclyffe Hall, *Adam's Breed* (1926; London, 1957), 185.
11. See Sonja Ruehl, 'Inverts and Experts: Radclyffe Hall and the Lesbian Identity', in Judith Newton and Deborah Rosenfelt (eds.), *Feminist Criticism and Social Change* (London, 1985); Jean Radford, 'An Inverted Romance: *The Well of Loneliness* and Sexual Ideology', in Jean Radford (ed.), *The Progress of Romance* (London, 1986); Clarie M. Tylee, *The Great War and Women's Consciousness: Images of Militarism and Womanhood in Women's Writings, 1914–64* (Basingstoke, 1990), all of whom have excellent discussions of the uses of sexology and its potential for the formation of a reverse discourse.

12. Radclyffe Hall, 'Miss Ogilvy Finds Herself' (1934), in Sandra M. Gilbert and Susan Gubar (eds.), *The Norton Anthology of Literature By Women* (New York, 1985), 1447.
13. Quoted in Baker, *Our Three Selves*, 244.
14. Sandra Gilbert and Susan Gubar, *No Man's Land: The Place of the Woman Writer in the Twentieth Century*, ii (New Haven, 1989). The arguments against Gilbert and Gubar's thesis about the socially and sexually liberating effects of the First World War for women have been made cogently by Jane Marcus, 'The Asylums of Antaeus: Women, War and Madness—Is there a Feminist Fetishism?', in H. Aram Veeser (ed.), *The New Historicism* (London, 1990); Tylee, *The Great War and Women's Consciousness*; and Ouditt, *Fighting Forces, Writing Women*. See Angela Woolacott, *On Her Their Lives Depend: Munitions Workers in the Great War* (Berkeley, 1994) for a judicious and partly critical summary of the objections. Gilbert and Gubar are undoubtedly correct about Hall's position, although they do not investigate its basis.
15. Ouditt, *Fighting Forces, Writing Women*, 44.
16. Ruehl, 'Inverts and Experts', 168.
17. Havelock Ellis, *Studies in the Psychology of Sex, ii: Sexual Inversion* (Philadelphia, 1922), 201.
18. Ibid. 251.
19. Sigmund Freud, 'Three Essays on the Theory of Sexuality', in *The Standard Edition of the Complete Psychological Works of Sigmund Freud*, vii (London, 1964), 157–8.
20. Sigmund Freud, 'Civilization and its Discontents', in *The Standard Edition of the Complete Psychological Works of Sigmund Freud*, xxi (London, 1964), 111–12.
21. W. T. Stead, 'The Conduct of our War in South Africa', in *War against War in South Africa*, 8 Dec. 1899 (London), 114. I am indebted for this reference and a suggestive discussion of chivalry to Paula M. Krebs, 'Cannibals or Knights: Sexual Honor in the Propaganda of Arthur Conan Doyle and W. T. Stead', paper given at the Institute of Commonwealth Studies, June 1994.
22. Radclyffe Hall, 'Fraulein Schwarz', in *Miss Ogilvy Finds Herself* (London, 1934), 154.
23. Ellis, *Sexual Inversion*, 28.
24. Herbert Spencer, *Social Statics* (London, 1851), 410.
25. See Tylee, *The Great War and Women's Consciousness* for an alternative argument about the status of masculinity in the story. I would disagree with her assumption that instinctual and chivalric masculinity amount to the same thing.
26. Nora Bomford, 'Drafts', in Catherine Reilly, *Scars upon my Heart: Women's Poetry and Verse of the First World War* (London, 1981), 12.
27. Compare Paul Fussell's discussion of the First World War's effects on the language of militarism with Graham Dawson's analysis of the romantic hero in the 1920s cult of Lawrence of Arabia, in Graham Dawson, 'Lawrence of Arabia', in Michael Roper and John Tosh (eds.), *Manful Assertions* (London, 1991).
28. For a brief but useful discussion of the opposing temporalities of the war in *The Well*, see Alison Hennegan, Introduction, in *The Well of Loneliness* (London, 1981).

29. See Tylee's parallel argument about Hall's treatment of masculinity in which she says that Hall 'locks herself into a paradox. Stephen is to be manly but not like a man' (*The Great War and Women's Consciousness*, 179). For a quite different reading of Hall's problem with the female invert's relationship to masculinity, see Teresa de Lauretis's argument about fetishism and lesbian desire in *Practice of Love: Lesbian Sexuality and Perverse Desire* (Bloomington, Ind., 1994), esp. 203–53.
30. Jean Radford, 'An Inverted Romance', 108–9, makes the point that Stephen's social status also fits with the tradition of the romance which is an important generic model for Hall in *The Well of Loneliness.*
31. Ibid. 107.
32. Ruehl, 'Inverts and Experts', 173.
33. Radford, 'An Inverted Romance', 107.
34. Benedict Anderson, *Imagined Communities: Reflections on the Origin and Spread of Nationalism*, rev. edn. (London, 1991), 7.

9
Flies and Violets in Katherine Mansfield

Con Coroneos

Of the writers discussed in this book, Katherine Mansfield was one of the few who entered a militarized zone in the Great War, and perhaps the only one who entered it for the 'wrong' reason. She did not go to drive an ambulance, to report, to propagandize or to mourn. Instead, she went to pursue a love affair with Francis Carco, a French soldier who was stationed just east of Dijon.[1] At Carco's invitation, she left England on 15 February 1915 for the French town of Gray, located in a zone forbidden to women visitors. Mansfield's first thought was to masquerade as a pregnant wife. She settled on the ruse of visiting a sick relative (with Corporal Carco pretending to be a helpful stranger) and just managed to get past the authorities: 'The last old paman who saw my passport, "M le Colonel" . . . nearly sent me back.'[2] She spent four days with Carco and then returned precipitately to England.

This unusual event took place when Mansfield was 26. Born in New Zealand in 1888, she had been writing stories and critical reviews in England since she was 20. The link with Carco came about indirectly through *Rhythm*, the short-lived literary journal established by J. Middleton Murry and Michael Sadleir in 1911. Mansfield was one of the first contributors. She had already published a collection of satiric sketches, *In a German Pension* (1911). By the summer of 1912, she had become assistant editor of the journal and was living with Murry, whom she was to marry in 1918. Carco, also a writer, was a foreign correspondent for *Rhythm*,[3] and acted as a guide for his editors when they visited Paris at the end of 1913, though the journal itself was by then defunct. Twelve months later Mansfield was going through the first of several estrangements from Murry, and involved in a passionate correspondence with Carco, now in the war zone. Although the affair itself was short-lived, it had a literary after-life. Each writer drew on aspects of the other in later work.[4] Moreover, Mansfield twice returned briefly to Paris in March and May 1915 to stay in Carco's unoccupied flat. During these visits she wrote 'An Indiscreet Journey', a story based upon the illegal adventure.

Christiane Mortelier remarks, almost pardonably, that the episode brings together 'Mansfield in love, Mansfield at war and Mansfield at work in quite an extraordinary way'.[5] The event has obvious local significance. But then it occurred very early in the war, and its relevance to Mansfield's subsequent work is far from clear. Mansfield was to live for only another eight years. In this time, she published two more volumes of stories: *Bliss* (1920) and *The Garden Party* (1922). A further two were published by Murry after her early death in 1923: *The Doves' Nest* (1923) and *Something Childish* (1924). These collections, on which her reputation tends to rest, consist mainly of stories written after 1914. Thus, the most productive phase of her short writing career coincides with the duration of the war and its immediate aftermath. How significant is this historical conjunction for her work? Almost a year to the day after the Armistice, Mansfield wrote a fierce attack on Virginia Woolf's novel *Night and Day* (1919):

> My private opinion is that it is a lie in the soul. The war has never been: that is what its message is. I don't want (G. forbid!) mobilisation and the violation of Belgium but the novel cant just leave the war out. There *must* have been a change of heart. It is really fearful to me the 'settling down' of human beings. I feel in the *profoundest* sense that nothing can ever be the same—that as artists we are traitors if we feel otherwise: we have to take it into account and find new expressions new moulds for our new thoughts feelings.[6]

This passionate statement seems to promise her own reader an exceptionally focused encounter with what Maurice Blanchot calls 'the writing of the disaster'. Yet this is not obviously the case. Although Mansfield often refers to the war in her letters and journal, there seems to be no question of a developed war response, a clearly defined polemics or irenics, let alone a solid body of 'war writing'. Her main collections contain only two stories which deal explicitly with war experiences. One is 'An Indiscreet Journey' (1915; published 1924), and the other is 'The Fly' (1922; published 1923).

Mansfield's work raises in an exemplary way the problem of literary response to war. What evidence is there of a response? How can silence be read? And in what ways is a response itself shaped, as Blanchot suggests, 'under the surveillance of the disaster'?[7] Mansfield's two war stories, as they will be called here, emerge from very different kinds of experience. 'The Fly' was written not only well after the war but in Mansfield's full awareness that her illness was incurable.[8] The pressures of memory and suffering which accompanied its composition make the adventurism of the Carco episode seem precious and impoverished. Yet the conjunction of the heart, writing, and the war which Mortelier finds in the earlier case is also fundamental to Mansfield's attack on *Night and Day.* The following discussion considers how this conjunction works in Mansfield's two war stories.

'She's done for!', notes Woolf with pleasure, after reading the story 'Bliss'. The mind behind the work is 'a very thin soil, laid an inch or two deep upon very barren rock', and the story leaves an impression of Mansfield's 'callousness & hardness as a human being'.[9] But a few lines later, Woolf checks herself. Is it really fair to read human failings into bad art? Her destruction of Mansfield is a case of what in another connection she calls 'bending her pen' to find fault, a tendency which she attributes to 'an instinct of self-preservation at work. If she's good then I'm not.'[10]

The rivalry between Woolf and Mansfield has attracted a good deal of attention, usually to Woolf's disadvantage. Such professional jealousy is hardly novel, and to construct it merely as a literary scandal is to underestimate the terms Woolf uses and the extent to which they reflect Mansfield's own criticism of Woolf. If 'Bliss' is callous, *Night and Day* betrays Woolf's 'aloofness, her air of quiet perfection, her lack of any sign that she has made a perilous voyage—the absence of any scars'.[11] Moreover, both Woolf and Mansfield detect signs of a kind of emotional atrophy in Dorothy Richardson as well. For Woolf, the sense of disquiet created by *Revolving Lights* (1923) arises from 'feeling that the accent upon the emotions has shifted

[. . .] What was important to Maggie Tulliver no longer matters to Miriam Henderson.' The same unease is felt when innovative artists (she cites Chaucer, Donne, and Dickens) show that the heart is not a stationary body but moves relative to constant emotions: 'That is what Miss Richardson is doing on an infinitely smaller scale. Miriam Henderson is pointing to her heart and saying she feels a pain on her right, and not on her left. She points too didactically. Her pain, compared with Maggie Tulliver's, is a very little pain.'[12] For Mansfield, *The Tunnel* (1919) displays Richardson's mind as a 'brilliant [. . .] machine': 'Anything that goes into her mind she can summon forth again, and there it is, complete in every detail, with nothing taken away from it—and nothing added.'[13] And again in the case of *Interim* (also 1919): 'she leaves us feeling, as before, that everything being of equal importance to her, it is impossible that everything should not be of equal unimportance'.[14] Each example presents a clever, artful, writerly mind which is out of touch and beyond being touched: too calloused to feel deeply, unable to judge what matters, or else incapable of bearing scars.

How would the creator of Maggie Tulliver have responded to the Great War? The impossibility of this question is not only biographical. These critical judgements were all made over the five years immediately following the First World War, and the vocabulary of feeling and scarring—not to mention Woolf's phrase 'She's done for!'—is thus locally resonant. There is, moreover, another significant context. One characteristic of the growing divergence between middlebrow and avant-garde writing from at least the 1890s is the decline of the heart of which Miriam Henderson's 'very little pain' may be taken as a symptom. The importance of this change is nowhere more evident than in the time of war, in which metaphors of the heart conventionally provide the most powerful names for *patria*, grief, or loss. The beating heart is indispensable to a good deal of First World War literature: the 'trench poetry', government and newspaper propaganda, and morale-boosting novels, such as those by May Sinclair and Mrs Humphry Ward. But how available is the heart as a means of authenticating exerience in the sensorium of literary modernism? This is an issue of the utmost importance for Mansfield. Recording a meeting with Lawrence in England, shortly before the Carco episode, she notes: 'We talked of the war and its horrors. I have simply felt it closing in on me and my unhappy love [concerning Carco], and all to no purpose.'[15] The war seems no more than the contracting horizon relative to the purpose of love. If this is perfectly understandable in the heat of an affair, there is nevertheless a feeling—perhaps churlish, in the context of a general readerly anxiety that the war should matter *most* for the writers that have engaged one's interest—that too often for Mansfield the true horizon is love, and that the war is a foreground impediment when it is not a background noise. To read her letters throughout the war (and more generally) is to be struck by an over-writing of love exemplified in this passage from a letter to 'Bogey' (Middleton Murry):

> I have loved you before for 3 years with my heart and my mind, but it seems to me that I have never loved you *avec mon âme* as I do now. I love you with all our future life—our life together which seems only now to have taken root and to be alive and growing up in the sun—I do not love you, but Love possesses me utterly love for you and for our life and for all our richness and joy. I have never felt anything like it before. In fact I did not comprehend the possibility of such a thing. [. . .] Bogey, come quickly quickly. My heart will break.[16]

At the end of the path is the kind of sub-Lawrentian Murryism which the master himself achieves when recalling the blissfully happy time he spent with Mansfield during early 1916 in a villa in Marseilles: 'And in that experience were laid the foundations of a conviction which has grown more solid with the years—that the only power which will ever put an end to wars is love between individual men and individual women. Only in that relation is the fundamental egoism of men and women really overcome.'[17] The love-dominance in Mansfield's letters comes as a surprise to the first-time reader, not only because of its utter self-absorption and apparent indifference to whether anything else—including the war—has significance, but also because it is so much at odds with the apparent anti-romanticism of much of her fiction. To complicate matters—or to bring them into a proper relation—it is a quality of heart which comes to define the act of writing itself. One month after the publication of her Richardson review, Woolf puzzles in her diary over an issue which seems decidedly old-fashioned: 'Am I writing The Hours from deep emotion?' She has been reading Mansfield's journal comments, appended to the posthumous collection *The*

Doves' Nest, on the need to write out of 'feeling things deeply'.[18] Mansfield's most dramatic statement of this appears in a journal entry dated 31 May 1919:

Shall I be able to express, one day, my love of work—my desire to be a better writer—my longing to take greater pains. And the passion I feel. It takes the place of religion—it *is* my religion—of people—I create my people: of 'life'—it *is* Life. The temptation is to kneel before it, to adore, to prostrate myself, to stay too long in a state of ecstasy before the *idea* of it. I must be more busy about my master's work.[19]

The feverish, exultant quality of this writing perhaps too easily recalls Mansfield's physical condition, by now hopelessly tubercular. If it seems to presage her decision to spend the last months of her life at Gurdjieff's Institute for the Harmonious Development of Man at Fontainebleau, it nevertheless deserves to be taken seriously as a statement about the relation between art and life. Her early espousal of a Wildean aestheticism changes under the influence of the philosophy of *Rhythm* in ways which exert considerable pressure in both her war stories. How this is so needs to be considered through the stories themselves.

Many of the details, incidents, and even the exact wording of various passages in 'An Indiscreet Journey' first appeared in Mansfield's journal as a combination of documentary record and fictionalization of the Carco episode.[20] In the more recognizable first part of the story, the English first-person narrator leaves Paris to seek her French lover in a town near the front. He has invented two French relatives for her—an Aunt Julie and an Uncle Paul who live in the town and have invited their 'dear niece' to visit them. This simple subterfuge is scarcely needed. The authorities at various checkpoints stamp her papers uninterestedly and wave her through. She meets 'her little corporal' at last. In the second part of the story, she returns to the café in which they have been regularly dining and is joined once more by her lover. In the final section, she and her lover are (still?) in the café, this time in the company of two other French soldiers. One of them celebrates a drink called 'mirabelle' (cherry plum liqueur), reputedly like whisky but without the hangover. Although it is past the soldiers' curfew, they persuade the café-owner to sell them some, and they begin to drink, hidden from the sight of the police, in the café's 'dark smelling scullery, full of pans of greasy water, of salad leaves and meat bones'.[21]

There have been some recent attempts to establish the war credentials of 'An Indiscreet Journey'. This is a task rather more difficult than the summary might suggest. Certainly, there are repeated references to soldiers, equipment, curfews, and damage, and Claire Tomalin speculates that the scene in which a convalescent soldier enters the smoky café is perhaps the first literary representation of the effects of gassing:[22]

In his white face his eyes showed, pink as a rabbit's. They brimmed and spilled, brimmed and spilled. He dragged a white cloth out of his pocket and wiped them.

'It's the smoke,' said someone. 'It's the smoke tickles them up for you.'

His comrades watched him a bit, watched his eyes fill again, again brim over. The water ran down his face, off his chin on to the table. He rubbed the place with his coat-sleeve, and then, as though forgetful, went on rubbing, rubbing with his hand across the table, staring in front of him. And then he started shaking his head to the movement of his hand. He gave a loud strange groan and dragged out the cloth again. (628–9)

Nevertheless, the story has the disconcerting effect of seeming to aestheticize or trivialize the war: 'What beautiful cemeteries we are passing!', says the narrator. 'Is there really such a thing as war?' (619). Claire Tylee's reading strategically contains this effect. At first the heroine 'refuses to take what she sees to heart'. She 'extravagantly dramatises her situation', 'her perceptions skim over the surface', her 'reactions are gaily superficial'. By the end, however, she has 'discovered the reality of war. She has adventured beyond the sphere of virgin ignorance, into the forbidden zone of masculine knowledge'. When she enters the scullery to drink the mirabelle, she 'has arrived at the squalid, profane reality of the war-zone. She realises what it is to take a proper taste of humanity.'[23]

But if it is indeed the case that Mansfield often *does* require her characters to become disillusioned, how clear is the function and position of the war in the story? Take the scene in the station buffet:

Through an open door I can see a kitchen, and the cook in a white coat breaking eggs into a bowl and tossing the shells into a corner. The blue and red coats of the men who are eating hang upon the walls. Their short swords and belts are piled upon chairs. Heavens! what a noise. The sunny air seemed all broken up and trembling with it.

A little boy, very pale, swung from table to table, taking the orders, and poured me out a glass of purple coffee. *Ssssh*, came from the eggs. They were in a pan. (620)

The source of the 'noise' is never named. There may be a pun on eggshells and military shells, and the little boy needs to be 'very pale' for a reason. The lack of nomination may well give the effect that the war is the far horizon of meaning, an absence so significant that to name it would be redundant in a way that the *Ssssh* of the eggs is not. But conversely, the noise is given no priority over the rest of the scene, and there remains the possibility that the aestheticized soldiers, cemeteries, and weapons are part of the story's texture rather than its motivation.

The question of horizon is clearly central to the issue of war writing in general and vital to the accusation of treachery which Mansfield threw at Woolf. According to Murry, 'no single one of Katherine's friends who went to the war returned alive from it'.[24] Her civilian experience in England included close contact with friends who were utterly hostile to the war—among them Lawrence and Bertrand Russell—and the emotionally devastating experience of the death of her brother, who was killed in a training accident in November 1915. Thus, less than a year after her trip to Gray she writes to Koteliansky:

On the mantelpiece in my room stands my brother's photograph. I never see anything that I like, or hear anything, without the longing that he should see and hear, too—I had a letter from his friend again. He told me that after it happened he said over and over—'God forgive me for all I have done' and just before he died he said 'Lift my head, Katy I can't breathe—

To tell you the truth these things I have heard about him blind me to all that is happening here—All this is like a long uneasy ripple—nothing else—and below—in the still pool there is my little brother.[25]

This range of emotional experience makes 'war' a very complex space. Imaginatively, it is not an object but a mental and geographical practice constituted through actual battle sites and cultural and mental space. The town of Gray, seventy-five miles behind the trenches, was the closest Mansfield came to actual fighting until 1918, when Big Bertha was shelling Paris. Writing from her Paris apartment about this terrifying experience of the shelling, Mansfield comments: 'Outside the window is the scenic railway—all complete & behind that pretty piece is the war—'.[26] What does 'behind' mean here—in other words, where is the horizon in wartime? Is it the front itself, in which case, what lies before it and how does the front construct it? If it is not, then what lies beyond the war, how is it mediated by the event, and how does it mediate the event, as horizons must?

Such questions have made it possible—and entirely plausible—for some critics to treat *Prelude* (published by the Woolfs' Hogarth Press in 1918) as a war work: a memorial to her dead brother which finds its terms of expression not in the tense and place of the Great War but much earlier and more remotely in the 1890s New Zealand of her childhood. Mansfield's journal entries in late 1915 and early 1916 encourage such a reading.[27] However, Mansfield's attack on Woolf's novel post-dates the writing of *Prelude* by several years, and what she says about both *Prelude* and *Night and Day* may be taken too portentously. In May 1920, for example, Woolf makes a note in her diary of Mansfield's most recent remarks on the form of her stories: 'This last one, [The] Man without a T[emperament], is her first in the new manner. She says she's mastered something—is beginning to do what she wants. Prelude a coloured post card.'[28] Whether or not Woolf (or Mansfield) is reliable here, there are, in fact, several occasions from 1913 until her death when Mansfield writes in journals or letters about finding a new form. Moreover, the very fact that details of war are oblique or displaced does not mean that they automatically constitute a structure of revelation. It is always difficult to countermand the power of the surface–depth model of reading, the model whereby the war is always the necessary *real*—such as implied by the modestly parenthetical comments in the second section of Woolf's *To The Lighthouse* (1927)—and the model which, in the case of 'An Indiscreet Journey', entices with the pious satisfactions of taking revenge upon lust and teaching superficiality a lesson.

Mansfield's first war story, in fact, puts up a very productive resistance to such a model. Consider the eye-catching sentence, *Policemen are as thick as violets everywhere.*[29] With this remark, which does not appear in the journal sketch, the narrator of the story warns her lover to keep hidden. Women, and affairs, are forbidden in the war zone, and both must be kept from the eyes of the police. But policemen do not go with violets, even if their uniforms are blue. If violets do indeed gather 'thickly', then it is not the kind of thickness ordinarily associated with a gathering of police. Then, there is an echo of the phrase 'as thick as thieves', perhaps too a suggestion of dullness, and more remotely yet a hint of violence.

The remark may indeed be 'absurd' or 'mad', typical of the narrator's scatty superficiality, and thus, by implication, of her misperception of war.[30] But the mode of 'An Indiscreet Journey' is much closer to the surrealism of Leonora Carrington or Alfred Jarry (the 'old pa-man' who stamped Mansfield's passport perhaps recalls Jarry's Pa Ubu) than to the bitter manners comedy of Mansfield's better-known stories of disillusion. This modal quality makes it extremely difficult to read the story as a straightforward learning plot. For a start, the story contains no Bovaryisms. This is exceptional in Mansfield. Both the representation of authentic consciousness and the formal effectiveness of her kind of short story often depend upon a violent recall from pleasurable self-imaging to a dull or shocking quotidian. Here, however, there is nothing to be recalled to—that is to say, nothing *excluded* from the narrative's curious democracy of semantic significance in which policemen can indeed resemble violets. The connectiveness of things is associative rather than logical and hierarchical. The remark scrawled on the back of the fabricated letter from 'Aunt Julie'—*venez, vite, vite*—thus prompts the narrator to reflect: 'Strange impulsive woman! My heart began to beat . . .' (622). She cannot buy fish from the old man at the station buffet because she can neither keep nor get rid of them: 'I am sure it is a penal offence in France to throw fish out of railway-carriage windows' (621). Moreover, from the beginning of the journey, details of time and place are oddly unattached:

> 'Does one go direct to X.?' I asked the collector who dug at my ticket with a pair of forceps and handed it back again.
>
> 'No, Mademoiselle, you must change at X.Y.Z.'
>
> 'At—?'
>
> 'X.Y.Z.'
>
> Again I had not heard. 'At what time do we arrive there, if you please?'
>
> 'One o'clock.' But that was no good to me. I hadn't a watch. Oh, well—later. (618)

Unlike Mansfield's other voyage tales, such as 'The Little Governess' (also written in 1915), where powerlessness creates intolerable anxiety, deprivation of agency in 'An Indiscreet Journey' always becomes something in which to take pleasure. The heroine has already been, already knows—indeed, is somehow so sufficiently at ease in her disoriented state to produce a highly aestheticized image of the surrounding houses: 'Strange and mysterious they looked in the ragged drifting light and thin rain, like a company of beggars perched on the hill-side, their bosoms full of rich unlawful gold' (626).

A good deal of twentieth-century war writing draws upon the great naturalist psychic texts of day-dream and hallucination. Where documentary naturalism reaches its representational limits, surrealism offers one obvious alternative. However, to read the mode of 'An Indiscreet Journey' simply in terms of the unrepresentability of war is to miscontrue the story's highly transgressive quality. The logic-testing simile *Policemen are as thick as violets everywhere* is a stylistic symptom of a transgressional urge which begins on the very first page when the heroine purloins a friend's Burberry and then treats it as her own. The whole work, in fact, masquerades in 'borrowed' clothes which are sometimes nothing more than a linguistic blind: the highly illegal adventure, for example, is converted into an 'indiscretion'. What then is being covered up? In the first place, not the war but sexual pleasure. The woman in the train to X taunts the narrator: '"You know what women are like about soldiers"—she raised a final hand—"mad, completely mad"' (622–3). Claire Tylee picks up on this comment with a general point about the eroticization of war: 'A young girl's innocent, thrilled ideas of the romance of soldiering is a fragile illusion, doomed by the disgusting reality. Mansfield's naive heroine is initially intoxicated by war, like May Sinclair or May Cannan, but a second dose reveals the tedium, the oppression, the exploitation.'[31] In one sense, Tylee is right. The second section ends with thoughts of the narrator, sitting alone in the café: 'this is the sort of thing one will do on the very last day of all—sit in an empty café and listen to a clock ticking until—' (627). When her lover's arrival is later announced, she says: 'For some silly reason I pretended not to hear, and I leaned over the table smelling the violets' (629). But Mansfield's heroine is not naïve, however 'innocently' she follows the three drunk soldiers into a scullery to drink hard liquor, nor is the fascination with soldiers the *pleine parole* of the story's interest in sexuality. The intoxicant in the story is not mirabelle but the idea of transgression, and it is this idea which brings policemen and violets together.

In her unreliable memoirs, Ida Baker, Mansfield's sometime companion, remembers Mansfield's description of her journey to the war zone 'as being constantly shadowed by the colour of violets'.[32] It is a tantalizing comment. There are no references to violets in the journal, and only three brief ones in the story itself, including the phrase already referred to. But there are many violets in Mansfield's other stories. Violets are worn ('Je ne parle pas français', 'Mr Reginald Peacock's Day'), bought, or given as gifts ('The Tiredness of Rosalind', *Prelude*, 'Psychology'), discarded ('Miss Brill'), cultivated ('Weak Heart'), discovered in nature ('Spring Pictures', 'Revelations'), and faked ('Pictures'). In addition to double-white, deep purple, and Parma violets are numerous bunches of pansies (a hybrid viola) which are attached to hats, placed on bosoms, and collected in bottles. The narrator in 'An Indiscreet Journey' leaves a spray of violets in a glass at the restaurant in the war zone.

What does a 'violet' mean for Mansfield? Or rather, which meanings are excluded and included out of the imposing range of possibilities offered by the *OED*? Presumably not medicinal meanings: the violet as laxative, expectorant, sleeping-pill, or remedy for the disease of the uvula (until the 1880s, when the first synthetic perfume was stabilized, many colognes were used internally as well as externally). Nor are class connotations a guide. Towards the end of the nineteenth century, flower names became popular. Mansfield had a cook called Violet; the wealthy Violet Schiff, patron of the arts, was Mansfield's friend; and in 1924, a year after Mansfield died, Middleton Murry married the middle-class aspiring novelist Violet le Maistre (1903–31). The violet may promise secrets and what Shelley calls 'the violet paths of pleasure'. It may also suggest a scent rather than simply a colour. *Violette de Parme* is, in fact, one of the few odours in Mansfield's highly visual sensorium. It is essence of romance. Highly evocative and thoroughly pervasive, it penetrates in the way an image never can, since shutting the eyes can never block it out. In its very romantic capabilities to block out reality, it brings with it an air of danger—the danger of what Meredith in *Modern Love* calls 'the violet breath of maidenhood' and what George Eliot in *Adam Bede* captures in her phrase 'An afternoon in which destiny [. . .] poisons us with violet-scented breath'.

Death by violets. If Ida Baker remembers correctly, and the journey upon which Mansfield's story is based was indeed coloured by violets, the story itself is awake to the danger of romantic intoxication. Transgression is at once the source and end of excitement. The police are as thick as violets because they are as oppressive as the smell of violets, because they are intoxicating, and because they too represent the heady fumes of the passional. Mirabelle is the drink without the hangover, and thus brings intoxication to a state of perfection by allowing it to blend seamlessly with sober reality. The significance of 'An Indiscreet Journey' as a war story does not lie in its details of gassing, military discipline, and war loss, relevant though these details are. It lies rather in its ability to rescue itself from romantic intoxication, the originating condition of the story, by displaying such intoxication as the condition and goal of the writing.

This disjunction between toxic romance and sober reality is of the greatest importance to Mansfield's ability to write the disaster. Discussing artists' journals, Maurice Blanchot notes that such journals are relatively modern and relatively rare; the writers who keep them tend to be 'the most literary of all'. The critic is naturally interested in what such journals say about artistic practice. But the truth of the journal, says Blanchot, lies not in such revelations but in the 'insignificant details which attach it to daily reality', for the journal is the means by which the writer memorializes herself, rescues herself from art.[33] Mansfield's interest in Dorothy Wordsworth's journals (substantial portions of which were first published in 1895) leads to a passage in her own journal uncannily resembling Blanchot's point. In his introduction to Dorothy Wordsworth's journals, the editor William Knight remarks:

> All the Journals contain numerous trivial details, which bear ample witness to the 'plain living and high thinking' of the Wordsworth household and, in this edition, samples of those details are given—but there is no need to record all the cases in which the sister wrote, 'Today I mended William's shirts', or 'William gathered sticks', or 'I went in search of eggs', etc. etc.

Mansfield carefully copies out this passage (exactly) and adds: 'There is! Fool!'[34] In many respects, Mansfield is Blanchot's artist—the literary artist, compulsive, dedicated, under the tyranny of writing, for whom the metaphors of 'sickness' and 'health' seem ungraciously suggestive, and for whom the forgetfulness of writing finds a cure in the more prosaic details of the journal which bind her to the living. If there is pleasure in the Wordsworthian eggs and sticks, there is also celebration for those 'moments when Dickens is possessed by this power of writing: he is carried away. That is bliss. It certainly is not shared by writers to-day.'[35]

It is a disjunction which seems to have no equivalent in Woolf, let alone George Eliot, and it is something which Mansfield often turns into a narrative trope. The artists portrayed in her works are always compromised. At best, they are sloggers, such as the overweight, impoverished heroine of 'Pictures'; at worst, they are frauds and gigolos, such as the sexually ambiguous hero of 'Je ne parle pas français'. The image of false or cheap art in Mansfield often takes the form of an 1890s decadent survival immersed in *violette de Parme.* The aspiring aesthete in Max Beerbohm's story 'Enoch Soames' produces a collection of poems entitled *Fungoids*; the narrator of 'Je ne parle pas français' comes up with the equally fashionable *False Coins, Left Umbrellas,* and *Wrong Doors.* A heightening of sensibility in the direction of hyperaesthesia; a development of style towards preciosity: these elements characterize the unhealthy characters and the highly artificial conversations in 'Bliss' and 'Marriage à la Mode'.

There is a fine line in Mansfield's work, however, between the art she attacks and the art in which that art is attacked. There is a sense in which she is always shadowing herself. Her cure is not always successful ('Bliss' is a famous case in point) because it is often part of the symptom. It may have escaped Mansfield that 'violet' is a euphemism for 'onion', a form of what Eric Partridge calls 'proletarian-ironic' which dates back at least to the 1880s.[36] The point of the euphemism, however, should not have escaped her heroine, who would have had to lean very close indeed to smell her glass of violets over the 'suffocating smell of onion soup' which fills the café. In a letter to a would-be lover who has misunderstood the signals, Mansfield writes playfully: 'I did not, swayed by a resistless passion say that I loved you. Nevertheless I'm prepared to say it again looking at this pound of onions that hangs in a string kit from a saucepan nail.'[37] In a substantial proportion of Mansfield's work, proletarian-ironic is elevated into a formal protocol. The technique of misnaming is already present as an elementary irony in the *German Pension* stories written well before the war. It continues into her later work most weakly as a kind of satiric misnaming—'Bliss', 'An Ideal Family', 'Such a Sweet Old Lady'. It becomes the most obvious way of countering the toxic effects of romantic illusions. In 'Life of Ma Parker' (1921), Mansfield describes the wretched life of the woman who cleans the flat of a 'literary gentleman'. Ma Parker recounts her history—the death of her husband, children, grandchildren, the squalor of 'black beedles', the poverty—with some encouragement from her employer: 'For occasionally he laid aside his tomes and lent an ear, at least, to this product called Life.'[38]

The artistic commodification of life blurs the distinction in Mansfield's work between onion and violet. This is nowhere more difficult to recognize than in the structure of disclosure already discussed in connection with the idea of the war as the *real*. 'The Singing Lesson' (1916) clarifies this aspect of her technique. A reluctant lover sends a wounding letter: '"the idea of settling down fills me with nothing but—" and the word "disgust" was scratched out lightly and "regret" written over the top'. As in many of her stories, love lies bleeding from the cruelty of the lover. In this case, however, the letter is hastily retracted with a telegram, and romance blooms again. But the sadism of the lover is all the more interesting because it is allowed to happen—whether or not it is plausible, it is what the story *wants*. The cruelty of the story, in fact, is less the calculated sadism of the lover, than the teacher's blissful reversal of feeling. The story works by knowing more and caring less. There is, of course, a sense in which such stories in Mansfield are nothing other than a 'caring' about feeling. But the artistry of the story depends upon an indifference which will allow the story to be told, an indifference which is the concomitant of a will to style; art itself becomes self-conscious in its relation to feeling: a complex synthesis of passion, disgust, and cruelty.

This is the *Rhythm* school of writing—what Murry in his essay 'Art and Philosophy' in the first number calls 'modernism'.[39] In this early use of the term, Murry means something deeply hostile to the Wildean aestheticism which first attracted Mansfield. 'Before art can be human it must learn to be brutal.' Modernism is 'an art that strikes deeper [. . .] drawing its inspiration from aversion, to a deeper and a broader field [. . .] in its pity and its brutality it shall be real.'[40] There is an element of this notion of the real in 'An Indiscreet Journey'. The only tears produced in the story are the angry tears of the adolescent boy waiter and the protective reflex of the soldier's damaged eyes. On neither occasion are tears shed for love or loss. Madame looks at the soldier's streaming eyes and remarks indignantly: 'Mais vous savez, c'est un peu dégoutant, ça' (629). In this remark, which has no basis in Mansfield's journal account, the idea of disgust is not even lightly erased and replaced by the word 'regret'. Disgust, disclosure of the real, the principle of aversion, the valorizing of pity, brutality, and the unsavouriness of truth: these ideals of *Rhythm* constitute the ironic indifferentiation of twentieth-century representations of war. It is an aesthetic which *already* contains the war. In this larger sense, a response to the war is condemned to repeat art. The war itself is the inevitable and most logical artistic commodity.

This version of the relation between art and life is under suspicion in 'An Indiscreet Journey'. But Mansfield's second war story, 'The Fly', pursues it to a different end. Old Woodifield has been visiting the boss, a successful businessman running an unspecified business.[41] The boss is the older man but, unlike Woodifield, blooming with health and success. Where mirabelle in 'An Indiscreet Journey' helps forgetfulness, whisky in 'The Fly' stirs the memory. Mr Woodifield, suitably primed, remembers a piece of news; he has been to France, and seen the war graves, nicely tended, of both his own son and the son of the boss. The boss just manages not to crumple at the unexpected news. Hastily getting rid of Woodifield, he sits down at his desk and prepares to weep in front of a large photograph of his boy. To his surprise, the tears do not come for the first time in six years. Just then he notices a fly has fallen into the inkpot. He rescues it, and it cleans itself. Just before it can fly away, the boss drops ink on it, and the process of cleaning begins again. The process is repeated twice more, until the boss decides it is the last time. The final ink-drop falls and the fly lies still. He carries 'the little corpse' on his pen to the bin. Refreshed and sitting down again, he cannot remember 'for the life of him' what it was that had been on his mind.

According to Middleton Murry, 'The Fly' is the 'perfect utterance' of the 'profound and ineradicable impression made upon [Mansfield] by the war'.[42] Presumably what he means by this is that the story is a complex rendering of grief, memory, and loss, and this seems to be the sense in which the story is usually anthologized. But there is a quality to the story which sits uncomfortably with this reading. The cruelty of the boss's treatment of the fly involves a curious affection and sensuousness; he breathes on the fly tenderly to bring it back to life, and the tactile pleasure of struggling legs—which links with old Woodifield's pleasure in the whisky, and numerous other closely registered details of touch and taste—produces further cruelty. This combination of the sensual and the cruel has a history in Mansfield's work. Intimations of 'The Fly' can be found in her early story 'Violet' (1913). The narrator fantasizes about a day in the country with Katharine Tynan,[43] drinking glasses of milk handed out by 'a red-faced woman with an immensely fat apron' and debating the 'direct truth of proverbs'. The red-faced woman disapproves of 'the one about a bird in the hand. I naturally prefer birds in bushes':

'But,' said Katharine Tynan, tender and brooding, as she lifted a little green fly from her milk glass, 'but if you were Saint Francis, the bird would not *mind* being in your hand. It would prefer the white nest of your fingers to any bush.'[44]

Over the next nine years, there are numerous further references to flies in Mansfield's stories, letters, and journal.[45] From 1918 the frequency of reference markedly increases, and several of them, grouped in mid-1919, are worth mentioning here. The first is an entry in her journal, suitably headed,

The Fly
December 31 4.45 p.m. Oh, the times when she had walked upside down on the ceiling, run up glittering panes, floated on a lake of light, flashed through a shining beam!

And God looked upon the fly fallen into the jug of milk and saw that it was good. And the smallest Cherubim and Seraphim of all, who delight in misfortune, struck their silver harps and shrilled: 'How is the fly fallen, fallen!'[46]

The second:

A little fly has dropped by mistake into the huge sweet cup of magnolia. Isaiah (or was it Elisha) was caught up into Heaven in a chariot of fire *once.*[47]

And finally:

Dark Bogey [Murry] is a little inclined to jump into the milk jug to rescue the fly.[48]

In these examples, the idea of suffering is complex. The threat of death goes hand in hand with sweet, encompassing nourishment and the possibility of transcendence. To be rescued from this is to be restored to the human from the divine. The fly is both the miniaturization of suffering itself, and the self-image of the sufferer who longs to lose herself.

These images gain further resonance in the context of an extraordinary sequence in Mansfield's journal, dated 21 June 1919, in which she describes the action and symptoms of lice, the bedbug, '*Hydatids*', '*The Egyptian disease*', '*Dysentery*' and '*Hydrophobia*'. She has been discussing these forms of illness with Dr Sorapure, a consultant at Hampstead General Hospital, who she had begun seeing in November the previous year.[49] Each of these forms of illness are evidently the product of knowledge coming about by virtue of the First World War. Thus Bateson saved lives in the Balkan War because he used himself as a guinea-pig, even letting his experimental lice feed off his own arm, and hydrophobia produces last stage symptoms of 'gasping and groaning as in gas-poisoning'. But the fascination of the diseases seems to arise from the relation between dependence and independence, and outside and inside: of what she calls 'the mysterious lives within lives'. In the first place, Mansfield is intrigued by the disintegration of her own body; she has been taught by Dr Sorapure to identify the symptoms of dying, and is on the alert for Death in a way which recalls precisely the ambivalent relation of the literary gentleman to Life. In the second place, however, she dwells upon the element of parasitism with fascination; she is seduced by this relationship, and makes some surprising larger connections: 'I had a sense of the *larger breath*, of the mysterious lives within lives, and the Egyptian parasite beginning its new cycle of being in a water-snail affected me like a *great* work of art. No, that's not what I mean. It made me feel how *perfect* the world is, with its worms and hooks and ova, how incredibly perfect.' She remarks: 'There is the sky and the sea and the shape of a lily, and there is all this other as well. The *balance* how perfect!'[50]

It is only a few months later that Mansfield condemns Woolf's artistic treachery as a 'lie in the soul', and it is difficult to imagine that her frame of mind had shifted substantially from the earlier comments. 'The Fly', however, develops what it means to have 'a change of heart', to remain loyal to art and to life, in an unexpected direction. The horizons of war and of art come together in the image of suffering as a longing for a kind of transcendent immersion. The action of the story depends, of course, upon resistance to such a longing—old Woodifield hanging on to life, the fly frantically cleaning its wings, the boss restored to vigour by finding himself incapable of grief. It refuses the indulgence of sweet suffering by returning to onion-life: the materialism of the boss's office with its sausage-like radiators, the rude health of the boss himself. This movement might thus suggest the saving movement of an act of writing which refuses, as Blanchot has it, the 'temptation to melt into the fiction of the universe, and thereby become indifferent to the tormenting vicissitudes of the near at hand'.[51]

But the issue of healthy art is more complex than this. Part of the much-discussed ambiguity of 'The Fly'[52] arises from its ideological containment of actions which sit uneasily between sadism and sentimentality—the boss's forgetfulness of his dead son, the loss of grief, the pleasure in old Woodifield's decrepitude, and, most notably of course, the treatment of the fly. A point of comparison is provided by Virginia Woolf, who seems to have drawn on 'The Fly' in at least two pieces of her own work: the story 'The New Dress' (1927) and the essay 'The Death of the Moth' (1942). In the essay, a moth is dancing ever more stiffly along a window-ledge in the sun. The narrator reaches out a pencil to help but to no avail. The moth is dying *naturally*:

> It was useless to try to do anything. One could only watch the extraordinary efforts made by those tiny legs against an oncoming doom which could, had it chosen, have submerged an entire city, nor merely a city, but masses of human beings; nothing, I knew, had any chance against death. Nevertheless after a pause of exhaustion the legs fluttered again. It was superb this last protest, and so frantic that he succeeded at last in righting himself. One's sympathies, of course, were all on the side of life.[53]

Woolf is too subtle to write 'Life' with a capital 'L' as Mansfield might have done; indeed, the close, sustained *enjoyment* of the pitiful struggle is sublimated into a paean to Death. This is not the way of Mansfield's response to the war. The element of sadism in 'The Fly' excuses itself through the idea of a 'truth to psychology' which is historically part of Mansfield's aesthetic and can free the reader—especially the immediate post-war reader—to participate in the spectacle of suffering without the anxiety of guilt. More profoundly, for Mansfield the suffering is necessary to make the writing healthy. Her war story is a form of self-inoculation; it understands the boss's action as a saving brutalism, a health *because* of sickness, behind which is a version of Woolf's instinct of self-preservation: 'if he's unwell then I'm not'.

NOTES

1. For a detailed account of the affair, see Antony Alpers, *The Life of Katherine Mansfield* (London, 1980), 173–9.
2. Mansfield to Frieda Lawrence, 20 Feb. 1915, in *The Collected Letters of Katherine Mansfield*, ed. Vincent O'Sullivan and Margaret Scott, i (Oxford, 1984), 150.
3. On Carco's life and writing, see Christiane Mortelier, 'The French Connection: Francis Carco', in Roger Robinson (ed.), *Katherine Mansfield: In from the Margin* (Baton Rouge, La., 1994).
4. The narrator of Mansfield's 'Je ne parle pas français' (written 1918) is usually taken to draw on Carco. For Carco's use of Mansfield, see Mortelier, 'The French Connection', 149–52.
5. Mortelier, 'The French Connection', 139.
6. Mansfield to Murry, 10 Nov. 1919, in *Collected Letters of Katherine Mansfield*, iii (Oxford, 1993), 82.
7. Maurice Blanchot, *The Writing of the Disaster*, trans. Ann Smock (Lincoln, Nebr., 1986), 4.
8. It would seem that Mansfield contracted gonorrhoea in 1910 and, as a consequence, had her damaged left fallopian tube removed in March 1910. She subsequently developed the symptoms of systemic gonorrhoea, including arthritis, heart trouble and pleurisy, and possibly tuberculosis. By 1918 her physical condition had deteriorated beyond recovery; she sought a variety of opinions and treatments, including painful injections and radiation therapy. Many of these details were first presented and argued in Claire Tomalin's *Katherine Mansfield: A Secret Life* (London, 1987).
9. Entry for 7 Aug. 1918, *The Diary of Virginia Woolf*, ed. Anne Olivier Bell, i (1915–19) (Harmondsworth, 1979), 179.
10. The quoted remark concerns her reluctance to review Dorothy Richardson's novel *The Tunnel* (1919). See the entry for 28 Nov. 1919, *The Diary of Virginia Woolf*, i. 315.
11. Katherine Mansfield, 'A Ship Comes into Harbour', review of *Night and Day*, *Nation and Athenaeum*, 21 Nov. 1919; repr. in *The Critical Writings of Katherine Mansfield*, ed. Clare Hanson (London, 1987).
12. Virginia Woolf, 'Romance and the Heart', review of Romer Wilson's *The Grand Tour* and Richardson's *Revolving Lights*, *Nation and Athenaeum*, 19

May 1923; repr. in *The Essays of Virginia Woolf*, ed. Andrew McNeillie, ii (London, 1988), 365–8.

13. Katherine Mansfield, 'Three Women Novelists', review of Dorothy Richardson's *The Tunnel*, *Nation and Athenaeum*, 4 Apr. 1919; repr. in *Critical Writings*, 49–50.
14. Katherine Mansfield, 'Dragonflies', review of Dorothy Richardson's *Interim*, *Nation and Athenaeum*, 9 June 1920; repr. in *Critical Writings*, 63–4.
15. *Journal of Katherine Mansfield*, ed. J. Middleton Murry, definitive edn. (London, 1954), 69.
16. Mansfield to Murry, 29 Dec. 1915, in *Collected Letters*, ii (Oxford, 1987), 242.
17. Murry's commentary, in *Katherine Mansfield's Letters to John Middleton Murry 1913–1922* (London, 1951), 85.
18. *The Doves' Nest* appeared some months after Mansfield's death at the beginning of 1923. Murry had included some excerpts from Mansfield's diary. The comments from Woolf appear in the diary entry for 19 June 1923, *The Diary of Virginia Woolf*, ii (1920–24) (Harmondsworth, 1981), 248.
19. *Journal*, under the heading '*May 31 Work.*', 161.
20. See *Journal*, 75–9.
21. Katherine Mansfield, *The Collected Stories* (London, 1988), 633. All further references are to this edition.
22. Introduction to Katherine Mansfield, *Selected Stories* (London, 1987), p. ix.
23. Claire M. Tylee, *The Great War and Women's Consciousness: Images of Militarism and Womanhood in Women's Writings, 1914–64* (Basingstoke, 1990), 85–91.
24. Murry's commentary, in *Journal*, 104.
25. Mansfield to S. S. Koteliansky, 19 Nov. 1915, in *Collected Letters*, ii. 200.
26. Mansfield to Murry, 3–4 Feb. 1918, in *Collected Letters*, ii. 56.
27. *Journal*, 96–8.
28. 31 May 1920, *The Diary of Virginia Woolf*, ii. 44.
29. Stress added. A phrase in one of Mansfield's letters written during her March stay in Paris recalls the phrase in the story and sets up an interesting tension between the illicit, the passional, and the idea of death. She is writing about Beatrice Hastings:

    'Of course everybody she ever knew has died a grisly death in this war —& the fact that Carco is going to Turkey seems to delight her beyond measure. Il ne reviendra jamais!

    Today everywhere they are crying voici les jolies violettes de Parme [. . .]'

    (Mansfield to Murry, [21 Mar. 1915], in *Collected Letters*, i. 160).
30. Introduction to Mansfield, *Selected Stories*, p. ix.
31. Tylee, *The Great War and Women's Consciousness*, 90.
32. Ida Baker, *Katherine Mansfield: The Memories of LM*, introd. A. L. Barker (London, 1985), 94.
33. Maurice Blanchot, *The Space of Literature*, trans. Ann Smock (Lincoln, Nebr., 1982), 29.
34. *Journal*, 210.
35. Ibid. 203.
36. Eric Partridge, *The Penguin Dictionary of Historical Slang* (Harmondsworth, 1972). There is a further fanciful but pleasing connection between violets and onions. In *A Natural History of the Senses* (London, 1990), Diane

Ackerman remarks that 'Violets contain ionone, which short-circuits our sense of smell. The flower continues to exude its fragrance, but we lose the ability to smell it. Wait a minute or two, and its smell will blare [*sic*] again. Then it will fade again and so on' (p. 9). The capacity of the nose to become intermittently virginal in the presence of violets is a nice complement to proletarian-ironic; onions are stylistically what ionones are physiologically.

37. Mansfield to Frederick Goodyear, [4 Mar. 1916], in *Collected Letters*, i. 248.
38. 'Life of Ma Parker', in *Collected Stories*, 304.
39. 'Art and Philosophy', *Rhythm*, 1/1 (1911), 12.
40. Editorial statement, 'Aims and Ideals', *Rhythm*, 1/1 (1911), 36.
41. In a letter to Dorothy Brett, 26 Feb. 1922, Mansfield describes the boss as a 'Bank Manager'. This detail has encouraged biographical readings (one of her father's positions was as bank manager) but it does not appear in the story. See *Katherine Mansfield: Selected Letters*, ed. Vincent O'Sullivan (Oxford, 1989), 248.
42. Murry's commentary, in *Journal*, 107.
43. Katherine Tynan (1861–1933), the Irish poet and novelist and leading member of the Celtic literary revival. Apart from volumes of tender poetry she wrote (after the date of Mansfield's story) two curious war novels, *The Holy War* (1916) and *Herb O'Grace* (1918).
44. 'Violet', in *Collected Stories*, 584. In the story, the narrator meets an old friend called Violet who has a 'secret' she wishes to forget. She has been kissed by a man who is engaged to another.
45. See Celeste Turner Wright, 'Genesis of a Short Story', *Philological Quarterly*, 34/1 (1955), 91–6.
46. *Journal*, 153.
47. Ibid. 161.
48. Ibid. 170.
49. For an account of Sorapure's treatment of Mansfield, see Tomalin, *A Secret Life*. In Ida Baker's *The Memories of LM*, she says that the MS of 'The Daughters of the Colonel' contained a dedication to Sorapure (128).
50. *Journal*, 167–8.
51. Blanchot, *The Writing of the Disaster*, 75.
52. Probably the fullest discussion of the story's difficulties takes the form of a debate in *Essays in Criticism*, 12 (1962), inaugurated as a 'Critical Exercise' in close reading by F. W. Bateson and B. Shahevitch which was then responded to in the Critical Forum section of the journal; see pp. 39–53, 339–51, and 449–52.
53. Virginia Woolf, 'The Death of the Moth', in *The Death of the Moth and Other Essays* (London, 1942), 11.

10

Mary Butts, Mothers, and War

MARY HAMER

WHAT kind of woman calls her own red hair scarlet? One who was not shy of the limelight, by all accounts. Asking us to look at her, even before she invites us to look with her, to join her in thinking again about the question of women, the voice of Mary Butts echoes imperiously still today. A brilliant, even ferocious intelligence, a demanding voice: there are no anodyne terms to present her in. And if you look to find her among her friends, you will not find them organizing to work together for the vote or exploring the extended options opened to women by the war. It is in the memories of men that the sense of her as a person survived, a big eager lawless redhead, on the lookout for excitement and parties. 'Paris was a dream. We didn't go to bed for a week and spent all our money on *such* binges! The last thing I remember was dancing solely supporting myself by the lobes of Cedric Morris' ears,' she wrote to Douglas Goldring.[1]

She is the hardest figure to recruit for any cause. In her own person she throws the regular terms of enquiry into disarray. Mary Butts was a woman who hated her own mother and though she gave birth to a daughter, Camilla, did not bring the child up herself. No one could say she was not a difficult woman, in almost any sense you care to name. When Patrick Wright brought her writing back to public attention in 1985, it was primarily to expose its enthusiastic rhetoric of blood and race.[2]

Yet it is her writing that makes Mary Butts a woman who cannot be dismissed. At the first encounter with one of her sentences, a reader wonders if she has ever heard the English language treated with such cavalier authority before: 'At breakfast, in a quicksilver mirror, she saw the men come in. The eagle over it had a sock-suspender in its beak, but between the straps and the distortion she did not like the look of them.'[3] Next, the reader asks, as Butts might have put it herself, whether she likes it. If rights are being assumed, might the move not be made at our expense?

But this almost tiresome originality, elliptical and clipped, is not a mere matter of style: the language changes in Butts's hands because she used writing as a way of feeling forward, feeling beyond and through the old ways of putting things together. The arbitrary and unfamiliar syntax, the odd juxtapositions, grow out of this. If the reader feels challenged, this is perhaps not a mistake. But more interesting than any demand for personal recognition, Mary Butts asked her readers to give up their old patterns of thought, the grammar of assumptions by which they held together their former picture of the world.

The noun 'intellectual' has an interesting history: in the Paris of the late 1890s the word was taken up as a term of abuse. It was used at the time of the Dreyfus affair against the writers and artists who were refusing to accept the explanations offered by the military authorities.[4] Now psychologists use it to indicate the way some people orientate themselves in the world, the ones who use thinking to organize their experience. Mary Butts was one of these. Though her formal education ended when her teachers learned she had planned to take a day off from Westfield College in London University to go to the Derby and asked her to leave, she confronted her experience with questions and she looked for some at least of her answers in books.[5] Although she chose stories as the form to record her discoveries, they are stories that record the observations of a moralist. She chose a life of pleasure in the world rather than seclusion, but in her fiction she posed the questions of a philosopher.

The story of her own life is not a comforting one. She was born on 13 December 1890, the first child of an elderly father and a much younger mother in a small country-house in Dorset. She grew up there, as she records in the last book she wrote, *The Crystal Cabinet: My Childhood at Salterns*, tuned to the life she found resonating in the landscape, the movement of the weather and the seas.[6] She claims to have been able to hold on to and even live within that visionary sense of the world that most people know only fleetingly. Her father made a friend of her, encouraging her to use his library, and he fended off attempts to pester her into young ladyhood. But when she was 14 he died, and his widow, her mother, sold some of his treasures to pay death duties and burned others, various volumes of classical literature that she considered indecent. She soon married again. Mary was sent away, and though it was a good school, St Leonard's, that she went to, where she was well taught, the breach with her mother was never healed.

The wildness that got her sent down from university before 1914 drove her after the war's end to a gesture that no one could take lightly. She left her husband, John Rodker, the painter, and her daughter, a baby of a few months, and set off for Paris with another man. She lived in Paris and travelled in Europe from then until the end of the decade, when the collapse of world markets seems to have been matched by a personal disintegration of her own. Her nerve and her money ran out at about the same time. She may have been undermined by a certain failure of response to the work she had been publishing for the previous ten years.

For she had been writing in all this time spent abroad, writing the whole day before convivial evenings that went on in bars and clubs until the small hours and beyond. She kept a journal from 1917 to 1927 and had been publishing her work since at least 1919, when Robert McAlmon arranged for parts of her first novel, *Ashe of Rings*, to come out in *The Little Review*. She was a protégée of Ford Madox Ford, who thought she had a streak of genius. Her first collection of short stories, *Speed the Plough*, appeared in 1923 after Alec Waugh had commended it to a publisher. Jean Cocteau drew the illustrations for her experimental work *Imaginary Letters* (1928). She published three novels, *Ashe of Rings* (1925), *Armed with Madness* (1928), and *The Death of Felicity Taverner* (1932).[7]

It is clear that this writing puzzled some home readers. By 1933 Ethel Smyth was turning in perplexity to Virginia Woolf, 'And who is Mary Butts?' Smyth asked; '& why can I only understand about ½ of every page she writes to be conscious of huge chunks in—say *death of Felicity Taverner* where I understand nothing of what is going forward.' She repeated her first question, 'Do you know who Mary Butts is?'[8] It seems likely that even for Butts herself, meeting incomprehension in her readers, it was getting harder to return a confident answer. Who can say what it had been costing her to produce her writing without the support of other women? Her family brought her home from Europe. Her companion, Cecil Maitland, had died earlier, and now she made a second marriage, to an artist called Gabriel Aitken, and went to live in a very small way at Sennen, in Cornwall.

At Sennen, Butts soon found herself alone again, poor and cut off from the company of the artists and writers whose sense of life had fed her own. She had to forge another means of connecting with the world and she set out to make a new identity, wooing the vicar and the local gentry, while establishing herself as a reviewer in London. She stopped publishing novels of contemporary life and wrote historical novels instead, *The Macedonian* (1933) and *Scenes from the Life of Cleopatra* (1935).[9] At this time too the right-wing pamphlets that Patrick Wright quotes, *Traps for Unbelievers* and *Warning to Hikers*, appeared, both published in 1932. The only link with her uncompromised younger self was her daughter Camilla, no longer a child but becoming a young woman. In the last two years of her life they spent about six months together.[10] Then in 1937 she died, after being found in a state of collapse, following a sudden haemorrhage from a perforated ulcer.

We are not altogether surprised if writers come to no good, but the apparent failure of a woman's life leaves us disturbed. It is hard to fend off the sensation of dismay that follows on telling the story of Mary Butts. Even to repeat it seems to carry risks for a woman, the danger of seeming not to know that this is not the way to live, the danger of exposing oneself as being like her, seeming to stand with her and invite the punishments of exile, isolation, and death that then came down. Silencing too: most of her books went out of print. It may be no accident that the publicly confessed admirers of her work have been almost all of them men: there was and is less hazard for a man in speaking out on behalf of such a woman.

Yet that negative interpretation of her life rests on assumptions that she herself continually used writing to examine, assumptions about what makes a good life, a good woman, a good man; in her own work Mary Butts steadily refrains from assuming that there must be a difference between what is expected of women and of men. In the course of the First World War, it has often been argued, the division between men and women was reinforced.[11] The chasm that opened, in the imaginary, during that time between soldiers and civilians also emphasized the difference between men and women. Only men could have the right to wear military uniform: however the war work women could find for themselves transgressed the boundaries of femininity as it had been known before 1914, women did not dress like warriors. Despite all that used to be claimed about the violent overthrow of familiar landmarks that took place during the First World War, culture's founding practice, the observation of sexual difference as a means to the subordination of women, was protected. It metamorphosed, if anything, into a stronger form.

It was as a critic of her own culture, its systems of beliefs and practices, that Mary Butts took up her stance, and it is in company with other cultural critics, particularly those with a background in psychoanalytic theory like the philosopher Luce Irigaray, that she can productively be read. Butts wrote stories and poems, not philosophy, but she anticipates Irigaray in calling the European idea of masculine identity a dangerous fiction and in demonstrating its dependence on a parallel fiction of the feminine.[12] In fictions of her own making, stories that refuse to anchor themselves by reference to conventional masculinity, she suggested that there were other ways of living a woman's life or a man's.

Butts believed that the war had not been an aberration but the likely outcome of ordinary ways, of the everyday habits of gendered lives. It had been incubated in the home. When she used fiction to explore the hatreds war licensed and the damage it left behind in minds and bodies, she repeatedly drew attention to patterns of kinship, gender, and belief. It was to these she sensed that the catastrophe was properly to be related. Rather than merely thinking of Butts as one among other modernist readers influenced by G. S. Frazer's *The Golden Bough*, we might do better to situate her as an originator, by the side of Jane Harrison, the classical scholar whose pioneering work in anthropology led Lévi-Strauss to name her as the founding thinker in the development of structuralism, or with Joan Rivière, one of the first women analysts to challenge Freud's account of the feminine by developing one of her own.[13] In her war writings Mary Butts investigated the ways that religious feeling, the will to violence, and the understanding of gender interlocked in her culture of origin. Because she used writing itself to do it, rather than any of the disciplines taught in the universities, it can be easy to miss the intellectual force of her work.

In a sense, Butts never stopped writing about what had caused the war and the damage the war had done. The characters in her novels of contemporary life are still operating, often, in what we might call a kind of post-traumatic stress that is referred back constantly to the war. This chapter will concentrate, though, on three early pieces: a short story, the volume of *Imaginary Letters* that her friend Jean Cocteau illustrated, and the novel *Ashe of Rings*.

From the first, Butts took up a strong position. Her story 'Speed the Plough', which opened and gave its name to the collection that was meant to bring her to the attention of readers in Britain, begins with a familiar and even sacred topic for the period, an account of a soldier lying in hospital and his return to consciousness. Yet within a very few lines it sets inexorably about discomfiting the reader, particularly the woman reader, for it starts with a challenging dismissal. Unusually, the soldier is not grateful to his nurses but offended by their lack of charm.

We learn that the patient has been lamed for life and is bound to be assaulted for years by nightmare images from his war experience, but any simple reflex of sympathy on our part is blocked by our discomfort with his fantasies. As the soldier drifts back to awareness of the world, he clings to the images of teasing young women drawn in an illustrated paper and gradually begins to imagine for himself the kind of clothes that they would choose: it is the names of expensive fabrics, crêpe, georgette, velour, aerophane, that he repeats as the litany that will save him. There is a certain surprise for readers in discovering that his dreams about undressing the girls in the paper should dwell so lovingly on bales of fabric.

His doctors, realizing that he is increasingly withdrawn and has made no progress for months, send him down to the country to work on a farm. Here, the passion for beauty that could find no satisfaction in the hospital, least of all in the presence of the women he found there, begins to be appeased. Not by sunsets or a Wordsworthian exchange with the landscape, but by his capacity to respond to what looks like the product of artifice in the natural world, objects that seem to exhibit a managed or stage-managed beauty, one produced by human work and intention. 'The sheen on the new grass, the expanse of sky, now heavy as marble, now luminous; the embroidery that a bare tree makes against the sky' (16).[14] Gradually the images that had paraded obsessively beyond his control in his hospital dreams enter his consciousness and are reintegrated there. He sees the thin ice crackle under his boots and remembers both the effect of diamanté and the word for it. His experience, the language he had been used to naming it in, his identity, are coming back to him. Pleasure returns, too, in the memory of the glamorous stars he used to watch at the music-hall.

In the hospital, when he saw himself in the mirror, he had wept and felt he could only contaminate the world he had loved by returning to it. In the farmyard, seated among the cows that he turns out to have a special gift for milking, the soldier regains his self-respect. This does not mean, however, that he is healed by the natural world as he encounters it in the milkingshed—not in the least. His sense of decency is revolted by what he finds there and it prompts the first coherent reflection of his restored consciousness: 'The warm milk whose beauty had pleased began to nauseate him. There was a difference in nature between that winking, pearling flow and the pale decency of a Lyons' tea-jug.' (18) Soon he is clear that what he has seen is 'dirty, yes, dirty, like a man being sick. In London we're civilised . . .' (20).

That evening his vision of 'fine delicate life' is confirmed when he sees a beautiful, well-dressed woman, 'some sort of actress', getting into her car to return to London. The disparaging comments of the people in the pub make him angry: he is increasingly clear that he doesn't belong here and must get back to the city. The story ends with the soldier reinstated, as the reader recognizes, in the former life to which his incoherent hospital dreams harked back; he is serving a society girl in a fitting-room, on his knees, pinning French brocade around her.

There can be little doubt that conventional thinkers were meant to find this mocking tale utterly provoking. It closes with the former soldier kindling in sympathy with the complaint of the spoiled young woman: 'When the war starts interfering with my clothes . . . the war goes under' (26). The writer has no time for patriotism. She goes out of her way to make light of it: it is girls with foreign names and foreign fashions that the recovering soldier yearns for. The women of the hospital 'distressed him. They were not like the Kirchner girls in the worn *Sketch* he fingered all day. . . . Coquetterie, mannequin, lingerie, and all one could say in English was underwear' (11).[15] To find pleasure and the words to put it into, the story suggests, you have to look outside Britain, to another sensibility, another language. It is the names of fabrics, velour, organdie, brocade, and of the women that wear them, names that deliberately aspire not to be English, that inflame desire and inspire loyalty in this story.

If Butts wants to dismiss patriotism, it is in the interest of making space for something more important. It is about the order of civilization itself that she wants to pose questions, the terms that are used for making sense of experience. She starts by asking questions about what makes a man. The hero of her story, whose name we never know, needs his sense of beauty satisfied before he can regain his hold on life, and this beauty locates itself for him in the work of artifice, not the world of nature. It is shamelessly unnatural versions of femininity that confirm his sense of what is real and of who he is himself, mannequins with their patently false names, 'Suzanne and Verveine, Ambre and Desti', and the stars of the music-hall, Gaby, Delysia, and Polaire, women whose bodies are transformed for exhibition by art.[16] It is the going beyond the given in nature that he needs: the unmade-up prettiness of some of the nurses only irritates him. He yearns for the women who brush their lids with 'violet from an ivory box' (15).

What is this male identity that is held in place by a fiction of the female? Not an uncompromisingly heterosexual one. We are told that the soldier had a fine body and that his training had developed it to advantage, but there is no mention of sexual desire in exploring his relation to women. The story implies something more troubling, that stripped of fantasy women's bodies threaten him with psychological disintegration. It claims that beside the 'embroidery a bare tree makes against the sky' a cow was 'an obscene vision of the night' (16), a visitation from something properly kept out of sight, an eruption, as the psychoanalysts might say, from the unconscious. As he improves, literally getting to grips with it in the milking-shed, the soldier gropingly recognizes the maternal body in the cow that he is milking. And he wonders how to connect this reality with the artificial versions of womanhood that he finds so fascinating: 'Dimly he realised that this was where most of life started, indifferent of any later phase. "Little bits of fluff," Rosalba and all the Kirchner tribe . . . was Polaire only a cow . . . or Delysia? . . .' (19).

He senses that some link is missing, a link that might be made between the artifice of femininity and the brute facts—unmediated by language—of the mother's body. As this body erupts into the text it will remind some of today's readers of Irigaray and of her theory that it is on the suppression of the body of the mother that Western culture, with its fantasies of masculine and feminine, takes its stand.[17] In the story Butts writes, this body is part of an integrated system of meanings that exist just beyond the soldier's grasp. Intuiting this seems to set him free to stand poised between the elements, the four elements of what used to be called the natural order. Once he has reached understanding, the story reports: 'The light had now the full measure of day. A wind that tasted delicately of shingle and the turf flew to meet him' (19).

With a new clarity the soldier turns away from a heterosexual positioning, the story seems to imply, not from incapacity but by choice. He makes the move supported by the memory of artifice, the spectacle and language, the lyrics of the music-hall. Though the farmer sees him as a born dairyman and invites him to come and look at the new bull, the soldier declines this offer of a place in the heterosexual order and goes back to town, to take up his old employment in the dress business. He returns to a job that had never been called man's work: the history associating men interested in fashion, design, and decoration with homosexual desire was already a long one.[18] Butts constructed her story to show that the move was not a change of direction for him, but a confirmation of choices made earlier, outside the conditions of war, before soldiering made a man of him. The meaning of those choices has been reframed: masculinity, health, and heterosexuality no longer overlap, but have been pushed apart to lie side by side, inviting a closer examination of what they might have in common.

Luce Irigaray, whose name keeps cropping up when you think about Mary Butts, has succinctly theorized the part images of women are called upon to play in Western culture. Fantasies of the feminine, she argues, have been concocted in the West only in order that they may support another fantasy, the fantasy of male identity. In 'Speed the Plough' Butts seems to be dramatizing something very like this dependence. In this story, the man's hold on his own identity, at first as tenuous as his grasp of the *Sketch* with its drawings of pert, half-dressed girls, gets more confident as he locates himself more firmly in relation to the parade of femininity.

But what about living women, how do they make sense of who they are? What has happened to Mary Butts herself? Where is she in this tale? She is telling a story about an image of the feminine created in the world of fashion, one that women must put on in order to become 'womanly', and to that extent her work might be said to anticipate Joan Rivière's insights in her paper 'Womanliness as a Masquerade', published a few years later, in 1929.[19] Butts goes further than Rivière, however. She tells a story that does not stop at dramatizing the masquerade, but also explores how it is received, examines the sources of its power.

For the man in this story it is in fabrics, even the feel of their names in his mouth, crêpe velour, crêpe de Chine, the recall of their textures, that the magic of what is feminine is encoded. His job involves pinning these fabrics around women's bodies, a point that the story returns to. There is both intimacy and distance in that image. The sense of touch is at once satisfied and tantalized. Permitted to approach a woman's body it holds back and contents itself with the pleasure of surrogate textures. This paradox is crystallized in the picture of the well-dressed woman glimpsed getting into her car, with her furs, glossy boots, and rich, thick gloves, and then *going away*. Distance is crucial in this equation: the desire for closeness is balanced by a fear which insists on creating and maintaining distance. Once again a theorist of the psyche comes to mind: Mary Butts has described a form of desire very close to masochism as it has been reinterpreted by Gaylyn Studlar using the work of Gilles Deleuze.[20]

The man in her story cannot speak, in his fantasy, to the woman he is serving because his mouth is full of pins, and, at the end, when he is back in the showroom and on his knees, a girl's petulance fills him with gratified excitement. The idea of masochism makes many people uncomfortable because ritualized pain and humiliation play such an important part in it. But Deleuze has reminded us that humiliation is only one way of registering and trying to master an imbalance of power, a state of inequality; it may be used to gesture wordlessly back to the fact that the woman who is the first source of these intense and contradictory feelings is no one but the mother of early experience, so much more powerful than the longing child. A hint of masochism in the air and thoughts of mother are not far away.

Although the person looking for masochistic pleasure is often represented as a man, there seems no reason why women should not also have a taste for it. They too might want closeness to their mother, yet fear her power to exact total submission. The recollections of the man in the story seem to involve the suppression of speech; he remembers being speechless, as well as on his bended knees, unable to speak because his mouth is full of pins. A young woman might well fear having to pay too high a price in self-censorship for staying close to her mother. Carol Gilligan and Lyn Mikel Brown have argued that it is older women who teach a girl what she may and may not say, may and may not admit that she knows.[21] Is it in the place of the kneeling figure that we should look for Mary Butts? Perhaps she too would like to be able to walk away, as her protagonist does at the end of the story, from the overwhelming immediacy of maternal flesh.

Imaginary Letters (dated 1924 though not published until 1928) does not take the form of a conventional fiction, but consists of a sequence of eight letters, one of them largely taken up by a poem.[22] The letters are written in Paris and addressed to the mother, who lives on the shores of the Black Sea, of a fictional young man named Boris. The whole thing runs to only eighty pages and is accompanied by five line drawings by her friend Jean Cocteau. It was the first time that Cocteau had done the drawings for a book he had not written himself, and it is likely that he became involved in the project because Butts was trying, like the rest of his friends, to encourage him to get on with his work in order to fight the depression that followed on the death of his lover, Raymond Radiguet, in 1923. Cocteau himself worked in the way that Butts does here, in this piece that is close to a form of autobiography, using writing as a way to explore and make sense of experience as it was still happening. From 1916 onwards writing letters to his own mother was one of his most important ways of doing it.

The subject of *Imaginary Letters* is ostensibly Boris Polteratsky, a young Russian *émigré*, a painter the writer had taken up and tried to help. The scenario sketched in the letters is one that seems to have been often repeated in Mary Butts's own life, if her casual biographers, who passed on stories about her in the course of other reminiscences, are to be believed.[23] She was always taking up with men who risked being dismissed as effeminate, erratic characters in manifest need of the care that she was so generous in offering. In the letters the writer explains how she had seen that this young man, Boris, was close to going under and was experienced enough herself to imagine the sort of grim little Paris funeral that he would end at the centre of, so she had made up her mind to take him in. She carried him off to the countryside, fed him up, and encouraged him in his work as a painter.

As she tells it, the story is ending in disappointment. Boris may be fascinating, but he is also tantalizing and unsatisfactory. 'He has a fine intelligence which it pleases us to see at last in use. He has led us a pretty dance. He is cruel, devoted, jealous, double-willed, capable of every perversion of sentiment. He is a gentleman, a saint, a cad, and a child who should not be let out alone' (10). The tone is both measured and unstable, an instrument of diagnosis: it is with the hope of understanding the cruelty she has suffered herself at this boy's hands and of analysing the mystery of his double will that she has undertaken this writing.

The real subject of enquiry in the *Letters* is the failure of relationship between the writer and this young man, a relationship of a kind to make many readers uneasy. It is a dispiriting story for her to repeat, one of minor betrayals, dishonesty, and hopes raised only to be disappointed. Although she had nursed him back to health, Boris neglects her and is careless of her welfare in every way, making her stand in the cold or wait without news of him late into the night. 'He has just come in. A little late, even for Paris bed-time. In the middle of the morning. Whisking like a kitten after the tail of last night's amusements. He had left me ill, with the promise to come home and look after me before two, as a sign of a now amended life, and perfect "sagesse"' (16–17). He makes off with her savings and is then much too sensitive to bear a word of reproach. But there is something about him that she can't help loving, something that a late twentieth-century reader warms to when she calls it 'an enchanting facility', though they may care less for it under some of the other names, such as 'a princely spirit', that she uses. There is an instinctive understanding between them. He makes her laugh; she loves his style.

When he first knew her, Boris had suggested that they might become lovers, but he had recoiled very quickly from this advance. It is the most wounding part of his behaviour, his denial of her sexuality. Everything else she has to offer he has taken. It is not merely a question of money or possessions. Boris has accepted a high degree of emotional and psychological intimacy. The writer has experienced this as giving 'the attentions, devotions, sacrifices of an adored mistress' and it is simply too painful for her, when she finds he turns away from her sexually, to live 'with every link but the link of bodies' (32). Boris asks her to live as if her sexuality were not a reality to either of them, to play out the fiction of the mother, the woman without desire, as if it were indeed the truth.

He manages his own pleasure elsewhere. This part of his life is lived out with what the writer calls 'little boys' and men whom he claims to hate immediately afterwards. She bravely claims to have no objection to the little boys, who are vivid and amusing: in itself pederasty, as she names it, does not disgust her. But she has her doubts about the authenticity of the choice, in Boris's case. There is an element, she suspects, of something that does not make sense. Knowing what she does about the deep sympathy that comes into play quite instinctively between the two of them, she dares to claim to see through this case, at least, of homoerotic desire. Waking from a nap to find him asleep at her feet, she decides 'our position was absurd; this pederasty nonsense, and in his case a lie' (32). This was a brave gesture by almost any standard. At the very least there is no reason to believe that the assertion would have been welcomed by Boris and his friends.

Meanwhile, publishing her account involved Butts in revealing to the world that she knew what it was to be devastatingly humiliated as a woman: it was as self-exposing for her to publish this as it had been for Freud to use his own dreams to demonstrate the techniques of dream-analysis. Freud, as we know, took years to harden himself to the risk.[24] Dignified by no title, no degrees, no institutional affiliation to back her, Butts staked out her claim to know.

What has gone wrong with Boris? The question needs an answer for the sake of others besides herself for, as the writer assured her readers, a number of the men women would most like to have as lovers, the choicest men, were turning away from women. In the very moment that she is admitting that Boris and she have now repeated the same cycle of relationship many times and cannot get beyond it, the writer turns to address a woman she has never met, to appeal to the far-away mother of Boris, in letters that she declares she does not even mean to post.

It is one way of tackling the puzzle that Butts had already identified in 'Speed the Plough', where the figure of the maternal is shown as so central, but so hard to come to terms with. There was nothing wrong with the cow in that story—it was even described as 'a gentle beast'—but it did not seem very intelligent; it just stared at the soldier when it turned its head. Perhaps it is specially difficult for us in the West and not only within individual families to imagine mothers thinking. In the *Letters* Butts struggles with that denial. As writer she takes up the position of a mother rather than a lover in the text, and it allows her in her opening sentences to raise the question of what a mother might know: 'I do not know what you think about being a mother; it's an odd department of one's existence, but I suspect that you love your son. And you are more than naturally cut off from the very little a mother can know' (9). In defiance of the cultural arrangements which assume that a mother does not know, that knowledge is dispensed by paternal authority, these letters will seek for a mother's knowledge. The effort of contradiction this involves is clearly illustrated: the writer cannot describe her own experience as knowledge, but begins with the docile disclaimer 'I do not know'. She writes to the unknown woman as one mother to another. Boris, she says, is 'your fleshly and my ghostly son' (59). When she says, 'we mothers must hang together', she reminds the reader, with a bitter gaiety, that she is making a pun, and that what mothers might have in common is the experience of having their voices and lives violently choked off. There is no chance that she will get an answer to her questions, but she offers what she knows about Boris after looking after him like a mother, and she asks the woman who gave him birth if she can explain her son. If only it could be had: her appeal for the mother's answer, her explanation, is uttered without hope.

Meanwhile, in the name of both of them, the writer advances a theory of her own. Boris is a symptom, a sign of a distress that is universal, only one of many such little displaced boys 'spat out' by 'the war that confounded all shores', to run about Paris (53). He is troubling in his own right, but he also implies the existence of other scattered fragments of families, like his own mother, the old lady living in Yalta and taking in sewing, and his sister, who has to give piano lessons now. For what, asks Butts, has this violent social transformation taken place? Though she knows that Marx and Russell would have political explanations of what is going on, and she quotes them, she cannot resist the idea that it is men themselves that are at the root of it, or men as their sons learn to know them. Again and again she asks the other mother if it is something the father has done that caused the damage. She has picked up the echo of a deep-seated hatred and divined that a need to reject his father is shaping Boris's behaviour in some way. She guesses that male violence may be the problem: did the father beat his son, she asks?

Though it is with such difficulty that a mother's voice is besought, there is no problem with hearing what the father has to say. And though qualms about fathers may be uttered, the writing never asks whether a father's opinions might be as open to question as his behaviour. A quotation from Whitehead's newly published *Science and the Modern World* stands at the head of *Imaginary Letters*: though she may write sceptically of 'old Freud', Butts distinctly frames her writing with reference to a knowledge and an intellectual authority that is male.[25] In that framing she may reproduce the trap from which she is trying to extricate her own understanding. The voice of which she is least sceptical, the one that she appears never to question, is the voice of the writer's father. Years ago he had already given her his own guide to the Russian temperament: 'when I was a child, my father once said: "I fought them in the Crimea, but when you are grown up and meet many races, I think you will find that it is only the Russians whom you will understand. They are children, and gentlemen, and mad. Add to them tenacity and control and you have us' (11).

His daughter does not appear to notice that there is no place for grown women, the women who will be mothers, in her father's account, or to wonder if the madness he brags of so gaily might have something to do with this. She makes no connection between madness and cruelty, madness and destruction, madness and war. She manages to read the admission that the way her people live is ordered and kept in place by something crazy as a proud boast, because it is made in a father's voice.

Echoing the 'science' of race produced in the nineteenth century, a form of knowledge created in the service of subordinating whole peoples to the greed of white Western Europe, this voice is scarcely to be relied on.[26] It has learned what it 'knows' on the field of conquest. The daughter, in contrast, has patiently assembled her knowledge of Boris from daily interactions, out of the exchanges from which living is made up. She is prompted to ask questions about the complexities of human development, about the way young men acquire their gender as they experience their parents, while the father's 'knowledge' presents a regiment of clones, a company of lead soldiers dropping one after another from the same mould.

The question of daughters is not overtly raised. To understand what happens in the case of young women the reader can only observe the moves Butts herself makes in *Imaginary Letters.* Rather unfortunately, it seems that the only steady and deep-seated connection available for her as writer lies in continuing to be her father's daughter, in being true to the memory of this father and the 'knowledge' he imparted. In the absence of the mother and her voice, her writing, no other support for the daughter's identity as a thinking being seems to offer itself. To the reader's dismay, the choice has evidently been embraced, and on her return from a trip back to England the writer casually pronounces herself 'restored by connection with her race'. If there are things to affright readers of our own day in her rhetoric, as Wright has justly pointed out, it as well to be clear where that language got its appeal for Mary Butts.

Ashe of Rings was the first full-length novel she published, and it begins with a father, or a man who is determined to be one. When she set out to retell her own history, by means of the little red-haired daughter, Van, Butts did not think to start with the mother. She drew a daughter like Athene, one born completely formed from out of her father's head. Antony Ashe is found brooding over the ancestral house and lands which he wants to pass on to a child of his own. On this family inheritance he puts an extraordinary value, apparently recognizing an immanent life in it to which he is responsible. He is its priest, no less. He does not have such respect for the more familiar form of life that he encounters in his wife. Making his own calculations, he selects a suitable woman to breed from among the neighbouring families. He loses no time in changing her name to Melitta and beginning to train her taste.

The child that is born is a daughter, but he does not seem

disappointed. In a ritual that is carefully distinguished from the Christian one, a ceremony private to his own family, he himself names her Vanna and sets out to form her aesthetically too. The little girl is favoured with an exceptional education: on the wall of her schoolroom are pinned a plan of the Eleusinian precinct, a Degas ballet, and a design for a ballet by Picasso. Her father and the male tutor he has engaged teach her to play at acting scenes out of Homer. She may be born of woman but all the rest of her has been formed by men.

What happens to the mother in this household and in the story that is being told? Melitta is first separated from her daughter; the father's rights, the rights of the old family, take precedence, as his insistence on the naming ceremony shows. Yet the weakening of Melitta's tie with her daughter is also represented as something she has brought about by her own negligence: she didn't breast-feed and wonders if it was a mistake. She is ignorant. How could a man of her husband's learning entrust such a woman with the education of his daughter? White woman speak with forked tongue, as they used to say in the old westerns: in this matter of fathers, Mary Butts both knows and does not know. She shows her readers a woman robbed of her daughter, she gestures helplessly towards the ruthless division between women on which patriarchal authority supports itself, and yet at the same time she represents the mother's loss as a just one. She can do this because she speaks in the language of the father, she constantly holds back from identifying with the mother's feelings or supporting them. As a result, she records Melitta's pain and confusion only to belittle them. We are invited to read them as the effusions of an inferior being.

Her sexuality too is turned into a means of humiliation: Melitta is a young woman and she takes a lover. She isn't allowed the triumph of escaping the surveillance of her husband: it is only what he expected. Her qualms, her unease about betraying him, are represented as further signs of inferiority, part of her subjection to the Christianity that he has left behind, to take up an older, more distinguished form of religion. Melitta's real solecism is to trespass with the passion he has such contempt for in the sacred places of that faith: Melitta used to meet her lover up in the ancient earthworks, the Rings, that stand above the old family house. When her husband finds out, he draws himself up to accuse her of violating 'the temenos of his race'

(51).[27] What does he worship up there in the place that he glorifies with that name, 'temenos', that was given to the sacred space marked off and dedicated to a god in ancient Greece? Perhaps we may guess that it is a story about families and how they are perpetuated, one in which the idea of generation itself may be as important as the notion of generations and their succession. We have been led to suspect that there may be room only for 'gentlemen and children' in that account: no wonder he did not want Melitta bringing the story of her own desire, the desire of the mother, into that place.

In the world where Van finds herself as a young woman, the world that the greater part of the novel is set in, it is wartime. Destruction is at work: it can be seen in the marks that are left on the bodies even of the young men who escape from it with their lives, the shrapnel wounds that leave 'pits of drawn skin, tight and blue' (275). But there is a lot of cruelty about on the home front too. It seems as if something in the writer wants us to think that war merely makes evident a savagery that is structured into the ordinary social arrangements between men and women. Van's intimacy with a young *émigré*, a painter called Serge, is threatened by his hankering for cruelty. She is trying to wean him from a relationship with another woman, Judy, who shares his taste for hurting other people. There is treachery among these civilians as well as violence: in a frightening scene that takes place at night, Van is threatened with rape at the hands of a male relative who is egged on by Judy. For a moment, in their revulsion, readers are reminded that fellow feeling between women is not absolutely unknown. That in turn opens the way to considering a new possibility. Family loyalty has been revealed as no more reliable than the loyalty of one woman to another: is it conceivable, the story asks *sotto voce*, that without solidarity between women, no family loyalty can be relied on at all? When women are made to stop feeling connected with each other, is there any end to the cruelty that will ensue?

The possibility that is opened out by the narrative at this point is one that the heroine, Van herself, never comes to formulate. She speaks a different language, one that names Melitta, her mother, as the true source of the war. Melitta works for the Red Cross, but Van suggests that her work is in some kind of collusion with the work of keeping the war going. 'What's a war without Melitta? It might stop', she jeers (223). The novelist, good daughter of the father that she is, both knows and does not know. She cannot see how she is caught up herself in the destruction she is so frantic to put a stop to. The attack on Melitta is shocking because it is mad and cruel, but also in a sense because it is true. Melitta is an ordinary sort of woman, but she has played her part in keeping the order going that has produced war. An important task of hers, as the mother of a daughter, was discouraging the will to understand, the daughter's use of her intelligence: 'men don't like women who learn things,' she said (66), taking charge of her daughter's education.

In 'Speed the Plough' Butts had tried to clarify the relations between the wounded man, the feminine, and the mother in order to understand the cultural dynamic that produced war. In *Ashe of Rings* her attempt to follow that enquiry through by looking into the life of a family like her own was more compromised. She wanted to present herself through the figure of Van as the true heir of her father. It is a point of pride with the author that Van herself is not cruel. But it is equally clear that pride is taken in a sort of cruelty that is ritual and institutionalized at the heart of her family. Out on the lawn in front of their house is the place where she is taught to remember that her ancestor, Florian, suffered crucifixion and hung looking out to sea for many hours before he died. They honour the memory of torture, make a religion out of it. Elsewhere Butts had divined something cruel in the way gender and sexuality were used to organize identity in families ruled by fathers. In *Ashe of Rings* that cruelty is sanctified and endorsed, represented as a memory to be perpetuated, a family heritage. Van's own identity is bound up with it.

What would make her free? For she is not happy as a grown woman, although she has taken possession of her inheritance: 'I, who am true Ashe, am hungry and lonely' is her complaint (149). In spite of herself Mary Butts can guess what is wanted. 'What would it be like', Van cries, 'to have a mother who would stand the truth?' (306). But she cannot quite believe in this desire or maintain it, can't imagine her mother as a woman like herself, a woman who might share her brains. Instead, towards the close of the novel Melitta, the bad mother, suffers a conversion into a woman who accepts her daughter without attempting to shape or censor her.

Looking back, more than ten years after its first publication, the writer admitted that her happy conclusion had far too much wish-fulfilment about it, that she hadn't really known how to close the gap between mother and daughter. She saw, after that long interval, that it was really 'a War-fairy-tale' that she had written: 'because it is a fairy-story, it had to end happily . . . Yet one sees now that that would not necessarily have been the true end; that, as things are, there would have been far less chance of peace for the Ashe-children.'[28] But Mary Butts knew that the story just as she had written it was not without truth, for it spoke of the heart's desire as best it could: she could not bring herself to change it. Let it stand, she said, and sent it out again into the world.

NOTES

1. Douglas Goldring, *The Nineteen-Twenties* (London, 1945), 214.
2. Patrick Wright, *On Living in an Old Country* (London, 1985), 93–134.
3. *Armed with Madness, The Taverner Novels*, repr. (New York, 1992), 7.
4. A conspiracy supported by anti-Semitic feeling in the army had led to Alfred Dreyfus, a Jewish artillery officer, being falsely accused of endangering the national security of France by delivering secret documents to a foreign government. He was found guilty and sent to Devil's Island in 1894, but his wife would not allow the case to rest and persisted in her attempts to clear his name. In 1898 Émile Zola published an open letter to Faure, the president of the French Republic, demanding that the case should be reopened: not till 1906 was the original verdict finally reversed. See Pascal Ory and Jean-François Sirinelli, *Les Intellectuels en France: De l'Affaire Dreyfus à nos jours* (Paris, 1986), 5–8.
5. Butts's autobiography (see n. 6) is not exact in its dating of events, but it implies that she was a student at Westfield from 1909 to 1912 and did not complete her third year. After leaving college, she worked for the LCC and the National Council for Civil Liberties. During the First World War her circle included Ezra Pound, HD, Richard Aldington, May Sinclair, and Ford Madox Ford. In 1918 she married John Rodker. The first biography of Mary Butts, by Nathalie Blondel, is forthcoming.
6. *The Crystal Cabinet: My Childhood at Salterns* (London, 1937). The MS Butts left at her death was not published in full in 1937. It had been severely edited, partly by herself but also by her literary executor, Angus Davidson, reducing it in length by about a quarter. The whole of the original text can be found in the Carcanet edition (Manchester, 1988), illustrated with photographs and introduced by her daughter, Camilla Bagg. There is an afterword by Barbara Wagstaff. Subsequent references to *The Crystal Cabinet* are to this edition.

7. No bibliography of Mary Butts's work has been published. Extracts from her journal were published by R. H. Byington and Glen E. Morgan in *Art and Literature* (Lausanne), vii (Winter 1965), 163–79. *Ashe of Rings* was published by the Contact Press in Paris in 1925 and reissued by Wishart in London in 1933. *Speed the Plough* came out with Chapman and Hall in 1923; some stories have been reprinted in the 1988 Carcanet selection, see below n. 14. 'At the Sign of the Black Manikin', Paris, published *Imaginary Letters* in 1928 and in 1979 it was reissued by Talonbooks of Vancouver. *Armed with Madness* and *The Death of Felicity Taverner* were both published in London by Wishart, in 1928 and 1932 respectively, and were reissued in a single volume by McPherson, New York, in 1992, under the title *The Taverner Novels.* In the same year McPherson issued a selection of the short stories under the title *From Altar to Chimney-Piece.*
8. Letter, 25 Mar. 1933, Berg Library.
9. She also signed a contract for a third novel, *Julian the Apostate,* with Heinemann, who were her London publisher at that period, though it does not appear to have been completed. *Scenes from the Life of Cleopatra* was reissued by the Ecco Press of New York in 1974.
10. Personal communication, Camilla Bagg. The pleasure she was taking in her daughter can be glimpsed in a brief reference in *The Crystal Cabinet*; 'what my fourteen-year-old daughter today calls cheerfully "Sex",—' (45).
11. See Claire M. Tylee, *The Great War and Women's Consciousness: Images of Militarism and Womanhood in Women's Writings, 1914–64* (Basingstoke, 1990).
12. See Luce Irigaray, *Speculum of the Other Woman* (Ithaca, NY, 1985).
13. Joan Rivière, 'Womanliness as Masquerade' (1929), repr. in Victor Burgin, James Donald, and Cora Kaplan (eds.), *Formations of Fantasy* (London, 1986).
14. References to 'Speed the Plough' are to the 1923 edition. The story has been reprinted in Natalie Blondel (ed.), *With and without Buttons* (Manchester, 1991). Two later collections of stories by Butts were published, *Several Occasions* (London, 1932) and *Last Stories* (London, 1938), a selection made by her friend Bryher after Butts died.
15. Ellipses in original. *The Sketch,* which proclaimed itself 'The Best Paper for Society and Fashion', was published weekly at 6*d.* It contained photographs of society figures and stars from the world of entertainment. Several of the ones mentioned by name in 'Speed the Plough', including Delysia and Lee White, were featured in wartime issues. The *Sketch* of 5 Jan. 1916 carried a prominent notice about Raphael Kirchner (1876–1917) and his drawings, which the magazine had secured exclusive rights over after they had noticed that every issue with a Kirchner girl in it sold out: 'Raphael Kirchner is now a household word. Nearly every dug-out has an example of his beautiful work hanging on its walls. Nearly every cabin of His Majesty's ships-of-war is made more cheery by his fascinating paintings.' A number of details connect the story with a date in 1916. The *Sketch* of 19 July 1916 carries a feature on Lee White and the song about ducks that Butts quotes from the revue *Some (More) Samples.* The fashion details in this story locate it precisely too: georgette was a fabric that first came on the market in 1914; the vee necks that are described were first introduced in 1916; the handbag, or satchel as it is named, carried by the hospital visitor, was an accessory that women had taken to only since about

1908. See John Peacock, *Twentieth-Century Fashion: The Complete Sourcebook* (London, 1993); Frances Kennett, *The Collector's Book of Twentieth-Century Fashion* (London, 1983); A. Mansfield and P. Cunnington, *Handbook of English Costume in the Twentieth Century* (London, 1973).

16. For further information on these women and the artifice they used to present themselves as spectacles, see Peter Leslie, *A Hard Act to Follow: A Music-Hall Review* (London, 1978); James Gardiner, *Gaby Deslys* (London, 1986); Jean Cocteau, *Souvenir Portraits* (London, 1991).
17. See Irigaray, *Speculum of the Other Woman.* For an accessible account of Irigaray's thought, see Margaret Whitford, *Luce Irigaray: Philosophy in the Feminine* (London, 1991).
18. See William Stewart and Emily Hamer (eds.), *The Queer Encyclopedia* (London, 1994).
19. Rivière, 'Womanliness as a Masquerade', 35–44.
20. Gaylyn Studlar, 'Masochism, Masquerade, and the Erotic Metamorphoses of Marlene Dietrich', in Jane Gaines and Charlotte Herzog (eds.), *Fabrications: Costume and the Female Body* (London, 1991).
21. See Carol Gilligan and Lyn Mikel Brown, *Meeting at the Crossroads: Women's Psychology and Girls' Development* (Cambridge, Mass., 1992).
22. References to *Imaginary Letters* are to the 1979 reprint.
23. For those who wrote about Butts in their memoirs, see Wright, *On Living in an Old Country*. See also Nathalie Blondel's 'Afterword' to *With and without Buttons*, and Barbara Wagstaff's 'Afterword' to the Carcanet edn. of *The Crystal Cabinet.*
24. *The Interpretation of Dreams* was not published until the end of 1899, though it was substantially complete by 1896; in his preface to the first edition Freud spoke of what it cost him to reveal himself in it.
25. A. N. Whitehead, *Science and the Modern World* (Cambridge, 1927).
26. Under the auspices of the disciplines of anthropology, linguistics, and physiology, in the course of the 19th century, a framework of thought was constructed to demonstrate 'scientifically' that differences in physical, moral, and intellectual ability were distributed between human individuals according to the 'race' they were born into. See e.g. Steven Gregory and Roger Sanjek (eds.), *Race* (New Brunswick, 1994).
27. References to *Ashe of Rings* are to the 1933 edition.
28. See afterword to the 1933 edition.

11
HD's War Neurotics

TRUDI TATE

AT the beginning of August 1914 the modernist writer Hilda Doolittle learned that she was pregnant.[1] The baby was still-born in May 1915—killed, HD believed, by the Great War. Not long before the child was born, HD had been shocked by some bad news: the sinking of the passenger ship *Lusitania*, in which 1,200 civilians died. Whether medically true or not, HD's view that the war indirectly killed her child is a significant and by no means unusual response. HD proposes a direct relationship between violent public events and the private lives of civilians during wartime; she suggests that civilians, like soldiers, may have been subject to crippling war neuroses—an idea which recurs throughout her war writing.

It might be tempting to read this specifically as a woman's response to the Great War, a feminist protest that the public violence of war has permeated even the most private of spaces: the unborn child in the womb. Yet HD's work resists precisely this kind of rigid gendering. Rather, she explores the peculiar effects of trauma on both women and men, and the uneven ways in which the war penetrates civilian society. She does this through her representations of war neurosis: a disorder usually associated with soldiers, and commonly, if inaccurately, known as 'shell-shock'.[2]

Civilian War Neuroses

Did civilians suffer from war neuroses during the Great War? The medical journal the *Lancet* did not think so for the first year of the war. As late as September 1915 it was arguing that no one, whether soldier or civilian, would suffer any long-term mental problems as a result of the conflict. Indeed, it claimed, because civilian neuroses were caused largely by boredom, the excitement of the war ought to make them diminish, if anything. For civilians, the *Lancet* argued, 'the spectacle of millions of men abandoning home, family, ambition, money, and laying down their lives for a principle is so glorious as to transfigure "the pictures of mangled bodies and human beings gasping in their dark struggle against death"'.[3] (The quotation comes from the superintendent of a lunatic asylum.) The term 'spectacle' is striking here. Soldiers—men—are seen to have a symbolic function; their bodies form a grotesque 'picture' whose meaning transcends and redeems its own horror. Civilians do not see this 'picture', of course: they imagine it. And when civilians actually did imagine some of the horrible sights of the Great War, they became susceptible to war neuroses, as the *Lancet* found itself reporting only a few weeks later.

A woman was admitted into Leicester Mental Hospital as a direct result of war news: five of her seven sons at the front had been wounded. The Dorset County Asylum reported that 'stress was frequently a well-recognised cause of mental breakdown, and that not a few cases were associated with the war, both among the wives of soldiers and young recruits'.[4] By March 1916 the *Lancet* had come to accept the reality of civilian war neuroses, arguing: 'While the stress of war on the soldier is discussed, it should not be forgotten that the nervous strain to which the civilian is exposed may require consideration and appropriate treatment.'[5] Even in Britain, symptoms of war shock among civilians were 'by no means uncommon'.

Eventually the idea of non-combatant war neurosis was commonplace enough to be the subject of a mild joke; in February 1918 the *Lancet* drew attention to a court case about the sale of some dubious milk: 'The defendant claimed that the milk reached the consumer exactly as it came from the cows, but it was drawn at a time when there was an air raid and the animals were suffering from shell shock.' The defence was unsuccessful, and the dealer was fined. None the less, the *Lancet* declared, 'there can be little doubt that such a defence might well be valid', for, like humans, cows are susceptible to stress or fright which can impair the quality of their milk.[6]

Civilian war neuroses are discussed by a number of other medical writers during and after the war. In *Shell Shock and its Aftermath* (1926), Norman Fenton notes:

The nervous effects of war strain on civilians is brought out by Redlick [in a 1915 article], who, studying them during the war, frequently found insomnia among peasants, who had never before known anything of sleeplessness, dreams about war disturbing their sleep. Variations in body temperature and modifications in heart action without apparent adequate cause were also common occurrences among the civilians Redlick studied.[7]

Clearly, British civilians suffered much less direct violence than French civilians in the battle zones. But they were subject to trauma none the less. Edwin Ash's propagandistic book *The Problem of Nervous Breakdown* (1919) argues that British civilians showed tremendous 'stability of nerve' during the war; the terror of attack served to strengthen the 'national nerve'; like steel, it has been tempered by the 'experiences of red-hot war in our midst'. Even as Ash invokes an unshakeable 'British nerve' (the opposite, it seems, of British 'nerves'), he acknowledges that civilians were susceptible to neurotic symptoms. He goes on to claim that, while civilian neuroses existed during the war, they were generally similar to the neuroses of peacetime. None the less, there were cases in which 'complete mental imbalance occurred, and stricken persons became deluded into the false belief that they were pursued by spies, or suspected of spying, or being persecuted by the Government in various mysterious ways'.[8] In other words, war neuroses were *not* always the same as peacetime neuroses: some were specific to the experience of the war, whether real or fantasized. (It is also worth noting that a sense of being mysteriously persecuted was not always a delusion. As Phillip Knightley notes, many people were wrongly arrested and persecuted as spies during the First World War.[9]) Finally, Ash admits that civilians subjected to mechanical violence, such as bombing raids, often exhibited symptoms like those of 'shell-shock of the battlefield': 'loss of voice, paralysis, [. . .] sleeplessness, terrifying dreams', and so forth.

We find, then, that the idea of civilians suffering from war neuroses was by no means unknown during the Great War. Later work on what is now called 'post-traumatic stress disorder'[10] draws explicit parallels between civilian disaster survivors and combat veterans: their symptoms, it is argued, are often remarkably similar. Survivors of war, floods, earthquakes, rape, the atomic bombs, and the Nazi concentration camps often exhibit similar traumatic symptoms.[11] In *Beyond the Pleasure Principle*, published not long after the end of the war, Freud noted the similarities between civilian survivors of railway disasters and shell-shocked soldiers.[12] Civilian experience of violence and terror, whether public and shared (railway accidents, floods, war) or individual and private (rape), can produce serious traumatic symptoms. Direct experience of pain, loss of autonomy, and fear of mutilation or death can produce mental disturbance, often expressed in the body, for many years afterwards.

Witnessing at a Distance

Does this help us to understand HD's view that her child was killed by the trauma of war? If the shock had been caused by the air raids on London, for example, then the models of war neuroses or post-traumatic stress disorder might readily be applied. But HD's case is striking precisely because it is *not* a response to direct violence. 'I had lost the first [child] in 1915', she remembered many years later, 'from shock and repercussions of war news broken to me in a rather brutal fashion.'[13] It was a story which did the damage.

HD was deeply troubled by her memories of the Great War and the death of her first child, and she rewrote them many times throughout her life.[14] In *Asphodel*, an early memoir of the war years, she states bluntly of the protagonist's stillborn child: 'Khaki killed it.'[15] In a letter to Norman Holmes Pearson in 1937, she wrote: 'In order to speak adequately of my poetry and its aims, I must you see, drag in a whole deracinated epoch. Perhaps specifically, I might say that the house next door was struck another night. We came home and simply waded through glass, while wind from now unshuttered windows, made the house a barn, an unprotected dug-out.'[16] This might be the 'carnage on Queen's Square' imagined in *Bid Me to Live*, HD's best-known war novel. Though the damage to London was minor compared with the devastation of the battlefields, it none the less had a profound effect on those who lived through the aerial bombardments—the first of their kind in Britain.[17] 'What does that sort of shock do to the mind, the imagination', HD wrote to Pearson, '—not solely of myself, but of an epoch?' (72). Her analysis with Freud, she wrote some years later, was partly to gain skills which might help 'war-shocked and war-shattered people' from the Great War in the period leading up to the next war.[18]

In 'Magic Mirror', an unpublished memoir written in the 1950s, HD remembers receiving the news of the *Lusitania*, recounting the memory through the characters of Rafe and Julia in *Bid Me to Live* (originally entitled 'Madrigal'): 'Rafe Ashton (though not so stated in Madrigal) destroyed the unborn, the child Amor, when a few days before it was due, he burst in upon Julia of that story, with "don't you realize what this means? Don't you feel anything? *The Lusitania has gone down.*"'[19] We should be cautious about accepting this at face value, however, as Friedman notes: 'Here and later in a repetition of this memory, H.D. added to the typed manuscript the pencilled words: "(But this never happened. Surely this was fantasy.)"'[20] HD's memories of the war were written and rewritten over a period of more than forty years, the act of writing itself compounding them with fantasy. Fantasy might be constituted differently from the memory of real events, but it can be equally disturbing. And as time passes, the distinction between real and fantasized memories can become blurred.[21] But whether memory or fantasy, HD's response to the news of the *Lusitania* provides some useful insights into her thinking about the war. The sinking became one of the great scandals of the war, forcing civilians in Britain (and to some extent in the United States) to realize that they too were serious targets.

The Sinking of the Lusitania

In February 1915 Germany established a submarine blockade around the entire United Kingdom, which then included all of Ireland.[22] Any vessel in this zone was declared to be a legitimate target, subject to attack without warning. The sea was the site of a major imperial struggle, as each nation attempted to cripple the other's economy and starve out its civilians, and was a significant factor, it is argued, in Britain's eventual victory.[23]

On 1 May 1915 the *Lusitania* departed from New York, carrying nearly 2,000 passengers and a secret cargo of war munitions for Britain. A number of passengers had received letters and telegrams warning that the ship was likely to be attacked. The morning that it sailed, the *New York Tribune* published a notice from the Imperial German Embassy in Washington warning that all ships entering the war zone were at risk of being destroyed. These warnings were ignored, however, and the ship sailed. At about 2 p.m. on 7 May, a German U-boat torpedoed the *Lusitania* as it passed by the south coast of Ireland. A second explosion, caused either by the munitions cargo or by one of the ship's engines, followed a few seconds later. The attack was not planned, as it happens, but this was not known at the time. Within twenty minutes, the ship, which was 790 feet long, had completely sunk. Incompetence, confusion, and cost-cutting by the shipping company meant that crew did not know how to use the lifeboats properly. The *Lusitania* sank rapidly at an angle, which made their task even more difficult. Passengers were crushed by falling lifeboats and killed trying to get off the ship; others were drowned. Bodies were washed up on the Irish coast for several days afterwards. Some were buried in mass graves; others were returned to the United States. (The corpses of the first-class passengers were embalmed before being sent back.) The newspapers printed pictures related to the disaster every day for about a week afterwards. In all, nearly 1,200 passengers and crew died; all of them civilians. Around 198 of the dead were American citizens—neutrals at this stage of the war. One passenger went into labour when the ship began to sink; both she and the baby were drowned.

Though the event had little military significance, the sinking of the *Lusitania* became a key symbol in the British propaganda campaign to bring the United States into the war. It was widely reported in all the British papers, with outraged commentary about German barbarism.[24] *The Times* devoted several pages to the story every day for about a week from 8 May, running alongside its rather positive reports of the disastrous Gallipoli campaign. The British papers reported that the sinking of the *Lusitania* was crassly celebrated in Germany: a story which was generally untrue, but which was used by the British government to revive civilian support for the war.[25] It was an important issue within the United States, too, and was frequently cited during the presidential campaign of 1916. When the US entered the war on Britain's side in April 1917, the *Lusitania* was seen by many people as a key factor in this decision. (In Willa Cather's war novel *One of Ours,* for example, one of the American characters cites three reasons for enlisting: 'Belgium, the Lusitania, Edith Cavell'[26]—all represented in newspapers and propaganda as examples of violated 'femininity'.) However, the *Lusitania* was less the *cause* than the *justification* of the American entry into the war: its function was imaginary or ideological.

But this is precisely its importance in our understanding of HD's response it. As I have already argued, it is well established that civilians, like soldiers, will suffer from war neuroses if they are subjected to violence. HD takes this point further, however, to suggest that violent events can cause physical or psychic shock *even to people who are not present.* Witnessing such events at a distance, or being exposed to them indirectly, discursively, through language, can cause war neuroses, just as some soldiers suffered from shell-shock without ever going into battle. In other words, HD's response to the sinking of the *Lusitania,* like her writings about the First World War, suggest that the stories which circulate in a society can damage people's bodies, or send them mad.

It is this imaginary effect of war that HD addresses in her war fiction. I want to look at two of her prose works about the Great War: 'Kora and Ka', a short story about a man who is still suffering from the war in the late 1920s, and *Bid Me to Live,* a novel about a woman's war experiences during 1917. Both stories deal with the problem of being a witness—indirectly —to the violence of the war,[27] and both ask how this interacts with structures of gender. But neither work posits a simple parallel between gender and violence; nor does it suggest that 'the war at home is also a war in the home'.[28] We need to resist the urge to find simple parallels and causal relationships between gender conflict and military conflict.[29] Nor am I convinced that HD is trying to define 'women's experience' or 'women's consciousness' of the Great War. Rather, her works explore how femininity is constituted in relation to the war. Furthermore, HD's writing also recognizes masculinity as a tenuous and contested construction; here her war fiction can productively be read in relation to soldiers' writings of the same period, as I have done elsewhere.[30] Neither femininity nor masculinity emerges as a single, unproblematic structure in her fiction; nor does she set up masculinity as the 'cause' of war, as some later feminist writers have attempted to argue.

'Kora and Ka' is a particularly interesting story in this context:

a story written by a woman which explores a man's reactions to the Great War. Like *Bid Me to Live*, this story demonstrates that the collective trauma of war spreads far beyond its immediate time and place, and can have a profound effect on the lives of both women and men.

'Kora and Ka'

'Kora and Ka' was completed in 1930 and published privately in 1934.[31] It is a strange, impenetrable piece of writing, and has received very little critical attention. The story is worth looking at in some detail, however, for it provides a striking study of the effect of war neuroses in the decade following the war.[32] 'Kora and Ka' has two main characters: Kora, a woman who has left her husband and children, and John Helforth, the man she lives with now. (The name John Helforth was also one of HD's writing pseudonyms, under which she published a short novel entitled *Nights*, in 1935; this further complicates the imaginary gender relations in the text.) Helforth suffers from the delusion that his mind has been occupied by a 'Ka'—a spirit from Egyptian mythology which lives on after the body has died. The story is narrated by Helforth in two interwoven voices: his own, and the Ka's. This makes it difficult to follow, partly because it is a representation of a nervous breakdown, narrated from within.

The story opens with a struggle between Helforth and the imaginary spirit as it tries to take over his mind. The struggle is centred on the act of looking, an act which is mentioned many times in the first few pages of the story. 'Helforth must see everything,' we are told, but his eyes trouble him. He suffers from hallucinations, some of them very like Septimus's visual delusions in *Mrs Dalloway* (1925). At work he sees the under-manager 'as under layers of green water, violet-laced'; the figures in his ledger shine 'violet-laced, nine, six, up through transparent seaweed' (188). He decides to see a doctor, and hallucinates as the doctor tries to test his eyes. The doctor asks him to read from a printed chart:

> As the huge page loomed before Helforth, he felt himself grow smaller. Helforth felt himself draw away, back and back, the length of the doctor's room and out of the wall behind it. Helforth became Helforth, minute at the minimizing other-end of an opera-glass. [. . .]

> A globe rather like the shape of the Venetian glass that Kora had set on the table last night, again reminded Helforth that man was a microbe. He saw a world like a drop of water and himself enclosed in it. (189)

The doctor diagnoses 'nerves' and recommends that Helforth stop working. But work is not the cause of his nervous disorders, though this does not become clear until half-way through the story. Helforth's illness dates from the war, some ten years earlier, and its symptoms are uncannily similar to war neuroses: hallucinations, a sense of dissociation, loss of certainty about his sexual identity. What is so striking about this, however, is that Helforth has not in fact been a soldier; his distress arises not from battle experience, but from the lack of it.

Out of the confusing chronology of the story and Helforth's disordered mind, one thread clearly emerges: his memory of the war. Both of his older brothers went to the front and both have been killed. Helforth was meant to avenge them, but the war ended before he was old enough to enlist. He blames their mother. 'Mother could have kept Larry at home,' he says:

> I was too young. Larry was of course vicious to have told me, in precise detail, all that he did. It was a perverse sort of sadism. I loved Larry. I would have gone on, loving men and women if it hadn't been for Larry. How could I love anyone after Larry? My mother used to say, '*Bob* would have been too noble-minded to have regretted Larry.' Bob? But Bob went that first year, dead or alive he was equally obnoxious. He was the young 'father', mother's favourite. I was sixteen. By the time I was ready, the war actually was over. Mother reiterated on every conceivable occasion, 'Larry is only waiting to get out there.' I don't know what mother thought 'there' was. It was so near. It was 'here' all the time with me. Larry was sent to avenge Bob, I was to be sent to avenge Larry. It was already written in Hans Anderson [*sic*], a moron virgin and a pitcher. We were all virgin, moron. We were virgin, though Larry saw to it that I was not. Larry. (197)

Larry has initiated Helforth into various kinds of adult experiences, providing him with an identity as a bisexual man—an identity he values, and wants to maintain.[33] But when Larry is killed, war stories and sex stories become confused, and Helforth regresses into an angry, infantile state, raging against his dead brothers, his mother, Kora's children.

War-neurotic soldiers often suffered from regression. In an

essay published in 1920, Maurice Nicoll described a number of case-studies; one soldier regressed to the age of 12, and then to the age of 5, then relived his own life up to his departure for the war. Another regressed into very young infancy, becoming 'as much a tyrant as a baby', and demanding to be fed every two hours. Responding to the war through regression, wrote Nicoll, 'is the exact opposite of adaptation by progression, the psychic movement being inwards, away from the level of reality-consciousness, towards a level of phantasy-consciousness. The movement may be slow or sudden; it may be arrested early or it may go so far that the patient becomes blind, deaf, dumb, and quadriplegic or psychically infantile, or both.'[34] The war neurotic is trying to run away from the war, not physically, '*but psychically*', writes Nicoll; one way of doing this is to retrace his own '*ontogenetic development*'.[35]

Where combatants often tried, unconsciously, to escape the war through illness, HD suggests that civilian men might flee into illness for the opposite reason—to enter the war and share its suffering. Helforth also tries to assert an unambiguous masculinity within the household, but it rapidly fragments into hallucination and despair:

> I will to be John Helforth, and Englishman and a normal brutal one. I will strength into my body, into my loins. [. . .] I insist on masculinity and my brutality. (194–5)

> I have meant to be robust; I have meant to smash furniture. I find myself seated on the low rush-bottomed arm-chair. I beat my hands on its sides [. . .] I say 'when are we going back? I can't stay here forever. It is her [Kora's] turn, at this moment, to retaliate, she does not. Then I sway. Ka is coming [. . .] I hear a voice, it is only Kora but still I say, 'Ka shan't get me.' [. . .] I go on, I say, 'cow', I say, 'mother, mother, mother.' Then I fling myself down, anywhere, head on the table, or head that would beat through the wooden floor to the rooms that lie beneath it, 'Larry'. (195–6)

Helforth is dangerous and self-destructive, like a severely disturbed child. He is undergoing psychoanalysis for his problems, and he is encouraged to speak about them with Kora. He blames his mother for the death of his brother Larry (199). 'Kora says my attitude is fantastic'—that is, a product of fantasy—'and linked up with mother-complex'—another symptom found among war-neurotic soldiers.[36] Helforth disagrees:

I say I do not think so. I explain it lucidly, as if she herself were a complete outsider, and herself had never heard of that war. I demonstrate how, systematically, we were trained to blood-lust and hatred. We were sent out iron-shod to quell an enemy who had made life horrible. That enemy roasted children, boiled down the fat of pregnant women to grease cannon wheels. He wore a spiked hat and carried, in one hand, a tin thunder-bolt and, in the other, a specialised warrant for burning down cathedrals. He was ignorant and we were sent out, Galahad on Galahad, to quell him. His men raped nuns, cut off the hands of children, boiled down the entrails of old men, nailed Canadians against barn doors . . . and all this we heard mornings with the Daily Newsgraph and evenings with the Evening Warscript. The Newsgraph and the Warscript fed out belching mothers, who belched out in return, fire and carnage in the name of Rule Britannia. (199)

Helforth speaks as if he were an ex-soldier, explaining the war to a civilian. He tells Kora horrible tales from the war, but they are instantly recognizable not as real atrocities, but as famous (and untrue) propaganda stories from the newspapers: raped nuns, mutilated children, crucified Candians.[37] A key aim of atrocity propaganda was to produce support for the war. British propaganda was extremely successful, generating the 'right' kind of disgust and hatred, and rekindling civilian interest in the war. Yet HD suggests it might also have another effect, producing a profound kind of sickness—a war-neurotic response to stories which were simply unbearable to imagine, and which displaced stories of real suffering. More than this: the story raises questions about true and false stories of the war, exploring the ways in which civilians are placed, distant from the actual events, and unable to tell the difference.

As a young man, Helforth equates manhood with soldiering. But the war ends before he is old enough to go, locking him into a state of eternal childhood—'a small lout in my mother's drawing-room' (195)—struggling against a sense of guilt and the imaginary power of his now-absent mother, for whom Kora is partly a substitute. Helforth's war fantasies lead him into a war-neurotic 'mother-complex'. He sees the newspaper stories as producing monstrous women ('belching mothers') who in turn produce more propaganda ('fire and carnage') to keep the war going. 'I did not realise,' he says later, 'that *nothing* depended on me, that a row of aunts was choros out of Hades, that the "family" was only another name for warfare and sacrifice of the young' (200). Some of Helforth's hatred is directed towards Kora, too, a mother who has left her husband and children to be with him. Kora misses her children, which makes Helforth jealous and resentful.

Perhaps the most striking aspect of this passage is Helforth's use of 'we'. If he is a man, he must have experienced the war; if not in reality, then in fantasy. For the war isn't just 'out there', but is '"here" all the time', in Helforth's head. His identity keeps merging with the dead men he has loved, to the point that he feels he really has shared their war experiences. He fantasizes about his own body in pieces, his feet as amputated lumps (185), his face seared away. These fantasies challenge familiar representations of war as a shared masculine 'truth'—an idea satirized, particularly, through the use of images from propaganda. It also reminds us that there was no single masculine experience of war. Despite the vast mobilization, the majority of British men were actually civilians, and found themselves located in an odd position in relation to the discourses of soldiering and masculinity.[38] In 'Kora and Ka', HD suggests that some men enacted a masquerade of masculinity, imitating the illnesses of men at war.

Bid Me to Live

Bid Me to Live was written and revised during the late 1930s and 1940s, but not published until 1960, shortly before HD died.[39] It is a survivor's account of the First World War, written and revised in the years surrounding the Second. The novel focuses on one character: a civilian woman named Julia who suffers from war neuroses. The novel also traces specific ways in which the war permeated civilian lives during 1917, from the direct experience of the Zeppelin raids on London,[40] to the indirect and imaginary effects of battles taking place out of sight—in the sea off Cornwall, for example, or in France, where Julia's husband Rafe is a soldier. (The central characters are based closely on HD and her husband Richard Aldington, from whom she became estranged during the war.[41]) The war is also felt through the presence of a 'multitude' of soldiers in London: 'heroic angels' who are really doomed men waiting to face injury, madness, and death.[42]

The war transforms the city of London, both physically and imaginatively. Zeppelins, frightening figures out of science fiction, appear like whales in the sky:

Superficially entrenched, they were routed out by the sound of aircraft; she stumbled down the iron stairs (that was the Hampstead flat) and bruised her knee. Just in time to see the tip-tilted object in a dim near sky that even then was sliding sideways and even then was about to drop. Such a long way to come. It drifted from their sight and the small collection of gaping individuals dispersed. Leviathan, a whale swam in city dusk, above suburban forests. (11)

At this stage of the novel, Julia and Rafe are both living as civilians in London, reading, writing, working on their Greek translations. Their similar occupations suggest equality and perhaps harmony between a woman and a man,[43] but the city they inhabit has become unsettled and is threatening violence. The war will transform London into a place of dread and emptiness:

City of dreadful night, city of dreadful night. She saw the railed-in square, the desolation of the empty street. It was a city of the dead. There were no lights visible in the blocks of walls that surrounded them, iron balconies gave on to the square and the plane-trees stood stark metal. They lifted metallic branches to a near sky that loomed now with a sudden spit of fire. A volcano was erupting. Along streets empty of life, there were pathetic evidences of life that had once been, an ash-tin, a fluttering scrap of newspaper, a cat creeping stealthily, seeking for stray provender. Ashes and death; it was the city of dreadful night, it was a dead city. (109)

There are obvious echoes of T. S. Eliot in this passage—another non-combatant whose work is complexly engaged with the effects of the First World War[44]—as well as direct references to James Thompson's despairing poem 'The City of Dreadful Night' (1874). The city is represented as stark, dry, and empty—unlike the war zone, which we know to be muddy and full of bodies, both dead and alive.

In *Paint it Today*, the city at war is depicted as a sinking ship (in another echo of the *Lusitania*, perhaps): 'Small city railings splintered and city parks infested with a black trail of livid, wretched creatures who shivered against each other as the crash came nearer. Who woke as from a dream when distant rumblings died away, and scurried like black rats fleeing the sinking wreck, washing up on the pavements [. . .]'.[45]

When the Zeppelin ('Leviathan') in *Bid Me to Live* attacks the city, Julia receives a minor injury as she runs for shelter. The very insignificance of the injury—in a book about a war which killed and mutilated people in their millions—directs us towards a more important aspect of the passage, in which Julia imagines such a fall with a child in her arms. 'Suddenly [. . .] her mind, which did not really think in canalized precise images, realized or might have realized that if she had had the child in her arms at that moment, stumbling as she had stumbled, she might have . . . No. She did not think this. She had lost the child only a short time before' (11–12). Like HD, Julia has lost a newborn child during the war, and she has the peculiar sense that the war will kill the child for a second time.

At the end of this scene, Rafe decides to enlist. This decision takes Rafe and Julia into separate worlds, where gender difference and the distinction between combatant and civilian seem to be identical. When Rafe returns later, now an officer on leave, Julia realizes that they have both been completely changed by their separate war experiences. He is no longer the same person she married (16); he is a stranger, 'not-Rafe' (45), an uncanny presence who looks like her husband but is somehow not the same. Rafe has been altered by his experience of being a soldier, while Julia has been changed by the loss of her child. At the beginning of the book, Julia sees the experiences as parallel, and resents being told about the men's suffering. 'I spared you what I went through,' she thinks, but 'you did not spare me. I did not tell you; my agony in the Garden had no words' (46). Such a loss, she argues, is specific to women, kept in the private sphere, with no shared language to express it—unlike the suffering of war, which Rafe has tried to describe to her.

Is this an example of the 'battle of the sexes' which critics such as Gilbert find running as a counter-narrative to the war?[46] Is Julia cast as Rafe's victim; is this a novel about women's suffering at the hands of men? It seems to me that, from the very first paragraph, *Bid Me to Live* problematizes precisely these issues:

> Oh, the times, oh the customs! Oh, indeed, the times! The customs! Their own, specifically, but part and parcel of the cosmic, comic, crucifying times of history. Times liberated, set whirling out-moded romanticism; Punch and Judy danced with Jocasta and Philoctetes,

> while wrestlers, sprawling in an Uffizi or a Pitti, flung garish horizon-blue across gallant and idiotic Sir Philip Sidney-isms. It was a time of isms. And the Ballet.
>
> They did not march in classic precision, they were a mixed bag. Victims, victimised and victimising. Perhaps the victims came out, by a long shot, ahead of the steady self-determined victimisers. (7)

Out of a nightmarish vision of history, flung out of chronology into an anachronistic, violent dance (Punch and Judy, Jocasta and Philoctetes), the relationship between victim and victimizer is rendered uncertain. Who is the victim, who the oppressor, in this scene? It is by no means clear, and remains ambiguous, despite the sympathetic focus on Julia, throughout the novel. Julia and Rafe—woman and man; civilian and soldier—are simultaneously victim and victimizer, in their marriage, in the war, and in their relationships with others. To complicate matters further, Rafe has volunteered for the war; does this modify his sense of being its victim?[47] Rather than reading *Bid Me to Live* as an expression of sex warfare, or as a competition in suffering, I would argue that the novel shows how the war, as both experience and discourse, *interpellates* women and men differently, constructing them differently as gendered subjects.

But the difference is endlessly modified by other structures of power and difference. When Rafe comes home on leave, for example, he dreams about the war and mutters about ghastly sights in his sleep. He is suffering from a mild form of war neurosis, an illness which makes him seem even more of a stranger to Julia. The difference between woman and man, soldier and civilian, seems to extend even into the unconscious. But this structure is disrupted only a few pages later, when Julia wakes from a brief sleep with a 'muddle of poisonous gas and flayed carcasses' in her head (39). These are *Rafe*'s nightmares which have spilled into *her* unconscious, just as traces of poisonous gas are transferred from his body into hers when they kiss (39). Rigid distinctions between woman and man, civilian and soldier, are broken down even as they are invoked. (Similarly, in Rebecca West's novel about shell-shock *The Return of the Soldier* (1918), the civilian narrator suffers from war-neurotic dreams about the trenches.) Traces of the horror faced by soldiers overflow into civilian lives, just as HD believed that the distant suffering of the *Lusitania* victims had a concrete effect upon her body, and killed her child.

As the war progresses, Julia too begins to suffer from war-neurotic symptoms, dissociated from her surroundings, at times on the verge of madness. She is most disturbed by big groups of soldiers in London, men 'who might be ghosts to-morrow, the latest vintage (1917) grapes to be crushed' (119). She goes to the cinema and is surrounded by soldiers. The narrative interweaves images from the film with Julia's vision of the crowd of doomed men. Fragments of the soldiers' song 'Tipperary' are scattered throughout the scene as Julia alternates between seeing the men as objects—spectacles—and identifying with them.

The film they are watching involves a long and rapid car journey down a mountain:

> She was part of this. She swerved and veered with a thousand men in khaki, toward destruction, *to the sweetest girl I know.* But no. A swift turn, a sudden slide of scenery, a landslide of scenery projected the car, its unknown mysterious driver onto a smooth road. He was rushing along a level road, such a road as lines the waterways outside Venice, on the way to Ravenna. Was he rushing to Ravenna? Where was this? It was outside, anyway. *Good-bye Piccadilly, good-bye Leicester Square.* They were all rushing toward some known goal. (123–4)

Watching the soldiers from above, Julia feels she is 'gazing into a charnel-house, into the pit of inferno', as the men sing with the 'voices of heroic angels, surging on toward their destruction, *pack all your troubles in your old kit bag and smile, smile, smile*' (126).

Like 'Kora and Ka' and HD's memory of the sinking of the *Lusitania, Bid Me to Live* is concerned with the problem of being a witness to the slaughter of war—but a witness who does not actually *see* the worst of what happens. As witness, Julia can only imagine what the soldiers have to face. She is exposed to the war discursively, through stories and fantasies of the men's suffering. How can the culture of war be represented? Does HD, a woman, civilian, and survivor, have the right to write of such things? Her war writings are troubled by these questions, torn between guilt and self-righteousness; staking a civilian claim to war experience—and suffering—yet strongly aware of the greater suffering of the combatants. Helplessness in the face of others' suffering[48]—whether witnessed or imagined—was a significant cause of war neuroses in both civilians and soldiers during the Great War.

Yet *Bid Me to Live* also contains some remarkably callous moments. When Rafe and Julia remember seeing and touching a Michelangelo statue before the war, Julia thinks: 'Yes—that was it, the very touch of the fingers of Michelangelo had been transferred to theirs. Their feet, their hands were instilled with living beauty, with things that were not dead. Other cities had been buried. Other people had been shot to death and something had gone on. There was something left between them' (72). Julia wavers between compassion and indifference—or even, as here, a perverse kind of pleasure—in the invisible suffering of others.[49]

Julia is a civilian war neurotic. Like Helforth, she suffers from dissociation, unsure of the limits and function of her own body, and struggling to place her life story within the larger narratives of history. Yet at times the experience of dissociation is strangely pleasurable, as she sees the world as 'magic lantern slides' (174), and wishes she could live in two dimensions (175). Where Helforth regresses into infancy and 'mother-complex', Julia meditates on her own maternity, both lost and potential, retreating (in a striking echo of Lawrence) into an imaginary, utopian space which she calls the *gloire*. 'I want to explain', she writes to Rico (the Lawrence figure in the novel),[50] 'how it is that the rose is neither red nor white, but a pale *gloire*':

> Perhaps you would say I was trespassing, couldn't see both sides, as you said of my Orpheus. I could be Eurydice in character, you said, but woman-is-woman and I couldn't be both. The *gloire* is both.
>
> No, that spoils it; it is both and neither. [. . .]
>
> The child is the *gloire* before it is born. The circle of the candle on my notebook is the *gloire*, the story isn't born yet.
>
> While I live in the unborn story, I am in the *gloire*.
>
> I must keep it alive, myself living with it. (176–7)

This is a profoundly unsettling moment in the novel, as Julia imagines escaping from the war into a utopian, maternal space. The scene could perhaps be read as an attempt to offer another kind of cultural imaginary—a feminine (or feminist) alternative to the culture which produced the terrible suffering of the Great War. But I find this interpretation unconvincing. While Julia meditates privately on the *gloire*, the war continues; millions more will suffer and die before it is over. Her mediation cannot change this; nor will it help to prevent another, larger war which was to prove much more disastrous for civilians—as HD knows very well when she completes the novel in the late 1940s. If anything this scene functions as a critique of theories which seek to analyse war purely in terms of gender.

Throughout her writings, HD explores and often dissolves the boundaries of subjectivity. At the same time, her war fiction represents subjects (Julia, Helforth) who are threatened to the point of severe neurosis by the war's reshaping of subjectivity. Not all transgressions of boundaries are liberating, either for women or for men.

NOTES

1. A shorter version of this chapter appears in Sarah Sceats and Gail Cunningham (eds.), *Image and Power* (London, 1996). For biographical information on HD, see Barbara Guest, *Herself Defined: The Poet H.D. and her World* (London, 1985); Susan Stanford Friedman, *Psyche Reborn: The Emergence of H.D.* (Bloomington, Ind., 1987); Friedman, *Penelope's Web: Gender, Modernity, H.D.'s Fiction* (Cambridge, 1990); Rachel Blau duPlessis, *H.D.: The Career of that Struggle* (Brighton, 1986); Friedman and duPlessis (eds.), *Signets: Reading H.D.* (Madison, Wis., 1990). On HD's writing of the Second World War, see Susan Edmunds, *Out of Line: History, Psychoanalysis, and Montage in H.D.'s Long Poems* (Stanford, Calif., 1994).
2. For the history of the term 'shell-shock', see e.g. Harold Merskey, 'Combat Hysteria', in *The Analysis of Hysteria* (London, 1979); Merskey, 'Shell Shock', in G. E. Berrios and H. Freeman (eds.), *150 Years of British Psychiatry, 1841–1991* (London, 1991).
3. 'Insanity and the War', *Lancet*, 2 (4 Sept. 1915), 553. Hysterical breakdown among soldiers was in fact documented as early as December 1914; recognition of the condition was uneven in the profession, and there was considerable debate over whether war neuroses were primarily physical or psychological in origin. See Chris Feudtner, '"Minds the Dead have Ravished": Shell Shock, History, and the Ecology of Disease Systems', *History of Science*, 31/4 (1993), 384.
4. 'Incidence of Mental Disease directly due to War', *Lancet*, 2 (23 Oct. 1915), 931. See also Eric Leed, *No Man's Land: Combat and Identity in World War I* (Cambridge, 1979). Feudtner notes that C. Stanford Read's study *Military Psychiatry in Peace and War* (London, 1920) found that nearly 25% of war-neurotic soldiers in one hospital had not been to the front line. Feudtner also points out that this kind of breakdown became more common as the war progressed ('Minds the Dead have Ravished', 386, 412 n. 20, 413 n. 35). See also Ruth Leys's fascinating work on psychoanalysis and war neuroses 'Traumatic Cures: Shell Shock, Janet, and the Question of Memory', *Critical Inquiry*, 20/4 (1994), 623–62; 'Death Masks: Kardiner and Ferenczi on Psychic Trauma', *Representations*, 53 (1996), 44–73.

5. 'War Shock in the Civilian', *Lancet*, 1 (4 Mar. 1916), 522.
6. 'Shell Shock in Cows', *Lancet*, 1 (2 Feb. 1918), 187–8.
7. Norman Fenton, *Shell Shock and its Aftermath* (London, 1926), 149.
8. Edwin Ash, *The Problem of Nervous Breakdown* (London, 1919), 275.
9. Phillip Knightley, *The First Casualty: The War Correspondent as Hero, Propagandist, and Myth Maker from the Crimea to Vietnam* (London, 1975).
10. According to Harvey Schwartz, this term emerged after the Vietnam war (Schwartz (ed.), *Psychotherapy of the Combat Veteran* (Lancaster, 1984), p. xi).
11. Bruce I. Goderez, 'The Survivor Syndrome: Massive Psychic Trauma and Posttraumatic Stress Disorder', *Bulletin of the Menninger Clinic* (Kansas), 51/1 (1987), 97.
12. Freud, *Beyond the Pleasure Principle* (1920), Pelican Freud Library, xi (Harmondsworth, 1984), 281. Merskey, 'Shell Shock', 246–7.
13. HD, *Tribute to Freud*, rev. edn (Manchester, 1985), 40.
14. See Gary Burnett, *H.D. Between Image and Epic: The Mysteries of her Poetics* (Ann Arbor, Mich., 1990); Burnett, 'H.D.'s Responses to the First World War', *Agenda*, 25/3–4 (1988), 54–63.
15. HD, *Asphodel*, ed. Robert Spoo (Durham, NC, 1992), 108.
16. HD, Letter to Norman Holmes Pearson, ed. Diana Collecott, *Agenda*, 25/3–4 (1988), 72.
17. These are described in a strange, uneasy scene in Woolf's *The Years* (1937). See Gillian Beer's discussion of aeroplanes and air raids in Woolf's writings: 'The Island and the Aeroplane: The Case of Virginia Woolf', in Homi Bhabha (ed.), *Nation and Narration* (London, 1990), 265–90.
18. HD, *Tribute to Freud*, 93. See also Claire Buck, *HD and Freud: Bisexuality and a Feminine Discourse* (Hemel Hempstead, 1991).
19. HD, 'Magic Mirror' (1955), quoted in Friedman, *Psyche Reborn*, 29.
20. *Psyche Reborn*, 301 n. 20.
21. This point is explored by Lynn Hanley, *Writing War: Fiction, Gender and Memory* (Amherst, Mass., 1991), ch. 1.
22. For this discussion, I have drawn upon the following historical accounts: J. M. Winter, *The Experience of World War I* (Oxford, 1988); Thomas A. Bailey and Paul B. Ryan, *The Lusitania Disaster: An Episode in Modern Warfare and Diplomacy* (New York, 1975); Des Hickey and Gus Smith, *Seven Days to Disaster: The Sinking of the Lusitania* (London, 1981); Edwyn A. Gray, *The Killing Time: The U-Boat War 1914–18* (London, 1972); C. L. Droste, *The Lusitania Case*, ed. W. H. Tatum (1916; London, 1972); Colin Simpson, *Lusitania* (London, 1972), as well as reports from *The Times* and the *Manchester Guardian*, 8–15 May 1915. The newspaper reports are not at all reliable, however, and I have not used these for factual information.
23. Civilian morale is considered to have been an essential factor in the outcome of the war. See e.g. John Turner (ed.), *Britain and the First World War* (London, 1988), 5.
24. *The Times*, for example, calls it an 'outrage', a 'crime', a 'wholesale massacre', and an action of 'diabolic character'(10 May 1915, p. 5).
25. For details of the propaganda campaigns around the *Lusitania*, see Arthur Ponsonby, *Falsehood in War-Time* (London, 1928) and H. C. Peterson, *Propaganda for War: The Campaign against American Neutrality, 1914–1917* (Princeton, 1939), ch. 5.
26. Willa Cather, *One of Ours* (1922; London, 1987), 236.

27. Questions about the difference between witnessing and seeing arise even more intensely in the Nazi holocaust: see Shoshana Felman, 'In an Era of Testimony: Claude Lanzmann's *Shoah*', *Yale French Studies*, 79: *Literature and the Ethical Question* (1991), 39–81. See also Shoshana Felman and Dori Laub, *Testimony: Crises of Witnessing in Literature, Psychoanalysis, and History* (New York, 1992).
28. Friedman, *Penelope's Web*, 139.
29. Here, my argument is directly opposed to Sandra Gilbert's reading of the war as a metaphorical 'battle of the sexes'. 'Soldier's Heart: Literary Men, Literary Women, and the Great War', in Sandra Gilbert and Susan Gubar, *No Man's Land: The Place of the Woman Writer in the Twentieth Century*, ii: *Sexchanges* (New Haven, 1989).
30. I read HD alongside a range of other writers of the Great War, including a number of soldiers, in my forthcoming study of modernism and the War. For recent discussions of masculinity, see Peter Middleton, *The Inward Gaze: Masculinity and Subjectivity in Modern Culture* (London, 1992); Graham Dawson, *Soldier Heroes* (London, 1994); Kaja Silverman, *Male Subjectivity at the Margins* (London, 1992). See also Judith Butler and Joan W. Scott (eds.), *Feminists Theorize the Political* (London, 1992); Sally Ledger *et al.* (eds.), *Political Gender* (Hemel Hempstead, 1994).
31. '*Kora and Ka' and 'Mira-Mare'* (Dijon, 1934); repr. in Bronte Adams and Trudi Tate (eds.), *That Kind of Woman: Stories from the Left Bank and Beyond* (London, 1991). References to 'Kora and Ka' are from this edition.
32. For the history of war neuroses, see Martin Stone, 'Shellshock and the Psychologists', in W. F. Bynum, Roy Porter, and Michael Shepherd (eds.), *The Anatomy of Madness: Essays in the History of Psychiatry*, ii (London, 1985); Leed, *No Man's Land;* Ted Bocagz, 'War Neurosis and Cultural Change', *Journal of Contemporary History*, 24, (1989), 227–56; Elaine Showalter, *The Female Malady: Women, Madness and English Culture, 1830–1980* (London, 1987).
33. HD was very interested in the possibilities of bisexual identities around the time that she was writing 'Kora and Ka'. Her male lover of that period was Kenneth Macpherson, a bisexual whom HD's lesbian companion, Bryher, had married in 1927. When HD consulted with Freud, around the time that the story was published, she reported to Bryher that Freud described her as the 'perfect bi-'. See duPlessis, *H.D.* 83, 144 n. 20; Friedman and duPlessis (eds.), *Signets*, 227.
34. Maurice Nicoll, 'Regression', in H. Crichton Miller (ed.), *Functional Nerve Disease* (London, 1920), 102–5; Leys, 'Traumatic Cures', 633. See also W. H. R. Rivers, *Instinct and the Unconscious*, 2nd edn. (Cambridge, 1922), ch. 18.
35. Nicholl, 'Regression', 102; italics in original.
36. H. Crichton Miller described twenty-eight examples of combatant 'mother-complexes', speculating that it might be a factor in more than 20 per cent of war-neurotic cases (Miller, 'The Mother Complex', in Miller (ed.), *Functional Nerve Disease*, 115–28).
37. See e.g. Peter Buitenhuis, *The Great War of Words: Literature as Propaganda 1914–18 and After* (London, 1989); Ponsonby, *Falsehood in War-Time*; Arthur Marwick, *The Deluge: British Society and the First World War*, 2nd edn. (Basingstoke, 1991).
38. Approximately 6m. British men (12.5% of the male population) served

in the war. This includes mechanics, cooks, medical workers, and many other non-fighting members of the armed forces (Winter, *The Experience of World War I,* 119; Eric Hobsbawm, *Age of Extremes: The Short Twentieth Century, 1914–1991* (London, 1994), 44).

39. Friedman, *Penelope's Web,* 364. The introduction to the 1984 Virago edition dates the writing of the novel incorrectly. For a detailed discussion of *Bid Me to Live* as a war novel, see Claire M. Tylee, *The Great War and Women's Consciousness: Images of Militarism and Womanhood in Women's Writings, 1914–64* (Basingstoke, 1990).

40. The early Zeppelins were extremely vulnerable, but by 1917 the Germans had developed an improved airship which flew at high altitudes and was difficult to shoot down, 'rendering obsolete the entire British air defence system' (Guy Hartcup, *The War of Invention* (London, 1988), 158–60). Compared with attacks on civilians during the Second World War, the Zeppelin raids killed a very small number of people. But we should not underestimate their imaginary effects; for the first time, British civilians found themselves targets of a war which was actually being fought elsewhere. It was also the first time that civilians came under attack from the air, and was much more terrifying than the low casualty figures might suggest.

41. See Caroline Zilboorg (ed.), *Richard Aldington and HD: The Early Years in Letters* (Bloomington, Ind., 1992).

42. HD, *Bid Me to Live* (1960; London, 1984), 123, 126. Subsequent references are to this edition.

43. This works against Gilbert's claim that women inevitably felt liberated by the war, and is closer to the lament, found in much writing of the period, that the war destroyed culture and civilization, for women as well as for men.

44. See Maud Ellmann, *The Poetics of Impersonality: T. S. Eliot and Ezra Pound* (Brighton, 1987); Peter Middleton, 'The Academic Development of *The Waste Land*', *Glyph Textual Studies,* 1 (1986), 153–80; David Roessel, '"Mr. Eugenides, the Smyrna Merchant" and Post-war Politics in *The Waste Land*', *Journal of Modern Literature,* 16/1 (1989), 171–6; Stan Smith, *The Origins of Modernism* (Hemel Hempstead, 1994), ch. 7.

45. HD, *Paint it Today* (New York, 1992), 45. The narrator of this strange and awkward novel says that the post-war 'convalescence' is 'even more painful' than the war itself (67). *Paint it Today* was written in 1921. Friedman, *Penelope's Web,* 141, 362.

46. Gilbert, 'Soldier's Heart'. For a detailed critique of Gilbert's argument, see Claire M. Tylee, '"Maleness Run Riot": The Great War and Women's Resistance to Militarism', *Women's Studies International Forum,* 11/3 (1988), 199–210.

47. Richard Aldington enlisted because he feared—with good reason—that he would soon be conscripted. Conscription was introduced for single men in January 1916 and for married men in May 1916. Zilboorg, *Richard Aldington and H.D.,* 21; John Gooch, 'The Armed Services', in Stephen Constantine, Maurice Kirby, and Mary Rose (eds.), *The First World War in British History* (London, 1995), 189.

48. For a fascinating discussion of similar issues in war poetry by women see Jan Montefiore, '"Shining Pins and Wailing Shells": Women Poets and the Great War', in Goldman (ed.), *Women and World War I,* esp. 58–62.

49. The passage also draws on HD's continuing interest in the ancient world

and its lost cities. See also her poem 'Cities' in *Sea Garden* (1916), discussed by Jane Gledhill, 'Impersonality and Amnesia: A Response to World War I in the Writings of H.D. and Rebecca West', in Goldman (ed.), *Women and World War I*, 175–7.

50. For HD's relationship with Lawrence, see Carol Siegel, *Lawrence among the Women: Wavering Boundaries in Women's Literary Traditions* (Charlottesville, Va., 1991); Helen Sword, 'Orpheus and Eurydice in the Twentieth Century: Lawrence, H.D., and the Poetics of the Turn', *Twentieth Century Literature*, 35/4 (1989), 407–28; Peter E. Firchow, 'Rico and Julia: The Hilda Doolittle–D. H. Lawrence Affair Reconsidered', *Journal of Modern Literature*, 8/1 (1980), 51–76; Jane Gledhill, 'Impersonality and Amnesia', 178–82; see also Paul Delany, *D. H. Lawrence's Nightmare: The Writer and his Circle in the Years of the Great War* (Hassocks, 1979).

12

Gertrude Stein and War

ELIZABETH GREGORY

> And then there was another Sunday and we were at Béon again that Sunday, and Russia came into the war and Poland was smashed, and I did not care about Poland, but it did frighten me about France—oh dear, that was another Sunday.
>
> And then we settled down to a really wonderful winter.
>
> (Gertrude Stein, *The Winner Loses: A Picture of Occupied France*)

IT has been argued that the peculiar literary project with which Gertrude Stein's name is typically associated involved a non-hierarchic utopian aspect. Sometimes described as cubist for its presentation of its objects from many angles at once, Stein's semi-grammatical work (i.e. at Chomsky's second level of grammaticality—not devoid of meaning but not fully clear either) is characterized as well by some combination of frequently repeated phrases, modulating more or less gradually over long spans of page, a glancing focus that often conveys the sense that a subject-matter exists without clarifying quite what it is, and a preference for present tense. Though the style varies over time and between texts, the large effect is an insistence on multiplicities of possible readings. In insisting so, this 'Steinese' undermines the notion of hierarchy implicit in the view that one may master a text's meaning, and raises questions about hierarchies of all kinds.[1] Stein's language has also been linked to the Kristevan semiotic and understood to re-create through its rhythms and its play with sound the pleasures of vocal interaction within a mother–child dyad. Such an honouring of the pre-symbolic over mature language use has also been read as a challenge to standard hierarchies. Through such means, Harriet Chessman argues, 'Stein creates forms of writing that resist the colonialism of reading's empires, and that playfully ask us to question our own desire for dominance'[2]. In place of structures of dominance, Chessman holds, Stein models interactions of tender intimacy, between reader and text (who must together make meaning out of Stein's writing) and between her characters.[3] Gender hierarchy comes into question here along with all other hierarchies and, relatedly, the subtext of lesbian love that Stein encodes in much of her work argues for the liberalizing of rules about who may acceptably love whom. Implied in all this subversion of the status quo shimmers a suggestion of a world animated principally by tenderness, sexual and other physical pleasure, and the intimate relations of family and friendship.[4]

Such non-hierarchic utopianism did not characterize all Stein's work, however, in terms of either structure or subject-matter. For instance, in some of her later work, written for a popular audience, she employs standard grammar to standardly determinate effect. And both her relationship with her companion Alice Toklas and her descriptions of it involved stereotypically gendered marital role-playing—i.e. Alice, the wife, acquiesced to and saw to the comfort of Gertrude, the husband. Relatedly, Stein's large ego led her to dwell on her desire for recognition as a genius and for the homage such a high position in the hierarchy of intelligence can claim. And she adopted a standardly masculine set of behaviours, including a preference for friendships with men (preferably brilliant men) in which she functioned as one among equals. These arrangements, though they operated on principles of hierarchy Stein is understood to denounce in other spheres, seem to have facilitated her psychological segue into turn-of-the-century Parisian society.

The contradictions between these two sets of behaviours suggest Stein's complexity, but in the long run her givings-in to the available order of things need not be understood to undermine the utopian strain in her work. Instead they would seem to complicate it with the desire of a living woman to function as an active member of the Parisian art world in the present; a desire realizable only, presumably, in a limited range of variation on familiar terms. Though they contradicted the principles on which she based her work, Stein took what means she found available to accomplish that end. In so doing she displayed a double-mindedness common to women writers of her period, who both questioned the hierarchical terms on which authority circulated in their world, and sought some of that authority for themselves.[5]

Some of this same contradictoriness characterizes Stein's response to war. Stein moved to France in 1903 and stayed there through both world wars, until her death in 1946. During the first war, she and Alice Toklas travelled extensively, conveying supplies to wounded soldiers. In the second war, though as Jews they knew the threat German anti-Semitism posed to them, they chose to remain in the occupied French countryside rather than return to their native United States.

Stein's decisions to remain in France during the wars emerged out of several interests. Shari Benstock's work has shown that Stein and many other American women writers, and particularly the lesbians among them, found in Paris an environment conducive to their work and to the happy living of their lives that they could not find in their native land. In addition, the situation of exile from homeland and from native tongue provided Stein with the distance necessary both to considered examination of the national character of America and Americans and, she argued, to radical experimentation with the English language. Paris had also the appeal for Stein it has had to millions of visitors, in its focus on pleasures of the most basic and satisfactory sort—gustatory, sensual, and aesthetic. For Stein these pleasures had a pre-eminent importance that made them necessities rather than touristic luxuries. While any and all of these reasons might explain Stein's remaining, it seems that the wars had their own appeal as well. Though the wars upset her mightily, they also afforded her some measure of enjoyment.

It will be the project of this chapter to explore the ways in which Stein's utopian project navigated the encounter with a world at war, a world in which tenderness and subversion of patriarchal norms would seem to have small place. Stein wrote quite a few poems and plays during the First World War—some concerned with the war explicitly, others not, but all addressing the world in which Stein moved. In 1932 she rendered her war experience in standardly realistic narrative form in her *Autobiography of Alice B. Toklas*, the most successful of her popular works. This was the first of a series of realistic texts in which she presents herself as a character involved in a war. The others in this series draw on her Second World War experience, either exclusively or in combination with her experience of the First World War: *Paris France* (1940), *The Winner Loses* (1940), and *Wars I have Seen* (1945). *Brewsie and Willie* (1945), a dialogue among American servicemen, draws on her war experience but does not include Stein as a character. *Mrs Reynolds* (written in 1940–3, published in 1952) returns to her non-realistic mode (though it is less obscure than some of her earlier work) to tell the story of a couple living in circumstances like those Stein and Toklas knew during the period of its composition. This chapter will not attempt to account for all Stein's writing about war, but will focus on a selection of the earlier material and look briefly at the Second World War writing. I will explore how Stein's written rendering of her war experiences balances what seem to be contradictory impulses, towards a world in which tenderness is valued most highly and towards patriotic jingoism.

By 1914 Stein had completed a novel, written in 1903 and published in 1950 as *Things as they Are*; a group of short stories called *Three Lives* (1909); and the non-generic *Tender Buttons* (1914). The latter two she published at her own expense, the first only made its way into print after her death. *Things as they Are* and *Three Lives* employ recognizable narrative techniques to tell unusual tales. *Things as they Are* reworks an early triangular lesbian romance of Stein's. *Three Lives*, based loosely on Flaubert's *Trois Contes*, tells the ordinary stories of three lower-class women. It is extraordinary precisely because their stories are so little told. With *Tender Buttons* Stein made a major departure from her earlier work. In it, she works to evoke the sense of her immediate experience of a series of domestic artefacts (in sections entitled 'Objects', 'Food', and 'Rooms'), rendering a mixture of what she perceived and her inner state as she perceived it. Thus the piece begins:

A CARAFE, THAT IS A BLIND GLASS
A kind in glass and a cousin, a spectacle and nothing strange a single hurt color and an arrangement in a system to pointing. All this and not ordinary, not unordered in not resembling. The difference is spreading.[6]

The passage comments on its own method—rendering this common subject of cubist painting through its perceiver's associations to it. Representing the influx of sensation and one's responses to it of course involves difficulties with communication to another perceiver, as do all such aestheticist attempts, since different viewers may perceive the same object differently and so not recognize the other's description of the process of perception. The result achieved here has an order ('not unordered'), but not the order we generally expect in description. The closing line suggests the expanding possibilities for a variety of readings that this text opens up, as well as the further departures from the expected to follow.

At the same time that Stein's new writing techniques challenge standard hierarchies of meaning, they also operate in a fairly usual way—as covers behind which Stein could express forbidden material while seeming not to. For instance, Stein fills *Tender Buttons* with allusions to sex, particularly lesbian sex. The title makes one such allusion, as does the following which seems to narrate an orgasm: 'Aider, why aider why whow, whow stop touch, aider whow, aider stop the muncher, muncher munchers.'[7] Her new techniques serve also to overturn literary conventions that preserve the status quo and create scenarios (especially that of the standard romance) in which women tend to be victimized.[8]

Gertrude Stein and the First World War

When the First World War broke out, Gertrude Stein and Alice Toklas were on a visit to England. They remained, tense and worried, for forty days, before obtaining a visa to return to Paris, which they found much changed from the cheerful city they had left. After a dreary winter full of Zeppelin alarms Stein and Toklas took off for Palma de Mallorca in Spain, where life was pleasant and Stein did some writing. But after Verdun, an anxiety to return to France sent them packing. They came back to:

> an entirely different Paris. It was no longer gloomy. It was no longer empty. This time we did not settle down, we decided to get into the war. One day we were walking down the rue des Pyramides and there was a ford car being backed up the street by an american girl and on the car it said, American Fund for French Wounded. There, said I, that is what we are going to do. At least, said I to Gertrude Stein, you will drive the car and I will do the rest.[9]

They spent the next two years driving around in a Ford (christened Aunt Pauline) as representatives of the American Fund for French Wounded, distributing food and visiting the sick first around Perpignan, then Nîmes, and finally Alsace. During this period Stein wrote quite a few poems and plays. A few of these, directly concerned with the war, she published in popular magazines in the United States. These were her first publications in such a context, her earlier work having been almost entirely published at her expense, for a limited audience.

The poems of this period involving the war introduce soldiers and a wartime milieu into the world of Steinese, and as with much of her work they are often difficult to read as clear statements. The war invoked here is clearly not that of the battlefield, however. Instead we get snippets of the war as Stein saw it, as it intersects with the dailiness of life in the towns and villages around Perpignan and Nîmes. For instance, in the poem 'Won' (1917) we see the arriving Americans crossing the path of Aunt Pauline in Nîmes.

Thousands of trucks.
And hundreds of marines.
And in between then.
Aunt Pauline losing oil.
We will see.
Can you think about a dish.
We will have a dish.
Radish.
That is good as food.
Aunt Pauline will justify herself.[10]

This poem speaks of the arrival of US soldiers, the winning of the war, good food, and the operation of Stein's car. The effect is to put all members of the set on a par, countering the emphasis on war and carnage that the soldiers may be made to represent (though in Stein's work they tend not to be) with an emphasis on homely concerns. Of course daily life may involve its own hierarchies and pains, and Stein's life certainly did, but in Stein's writing it is the pleasures and the co-operativeness of such life that get the emphasis.

The poem 'A Deserter' (1919) presents its central character as a whole person, giving a sense both of his identity beyond his crime and of the reasons behind it: 'I cannot forget Narcissus

Deschamps. He was a deserter. He had had them brothers killed in the war. He was a professor and took pleasure in a bout of box. He told us he was an automobile assayer. He worked very well and he got the colic and the police caught him. We know him.'[11] Here the focus falls not directly on the destructiveness of battle, though that is suggested, but on the humanity of the aptly named Narcissus Deschamps, who seems to have attempted to put his own interests first, escaping the front and returning to the life of the town, though ultimately unsuccessfully. The speaker's sympathy with him is apparent.

These poems are more accessible than the work Stein had been writing in the period just prior. In general Marianne DeKoven finds the new poems less interesting than their predecessors. 'Unlike the subjects of *Tender Buttons* or the early portraits, the subjects of the 1914–19 work are often all too readily discernible: the irritations and privations of domestic life in wartime exile in Mallorca, details of household management, casual observations on the lives of Gertrude's and Alice's acquaintances, and intimate exchanges—defensive, sharp, teasing, loving—between the two women.' She interprets Stein's purpose in using what she calls banal language in these pieces as a reverse-logic attempt to effect a '[dislocation of] the banal, and the patriarchal-hierarchical linearity on which the banal rests' and so to reveal the irrational, non-hierarchical substrata of mental life. But sometimes, she finds, the effect is only one of making this banal language 'not less, but more trivial'. Because the forms Stein employs in this period are more conventional and therefore seem more rational than those she employed earlier, DeKoven finds that they 'concea[l] rather than uncove[r] [the banal language's] genuine resonance in the irrational'.[12]

But the later work operates in a new context with a new set of concerns, and so it seems inappropriate to judge it by the same standard used for the earlier work. If *Tender Buttons* was anti-patriarchal because it refused clear statement, the war work achieves a similarly anti-patriarchal purpose by different means. In coming much closer to definite statement *per se*, this newer work also manages to offer a more direct statement of protest against the forces of destruction. In these poems and in others the humanity of the soldiers and of the people they are fighting for is stressed. The trivial concerns and pleasures of daily life are precisely the point. Where war promotes structures of domination over structures of mutual responsibility and undermines the values of dailiness and loving comfort, Stein's work—both her literary work and her relief work—reasserts those values. She brings food and clothing and cheerful conversation to the wounded, countering with tender intimacy the cruelties of the battlefield, an effort directly linked in principle to her attempts in the pre-war *Tender Buttons*. Her poems' characters are seen eating, asking for photographs, going to the theatre. For instance, in 'What does Cook Want to Do' (1916) we get a catalogue of options for pleasure:

> Will he go alone or does he want two tickets or three tickets or four. Does he want to spend his time here. Does he want an occupation. Has he pleasure in walking. Would he like to raise birds. Does he like a light house. Has he reason to be natural. Is he fond of water. Does he incline to make friends. Does he know how often he has an appetite. Is he eager to be called. Does he mean to go away.
>
> What does he want.[13]

The animating concern here is that desires be named and met. In 'Let us be easily Careful' (1916) we get discussions of housekeeping and food:

> He asks for a soup spoon. He says that is the only thing we forgot. We are also sending fruit knives. . . .
>
> Mutton. This is a subject. Were we displeased. Were we perfectly satisfied. Did we find it tenderer more than we expected. . . .
>
> Lettuce. He said they did not have lettuce. Green peas. They have green peas. All the rest. They have all the rest. They are a funny people. A drop of oil remains just what it is.[14]

Where Stein's pre-war work had stressed intimacy and the daily concerns of home life as a counter to structures of domination, it had done so within a framework that made its emphasis on the world of intimate relations barely recognizable to most readers. Her war work remains difficult to make plain sense of but the objects are recognizable, as is the texture of the lives she describes. In this rendering the work speaks more publicly, to a wider audience, and so, given the public nature of war, offers a more apprehensible and so Stein might hope a more effective protest.

Stein's emphasis on daily pleasures and the ordinary lives of people in extraordinary circumstances operates in a way similar to that which Lyn Bicker describes in the work of other women writers of the war period. Bicker, using Katherine Mansfield as a prime example, suggests that it was common for women writers to offer their protest against the inhumanity of war not through direct statement but through reference to the pleasures of home life. She explains this choice as based on a sense of what was considered seemly: 'in writing which was not intended to be political, triviality was the only tone available to women—or at least perceived as available'.[15] This explanation of the phenomenon might be revised to include the understanding that the definition of the trivial is exactly what is at issue. By choosing to represent ordinary scenes these writers attempt to redefine what is considered important, moving the emphasis from the destructive theatres of battle to the creative theatres of daily life.

While concerns about decorousness might constrain her fellow women writers of the period, Stein, as might be predicted, does not toe the line of seemliness for its own sake. Sometimes she does make direct statements about her views (or, if she is quoting another, the quoted voice takes on an authority within the poem). For instance, in a poem on their war work entitled 'The Work' (1917) published in the *Bulletin of the American Fund for French Wounded*, we get these direct statements:

> Not fierce and tender but sweet.
>
> This is our impression of the soldiers....
>
> Hurrah for America....
>
> This makes me sad. I hate to hear of them that they are not going to be well. We need them. Not to fight only but to live. You can imagine how I feel....
>
> I remember one [hotel] where the landlady told us of her son.... And a boy was an officer. Not one of her children. Were they fighting. They would never remain different in living. Let us hope they are not dying. I cannot tell you what it means to be fighting....
>
> A war is not a joke.
>
> Did he die there because he was mortal and we leave Rivesaltes. Be nice to me....
>
> It is astonishing that those who have fought so hard and so well should pick yellow irises and fish in a stream.[16]

The poem refuses to see the soldiers as warriors, presenting them instead as family members, needed by the communities they have left behind.

In 'Decorations' (1917) Stein transports her soldiers from the realm of war, fear, and loss into the realm of pleasure:

What did I do in the garden.
I played with soldiers.
You mean the soldiers prayed.
I mean the soldiers played.[17]

'We have eaten Heartily and we were Alarmed' (1916) includes several sections that address the war directly, one of them entitled 'Do be Dead': 'Soldiers fighting soldiers can walk all day without eating. This has been my experience. If anybody wants this let them assure them that it is tiresome. It must be fatiguing. Going and coming and thinking. All fronts are the same only the clay country is different. What do they care. They don't care about anything.'[18] In 'Our Aid' (1917), of the next of kin at what may be either a wedding or a funeral we are told 'All of them are worthy of a caress. | The little English that we know says, We cannot miss them. Kiss them.'[19] In both the poems that specifically treat the war and those that do not Stein argues against the principles of destruction. The anomalous style and odd juxtapositions of war images with images of ordinary life represent the entry of war into the daily lives of ordinary folk as absurd.

This sense of a sadness in the war and a need to assuage it is not the only mood Stein models in her treatments of the First World War, however. Her work brought her into much contact with soldiers, both French and American, and both she and Toklas enjoyed this greatly. The pleasantness of their exchanges comes to prominence in Stein's later work. In the retrospective account of the war in *The Autobiography of Alice B. Toklas* (1932) the war takes on a glamour and jauntiness, perhaps having to do with the self-interested falsifications of memory, perhaps with the desire to keep the tone of the book light in order to sell more copies, or yet to be ironic (to match the ironic tone of the whole). One episode suggests particularly well the revisionary role of war memory:

> Elmer Harden had been nursing french wounded in the american hospital and one of his patients, a captain with an arm fairly disabled, was going back to the front. Elmer Harden . . . said to Captain Peter, I am going with you. . . . [and] by the end of the week Captain Peter

had rejoined and Elmer Harden was in his regiment as a soldier. He fought well and was wounded. . . . Only the other day . . . Elmer made Captain Peter and Captain Peter is a breton admit that it was a nice war. Up to this time when he had said to Captain Peter, it was a nice war, Captain Peter had not answered, but this time when Elmer said, it was a nice war, Captain Peter said, yes Elmer, it was a nice war.[20]

Along with the sexual innuendo in this story, Elmer's sentiment on the war reinforces the impression that Stein–Toklas gives throughout of her own sense of the niceness of the war. The process by which Captain Peter arrives at his closing view on the war may parallel Stein's own revisionary process.

Another source of Stein's jauntiness would seem to lie in the fact that the war did have its pleasures for her. Part of the war's appeal, she explains, lay in the opportunity the war offered her of being with Americans (whom she found sympathetic) without having to submit to being in the United States (which she did not find so): 'We did enjoy the life with these doughboys. I would like to tell nothing but doughboy stories. They all got on amazingly well with the french. . . . Gertrude Stein always said the war was so much better than just going to America. Here you were with America in a kind of way that if you only went to America you could not possibly be.'[21] The absorbing war work and the company of lots of friendly young men energized Stein, who had always preferred male company anyway. Stein's biographer Richard Bridgman calls the war 'therapeutic' for her.[22]

The war seems to have been an occasion for many pleasant interactions, and for the excitement of extraordinary gestures. Stein's reminiscences echo the resistance fighters' nostalgia for the Second World War as one of the few moments in their lives when right and wrong were clear-cut. Aunt Pauline, the Ford Toklas and Stein drove, became the catalyst of many friendly encounters. This was due, first, to their policy of offering lifts to any soldier they passed hitch-hiking:

We drove by day and we drove by night and in very lonely parts of France and we always stopped and gave a lift to any soldier, and never had we any but the most pleasant experiences with these soldiers. And some of them were as we sometimes found out pretty hard characters. Gertrude Stein once said to a soldier who was doing something for her . . . you are tellement gentil, very nice and kind. Madame, said he quite simply, all soldiers are nice and kind.[23]

The car provided opportunities for further pleasant encounters by regularly breaking down. Whenever the car failed to respond to her cranking, or blew a tyre, or developed some other problem, Stein found men willing to help her.

This faculty of Gertrude Stein of having everybody do anything for her puzzled the other drivers for the [American Fund for French Wounded]. Mrs. Lathrop [the director] who used to drive her own car said that nobody did those things for her. It was not only soldiers, a chauffeur would get off the seat of a private car in the place Vendome and crank Gertrude Stein's old ford for her. Gertrude Stein said that the others looked so efficient, of course nobody would think of doing anything for them. Now as for herself she was not efficient, she was good humoured, she was democratic, one person was as good as another, and she knew what she wanted done. If you are like that she says, anybody will do anything for you. The important thing, she insists, is that you must have deep down as the deepest thing in you a sense of equality. Then anybody will do anything for you.[24]

Evincing a contradictoriness here not unlike that which characterized Stein's attitude toward hierarchy, the logic of this paragraph holds that the democrat is the one others will serve cheerfully.

As the war progressed, the two women adopted an expanding set of military godsons with whom they exchanged many letters. Stein–Toklas recounts the story of the favourite of these, named Abel. Her tale focuses on their encounters with him, specifically de-emphasizing the horrific aspects of his war experience. In his first letter from the front Stein relates that Abel expresses no surprise, everything being as had been described to him, except over the fact that there are no tables to write on. If he said anything about the fighting, Stein omits it. After the war, Abel, decorated along with his entire regiment with the legion of honour, visits his godmothers in Paris, his first trip to the capital. He likes the city but finds it frightening at night: 'The front had not been scareful but Paris at night was.'[25] Abel's special attraction for Stein may lie precisely in his like-minded refusal to allow the war to usurp his focus on the business of ordinary life—the presence or absence of writing-tables, for instance, or the differences between city and country.

Stein elides the war's bloody aspect not in this incident alone but throughout the text. Much of her war experience occurred far from the front, which explains something; her focus tends to be on her own experience. But even when she does come near the front she describes it only briefly:

> Soon we came to the battle-fields and the lines of trenches of both sides. To any one who did not see it as it was then it is impossible to imagine it. It was not terrifying it was strange. We were used to ruined houses and even ruined towns but this was different. It was a landscape. And it belonged to no country.
>
> I remember hearing a french nurse once say and the only thing she did say of the front was, c'est un paysage passionnant, an absorbing landscape. And that was what it was as we saw it. It was strange. Camouflage, huts, everything was there. It was wet and dark and there were a few people, one did not know whether they were chinamen or europeans. Our fan-belt had stopped working. A staff car stopped and fixed it with a hairpin, we still wore hairpins.[26]

Stein actively moves away in the course of these two paragraphs from discussion of the horrors of war and towards the concerns of the familiar, the homelike. The move is not complete, however; some element of the war's strangeness remains at the end in the reference to hairpins, which have become as unusual to the contemporary (short-haired) Stein as the nationless landscape she saw in travelling to Strasbourg in 1918.

When at one point Stein does mention death in relation to the war it is not directly connected with battle: 'Every now and then one of the american soldiers would get into the hospital at Nimes and as Doctor Fabre knew that Gertrude Stein had had a medical education he always wanted her present with the doughboy on these occasions. One of them fell off the train. He did not believe that the little french trains could go fast but they did, fast enough to kill him.'[27] Death here comes accidently, not as a result of malice, and it disappears from the narrative as swiftly as it enters. Such an approach shares much with Stein's dwelling on the ordinary in the work she composed during the war. By refusing to feature the war in her narrative, and reducing its 'large' concerns to a bit part, she challenges the common rankings of what kinds of thing matter. Again, as with the earlier material, what matters in this version of the war are relationships and ordinary pleasures.

As the quotations I've taken from the *Autobiography* demonstrate, Stein evolved a new, chatty style in this text and a peculiar but thoroughly readable realism. The new work's appeal lay in its anecdotal format—providing readers with insider glimpses of the lives of the rich and famous of the art world—and in its sharp, epigrammatic wit. Stein wrote the memoir at the urging of friends because she was short of funds and desirous of a wider public for her work (she described her motives, in *Stanzas in Meditation*, as 'need . . . pride | And . . . ambition').[28] The book became an immediate bestseller and established her as a major character in the eye of the public at large, though she had already been fairly well known. For this broader public, Stein presented herself as extremely good natured (and when bad natured, so honestly so that it counted as good natured after all); a comedian. Her emphasis then on the co-operative, even cheerful aspect of war fits with this lighter focus. Thus in the *Autobiography*, generic constraints reinforced the earlier refusal to allow the destructive aspects of war a featured place in her work.

Stein's ambition and her desire for popularity led her to this more direct form, which, given the basis of her earlier subversion in evasion of standard narrative form, might be understood as less subversive. But the new form brought its own possibilities for raising questions about the status quo (and in so doing it responds to the conundrum often raised in modernist literature classes about how such obscure texts can be considered anti-hierarchic when they are themselves available only to élite audiences trained to be patient with the kinds of difficulty they present to readers). For instance, the 'joke' of having an autobiography written by someone other than the 'self' being represented raises questions about the nature of identity (to what extent are we informed by those with whom we live and interact), about the fictionality of all autobiography (i.e. the selection and slanting necessarily involved), and conversely about the autobiographical quality of all fiction, while at the same time signalling that we cannot read this narrative entirely straight. The irony in the frame story asks readers to look more carefully than they otherwise might at the rest of the memoir's claims. Thus while the *Autobiography* leaves out direct mention of the sexual bond between Stein and Toklas, no other explanation is offered of their union either, leaving it to readers to decipher cannily.

Similarly, while the memoir may accurately express Stein's pleasure in her encounters with soldiers during the war, the whole narrative is presented so wryly, with such an air of irony, that its cheer-leader slant on the war cannot escape its taint entirely. One may take the ironic tone of the memoir's premiss as authorization to hear the opposite in all Stein's claims. However, since the irony throughout seems heavily mixed with sincerity (for instance, Stein's love of fame is admitted outright, and finally so is the fact that Stein has written the book), the grounds seem slim for taking her views on the war as *fully* ironic. Instead, the presentation renders well the contradictory emotions that the war evoked in Stein, which were divided between pleasant feeling for the memories of her own spirited wartime encounters and a more abstract horror over what the war threatened to do to the world of intimacy and daily pleasure she valued above all else.[29] On reflection it becomes plain that the two apparently diverse reactions have a common source: the happy response to the soldiers springs from the same impulse to intimacy and positive human interaction, as does the refusal to allow the destructiveness of war to take over one's view. War and soldiers, as Stein suggests in her later *Wars I have Seen*, are very different things.[30]

Gertrude Stein and the Second World War

With Europe's return to war in 1939, Stein and Toklas (now both in their sixties) retired from Paris to Bilignin, the village near Lyon where they had summered for years. In *The Winner Loses*, Stein recounts how they almost decided to return to the United States but finally were persuaded to stay. At first Stein argues against those who urge them to depart that 'it would be awfully uncomfortable and I am fussy about my food', and determines to stay put, 'cut box hedges and forget the war'.[31] Toklas feels less sure, however, and they again consider departure. The argument of a neighbour closes the discussion:

> 'Well,' said Doctor Chaboux, reflecting, 'I can't guarantee you anything, but my advice is stay. I had friends,' he said, 'who in the last war stayed in their homes all through the German occupation, and they saved their homes and those who left lost theirs. No,' he said, 'I think unless your house is actually destroyed by a bombardment, I always think the best thing to do is to stay.' He went on, 'Everybody knows you here; everybody likes you; we all would help you in every way. Why risk yourself among strangers?'[32]

Though the risks for two Jewish women might seem to be greater than for Dr Chaboux's other friends, the attractions of home and life among friends win out over the presumed greater safety of life in the United States.

Having once decided to remain, Stein carried on her double life as a writer, penning both her series of cheerful patriotic memoirs in the fairly standard narrative form and a rather down-hearted and obscure novel called *Mrs Reynolds.* Though they take different tacks, both the esoteric and the popular texts are animated by a shared delight in the rituals of daily life and intimate relationship. The more public narratives maintain a fairly jaunty tone, or, when they admit to fear, as in the epigraph with which this chapter began, they undercut that admission swiftly with humour and an assertion of pleasure at home. In general, Stein is represented by her biographers as having had little political awareness, but the refusal of such awareness can itself be understood as a political decision. In *Mrs Reynolds,* however, Stein accedes to the pressure of the world outside and creates a narrative in which politics trouble the home life of her heroine. Two dictator figures—Angel Harper, representing Hitler, and Joseph Lang, representing Stalin, threaten the world's peace and cause the characters to despair for a while. In her epilogue to the text, Stein explains:

> This book is an effort to show the way anybody could feel these years. It is a perfectly ordinary couple living an ordinary life and having ordinary conversations and really not suffering personally from everything that is happening but over them, all over them is the shadow of two men, and then the shadow of one of the two men gets bigger and then blows away and there is no other. There is nothing historical about this book except the state of mind.[33]

Once again, Stein employs ordinariness and its pleasures as a counter to the forces of destruction. But in this later work, rather than figuring the victory of tenderness that she desires in the exile of the unhomely from her text, she includes it and renders the contest. But it does not reduce to a simple 'us versus them' dynamic. In *Mrs Reynolds* as elsewhere Stein expresses interest as well in the humanity of the 'enemy'—even her Hitler figure comes in for some understanding here, though finally she concludes he must die.

In *The Winner Loses,* one of her memoirs of the period, Stein makes the case that those who go to war to conquer others lose in the long run. She concludes by looking forward to the time when 'everybody will find out . . . that the winner loses, and everybody will be, too, like the French, that is, tremendously occupied with the business of daily living, and that that will be enough'.[34] Similar sentiments animate the one-page 'Reflection on the Atomic Bomb' (1946), one of Stein's last pieces:

> They asked me what I thought of the atomic bomb. I said I had not been able to take any interest in it.
>
> I like to read detective and mystery stories, I never get enough of them but whenever one of them is or was about death rays and atomic bombs I never could read them. What is the use, if they are really as destructive as all that there is nothing left and if there is nothing there nobody to be interested and nothing to be interested about. . . . Sure it will destroy a lot and kill a lot but it's the living that are interesting not the way of killing them . . .[35]

Interest in people and in ways of living well animates her to the end.

But while the excitements of war held no temptations for her, in the Second World War as in the First, Stein enjoyed very much her encounters with soldiers, particularly American soldiers. In *Brewsie and Willie* she features two GI friends, in post-VE Day France, who discuss with a number of others the world that awaits them back home in the States. The soldiers, speaking very colloquially and frankly, remark on how much they have learned in Europe about the business of daily living (battlefield experience gets very little mention throughout) and worry about returning to the US to live out their lives merely as employees, not as whole people. While Stein's enthusiasm for soldiers (both the First World War doughboys and the GIs of the Second World War) and her pleasure in her wartime activities, especially during the First World War, may initially seem antithetic to the principles of intimacy and subversion of hierarchy and of the status quo that run her experimental work, they develop from the same impulse.

Stein's response to the First World War was a redoubled celebration of the principles of value in the ordinary pleasurable and co-operative aspects of life, as counter to patriarchal structures of domination. The war seems to have led her to express herself more directly, in order to reach a wider public. Later she developed this directness even further with the *Autobiography* in order to sell more books to an audience waiting to be entertained. Even later, with the Second World War, she expressed a variety of feelings about war for a variety of audiences. In the different contexts, the affect she connects to war changes. Sometimes it seems merely an occasion for adventure, at other times a source of great distress. Stein's experience of the war was complex, as was that of many others, and her war writing reflects that complexity. All these texts share a concern for the happiness of the ordinary lives of men and women, with an emphasis on home life (particularly as practised in France) as the effective environment for its preservation. In representing the world she lived in, devastated by war not once but twice over thirty years, Stein could not represent a utopia. Instead the worlds she represents are full of conflicts and contradictions (and have the advantage over utopias of real-world existence and so of the possibility of real pleasure, even though mixed with pain). But the utopian impulse remains and directs her ongoing protest against the destructiveness and cruelties of war. For the most part, she protests by eliding the evidence of violence around her, refusing to honour it with mention, and focusing on pleasure instead.

NOTES

1. See Marjorie Perloff, *The Poetics of Indeterminacy: Rimbaud to Cage* (Princeton, 1981), 67–108.
2. Harriet Scott Chessman, *The Public is Invited to Dance: Representation, the Body and Dialogue in Gertrude Stein* (Stanford, Calif., 1989), 8.
3. For other readings in this vein, see Marianne DeKoven, *A Different Language: Gertrude Stein's Experimental Writing* (Madison, Wis., 1983); and Lisa Ruddick, *Reading Gertrude Stein: Body, Text, Gnosis* (Ithaca, NY, 1990).
4. The relationship between intimacy and repetition that Stein works with is suggested in the following passage from her essay 'Poetry and Grammar': 'you can love a name and if you love a name then saying that name any number of times only makes you love it more, more violently more persistently more tormentedly. Anybody knows how anybody calls out the name of anybody one loves. And so that is poetry really loving the name of anything and that is not prose. Yes any of you can know that' (Gertrude Stein, *Lectures in America* (1935; Boston, 1985), 232).
5. For more extensive exploration of this dynamic, see my 'Stamps, Money, Pop Culture and Marianne Moore', *Discourse*, 17/1 (1994), 123–46.
6. *The Selected Writings of Gertrude Stein*, ed. Carl Van Vechten (1934; New York, 1962), 461.

7. Ibid. 476.
8. Janice Doane points out that 'Lena', the first of the stories in *Three Lives*, 'demonstrates the disastrous effects of a conventional plot', since Lena is left 'not only devastated but dead, while her mate, roughly of the same caliber, is encouraged and left to contentedly carry on' (*Silence and Narrative: The Early Novels of Gertrude Stein* (Westport, Conn., 1986), p. xxiv).
9. *Autobiography of Alice B. Toklas*, in *Selected Writings*, 159.
10. Gertrude Stein, *Bee Time Vine and Other Pieces: 1913–1927* (New Haven, 1953), 187–8.
11. Gertrude Stein, *Reflection on the Atomic Bomb* (Los Angeles, 1973), 40. In *The Autobiography* (175) 'Alice' refers to this poem as an example of Stein's work during an especially prolific period: 'It was during these long trips [to villages around Nîmes to collect sick soldiers] that she began writing a great deal again. The landscape, the strange life stimulated her. . . . She wrote at that time the poem of The Deserter, printed almost immediately in Vanity Fair.'
12. DeKoven, *A Different Language*, 90–1. Of the instances she considers failures, DeKoven goes on to note: 'Stein does not go far enough in the subversion of conventional meaning, the necessary basis of experimental writing. If this writing is not sufficiently dedefined, multiplied, and fragmented, it cannot be anything more than solipsistic records of daily trivia, interesting only as documents of Stein's domestic life' (ibid. 92).
13. Gertrude Stein, *Painted Lace and Other Pieces: 1914–1937* (New Haven, 1955), 31.
14. Ibid. 33.
15. Lyn Bicker, 'Public and Private Choices: Public and Private Voices', in Dorothy Goldman (ed.), *Women and World War I: The Written Response* (Basingstoke, 1993), 103.
16. 'The Work', in *Bee Time Vine and Other Pieces*, 189–94.
17. *Bee Time Vine and Other Pieces*, 186.
18. *Painted Lace*, 40.
19. *Bee Time Vine and Other Pieces*, 184–5.
20. *Autobiography*, in *Selected Writings*, 187–8.
21. Ibid. 173–4.
22. Richard Bridgman, *Gertrude Stein in Pieces* (New York, 1970), 231.
23. *Autobiography*, in *Selected Writings*, 164.
24. Ibid. 164–5.
25. Ibid. 166.
26. Ibid. 176–7.
27. Ibid. 174.
28. *Stanzas in Meditation*, in *The Yale Gertrude Stein*, ed. Richard Kostelanetz (New Haven, 1980), 384.
29. As a woman of scientific training dedicated in some measure to principles of objective observation in her literary work, Stein recognized even war as part of human experience, and as such she found it interesting.
30. Stein, *Wars I Have Seen* (London, 1945), 3–4.
31. *The Winner Loses*, in *Selected Writings*, 623.
32. Ibid. 624.
33. *Mrs. Reynolds and Five Earlier Novelettes* (New Haven, 1952), 267.
34. *Selected Writings*, 637.
35. *Reflection on the Atomic Bomb*, 161.

Notes on the Contributors

GILLIAN BEER is King Edward VII Professor of English at the University of Cambridge and President of Clare Hall. Among her books are *Darwin's Plots* (1983), *George Eliot* (1986), and *Open Fields: Science in Cultural Encounter* (1996). She is currently at work on a study of the idea of the island in English culture from the nineteenth century.

NATHALIE BLONDEL is a lecturer and Mary Butts Research Fellow in the School of Literary Studies, University of the West of England, Bristol. She has edited collections of writings by Jane Bowles and Mary Butts, including *With and Without Buttons: Selected Stories of Mary Butts* (1991), and is the author of the first critical biography of Mary Butts, forthcoming.

CLAIRE BUCK is Reader in English at the University of North London and has published articles on modern poetry and feminist theory. She is the author of *HD and Freud: Bisexuality and a Feminine Discourse* and editor of *The Bloomsbury Guide to Women's Literature.* Currently she is working on *Models of Maternity,* which will explore the uses of the maternal in contemporary feminist theory.

MARY CONDÉ is a lecturer in the School of English and Drama, Queen Mary and Westfield College, University of London. She is currently editing a book on Caribbean women's fiction with Thorunn Lonsdale for Macmillan.

CON CORONEOS teaches in Cambridge. He has recently completed a book entitled *Space, Conrad, Modernity* and is currently working on a study of the pervasion of eugenic ideas into mass culture, with particular reference to film.

ELIZABETH GREGORY is an Associate Professor of English and Director of the Women's Studies Program at the University of Houston. She is the author of *Quotation and Modern American Poetry: '"Imaginary Gardens with Real Toads"'* (1996). Recent articles include an essay on Helen and Penelope in *Helios.*

MARY HAMER is a Fellow of the W. E. B. Du Bois Institute for Afro-American Research, Harvard, and a former fellow of the Bunting Institute, Radcliffe College; she also teaches in Cambridge, England. Recent publications include *Signs of Cleopatra: History, Politics, Representation* (1993) and *Writing by Numbers: Trollope's Serial Fiction* (1987).

TRACY HARGREAVES is a lecturer in modern literature at Leeds University. She has published essays on Woolf, biography, and popular culture and is currently working on Ethel Smyth.

JANE POTTER is currently completing a D. Phil. on literature of the First World War at Wolfson College, Oxford.

SUZANNE RAITT is an Associate Professor of English at the University of Michigan. She is author of *Vita and Virginia: The Work and Friendship of V. Sackville-West and Virginia Woolf* (1993) and editor of Virginia Woolf's *Night and Day* for World's Classics and Katherine Mansfield's *Something Childish and Other Stories* for Penguin. She is currently working on a critical biography of May Sinclair.

HELEN SMALL is Fellow and Tutor in English Literature at Pembroke College, Oxford. She is author of *Love's Madness: Medicine, the Novel, and Female Insanity 1800–1865* (1996) and co-editor of *The Practice and Representation of Reading in England* (1996). She has co-edited *Little Dorrit* for Penguin and is currently working on a book about the representation of age in English literature.

TRUDI TATE is a lecturer in the English Department, University of Southampton and a Visiting Research Fellow at Clare Hall, Cambridge. She is editor of *Women, Men and the Great War: An Anthology of Stories* (1995) and is currently completing a book on modernism and the First World War, to be published by Manchester University Press.

Select Bibliography

For references to individual writers and works, see notes to chapters.

ALBERTI, JOHANNA, *Beyond Suffrage: Feminists in War and Peace, 1914–28* (Basingstoke, 1989).

ANDERSON, BENEDICT, *Imagined Communities: Reflections on the Origin and Spread of Nationalism*, rev. edn. (London, 1991).

BAYLISS, GWYN, *Bibliographic Guide to the Two World Wars* (London, 1977).

BEER, GILLIAN, *Arguing with the Past: Essays in Narrative from Woolf to Sidney* (London, 1989).

BENSTOCK, SHARI, *Women of the Left Bank: Paris, 1900–1940* (London, 1987).

BLANCHOT, MAURICE, *The Writing of the Disaster*, trans. Ann Smock (Lincoln, Nebr., 1986).

BRACCO, ROSA, *Merchants of Hope: British Middlebrow Writers and the First World War, 1919–39* (Oxford, 1993).

BRAYBON, GAIL, *Women Workers in the First World War* (London, 1989).

—— and PENNY SUMMERFIELD, *Out of the Cage: Women's Experiences in Two World Wars* (London, 1987).

BRENNAN, TERESA (ed.), *Between Feminism and Psychoanalysis* (London, 1989).

BUCK, CLAIRE, *HD and Freud: Bisexuality and a Feminine Discourse* (Hemel Hempstead, 1991).

BUITENHUIS, PETER, *The Great War of Words: Literature as Propaganda 1914–18 and After* (London, 1989).

BUTLER, JUDITH, *Gender Trouble: Feminism and the Subversion of Identity* (London, 1990).

—— and JOAN W. SCOTT (eds.), *Feminists Theorize the Political* (London, 1992).

CHESSMAN, HARRIET SCOTT, *The Public is Invited to Dance: Representation, the Body, and Dialogue in Gertrude Stein* (Stanford, Calif., 1989).

COLLIER, PETER, and JUDY DAVIES (eds.), *Modernism and the European Unconscious* (Oxford, 1990).

CONDELL, DIANA and JEAN LIDDIARD (eds.), *Working for Victory? Images of Women in the First World War, 1914–18* (London, 1991).

CONSTANTINE, STEPHEN, MAURICE KIRBY, and MARY ROSE (eds.), *The First World War in British History* (London, 1995).

Cooper, Helen M., Adrienne Auslander Munich, and Susan Merrill Squier (eds.), *Arms and the Woman: War, Gender and Literary Representation* (Chapel Hill, N.C., 1989).

Dawson, Graham, *Soldier Heroes* (London, 1994).

de Lauretis, Teresa, *Practice of Love: Lesbian Sexuality and Perverse Desire* (Bloomington, Ind., 1994).

Eksteins, Modris, *The Rites of Spring: The Great War and the Birth of the Modern Age* (London, 1989).

Elam, Diane, *Feminism and Deconstruction* (London, 1994).

Elshtain, Jean, *Women and War* (Brighton, 1987).

Enser, A. G. S., *A Subject Bibliography of the First World War*, 2nd edn. (Aldershot, 1990).

Felman, Shoshana, and Dori Laub, *Testimony: Crises of Witnessing in Literature, Psychoanalysis, and History* (New York, 1992).

Field, Frank, *British and French Writers of the First World War* (Cambridge, 1991).

Fussell, Paul, *The Great War and Modern Memory* (Oxford, 1975).

Gilbert, Martin, *The Routledge Atlas of the First World War* (1970; 2nd edn. London, 1994).

Gilbert, Sandra, and Gubar, Susan, *No Man's Land: The Place of the Woman Writer in the Twentieth Century*, ii: *Sexchanges* (New Haven, 1989).

Gillis, John (ed.), *The Militarization of the Western World* (New Brunswick, 1989).

Goldman, Dorothy (ed.), *Women and World War I: The Written Response* (Basingstoke, 1993).

Goodwin, Sarah Webster, and Elisabeth Bronfen (eds.), *Death and Representation* (Baltimore, 1993).

Gregory, Adrian, *The Silence of Memory: Armistice Day 1919–1946* (Oxford, 1994).

Hanley, Lynne, *Writing War: Fiction, Gender and Memory* (Amherst, Mass., 1991).

Hardwick, Joan, *An Immodest Violet: The Life of Violet Hunt* (London, 1990).

Hartigan, Richard Shelly, *The Forgotten Victim: A History of the Civilian* (Chicago, 1982).

Haste, C., *Keep the Home Fires Burning: Propaganda in the First World War* (London, 1977).

Henig, Ruth, *Versailles and After, 1919–1933* (London, 1984).

Higonnet, M. R., Jane Jenson, Sonya Michel, and Margaret C. Weitz (eds.), *Behind the Lines: Gender and the Two World Wars* (New Haven, 1987).

Hobsbawm, Eric, *Age of Extremes: The Short Twentieth Century, 1914–1991* (London, 1994).

HUSSEY, MARK (ed.), *Virginia Woolf and War: Fiction, Reality, and Myth* (Syracuse, N.Y., 1991).

HUSTON, NANCY, 'The Matrix of War: Mothers and Heroes', in Susan Rubin Suleiman (ed.), *The Female Body in Western Culture* (Cambridge, Mass., 1986).

HYNES, SAMUEL, *A War Imagined: The First World War and English Culture* (London, 1990).

JOLL, JAMES, *The Origins of the First World War*, 2nd edn. (London, 1992).

KHAN, NOSHEEN, *Women's Poetry of the First World War* (London, 1988).

KNIGHTLEY, PHILIP, *The First Casualty: The War Correspondent as Hero, Propagandist, and Myth Maker from the Crimea to Vietnam* (London, 1975).

LEED, ERIC, *No Man's Land: Combat and Identity in World War I* (Cambridge, 1979).

MARCUS, JANE, 'The Asylums of Antaeus: Women, War and Madness—Is there a Feminist Fetishism?' in H. Aram Veeser (ed.), *The New Historicism* (London, 1990).

—— (ed.), *Virginia Woolf: A Feminist Slant* (Lincoln, Nebr., 1983).

MARWICK, ARTHUR, *The Deluge: British Society and the First World War*, 2nd edn. (Basingstoke, 1991).

MEE, CHARLES L., *The End of Order: Versailles 1919* (London, 1981).

MIDDLETON, PETER, *The Inward Gaze: Masculinity and Subjectivity in Modern Culture* (London, 1992).

NICHOLLS, PETER, *Modernisms* (Basingstoke, 1995).

OUDITT, SHARON, *Fighting Forces, Writing Women: Identity and Ideology in the First World War* (London, 1994).

PARFITT, GEORGE, *Fiction of the First World War* (London, 1988).

PICK, DANIEL, *War Machine: The Rationalisation of Slaughter in the Modern Age* (New Haven, 1993).

PONSONBY, ARTHUR, *Falsehood in War-Time* (London, 1928).

PUGH, MARTIN, *Women and the Women's Movement in Britain 1914–1959* (Basingstoke, 1992).

RAITT, SUZANNE, *Vita and Virginia* (Oxford, 1993).

REILLY, CATHERINE (ed.), *Scars upon my Heart: Women's Poetry and Verse of the First World War* (London, 1981).

RILEY, DENISE, *Am I that Name? Feminism and the Category of 'Women' in History* (London, 1988).

ROSE, JACQUELINE, *Why War?* (Oxford, 1993).

—— *States of Fantasy* (Oxford, 1996).

RUTHERFORD, ANDREW, *The Literature of War: Studies in Heroic Virtue*, rev. edn. (Basingstoke, 1989).

SANDERS, M. L., and PHILIP M. TAYLOR, *British Propaganda during the First World War* (Basingstoke, 1982).

SCOTT, BONNIE KIME (ed.), *The Gender of Modernism: A Critical Anthology* (Bloomington, Ind., 1990).

SHARP, ALAN, *The Versailles Settlement: Peacemaking in Paris, 1919* (Basingstoke, 1991).

SHOWALTER, ELAINE, *The Female Malady: Women, Madness and English Culture, 1830–1980* (London, 1987).

SMITH, STAN, *The Origins of Modernism* (Hemel Hempstead, 1994).

STEVENSON, RANDALL, *Modernist Fiction* (Hemel Hempstead, 1992).

TANNER, JANET, *Women and War* (London, 1987).

TATE, TRUDI (ed.), *Women, Men, and the Great War: An Anthology of Stories* (Manchester, 1995).

TAYLOR, A. J. P., *English History 1914–1945* (Oxford, 1965).

TAYLOR, PHILIP M., *Munitions of the Mind*, rev. edn. (Manchester, 1995).

TERRAINE, JOHN, *White Heat: The New Warfare 1914–1918* (London, 1982).

THOM, DEBORAH, 'The Bundle of Sticks', in Angela John (ed.), *Unequal Opportunities* (Oxford, 1986).

THOMAS, GILL, *Life on all Fronts: Women in the First World War* (Cambridge, 1989).

TROTTER, DAVID, *The English Novel in History 1895–1920* (London, 1993).

TURNER, JOHN (ed.), *Britain and the First World War* (London, 1988).

TYLEE, CLAIRE M., *The Great War and Women's Consciousness: Images of Militarism and Womanhood in Women's Writings, 1914–64* (Basingstoke, 1990).

WALL, RICHARD, and J. M. WINTER (eds.), *The Upheaval of War: Family, Work and Welfare in Europe, 1914–1918* (Cambridge, 1988).

WEINTRAUB, STANLEY, *A Stillness Heard round the World: The End of the Great War: 1918* (Oxford, 1985).

WILLIAMS, SUSAN A., *Women and War* (Hove, 1989).

WILSON, TREVOR, *The Myriad Faces of War: Britain and the Great War, 1914–1918* (Oxford, 1986).

WINTER, J. M., *The Great War and the British People* (Basingstoke, 1986).

—— *The Experience of World War I* (Oxford, 1988).

—— *Sites of Memory, Sites of Mourning: The Great War in European Cultural History* (Cambridge, 1995).

WOOLLACOTT, ANGELA, *On her their Lives Depend: Munitions Workers in the Great War* (Berkeley, 1994).

WRIGHT, ELIZABETH (ed.), *Feminism and Psychoanalysis: A Critical Dictionary* (Oxford, 1992).

ZIZEK, SLAVOJ, *The Metastases of Enjoyment: Six Essays on Women and Causality* (London, 1994).

Index